be returned on or before

KT-512-593

THE IRAQ WAR

Campus Library Services Limited

52934

WARWICK SCHOOL

Also by Martin Walker

The National Front: The Extreme Right in Britain

Powers of the Press: The World's Leading Newspapers

The Waking Giant. Gorbachev and Perestroika

Martin Walker's Russia: A Perestroika Journal

The Cold War: A History

The President They Deserve

America Reborn: A 20th-Century Narrative (published in the U.K. as *Makers of the American Century*).

The Caves of Perigord

THE IRAQ WAR

As Witnessed by the Correspondents and
Photographers of United Press International

Edited by Martin Walker

Brassey's, Inc.
Washington, D.C.

Copyright © 2004 by Brassey's, Inc.

Published in the United States by Brassey's, Inc. All rights reserved. No part of this book may be reproduced in any manner whatsoever without written permission from the publisher, except in the case of brief quotations embodied in critical articles and reviews.

Library of Congress Cataloging-in-Publication Data

The Iraq War as witnessed by the correspondents and photographers of United Press International / edited by Martin Walker. — 1st ed.
    p. cm.
    ISBN 1-57488-798-X (pbk : alk. paper)
1. Iraq War, 2003.   I. Title: Iraq War.   II. Walker, Martin, 1947–   III. Title.
DS79.76.I728 2004
956.7044′3—dc22

                                                    2003016231

Printed in the United States of America on acid-free paper that meets the American National Standards Institute Z39-48 Standard.

Brassey's, Inc.
22841 Quicksilver Drive
Dulles, Virginia 20166

First Edition

10 9 8 7 6 5 4 3 2 1

CONTENTS

FOREWORD

It has been said that journalism is the first draft of history. UPI's gripping report of the Second Gulf War certainly qualifies for that accolade. It gives a full account of the diplomatic maneuvers leading up to the conflict and to the military maneuvers of the conflict itself. It analyzes the various viewpoints of the U.S. government, its British ally, those European states that resisted the case for intervention, United Nations officials, Middle Eastern governments, and of Arab public opinion with scrupulous fairness. And once the actual fighting begins, it describes the shifting fortunes of the battlefield with extraordinary vividness from two very different vantage points — namely, that of the strategists who drew up the battle plan and that of the ordinary soldiers who had to slog it out across the desert or in sieges of dusty cities.

UPI's account is also a necessary history. We are inclined in retrospect to think of the Second Gulf War as something like a walkover. And, to be sure, the victory of the U.S.-led coalition was a truly remarkable achievement. It was a victory won at an impressively low cost in casualties (though we must never forget that every soldier's death is a family's tragedy). The Coalition's strategy sought to avoid casualties not only for its own soldiers and civilians but for enemy forces as well. Yet despite these self-imposed restraints, it brought the statue of Saddam Hussein crashing to the ground in central Baghdad a mere three weeks after the start of the conflict. If Gen. Tommy Franks, Gen. Richard Myers and Defense Secretary Donald Rumsfeld had achieved nothing else in their distinguished careers, they would still be admired as among the military commanders who won decisive victories by daring, speed and unexpectedness. From the standpoint of the military historian, this is a campaign that repays study. Here is the first full account of it.

Yet when the war was actually taking place, most of us were caught up in a fog of uncertainty. As coalition forces raced north towards Baghdad, there were small but disquieting reverses. Fedayeen terrorists in civilian clothes sniped at U.S. troops from behind genuine civilians. Those Iraqis who were liberated seemed unsure that their liberation was a permanent one and reacted nervously to the new status quo. And the strategy of engineering the gradual surrender of cities like Basra by destroying the symbols of Saddam Hussein's power inevitably took time and patience. These were new kinds of warfare. We watched fascinated but also unsure as to exactly how they would turn out. Some people worried that coalition forces were overstretched and vulnerable to counterattack. War never looks like a foregone conclusion when it is actually happening.

UPI's reporters convey these twists, turns and uncertainties of the war with skill, accuracy and foresight. Some examples here: Pamela Hess, reporting from the Pentagon, lays out its innovative and soon-to-be victorious strategy at a time when the journalistic consensus held that the war was leading to a "quagmire." Martin Walker gives a gripping eyewitness account of the Battle of Basra and of the courage and comradeship of the British soldiers he accompanied covering the final assault. Martin Sieff describes how Saddam had literally paved the way for U.S. armed columns to strike dramatically at the center of Baghdad by ordering a grandiose totalitarian architecture of wide avenues ideally suited to tanks. Claude Salhani, noticing the eerie silence of Middle Eastern leaders in the run-up to war, underscores the undiplomatic truth that the crisis was in part a failure of Arab leadership because the Arab world had failed to curb Saddam on its own. Several UPI reporters within Iraq note that the Iraqis were willing to welcome their liberators openly only when they were convinced that Saddam Hussein really had been defeated. Similar insights and observations occur on virtually every page.

We are still enmeshed in postwar Iraq. For the foreseeable future, U.S. and British soldiers are unlikely to have much difficulty in passing the purely military tests that their masters back home give them. But the political tests are harder to pass. Where we are giving advice and help from outside, we should encourage the governments of the region to introduce open and responsive political systems by being there to assist them when reform runs into trouble — as it is bound to do sometimes. And where we have direct responsibility as in Iraq, we should establish the seriousness and firmness of our commitment.

To return to the volume at hand, much of it was written and photographed under fire. Almost all of it began life as first-hand reports written on the same days as the events they describe. And all of it was written under the lash of the deadline. Yet it passes every test of accuracy and prescience and it gains immeasurably in vividness and force because it is the work of men and women who were there when

these things happened. I congratulate UPI's reporters and editors on their fine work and, in particular, Martin Walker on weaving their threads into such a persuasive pattern. In his skillful compilation, UPI's reports and analyses become history that is vividly told and shrewdly judged. This is how it was in Washington, New York, London, Paris, Moscow and Baghdad. As we cope with the rebuilding of Iraq and the postwar reordering of international relations, UPI has given us not only a fine account of how we got here but also some indispensable lessons on how we might avoid such needless crises in the future.

Margaret Thatcher
(Lady Thatcher was prime minister of Great Britain and Northern Ireland from 1979 to 1990.)

INTRODUCTION

In the early evening of Feb. 26, 1991, after a three-hour battle through minefields and dug-in Iraqi T-55 tanks that secured 1,600 prisoners, the M1 Abrams tanks of the Tiger Brigade of the U.S. 2nd Armored Division took the high ground of Mutla Ridge, almost immediately due east of Kuwait City. Spread out below them as they topped the rise was the junction of two 6-lane highways and the road north to Iraq that was to be called the Highway of Death.

What they also saw, according to the U.S. Army's official history, was "the largest target an armored brigade had probably ever seen. The previous night Air Force and Navy aircraft had begun destroying all vehicles spotted fleeing from Kuwait. Now the brigade added its firepower to the continuous air strikes. On the Highway of Death, hundreds of burning and exploding vehicles of all types, including civilian automobiles, were visible. Hundreds more raced west out of Kuwait City to unknowingly join the deadly traffic jam. Here and there knots of drivers, Iraqi soldiers and refugees fled into the desert because of the inferno of bombs, rockets, and tank fire. These lucky ones managed to escape and join the ranks of the growing army of prisoners."

The Highway of Death, stretching 30 miles north to the Iraqi border and another 50 miles to Iraq's southern city of Basra, was the graveyard of the army that Saddam Hussein had ordered to invade Kuwait the previous August. The American pilots called this long, vulnerable target the turkey shoot, the final destructive moment of a four-day ground war that cost the Iraqi forces 3,200 of the 5,000 tanks with which they had begun the war. They lost another 920 of their 1,700 BMP armored infantry vehicles, 200 of their 350 self-propelled guns and 2,300 of their 3,500 towed guns. The Iraqi air force no longer flew; its aircraft had been shot down, destroyed on the ground or had fled into neighboring Iran for safekeeping. Once the most formidable Arab force in the Middle East, the Iraqi military had been defeated and almost destroyed.

Almost, but not quite. There were enough loyal troops and tanks and guns to maintain Saddam Hussein's regime in power against the uprisings by the Kurds of the north and the Shi'ites of the south. At the Safwan cease-fire negotiations, U.S. Commander General Norman Schwarzkopf agreed to the request of Iraqi General Sultan Hashim Ahmad that the Iraqis be allowed to use their remaining helicopters, "since so many bridges and roads had been destroyed." In fact, the helicopters were the regime's trump card in crushing the uprisings. Saddam Hussein reasserted his brutal rule, frustrated repeated U.N. resolutions demanding that he surrender his remaining Scud missiles and weapons of mass destruction and played cat-and-mouse games with the U.N. Inspectors.

That, briefly, was why the Bush administration decided that Saddam Hussein's regime had to be fought all over again. Legally, it had a case. Saddam Hussein had not met the conditions of the original 1991 cease-fire, not least in giving a full accounting of Kuwaitis who had disappeared or had been made prisoners of war. He had not fulfilled the terms of successive U.N. resolutions. But there was an additional factor. The terrorist attacks of 9/11 on Washington and New York had convinced the Bush administration that the American security environment had changed forever. The prospect of a terrorist organization like al-Qaida obtaining chemical, biological or even nuclear weapons from a rogue state like Iraq could no longer be ignored. The new U.S. national security strategy, published in September 2002, said that regimes of such character and with such fearsome capabilities had to be tackled, with preventive military action if need be.

But only the United States had suffered that devastating attack of September 11. Other countries, including traditional American allies in Europe, shared neither American losses nor America's shock, and not all could embrace the new strategy. Already chafing over the Bush administration's refusal to join new international systems like the Kyoto Protocol on global warming and the International Criminal Court, France, Germany and other countries like Russia and China feared that the Bush administration was abandoning traditional international procedure for a muscular new American unilateralism. German Chancellor Gerhard Schroeder won an upset re-election victory by campaigning hard against "an American military adventure" against Iraq.

"Any community with only one dominant power is always a danger and provokes reactions," French President Jacques Chirac told *Time* magazine in February, as France took the lead in the intense U.N. arguments over Iraq. "That's why I favor a multipolar world, in which Europe obviously has its place."

There was an irony to Bush's new national security strategy. The strategy was based on the post-9/11 alarm about America's vulnerabilities, although at the same time the United States dominated the world as no single nation had since the days of the Roman Empire. The United States was the world's greatest financial and industrial power, its biggest exporter, with the most advanced technology and most productive agriculture. Above all, spending on defense more than the world's 10 next military powers combined, American predominance was simply beyond any military challenge on land, at sea, in the air or in space. The United States was not just richer and stronger, it was a technological generation ahead of any other military on the planet, possessing a degree of unbridled power and freedom to impose its own rules that made others nervous.

That was the background to the diplomatic challenge that America's allies, France and Germany, and America's less-than-friends, Russia and China, decided to mount in the one arena where they met the United States as equals — the Security Council of the United Nations. A body that still reflects the power realities of 1945, when World War II ended, the U.N. Security Council has 15 members. Ten delegate positions rotate among all the world's nations and each of the 10 has a vote. Five places are permanent — for Russia, China, France, Britain and the United States — and these "Big Five" all have the power to cast a veto against any resolution. To pass, a resolution has to get nine votes and not a single veto.

President George Bush went to the United Nations in September for a resolution that gave Saddam Hussein one last chance to readmit the U.N. inspectors, comply with the previous resolutions and cooperate in his own disarmament. Vice President Dick Cheney and Defense Secretary Donald Rumsfeld were far from convinced that this was a good idea. But the important British ally, Prime Minister Tony Blair, desperately needed a U.N. mandate to help beat back threats of rebellion in his own Labor Party majority in Parliament. And Secretary of State Colin Powell argued that the United Nations brought international legitimacy and the prospect of wide diplomatic support, which made it easier to obtain temporary military bases, overflight rights and financial and other help in postwar reconstruction.

Bush accepted the Blair–Powell argument, but in his address to the U.N. General Assembly in September 2002 he packaged it in a new and challenging way. Either the United Nations decided to live up to its own resolutions and enforce them or it risked becoming "irrelevant." Relieved that Bush had been sufficiently "multilateralist" to go to the United Nations, the Security Council gave the United States the resolution it wanted by a vote of 15–0. The catch was that the French said that a second resolution would be required before there could be any U.N. authorization of military action — even if the Saddam Hussein regime was still playing cat and mouse with the inspectors.

The inspectors went to work — and got just enough Iraqi cooperation to encourage them to continue. For the British and Americans, this was clearly not enough. For the French, Russian and Chinese — and for much of public opinion around the world — it was enough to make continuing with the inspections preferable to war. As the diplomats wrangled, and the 250,000 American and 45,000 British and 3,000 Australian troops began to gather in the Persian Gulf, Bush and Blair saw themselves pilloried as war-mongering bullies, and Blair faced a political fight for his life in his own Labor Party.

This was extraordinary. Saddam Hussein ran what was clearly one of the most evil regimes on the planet. This was widely known. The U.N. Human Rights Commission, in April 2002, adopted a resolution strongly condemning "the systematic, widespread and extremely grave violations of human rights and of international humanitarian law by the government of Iraq, resulting in an all-pervasive repression and oppression sustained by broad-based discrimination and widespread terror."

Amnesty International, in a special report on torture in Iraq, said:

> Torture is used systematically against political detainees in Iraqi prisons and detention centres. The scale and severity of torture in Iraq can only result from the acceptance of its use at the highest level. There are no attempts to curtail or prevent such violations or punish those responsible. This total disregard for a basic human right, the right not to be tortured or ill-treated, grossly violates international human rights law which prohibits torture in all circumstances.

> Torture victims in Iraq have been blindfolded, stripped of their clothes and suspended from their wrists for long hours. Electric shocks have been used on various parts of their bodies, including the genitals, ears, the tongue and fingers. Victims have described to Amnesty International how they have been beaten with canes, whips, hosepipes or metal rods and how they have been suspended for hours from either a rotating fan in the ceiling or from a horizontal pole often in contorted positions as electric shocks were applied repeatedly on their bodies. Some victims had been forced to watch others, including their own relatives or family members, being tortured in front of them.

Other methods of physical torture described by former victims include the use of *Falaqa* (beating on the soles of the feet), extinguishing of cigarettes on various parts of the body, extraction of fingernails and toenails and piercing of the hands with an electric drill. Some have been sexually abused and others have had objects, including broken bottles, forced into their anus. In addition to physical torture, detainees have been threatened with rape and subjected to mock execution. They have been placed in cells where they could hear the screams of others being tortured and have been deprived of sleep. Some have stayed in solitary confinement for long periods of time. Detainees have also been threatened with bringing in a female relative, especially the wife or the mother, and raping her in front of the detainee. Some of these threats have been carried out.

Some secret policemen, charged with these foul duties, were issued identity cards that listed their occupation as "Official Violator."

Knowing the regime's record, and recalling the 1991 uprisings against Saddam Hussein by the Kurds and Shi'ites, many in the Bush and Blair administrations assumed that the Iraqis would welcome the British and American troops as liberators. They were assured by Iraqi exiles, hoping to replace Saddam Hussein in power in a democratic Iraq, that few would fight for the "Beast of Baghdad."

This is the story of the 21 days that finally — after hard fighting, some resistance and a stunning demonstration of American military prowess and technology — proved them right.

MAPS

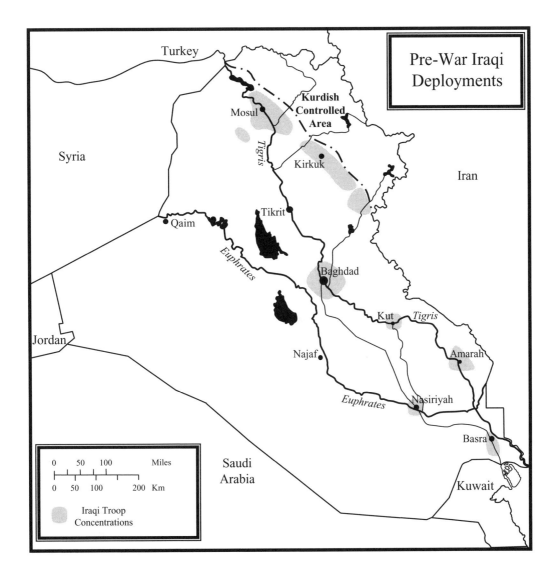

Turkey

Syria

Mosul

Kurdish
Controlled
Area

Tigris

Kirkuk

Iran

Qaim

Tikrit

Euphrates

Baghdad

Kut

Tigris

Jordan

Najaf

Amarah

Euphrates

Nasiriyah

Basra

Saudi
Arabia

Kuwait

| 0 | 50 | 100 | Miles |
| 0 | 50 | 100 | 200 Km |

Iraqi Troop
Concentrations

Pre-War Iraqi
Deployments

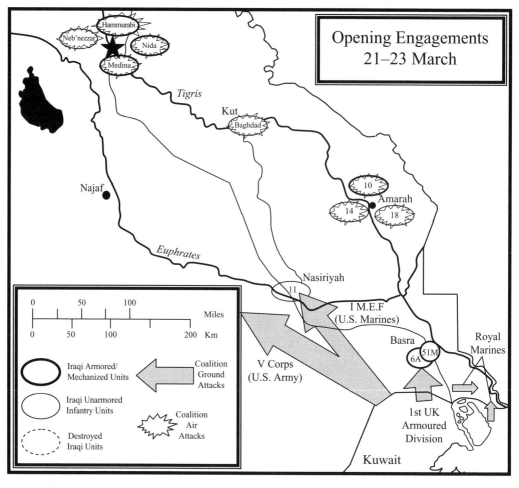

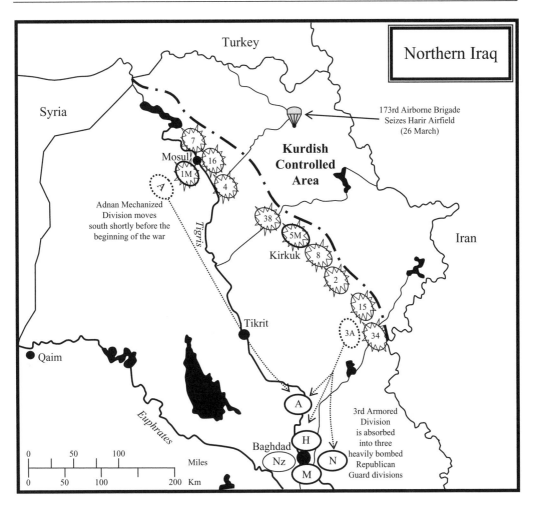

Northern Iraq

Turkey

Syria

Kurdish
Controlled
Area

173rd Airborne Brigade
Seizes Harir Airfield
(26 March)

Mosul

Adnan Mechanized
Division moves
south shortly before the
beginning of the war

Iran

Kirkuk

Tikrit

3rd Armored
Division
is absorbed
into three
heavily bombed
Republican
Guard divisions

Qaim

Baghdad

0   50   100
                    Miles
0   50   100   200 Km

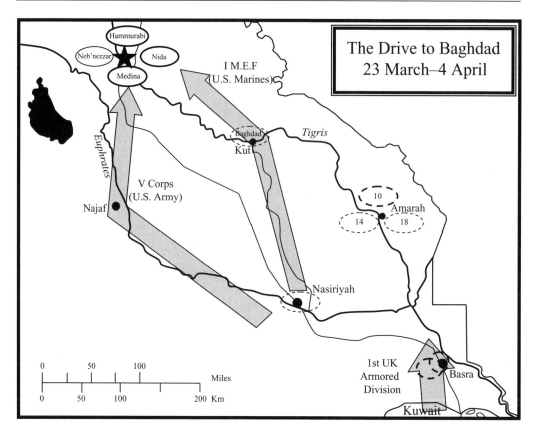

THE IRAQ WAR

CHAPTER 1
THE ROAD TO WAR

ABOARD THE USS KITTY HAWK, The Arabian Gulf, March 17 (UPI) — Aviation ordnancemen load an AIM-9M Sidewinder air-to-air missile onto an F/A-18 Hornet strike fighter aboard USS Kitty Hawk (CV 63) on March 17, 2003. The Sidewinder is a short-range, heat-seeking, air-intercept missile used by 28 different nations, including the United States. Kitty Hawk and her embarked Carrier Air Wing Five (CVW-5) are conducting combat missions in support of Operations Southern Watch and Enduring Freedom. Kitty Hawk is the Navy's only permanently forward-deployed aircraft carrier and operates out of Yokosuka, Japan. (U.S. Navy photo/Todd Frantom)

The great Arab void

CLAUDE SALHANI

WASHINGTON, Feb. 11 (UPI) — The noticeable absence from the international political scene in the months since the Bush administration started actively planning the removal of Iraqi leader Saddam Hussein has been a strong voice emanating from the Arab world. During this time of grave crisis, a number of voices have made themselves heard as the debate whether to attack Iraq has gathered momentum. Many are those who articulated the pros and cons of going to war with Iraq, from the White House, the Pentagon, the State Department, the CIA and the United Nations, as well as from Paris, London, Berlin, Moscow and Brussels.

Yet the Arab world seems to have gone mute.

It's quite disconcerting that as more than 100,000 American combat troops, hundreds of fighter aircraft and several naval battle groups converge on the Arabian Gulf in preparation for war, not a single Arab leader has tried to introduce a comprehensive initiative to avoid a U.S. invasion of an Arab country — a move that is bound to bring renewed havoc to the Middle East for years to come.

"This will be an Arab crisis that will have traumatic repercussions on the whole region,"

Hassan Hassouna, the Arab League representative in Washington, told United Press International.

During the 1990–91 Gulf War, when the United States led a coalition to oust Iraq from Kuwait, King Hussein of Jordan played a major role in trying to convince Saddam to avoid a military confrontation with the United States. The Jordanian monarch and President Hosni Mubarak of Egypt were especially active in their efforts to avoid a war. Although ultimately they failed, and the coalition put together by President George Bush père went to war in January 1991, at least there was some Arab effort at mediation. Today, besides some lip service from Syria and some meek efforts from the Arab League, there appears to be complete Arab inertia.

It is true there have been some low-level and behind-the-scenes diplomatic efforts by some Arab League members, but those would appear to be too little, too late. Hassouna told UPI a meeting of Arab foreign ministers is scheduled to convene in Cairo on Feb. 16 to discuss the situation.

"Out of this meeting something could happen," said Hassouna. A summit meeting "could happen beginning of March," the Arab League diplomat said. But by then, U.S. forces may well be on their way to Baghdad.

Why then are the Arabs so quiet this time, in contrast to the Gulf War that followed Iraq's invasion of Kuwait in 1990?

"It's a different case," explained Hassouna. "At the time it was a clear case of aggression. That was the focus. This time it is different. Whatever the Arab leaders do will depend on the report of U.N. weapons inspectors Hans Blix and Mohammad ElBaradei."

The inspectors are scheduled to report back to the U.N. Security Council on Feb. 14. Hassouna also pointed to a mini-summit held on Sunday in the Egyptian Red Sea resort of Sharm el-Sheikh that Mubarak hosted for Syrian President Bashar Assad and Libyan leader Moammar Gadhafi. And then there was an earlier meeting in Istanbul, Turkey, last month when foreign ministers from Turkey, Iran, Syria and Saudi Arabia met, some analysts believe, in an effort to try and convince Saddam to seek asylum in a friendly country and thus avoid a war.

Egypt, however, said Sunday that the upcoming summit of Arab League states — if it happens — will not ask Saddam to resign. Saddam's resignation would avoid a war. "I don't think any Arab country would interfere in Iraq's internal affairs," Egyptian Foreign Minister Ahmad Maher told reporters in Sharm el-Sheikh after the mini-summit. "It is the Iraqi people who should decide who rules over their country."

Of course, but so long as Saddam remains in power, the Iraqi people will not have much of a say in running their country, and they, unfortunately, will be the last ones to decide who rules them.

Regardless, these low-level gatherings of Arab leaders have attracted little attention and produced even less political impact. What is needed is an immediate summit meeting of Arab heads of state that could present a comprehensive initiative, offering a viable alternative to an American invasion of Iraq. But that is highly unlikely to occur for a number of reasons.

First, the Arab world as a whole is leaderless. Many of the older, more astute leaders who have ruled the Arab world since the post–World War II, post-colonization era have died and been replaced by their younger, and far less experienced, progeny.

With the exception of Egypt's Mubarak, the doyen of the Arab world's leaders, the rest of the Arab world is ruled by a new crop of leaders, still unaccustomed to dealing with the complexity of interregional intricacies. And even Mubarak has been largely removed from the Iraqi debacle, as he remains preoccupied with his own internal concerns. Saudi Arabia, the one-time oil-rich powerhouse of Arab world politics, is disadvantaged by King Fahd's invalidism and plagued by the harsh reality that it, too, faces internal dissent. Fifteen of the 19 Sept. 11 hijackers were Saudi citizens.

Syria, the other traditional leader in the Arab world, is governed by Bashar Assad, a young and inexperienced man who saw himself propelled into the top job after the death of his father, Hafez, in 2000. Bashar, by training an ophthalmologist who never had political vision, lacks the charisma and ambition to emerge as the new pan-Arab leader.

Jordan's charismatic King Hussein died in 1999, leaving control of the Hashemite kingdom to his untried son, Abdullah. The same holds true in Morocco, where King Mohamed VI ascended to the throne upon the death of his father, King Hassan II, also in 1999.

These recent changes in leadership have left the Middle East with a lack of experienced leaders who have any real influence beyond their individual borders. In addition, today, no Arab country is in a position to openly defy the United States.

The worst-case scenario

MARTIN WALKER

WASHINGTON, March 5 (UPI) — It is now eyeball-to-eyeball time at the United Nations. The British and Americans say they are quietly confident that they now have the nine votes needed in the Security Council and are hopeful of a 10th. But they might be bluffing. But Wednesday, the French, German and Russian foreign ministers issued a solemn joint statement from Paris that said, "We will not let a proposed resolution pass that would authorize the use of force." And France and Russia then warned they were prepared to use the veto. But they might be bluffing.

The salient fact is that the French and Russians simply do not know how far they can trust one another to carry out that veto threat — with all the profound consequences for their own relations with Washington that would follow. Nobody wants to be left isolated, wielding a solitary veto, when the music stops. That is why they reached the pact of Paris Wednesday, sealed with the presence of German Foreign Minister Joschka Fischer, whose country has no veto but launched the great rebellion against U.S. leadership in last year's German election.

In defying the American hyperpower, there might be safety in numbers. France, Russia and Germany can support one another and share the blame and pain much better than an isolated challenger. And pain and blame there will be. The wrath of the Bush administration, if frustrated by such a coalition or forced to go to war

in defiance of a U.N. veto, will be fierce. Suddenly, the stakes are far greater than the future of Saddam Hussein. Some of the most prominent institutions of global management are at risk.

Start with the United Nations. If the Franco-Russo-German view prevails, then that means that the United Nations has become a body that can veto the United States from acting in what it sees to be its vital national interest. No American president, and no U.S. Senate, can be expected to endorse such a limitation on American sovereignty. The United States will simply ignore it.

It is difficult to see much future for NATO in the face of such a direct clash between the Franco-Germans and the Anglo-Americans. That constant American support for the project of European integration, which has been a consistent principle of U.S. grand strategy since the late 1940s, could not be expected to continue.

It is equally difficult to see how the European Union can continue working toward its goal of "a common foreign and security policy" in the teeth of such a split between Britain and the traditional Franco-German core of that body. And the British are not alone; the governments of Spain and Italy, and the "New Europe" of the Poles and Czechs and Balts, line up with the Americans.

None of them wants to be part of a Europe that starts to look like a potential challenge to American interests. The EU would revert to being little more than a customs union. But there are other grim consequences looming. If Britain joins the United States in going to war without the backing of a second U.N. resolution, it is then an open question whether Saddam or Tony Blair falls first. There will be instant massed demonstrations in Britain and probably a wave of strikes. There will probably be a challenge to Blair's leadership in the National Executive Committee of the Labor Party, and that in turn would trigger a vote of confidence in Parliament — and possibly Blair's replacement by Chancellor of the Exchequer Gordon Brown.

Any Blair successor would face an excruciating dilemma. Would he keep the British troops in action — in the teeth of public and parliamentary opposition? Or would he back his fellow Europeans in Paris and Berlin, withdraw the troops — and destroy the Anglo-American alliance?

At that point, NATO is dead, and from Washington's perspective, the EU would start to look like a rival and far from friendly superpower. The restraint that both the United States and EU have displayed in their trade disputes would no longer be applied, and trade rivalries and tariff wars would probably destroy the World Trade Organization and plunge already weakened economies into serious recession.

All this for the wretched Saddam Hussein.

It's eyeball to eyeball time, and this is no longer about Iraq. It is about the resentment in Paris, Berlin and Moscow at being bullied into submission in a world run unilaterally from Washington. And it is about Washington's outrage at being told by the U.N. pygmies what the lone superpower may and may not do on the world stage.

If this worst-case scenario starts to sound like Sarajevo 1914, with the world plunging into unthinkable crisis because of diplomatic bumbling and miscalculation, that is precisely the threat that now looms at the Security Council.

Iraq dents Blair's EU ambitions

GARETH HARDING

BRUSSELS, Belgium, March 6 (UPI) — The war against Iraq has yet to begin, but the fallout from the conflict has already started to settle over Europe's political elites like a deadly dust.

Britain and Spain's backing for U.S. President George W. Bush's hard-line stance against Baghdad has led to a collapse in public support for the leaders of the two western European states. In London, recent opinion polls put the opposition Conservatives on a level pegging with Tony Blair's ruling Labor Party for the first time since the center-left swept to power in 1997 — largely as a result of hostility to the prime minister's bullish stance on Iraq. And in Spain, where more than 3 million protesters took to the streets in last month's antiwar demonstrations, the Socialists have now overtaken right-wing Premier Jose Maria Aznar to become the country's most popular party. But Blair and Aznar's unswerving support for Bush has not only dented their national standing, it may also halt their European ambitions. Both leaders favor creating the powerful new post of EU president and until recently were odds-on favorites for the prestigious position. Just six months ago, Blair bestrode the European political landscape like a colossus. With the largest parliamentary majority of any EU leader, he had free reign to conduct European policy as he saw fit. He could claim credit for pushing Bush down the U.N. path on Iraq. And sensing that the Franco-German relationship was cooling, the British prime minister forged a series of strong alliances with right-wing governments in Italy, Spain and Denmark. Now, in "old European" countries like France, Germany and Belgium, Blair is almost as reviled as Bush.

"People talk of the prime minister straddling the Atlantic. His footing may be secure in Washington, but it is not any longer in Europe," former French Minister for Europe Pierre Moscovici wrote in the Financial Times Wednesday. "By putting trans-Atlantic solidarity before European unity, he runs the grave risk of dividing Europe and cutting Britain off from the Franco-German partnership, which is after all much closer to European public opinion."

Given the level of animosity between Blair and French President Jacques Chirac, it is difficult to see Paris supporting the British premier's bid to become the EU's first president. It is also hard to see Chirac and German Chancellor Gerhard Schroeder forgiving Aznar for penning the infamous "letter of eight" European countries backing the U.S. position on Iraq.

Another possible candidate for EU president — Danish Prime Minister Anders Fogh-Rasmussen — may also pay the price for supporting Bush if European leaders decide to set up the high-profile post next year. Although Fogh-Rasmussen, who was widely praised for wrapping up membership talks with 10 EU applicant states in December, has been careful not to antagonize the French and Germans over Iraq, he was also a signatory of the Wall Street Journal letter. But it is not just "new European" leaders who have seen their EU stock fall; opponents of war may also have blown their chances of leading the bloc.

Belgian Prime Minister Guy Verhofstadt, who handled the 15-member club's response to the Sept. 11, 2001, attacks against the United States, has been tipped as a future EU president when current incumbent Romano Prodi steps down next year. German Foreign Minister Joshka Fischer has also hinted that he might be interested in the post of the EU's "top staffer." However, given both men's stubborn opposition to military action against Baghdad, it is hard to see the likes of Blair, Aznar and Italian leader Silvio Berlusconi backing their candidacies.

Simon Hix, a lecturer at the London School of Economics, says the Iraqi issue has led to a "real polarization" among Europe's current crop of leaders. "The traditional European method of consensus-building seems to have gone out of the window for the moment," he says, predicting "pretty acrimonious battles" over the choice of future EU leaders.

Of course, the present crisis may blow over quickly, and politicians who find themselves languishing in the opinion polls could bounce back. But EU leaders, like elephants, have long memories, and the next time they are asked to choose one of their own to lead the pack, they might find the task very tough indeed.

Walker's World: Battle for the U.N.

MARTIN WALKER

WASHINGTON, March 9 (UPI) — President George W. Bush is starting to face the nightmare that has eventually brought down every overwhelming power in history. A coalition of the jealous and the frightened, the resentful and the hostile, is slowly taking shape on the U.N. Security Council. Inspired initially by Germany, and now led by France and backed by Russia and China, this coalition seems to be forcing on the United States the grim choice of defying and

perhaps destroying the United Nations or surrendering to its uncertain moral authority. There are few hours remaining before Tuesday's crucial vote, time to be used by both sides of the debate to rally support among the anguished and undecided. The mathematics of the 15 votes on the Security Council are simple. The United States is backed by Britain, Spain and Bulgaria. In opposition, rallying behind the hopeful judgment of the U.N. inspectors that Saddam Hussein is buckling and they deserve more time, are France, Russia, China, Germany and Syria. That leaves the votes of Pakistan, Mexico, Chile, Guinea, Angola and Cameroon to be fought and bargained for. Unlike the five permanent members of the Security Council, none of these has veto powers. But they have votes that could prove to be decisive, because if the British and Americans can rally a majority of nine votes to their side, then China and Russia might just be persuaded to abstain. This would leave France isolated, and three former French prime ministers — all from President Jacques Chirac's own political party — have warned that a lonely veto on behalf of Saddam would not be in France's best interest. France, too, needs the cover that other votes could provide.

Hence, French Foreign Minister Dominique de Villepin has flown from New York to Africa this weekend to lobby the leaders of Guinea and Cameroon — former French colonies where France remains influential — and Angola. But American and British diplomats have also been active. And they have some serious diplomatic weapons to deploy to persuade the undecided countries to see things America's way.

Chile's top economic priority is its free trade agreement with the United States — which has yet to be ratified by a watchful and possibly vengeful U.S. Congress. Pakistan, where Islamic fundamentalists may well erupt in the streets, would like dearly to abstain. But the government of Gen. Pervez Musharraf is heavily dependent on U.S. aid and above all needs Washington's restraining hand on its neighbor, India.

Angola depends on the $5 billion a year it earns from oil exports — of which 63 percent go to the United States. The United States and Portugal (which broadly supports the Bush administration) between them account for 40 percent of Angola's imports. President Jose Eduardo

Dos Santos knows where his country's economic interests lie.

Many U.N. diplomats assume that Cameroon is a reliable vote for France, the former colonial power. Not so. The top three customers for its annual $2.3 billion oil exports are Italy, France and Spain — in that order. And Italy and Spain back Bush. Moreover, Cameroon's oil is running out, and the key to its future prosperity is a proposed 670-mile pipeline through Cameroon from landlocked Chad. That pipeline is being built by Exxon-Mobil and ChevronTexaco. Cameroon's economic interests are also with the United States.

Guinea is a police state and disaster zone, where electric power cuts mean the TV works only one day in four. The United States is its biggest trading partner, and President Lantana Conte's biggest concern is the security threat from neighboring Liberia. Guinea is also in default on loans from the World Bank and International Monetary Fund. Even though Conte is terminally ill from liver disease, Guinea's economic and strategic interests could steer him America's way.

Finally there is Mexico, which sells 80 percent of its exports to the United States, its partner in the North American Free Trade Association, and whose president, Vicente Fox, once looked to Bush as his closest international friend. But relations have cooled since the post-9/11 clampdown on U.S. immigration, and Mexico's media are outraged at what they see as American bullying over Iraq.

Unnamed U.S. diplomats have been quoted warning that a "no" vote could "stir up feelings" against Mexicans in the United States — like those that saw Japanese-Americans interned during World War II. In an on-the-record interview with Copley News Service last week, Bush warned "there will be a certain sense of discipline" in the way the United States judges unhelpful countries in the future.

The United States is prepared to play hardball to get those nine votes at the United Nations and break the opposing coalition. Ironically, even though its pressure of muscle and menaces may just win Tuesday's vote, American tactics could provoke deeper resentments — and a far more dangerous mood of resentful anti-Americanism for the future.

Blair is stronger than he looks

MARTIN WALKER

WASHINGTON, March 13 (UPI) — To understand why Tony Blair's political future may not be doomed, start with the fact that British voters like a fighter, and traditionally they have backed a fighter who sticks to his guns. The same instincts that rallied behind Winston Churchill in 1940 and Margaret Thatcher in 1982 are starting to come to Blair's aid today. Moreover, Blair is making the case that the current U.N. Security Council is not so much the home of wisdom and international legitimacy as the scene of a cynical French power play. And while accepting that they run a delightful country and make splendid wines, the British in general are no great fans of their neighbors across the Channel.

French President Jacques Chirac is routinely dubbed "The Worm" in Britain's top-selling daily, The Sun. And all of the doubts about too close a connection with Europe that have held Britain back from joining the euro currency are coming into play. The French, Blair told Conservative Party leader Iain Duncan-Smith Thursday, are being "completely intransigent." Blair's official spokesman went further, saying the French had "poisoned" the diplomatic atmosphere.

After months of plunging ratings that left his New Labor government barely ahead of the dispirited Conservative opposition, the polls have bottomed out and are beginning to shift towards Blair. Last month, just 11 percent told pollsters that Britain should wage war against Iraq without the backing of a second U.N. resolution. Last week, 19 percent said that. This week, 26 percent said they would support a war without the United Nations. And with a new resolution, 71 percent would support military action, with only 22 percent still opposed.

Blair faces real problems. A quarter of his members of Parliament, 121 of them, voted against their government over Iraq two weeks ago. One Cabinet minister, Clare Short, having attacked her leader as "reckless," is pledged to resign if Blair goes to war without the United Nations. Another, former Foreign Minister

Robin Cook, is reliably said to be "considering his position." A handful of MPs has talked of starting the process of launching a leadership election.

This is less serious than it sounds. Clare Short, development minister, who resigned from the Shadow Cabinet over the last Gulf War, represents the bleeding-heart wing of the party and is widely felt, in that classic British euphemism, to be "a sandwich or two short of a picnic." And after a hideously messy divorce that saw him eventually marry a much younger aide, Cook still suffers from his wife's account of his drinking himself regularly into a stupor and falling asleep with an empty bottle rolling at his side.

Even the rebels know their limits. Tony Banks, a populist type and former sports minister who voted against his government in the revolt two weeks ago, said: "It's very difficult to get rid of a leader of the Labor party. I've found no widespread indication within the parliamentary Labor party or in the party around the country that there would be a move to get rid of Blair. People have not come round to thinking like that yet."

Another rebel MP, Martin Salter, puts it this way: "Even among those who have fundamental problems with the government's policy towards Iraq, there is a grudging and genuine respect for his manifest personal convictions on the issue and for persuading America to put the issue to the United Nations. These people talking about getting rid of Blair are the usual suspects. I have spoken to a number on the hard left who believe that it has been a tactical mistake to personalize the issue. Just because we don't agree with the prime minister on this, it doesn't mean we should get rid of him."

Even loyal conservatives are worried about the results of toppling Blair. Former Daily Telegraph editor Max Hastings, writing in the latest Spectator, warns that Blair would almost certainly be replaced by his more left-wing finance minister Gordon Brown, a dour Scot who likes Big Government. And certainly until Brown shows himself ready for a challenge, there is no credible alternative to Blair — at least while hostilities threaten and British voters and the British press rally instinctively to "support our boys in the Gulf."

If the war goes well, the British troops are welcomed as liberators and Saddam Hussein's evil weapons are unearthed, Blair will be vindicated — and it will be payback time in British politics. If it all goes wrong, Blair will face mass demonstrations, some protest strikes and a firm challenge to his leadership at the proper time and place — the Labor Party conference in October. If there is a disaster, he may even resign before then — and this time with no golden parachute into a plum European job. The French would veto that, too. But for the moment, and not least because his brave and uncompromising performance at prime minister's question time in Parliament Wednesday, and because he has persuaded President Bush to keep trying diplomacy for a few days longer, his position is stronger than it may look. Having looked briefly into the abyss called Life After Tony, the Labor Party thinks that might be an even worse place to be than Iraq.

Europe backs U.S. stance on Iraq

GARETH HARDING

BRUSSELS, Belgium, March 18 (UPI) — As the United States prepares to launch a military strike against Iraq, there is a widespread belief on both sides of the Atlantic that Washington stands alone against Saddam Hussein and that most European states are either lukewarm or downright hostile to the use of armed force. The feeling has been fostered by the high-profile antiwar stance of the French and German governments and the strength of the peace protests that clogged the continent's capitals last month.

French President Jacques Chirac sought to capitalize Tuesday on the U.N. Security Council's hesitancy to a military strike, declaring, "France's viewpoint is shared by a large majority of the international community."

This may be true of Africa, Asia and Latin America, but even after U.S. President George W. Bush's decision to abandon diplomacy Monday, the majority of European countries support Washington's hard-line stance. A survey of the 27 countries that are either EU members or will be in the near future reveals that 16 back military action to disarm Saddam Hussein, seven are resolutely opposed to war and four are neutral or undecided.

British Prime Minister Tony Blair and his Spanish counterpart Jose Maria Aznar can lay claim to being Washington's most enthusiastic supporters. Both have backed Bush from the beginning of the standoff and Sunday joined the U.S. commander in chief for a war summit in the Azores islands. Portugal, which hosted the Azores meeting, and Italy have also advocated the use of strong-arm tactics to disarm Saddam Hussein despite huge opposition to war in the two Mediterranean states.

NATO founding member Denmark is another EU state to give its explicit backing to the U.S. military buildup in the Middle East. In a statement released after Bush's ultimatum to the Iraqi leader, Danish Prime Minister Anders-Fogh Rasmussen said: "The time has come to take a stance ... . It is unacceptable to make a mockery of the international community's authority."

The position of the Netherlands is clouded by the ongoing efforts to form a left–right coalition government following January elections, but Premier Jan-Peter Balkenende has been a staunch ally of Bush and has dispatched Patriot missiles to Turkey to protect the NATO state in the event of an attack by Iraq.

The position of the 10 ex-communist states of Central and Eastern Europe, however, leaves no room for doubt. Last month, the former Soviet bloc countries of Bulgaria, the Czech Republic, Estonia, Hungary, Latvia, Lithuania, Poland, Romania, Slovakia and Slovenia signed a letter of support for the U.S. position on Iraq, prompting an intemperate outburst from Chirac. Announcing plans to send over 200 troops to the Gulf Tuesday, Polish President Aleksander Kwasniewski said, "We agree with British Prime Minister Tony Blair, who said that, in order to keep the peace, you have to fight."

The Balkan states of Albania, Croatia and Macedonia — which are expected to join the EU in the coming years — also back Washington's muscular stance against Saddam Hussein.

Since January, European opposition to war has been led by France and Germany, with Belgium, Austria, Greece, Luxembourg and Sweden following more sheepishly behind. Ireland, Finland, Cyprus and Malta remain neutral or have not nailed their colors to the mast. So with only half a dozen or so EU, or future EU, member states categorically opposed to war, why has the old Continent managed to convey an image of pacifism, appeasement and anti-Americanism over the past months?

First, polls show that European public opinion is overwhelmingly against war, and last month's mass demonstrations rammed home this message in Technicolor detail.

Second, France, Germany and Belgium have waged an unrelenting rear-guard campaign against armed action, culminating in the three countries' decision to temporarily block military support for fellow NATO member Turkey.

Third, although the EU's 15 members are split down the middle over how to disarm the Iraqi regime, the Brussels-based bloc is not representative of Europe as a whole. Almost all the 12 countries queuing up to join the Union over the next four years are standing shoulder to shoulder with London and Washington.

Finally, both the American and European media have been happy to repeat the old canard about the United States acting "unilaterally" against Baghdad, despite military backing from Britain and Australia and the more passive support of dozens of other countries. Of course, the current U.S. president is far from assembling the type of broad coalition Bush Sr. stitched together in 1991. But to talk about the United States being isolated and EU states being isolationist merely panders to the views of those who see Americans as from Mars and Europeans from Venus.

It's not just France against war

CLAUDE SALHANI

LONDON, March 19 (UPI) — While France bore the brunt of the recent trans-Atlantic diplomatic dispute over Iraq, it should be noted that President Jacques Chirac's opposition to war is widely mirrored across much of Europe. Even here, in the United Kingdom, where Prime Minister Tony Blair has proved throughout these difficult months of intense behind-the-scenes diplomatic haggling to be President George W. Bush's best friend and ally, public opinion is far from supportive of the U.S.-led war effort.

Blair, many analysts believe, might be gambling his political career, betting on a quick, clean war. Britain's prime minister is hoping the conflict in the Middle East will meet with rapid success in its efforts to oust Saddam Hussein and identify, and neutralize, his weapons of mass destruction.

For the moment, Blair is riding strong, having won what one British newspaper called a "historic vote for war." The antiwar motion was defeated in the Commons on Tuesday, 396–217, giving the prime minister a majority of 179, despite the biggest Labor Party rebellion since he became prime minister. The government's motion for military action to disarm Iraq, "using all necessary means," was approved 412–149. In a passionate speech, Blair told Parliament he would resign if the members voted against military action, forcing him to withdraw British troops lined up to battle Saddam and his military forces. But already Robin Cook, a former foreign secretary and leader of the House of Commons, has resigned from the government. And on Tuesday, two more ministers — John Denham and Lord Hunt — resigned. However, Clare Short, the international development secretary, who had earlier threatened to quit, changed her mind, saying it would be "cowardly" to do so now.

Cook announced his resignation in an impassioned statement to Parliament on Monday. Cook, who for the first time in his 20-year political life addressed the House from the Back Benches, stated that while "France has been at the receiving end of bucketloads of commentary in recent days, it is not France alone that wants inspections. Germany wants more time for inspection; Russia wants more time for inspections, said Cook. "We delude ourselves if we think that the degree of international hostility is all the result of President Chirac."

While, indeed, Chirac did seem to be spearheading the antiwar, anti-Bush campaign, it is important to note that Russia, Germany, Belgium and other nations remain just as opposed

to U.S. unilateralism and to Bush's urge to act outside the framework of the United Nations. In fact, although their governments support Bush's initiative, the majority of Britons, Italians and Spaniards are just as opposed to going to war without a second U.N. resolution, as, too, are the United States' immediate neighbors and largest trading partners, Canada and Mexico.

So why is America's ire and frustration at France's refusal to accept the war option so vociferous?

It could be explained primarily because France — one of the five permanent members of the U.N. Security Council — repeatedly threatened to use its veto power, thus blocking any resolution that would automatically authorize the use of force.

While Russia and China — also veto-wielding permanent Security Council members — also opposed recourse to war, unlike Chirac their leaders were careful not to mention the possibility of using their right to veto. Putin, for example, simply said he was opposed to any new resolutions. France, on the other hand, showed no such reserve. Chirac, and his energetic foreign minister Dominique de Villepin, who actively campaigned to ensure the support of African countries currently sitting on the Security Council, kept reiterating that there was "no justification for use of force."

"Opposition to war," said Chirac in a televised address that closely followed Bush's ultimatum to Saddam on Monday, "was showed by a majority of countries." Part of this can be explained by the fact that France firmly sees a bigger role in international politics for Europe, which it sees itself, along with Germany, leading. In addition, most Europeans have a stronger desire to find a peaceful solution to the crisis, even if it means being more flexible with Saddam and according him more time. "Ironically," said Cook, "it is only because Iraq's military forces are so weak that we can contemplate its invasion."

Second, Chirac believes himself to be the political heir — and spiritual son — of Gen. Charles de Gaulle. As such, he believes he should stand up to American unilateralist policy in the good old Gaulist tradition.

This diplomatic squabble between France and the United States is nothing more than the continuation of a dispute started by de Gaulle with Gen. Dwight D. Eisenhower during World War II, when de Gaulle was in exile in London and Ike commanded the Allies. There is little doubt here that in his more quiet moments, Chirac must be asking himself what would the good general do in a similar situation.

It is also worth noting that some time after the war, once the dust of this dispute settles, historians will most certainly point out the importance of France's "mediating" role in this crisis. "Chirac's and France's position vis-à-vis this debate is proof that this crisis is not a clash of civilizations," said one high-ranking French official to United Press International. "France's, as well as Germany's position, shows that at least this is not a dispute between East and West."

In the final analysis, France will side with the coalition. As Bush's 48-hour ultimatum winds down, with Saddam still firmly in Baghdad and showing no signs of abdicating, hostilities will soon replace diplomacy.

In the words of Cook's departing comments to Parliament, "To end in such diplomatic weakness is a serious reverse."

CHAPTER 2
WAR PLANS

WASHINGTON, March 20 (UPI) — Secretary of Defense Donald Rumsfeld, (*left*) and Chairman of the Joint Chiefs of Staff Gen. Richard B. Myers brief members of the Pentagon press corps on the first day of the war with Iraq on March 20, 2003. (Michael Kleinfeld, UPI)

What is the war's "brand strategy"?

LOU MARANO

WASHINGTON, March 13 (UPI) — Every war needs a compelling brand proposition, and the Bush administration's default proposition is "This is about American prerogatives," a Manhattan consultant said.

"The consumer holds the brand, not you," said Tracey Riese, an amateur military historian who is president of brand strategy firm T.G. Riese and Associates. For a war against Iraq, many people are not buying the brand, she said. "It's not a question of what you call it. Thinking of something snappy to call the War of 1812 would not have rallied people to the cause." The problem for the administration of James Madison was that it was unable to create a sufficiently meaningful purpose for the war in the minds of many Americans. She advises clients that slogans, logos, and even company names — although important manifestations of the enterprise — are not the brand.

The best and most successful "branding" establishes an emotional connection between the "product" and those who will pay for it, she said. In war, citizens must pay the highest possible price. The more directly and passionately the cause can engage them emotionally, the more loyally and ardently they will support it. Using an example from the business world, Riese said the underlying brand principle at Disney is magic and happiness. Once the brand principle is understood, the organization must be structured to make it true. In Disney's case, this means delivering the happiness that people want to buy.

A government's ability to tap into the underlying emotional commitment of the public often determines the outcome of the war, Riese said. When a brand proposition has been strong and compelling, generally the outcome has been successful. Riese said that in 1776, American colonists transformed the Revolution from a contest between powers to a struggle for "liberty" by enlightened citizens. The Civil War, which began as a struggle between two economic systems and constitutional interpretations, took on new meaning when Abraham Lincoln reframed it as a battle for the soul of a nation "conceived in liberty and dedicated to the proposition that all men are created equal."

World War I, which Riese said was "the outsized result of a series of petty miscalculations," was "redeemed" when Woodrow Wilson, the leader of a late entrant, transformed it into the "war to end all war." When national leadership has failed to marshal a sense of larger purpose for war, its brand position never has resonated with the public, Riese said, and the outcomes have been more equivocal.

Riese said Korea was "fought to a stalemate." The interviewer said the original war aim — preventing the communist conquest of South Korea — was achieved. Surely the Chinese intervention, not the failure to make a compelling brand proposition, is the reason why the entire peninsula was not liberated. Riese replied that if the United States had found a larger purpose in pushing the North Koreans back across the 38th parallel, it might have been able to confront the Chinese. "People will pay more for what they value more. There was a limit to the price we were prepared to pay in Korea." Riese said the proposition for the war in Vietnam was so weak that it finally sapped the nation's will to fight. What about the freedom of the South Vietnamese?

"The brand proposition that the Johnson administration really tried to make had more to do with the containment of communism than with preserving the liberty of the South Vietnamese," she answered. "A brand has to be true in all its roots and aspects. Many Americans did not perceive the South Vietnamese as being as engaged in the struggle on their own behalf as the United States." (U.S. leaders did not do much to refute this perception, such as publishing South Vietnamese casualty figures.) "So the price for Americans seemed to be very high … . Certainly, Americans rallied around the idea of protecting the liberty of Berlin at certain times in our history (1948 and 1961)." The brand strategy, "This is about American prerogatives," although an "inherently isolating one" can nonetheless be pursued, she said.

"Lots of my clients have brand positions that are not necessarily compelling to a great number of people," Riese told United Press International. "And they can make a business decision to operate in that way, or to engage more people around a willingness to pay higher prices for what they deliver. You want an assessment of the long-range and the short-range costs and implications. Brands live a very long time. What are the costs and benefits of an American prerogatives strategy, say, 20 years hence?"

What about the proposition that the United States cannot allow itself to become subject to nuclear blackmail, particularly in the Middle East? Riese replied that this confuses a rationale for taking action — which is analogous to business operating strategy — with branding problems. It does not create a compelling reason to "buy" for most Americans or the global community at large. "First of all, it is too intellectual an argument," she said. "Most people cannot relate to an abstract outcome such as not succumbing to nuclear blackmail." She believes it is not emotionally powerful. "The reason for choosing a toothpaste is so your teeth don't fall out, but no toothpaste on the market is 'branded' on that basis. They are branded on the basis of: 'You will be more attractive and confident.' "

Second, it embodies the "lonely marshal" model of the character played by Gary Cooper in the 1952 movie classic "High Noon." The lawman will do for the town what the town will not do for itself. The basis for such a brand strategy would be to be feared and admired, even if not beloved, Riese said. "That strategy will appeal to a certain number of American 'customers.' " But she asked if enough such "customers" will back the war with vigor and commitment. "I think that a great number of Americans actually don't fancy that role for themselves in the world and would not feel proud of themselves in that role." Riese said some people see the "lonely marshal" position as principled and heroic. Others perceive it as arrogant and bullying. She believes that although a relatively small number of Americans will feel proud and affiliated with this model, a much larger number of "other constituents" will feel alienated, resentful and pushed around.

Riese does not doubt a military victory. "The question is: Once we prevail, what are we going to do, and who are we going to need?" "High Noon" ends with a fantasy, she said. "Gary Cooper gets to withdraw himself from the world. He gets to leave the town behind — and we don't. He left only because the town was stable and governable, and that's not going to be the case in Iraq."

Walker's World: Turkey's Decisive Hour

MARTIN WALKER

WASHINGTON, March 16 (UPI) — This could have been Turkey's proudest moment. The stars and planets had come together to present Turkey with a golden opportunity to resolve its financial, geopolitical and great regional problems, all in the same brief moment of time. By now, the U.S. Army's 4th Infantry Division could be rolling through the wild country south of Lake Van to the Iraqi border, ready to roll down and force Saddam Hussein's wretched forces to divide and meet a second front. Cruise missiles and U.S. warplanes and an aerial conveyor belt of cargo aircraft and combat helicopters could be streaming through friendly Turkish airspace.

Turkey's proud tradition of 50 years of NATO loyalty would have been upheld, and the country would have maintained a special place in America's friendships. Moreover, some $28 billion in cash and credits would have been on their way into the empty Turkish treasury, providing the financial cushion that the new government sorely needs. At the same time, Greek and Turkish Cypriots could be getting ready to vote in a referendum on the U.N. peace plan that could finally have ended their island's 29 years of partition. Rauf Denktash, the obdurate Turkish Cypriot leader, rejected the plan and refused to let his people vote. After the mass demonstrations of tens of thousands of Turkish Cypriots in favor of the plan, all the signs are that they would have voted "yes."

With the United States and European Union and the United Nations all urging a deal, Denktash could probably not have resisted the further pressure that could have put upon him by the Turkish government and Turkish military to settle. The Turks applied such pressure in December, but since then, distracted by the crisis over Iraq, they failed to do very much at all. And the wily old Denktash knows very well when his Turkish patrons — the only ones who recognize his tinpot self-proclaimed statelet — are seriously telling him it is time to deal.

The Turkish Cypriots are not the only ones who will suffer from the Denktash decision, and from Turkey's indecision. In fact, young Turkish Cypriots will start leaving the country for Istanbul, to get by roundabout routes to the Greek Cypriot half of the island, where they can apply for Republic of Cyprus passports that will qualify them to live and work anywhere in the EU.

But Turkey's own hopes of joining the EU have been significantly harmed. The EU does not want to take in only half an island, with a Berlin Wall–style border running through downtown Nicosia that is guarded by Turkish troops. In Europe, Turkey is blamed for failing to deliver Denktash. An EU spokesman noted last week that the legal situation was that Turkey could now be seen as occupying a piece of EU territory with its troops. And the new Turkish prime minister, Recev Tayyip Erdogan, can forget about any lingering Franco–German gratitude for his country's part in hampering the American war machine. That was plain last week, when the European Court of Human Rights ruled that Abdullah Ocalan, the Kurdish separatist leader who launched a guerilla war that cost 30,000 lives, had not received a fair trial and should be tried again.

Turkey, which had commuted his death sentence to life imprisonment as a way of mollifying EU concerns about its human rights record, was furious all over again.

All this means that Turkey's bid to join the EU's prosperity club, always an uphill struggle given EU concerns about taking in a poor, Islamic state that will soon have the EU's largest population, looks increasingly forlorn. To have simultaneously offended the United

States and the Europeans, and thrown away a much needed $28 billion, must be some kind of record for incompetent statesmanship.

And it could get worse. There are ominous signs that the Turkish military is gearing up to complicate the war on Iraq even further with a military incursion of its own into the Kurdish region of northern Iraq. Vast convoys of military trucks have been rolling to the border, and the Kurds fear the Turkish generals are planning to wipe out the remnants of the PKK Kurdish guerillas to prevent Iraqi Kurdistan from becoming the nucleus of an independent Kurdish state — and thus a dangerous magnet for Turkey's own Kurds.

In Washington Friday, Barhim Salih, prime minister of the Kurdish enclave in northern Iraq, urged the Bush administration to ensure that the Turks stayed out, warning, "It will create havoc." Other Kurdish leaders are vowing to fight the Turks if they cross the border — and the Turkish parliament's own decision precluded the presence in the region of U.S. troops that could have controlled the potential for Turk–Kurd clashes.

So far, the new Turkish government has done almost everything possible against their own national self-interest. If their army takes advantage of the Iraq war to invade the Kurds, it will be a march of self-destructive folly. It may not be too late. Premier Erdogan has called a special session of parliament Sunday that may — or may not — finally give the United States permission to send both its troops and warplanes across Turkish territory. The prospects look slim. The tragedy is that Turkey's prospects could all have been so different and so hopeful.

Comparing U.S. and Iraq forces

THOMAS HOULAHAN

WASHINGTON, March 18 (UPI) — Now that President Bush has given Saddam Hussein and his inner circle 48 hours to leave Iraq and Saddam has declined the offer, the stage is set for a military confrontation. If there is a ground war, the main thrust (right now, the only thrust unless the Turkish Parliament grants basing rights) would come from Kuwait. Leading the charge would be the Army's 3rd Infantry Division (Mechanized). The division is equipped with 203 Abrams tanks and 261 Bradley fighting vehicles. It would be supported by U.S. Marines and British army forces. The Marines have the equivalent of about two divisions, supported by 120 Abrams tanks. The British have the equivalent of a division, with 116 Challenger tanks (roughly equivalent to the Abrams in terms of protection and hitting power) and 145 Warrior infantry fighting vehicles. The 101st Airborne Division does not have all of its equipment yet, and won't for a week or two, so it probably wouldn't play a central role in the fighting if it broke out soon.

Right now, the 4th Infantry Division's equipment is on board ships off Turkey, and most of its troops are still in Texas. Its designation notwithstanding, the 4th Infantry Division (Mechanized) is actually an armored division, with 247 Abrams tanks and 217 Bradleys. The division has the combat power to create an effective second front in the north. If a ground war is delayed by several weeks, it might be possible to land the division's equipment and transport it through Turkey to the Kurdish Autonomous Region in time to take part in the fighting. The other heavy units that have been ordered to the Gulf are either still awaiting shipment or are so early in the transit process that they would not arrive in time to take part in a ground war. If there is a ground war, and if it is successful, questions will still be raised over why the government deployed so few divisions to unseat Saddam Hussein. Though this deployment may lead to Saddam's overthrow, it is nevertheless a serious violation of the "Powell Doctrine" of overwhelming force that served us so well in Operation Desert Storm.

On entering Kuwait, the 3rd Infantry Division would first encounter the Iraqi III Corps. The corps' 11th Infantry Division is deployed along the border. For armor support, the division has 17 to 25 decrepit T-55 tanks and 50 or so equally decrepit 122 mm towed artillery pieces. Unarmored divisions like the 11th are more sound than they were during the Gulf

War. On Feb. 24, 1991, there were 40 regular army truck-borne or foot-propelled infantry divisions in the Iraqi order of battle. Now there are 11. With 29 fewer light divisions to stock, Iraq is no longer forced to rely so heavily on old men and boys to fill them. More important, it no longer has to rely on politically unreliable soldiers to fill them. While 75 percent of Iraq's population was Shiite or Kurdish, almost 90 percent of the soldiers on the Saddam Line in the Gulf War came from these ethnic groups, which helps explain their lack of fighting spirit. Kurds are now exempt from military service, as are most Shiites. Still, these divisions are basically worthless. After the destruction of the handful of dug-in tanks backstopping the front line and an intense artillery barrage, there would almost certainly be a mass surrender.

Backing the 11th Infantry Division is the 51st Mechanized Division. The 51st Mechanized has around 140 tanks and 180 armored personnel carriers. Though many analysts theorize that only Republican Guard units would fight, most if not all of the regular army's heavy units would probably fight until they were destroyed. It is a little known fact that on the second day of Desert Storm's ground war, while analysts were chuckling about the previous day's mass surrenders, the Marines were savagely counterattacked by elements of two regular army heavy divisions. These attacks were essentially armored versions of the "Charge of the Light Brigade" and were broken by Marine tanks, antitank missile launchers, attack helicopters and Harrier jets. Said one Marine: "They had guts. If they hadn't been trying to kill me, I might have stood on my tank and cheered for them." Iraq's heavy units will probably have lost around 10 percent of their armor to air attack by the time they are encountered by coalition ground forces, but they will fight.

Guarding Basra would be the 6th Armored Division, which has around 180 tanks and 150 BMP infantry fighting vehicles. These BMPs are thinly armored firetraps that fire a weak, inaccurate 73 mm main-gun round and mount an equally inaccurate antitank missile that cannot penetrate American or British main battle tanks. However, they are better than the armored personnel carriers (which only have heavy machine guns) that the infantry of most regular army heavy divisions are equipped with. The type of infantry vehicle a heavy division is equipped with is an important clue to the capabilities of that division. BMPs only go to the better, more reliable units. So, if you see a unit equipped with BMPs, it's a good bet that the unit's officers and men will be a cut above their counterparts in other heavy units and will be more likely to fight well and with some dedication.

It should be added that there have been reports that the III Corps' two heavy units have been ordered to positions closer to Baghdad. The accuracy of the reports is uncertain, however. On one hand, it is difficult to believe that Saddam Hussein would essentially abandon Basra. On the other, he has made strange military moves before.

Halfway between the Kuwaiti border and Baghdad sits the Iraqi IV Corps, which consists of two virtually worthless divisions (the 14th Infantry and the 18th Infantry) and one of Iraq's better tank divisions, the 10th Armored. Like the 6th Armored Division to the south, the division's infantry units are equipped, with BMPs. Between the IV Corps and Baghdad's outer ring of defenses is the Republican Guard's Baghdad Motorized (truck-mounted) Division. With only a battalion of tanks and a battalion of BMPs, it doesn't have the combat power to be any more than a speed bump to an advancing American heavy unit. Like the Republican Guard's other two motorized divisions, the Baghdad Division is basically an armed rabble. The standard of manpower and leadership is very poor, and it would probably disintegrate on contact.

The outer defenses of Baghdad are manned by four Republican Guard Divisions and at least two commando brigades. Commando brigades are used to defend areas of tactical importance. These units fought doggedly in the Gulf War and can be expected to do so again if called upon. To the northwest of the city is the Hammurabi Armored Division, supported by the 26th Commando Brigade. To the northeast is the Nidah Armored Division. To the southeast is the Medina Armored Division. These three armored divisions have the best tanks and infantry fighting vehicles available to the Iraqi Army. To the southwest is the Nebuchadnezzar Motorized Division, which, like the Baghdad

Division, is too light to put up much resistance. Like the Baghdad Division, it would probably disintegrate on contact. Guarding the southern edge of the city is the 3rd Commando Brigade.

Baghdad itself would be defended by the division-sized Special Republican Guard. The possibility of house-to-house fighting in Baghdad is why a northern front is so important. Hope is an important factor in defense. If, at the time a southern thrust reached the outskirts of Baghdad, half of the Iraqi army was still intact to the north, one could reasonably expect fierce resistance from the Special Republican Guard. If, on the other hand, the men of the SRG looked to the north, saw the tanks of the 4th Infantry Division and realized that the entire Iraqi army in the field had been destroyed, they would be more likely to see the handwriting on the wall and quit.

The Iraqi army has three corps in the north, along the border of the Kurdish Autonomous Region. In the northern sector, the V Corps defends Mosul. The corps is made up of three poor light divisions (4th Infantry, 7th Infantry and 16th Infantry) and the 1st Mechanized Division, probably the least steady regular army heavy unit. It is also supported by the Republican Guard's Adnan Mechanized Division, with its 140 tanks and 180 BMPs. In the center, defending Kikuk, is the I Corps. It has a fairly solid heavy unit, the 5th Mechanized Division. However, it also has three virtually worthless infantry divisions, the 2nd, 8th and 38th. In fact, the 38th Infantry Division is considered by some analysts to be the worst division in the Iraqi army.

Those three divisions are supported by one of the Republican Guard's shaky motorized divisions, the Abed Division. The southern flank is held by the II Corps. That corps has two weak infantry divisions (the 15th and 34th) and a well-regarded armored division. About half of the 3rd Armored Division's infantry units are equipped with BMPs.

Even if the 4th Infantry Division were unable to establish a northern front, these three corps would be unlikely to move south to intervene in fighting around Baghdad. The two Republican Guard divisions might move south, though that would be dangerous once bombing started, but the V, I and II corps lack the transport to move.

As to reserves, Iraq doesn't have any to speak of. It has various "People's Militia" units, which are basically a joke. If they were to go into action against American or British forces, they would be slaughtered. However, these units are made up of older men who have had their fill of war against Iranians, Americans or both, so they probably wouldn't go into action. In the event of an invasion, most will probably find that they have pressing business elsewhere.

These are the lineups. Now, all that remains is for the fighting to commence and for events to take their course.

(Thomas Houlahan is the director of the Military Assessment Program of the William R. Nelson Institute at James Madison University.)

U.S. forces girding for short, furious war

PAMELA HESS

WASHINGTON, March 17 (UPI) — Around a dozen Tomahawk cruise missile–capable ships and submarines have moved from the Mediterranean Sea into the Red Sea and are poised to unleash their satellite-guided weapons on Baghdad, Pentagon officials confirmed Monday. A small number of U.S. Special Forces are in northern Iraq to track down Iraqi Scud missiles and chemical and biological weapons. Around 3,000 are based in Jordan, pending the start of the war. Five aircraft carriers and dozens of ships are in the Persian Gulf and Arabian Sea, ready to launch a furious but short air strike with precision munitions to provoke "shock and awe" in the Iraqi army and cause mass defections.

"We're locked and loaded," a senior defense official said Monday.

The coming war will be very different from Operation Desert Storm of 1991, when the goal was to repel Iraqi troops from its neighbor, Kuwait. It did so with 38 days of air strikes with

126,645 combat sorties, during which satellite-guided Tomahawks made their combat debut. It also saw the first use of laser-guided bombs. In all, the coalition dropped 96,000 tons of ordnance. The United States was responsible for all but 7,500 tons of it. More than 300 tons of the ordnance involved depleted uranium munitions, used to pierce heavy armor.

The war is expected to start with just over three days to a week of air strikes and missile launches, during which as many as 3,000 bombs and missiles will be fired, many of them at air defense sites around Baghdad. Others will target suspected chemical and biological weapons sites, surface-to-air missiles sites, communications facilities and military headquarters, including presidential palaces.

The force at the start of the 1991 ground war totaled 541,425 personnel — more people than are now on the entire active roster of the U.S. Army. There were also 257,900 coalition forces, including 45,000 Brits and 14,600 French. Saudi Arabia dedicated 100,000 troops to the effort, according to Pentagon documents. Now, 149,000 U.S. troops are in Kuwait. More than 100,000 military personnel are arrayed at other bases and on ships in the Middle East and in Europe, ready to participate in the strike to remove Saddam Hussein from power and rid Iraq of its weapons of mass destruction.

The Pentagon has not revealed the number of foreign forces that will be fighting with the United States if war is declared, but the number is certain to be far lower than in 1991. The United Kingdom has about 45,000 troops in the Gulf region, including 25,000 troops in Kuwait, and Australia has sent around 2,000.

The Persian Gulf War and 10 years of no-fly-zone and drive-zone strikes have significantly eroded the Iraqi military. The coalition destroyed roughly 3,700 of 4,280 Iraqi battle tanks, 2,400 of 2,870 armored vehicles, 2,600 of 3,110 artillery pieces and rendered ineffective 42 Iraqi divisions, according to the Pentagon.

From an army that once numbered more than 680,000 in 1991, Iraq is believed to have a ground force now of roughly 400,000, with as many as 300,000 more reservists on call-up status.

Using black market funds from the illegal sale of oil, Iraq has been able to rebuild its forces somewhat. Iraq now has an estimated 2,200 to 2,600 main battle tanks, 3,700 other armored vehicles and 2,400 major artillery weapons. It could have as many as 850 surface-to-air missile launchers and 3,000 antiaircraft guns, according to Anthony Cordesman, an Iraq expert analyst at the Center for Strategic and International Studies.

Iraq's army includes six Republican Guard divisions, the best-trained and most loyal forces to Saddam. They number around 100,000 men and are expected to heavily fortify Baghdad. Four special Republican Guard brigades numbering 12,000 to 25,000 are dedicated to Saddam's personal and government security.

Pentagon sources say at least one of the Republican Guard units may have been equipped with chemical munitions in the event of an attack on Iraq. Pentagon officials say they have intelligence indications but no proof.

"We suspect it, but do we have proof? No," an official told United Press International. They do not believe Iraq is likely to launch a pre-emptive chemical attack, as to do so would likely galvanize the world against Saddam. "If he gets in a shot before something starts, the floodgates would open as to who would support what," the official said.

Iraq launched 88 Scud missiles during the Persian Gulf War, including 39 at Israel. One Iraqi Scud killed 28 U.S. soldiers in Saudi Arabia, the single largest loss in Operation Desert Storm. A total of 146 Americans were killed in action in the Gulf War. There were 98 more casualties in the coalition. The total number of coalition soldiers wounded in action, including American, was 894. Thirty-five Americans died in friendly-fire accidents during the Gulf War.

U.S.: Iraq has no idea of U.S. power

PAMELA HESS

WASHINGTON, March 19 (UPI) — The Iraqi military has no idea what the first wave of the coming war will be like, a top U.S. Air Force official declared Wednesday. "I do not think our potential adversary has any idea what's coming," said Col. Gary Crowder, division chief of the plans directorate at Air Combat Command. "We would not have believed it possible" 10 years ago, he said.

What's coming is 10 times greater than what the Iraqis faced on the first night of the Persian Gulf War: As many as 3,000 precision weapons, fired at targets around Iraq in an intense volley meant to stun and overwhelm the military, according to Crowder. The Persian Gulf War began with between 300 and 400 precision weapons — mostly Tomahawk cruise missiles and laser-guided bombs from stealthy F-117 fighters — at around 125 targets. "There will be an order of magnitude larger in terms of numbers struck in the first 24 hours," Crowder said. "I think the effects that we are trying to create is to make it so apparent and so overwhelming at the very outset of potential military operations that the adversary quickly realizes that there is no real alternative here other than to fight and die or to give up."

The difference between then and now: Where only 36 aircraft were equipped with precision-guided munitions (PGMs) in 1991, nearly all of the roughly 600 combat aircraft arrayed around the Persian Gulf have "smart" weapons, according to Crowder. Most are equipped with the low-cost satellite-guided Joint Direct Attack Munition, a "dumb" bomb with a strap-on "IQ" — a motor, tail kit and guidance system that guides the weapon to its target using Global Positioning System data. "Our capability is dramatically improved," Crowder said. "If you're not dropping PGMs, you're probably not close to the fight."

In the Persian Gulf War, F-117 Nighthawks flew just 2 percent of the opening night sorties but took out 53 percent of the targets, Crowder said. Stealth will be equally as important in this coming battle but perhaps less necessary. Ten years of no-fly-zone enforcement has seriously degraded Iraqi air defenses in the northern and southern no-fly-zones, which together cover almost half of the country.

"It is a significantly less hostile place than it was on the opening night of the Gulf War," Crowder said.

In 1991, it took "vicious fighting" to gain air superiority over the Iraqis' then very robust air defense system. The steady attrition of the system's farther outposts means almost instant air superiority, so ground forces can push toward Baghdad quickly. Baghdad itself is expected to be the primary battlefield. CNN reported Wednesday that elite Iraqi Republican Guard soldiers are fanning out around the city, suggesting there may be heavy urban fighting, the most dreaded type of battle with the highest possibility of casualties, both military and civilian.

"Civilians who are not targets will be killed in the operation," Crowder said.

They could be victims of errant bombs, Iraqi missiles falling back to earth, Iraqi sabotage or simply being caught near a legitimate military target at the wrong time.

Crowder said U.S. forces are confident of a swift victory but aware that war is a chaotic, uncontrollable event.

"Quite frankly, we really have little clear understanding of exactly what will happen when we step across that line. I think there's going to be a wide variety of different reactions by the Iraqi people and the Iraqi military forces," Crowder said. "We have every reason to be confident. We're the finest military in the world. That said, if we go to war, all bets are off. But we wouldn't be doing this if we thought we were going to lose."

Baghdad will be very selectively targeted, with the United States using the smallest possible weapon on military targets to cause the least amount of damage to surrounding areas, he said. "Baghdad will not look like Dresden," he said, referring to the leveled German city in World War II. "You're not going to see that type of conflict."

Crowder said the military has evolved a new approach to war called "effects-based targeting," which allows the least amount of physical damage with the greatest impact on an enemy. Where once the military planned to destroy all targets, now the military goes to great lengths to determine which targets are critical nodes that, if taken down, hobble other targets. This allows selective targeting and frees up planes and missiles to target other key nodes simultaneously, hastening the collapse of the enemy.

The U.S. Air Force is likely to debut a new precision armored tank- and truck-killing weapon, the Sensor-Fuzed Weapon. This a large 1,000-pound canister filled with 10 submunitions, each with a parachute that controls its rate of descent and helps spread the bombs over a tank column or 30-acre battlefield. Each submunition contains four copper disks with infrared sensors. Each disk searches for separate targets and then triggers an explosion, which melts the metal and propels it toward the target. During the flight, the melted copper is shaped into a perfectly aerodynamic projectile that can pierce armor. The SFW has a triple redundant "dudding" mechanism, which should render the weapon harmless if it cannot find an appropriate target.

Bush: War on Iraq has started

WASHINGTON, March 19 (UPI) — President George W. Bush said late Wednesday that U.S. and coalition forces were in the "opening stages" of what he called a "broad and coercive campaign" against Iraq. "American and coalition forces are in the early stages of military operations to disarm Iraq, to free its people and to defend the world from grave danger," Bush said.

The war against Saddam Hussein's regime began about 90 minutes after the expiration of a 48-hour deadline Bush gave to the Iraqi leader and his two sons on Monday. Saddam was told to step down or face a U.S.-led military invasion.

In his approximately five-minute Oval Office address to the nation, the president cautioned that the war "could be longer ... than some predict." Bush said the first strikes were against "selected targets of military importance." The president added that the Iraqi leader has "no regard for convention of war or rules of morality." Bush said Saddam "has attempted to use innocent, men, women, children" as shields.

CHAPTER 3
TWENTY-ONE DAYS

Day 1 — Thursday, March 20

ABOARD THE USS HARRY S. TRUMAN, eastern Mediterranean, March 20 (UPI) — An F-14 Tomcat launches from the flight deck of the USS Harry S. Truman on Thursday, March 20, 2003, in the eastern Mediterranean. (John Gillis, UPI)

"(A)n improvised prelude to the major attack . . ."

MARTIN WALKER

As dawn broke over Baghdad, the shrill sound of air raid sirens filled the air, followed by loud bursts of antiaircraft gunfire. Then came bigger explosions that shook buildings. After months of bitter debate, and the dropping of 17 million propaganda leaflets by U.S. military aircraft, the U.S.-led attack against Iraq had begun. President George W. Bush called it "the opening stage of what will be a broad and concerted campaign" — and, fittingly, the target was Iraqi leader Saddam Hussein himself.

After forcing the diplomatic pace in the United Nations, Bush, on Monday, March 17, had given Saddam 48 hours to leave the country or face war. Ninety minutes after that deadline ended — and with a defiant Saddam still in place — precision bombs began falling on Baghdad.

Even British Prime Minister Tony Blair was taken by surprise by the raid when he was woken up and told the news at around 4 A.M. The Americans had jumped the gun. The allies had agreed to launch a full military offensive Saturday. Also, the limited raid was far from the planned "shock and awe" operation, calling for 3,000 tons of bombs to be to be dropped

23

on Baghdad in the first 24 hours. But U.S. administration officials said the attack had been an improvised prelude to the major attack, hoping to take advantage of a chance opportunity. American intelligence had been alerted by one of its best-placed intelligence assets in Baghdad that Saddam was meeting in a bunker with his top military and intelligence aides. Alerted by Central Intelligence Agency Director George Tenet, Bush decided to act fast before the Iraqi leader moved to another location.

For the Bush administration, the Iraq crisis had always been first and foremost about removing Saddam and only second about disarming Iraq. Senior officials argued in private that with Saddam deposed, dismantling Iraq's weapons of mass destruction — the chemical and biological stockpiles and Baghdad's alleged work on developing nuclear bombs — would drop easily into place.

Between 30 and 40 cruise missiles were launched at the two Baghdad targets in simultaneous attacks lasting around 50 minutes. Two hours later, a pale and drawn Saddam, wearing large dark-rimmed glasses, appeared on television to deliver a rambling, defiant speech full of exhortations to his people to resist the attackers. Addressing the United States, he said, "Draw your swords: I am not afraid." In contrast to his words, there was little emotion in his delivery, as he read from a note pad, flipping over the pages.

Although the raid had apparently failed to remove Saddam (to those who knew him, the speculation that the man on television might be a Saddam double seemed far-fetched), the fact that Washington had opened its offensive with a direct attack on the dictator will have scored points in the psychological war. Iraqis learned from CNN, al-Jazeera and other media that their leader had been the target of a U.S. attack. As a result, he was forced to emerge from his hiding place quickly to stop rumors that he had been hurt.

Saddam began his speech by mentioning the date so that his listeners would know it was not an earlier recording. Still, taken in conjunction with the clouds of leaflets that had been dropped on Iraq urging soldiers to surrender, and the promises of better conditions when Saddam was ousted, news of the attack would have left an impression of his vulnerability.

As for Saddam himself, there was first the shock of the attack. Saddam is known to move constantly among his many palaces and never to spend two nights in succession in the same location. Now he confronts the realization that someone close enough to him to have details of his normally secret movements had leaked his whereabouts to the enemy.

Observers noted that Saddam did not say he was not where U.S. intelligence had placed him. Not that it mattered. The Bush administration was seen to have struck the first blow at its No. 1 target.

Meanwhile, 350 miles to the south, the U.S. Marines had punched wide holes on the fences and sand berms that marked the frontier zone between Kuwait and Iraq and launched the land invasion. Dawn broke over the al Rumaila oil fields of southern Iraq to plumes of billowing smoke from torched wells, destroyed Iraqi military positions and the sight of Iraqi soldiers surrendering by the score.

United Press International reporter Richard Tomkins, embedded with the 5th Marines, saw the gas–oil separation plant six miles north of the Kuwaiti border burning fiercely in two places, set alight in an apparent scorched-earth move by the Saddam Hussein regime. Elsewhere on the horizon, at least four natural gas facilities were spewing flame and smoke in the distance. The facility, referred to on Marine Corps maps as GOSP-3, was the prime objective of Bravo Company, 1st Battalion, of the 5th Marine Regimental Combat Team, which crossed the border Thursday night at 1730 GMT (8:30 p.m. local/12:30 p.m. EST) in armored assault vehicles. It suffered less than a half-dozen casualties, and none of the wounds was life threatening.

Pushing though the border line from LD (line of departure) Florida, the Marines had to move through a narrow five-kilometer path — the Kuwaiti border berm, a tank ditch, an electric fence and then the Iraqi border berm. The task was made easier by a vanguard that destroyed the obstructions hours earlier. To a crescendo of distant explosions from U.S. aircraft, the Marines split into several columns and raced to their objectives.

"It's a good day to be a Marine," one man yelled from his 26-ton vehicle.

"They put up some minor resistance, kind of a show of face, I guess, and then surrendered," Staff Sgt. Gregory Craft said.

Craft said his unit took six prisoners in the inky black night while searching trenches, eerily illuminated by the burning remnants of an artillery battery vaporized by laser-guided bombs from planes. A small number of tanks were also engaged but did not fire back. The Iraqis had abandoned them and fled.

With the coming of dawn, a dribble of disheveled Iraqi troops began leaving their foxholes on the south side of the gas and oil plant in groups of three and four, waving makeshift white flags as they approached 1st Battalion troops. Before an hour had passed, they were coming out in larger groups. In the first two hours of Friday morning, more than 159 Iraqis had surrendered and more were continuing to approach U.S. troops, turning themselves in.

"We search 'em, search 'em for weapons, never mind the mementos and papers for now," Lt. Dave Denials, commander of the company's 1st Platoon, told his men. "And keep each other covered."

The prisoners, ranging from teenagers to older men, appeared thankful to turn themselves over. Many asked for food and water, which they were given once taken to positions in the rear.

"Hey, look, they're forming lines themselves," said Lance Cpl. Gregory Moll, looking at the detainees. "It looks like they've done this before. They all look so dirty, tired and hungry."

The attack Thursday night launched the ground war to topple Saddam and disarm him of suspected weapons of mass destruction. It came after troops spent two days in forward positions along the border, practicing the attack but also taking time out to listen to President George W. Bush on the radio announce the start of hostilities.

That start was readily apparent to them. As the president spoke, aircraft streaked overhead, heading north to Iraq. Four Marines — from Alpha Company — were wounded in the pre-dawn fighting: three from a land mine or other explosive device, one from a bullet to the thigh. One Marine was killed in the fighting: 2nd Lt. Therrel Shane Childers, 30, of Saucier, Miss. The wounded were tended and the prisoners were handed over to the British troops of the Royal Irish Regiment, who were securing the oil fields. And the Marines clambered aboard their troops' carriers and headed north.

The predictable leaders in the predictable capitals made predictable comments condemning the raids on Baghdad. Only the sharpness of the language differed.

Russian President Vladimir Putin's unusually tough criticism was surprising. At a meeting of senior members of the Kremlin Thursday, he warned the Bush administration that it was making "a big political mistake." He said, "Russia insists on an end as quickly as possible to military action."

French President Jacques Chirac was muted by comparison. As the point man for the antiwar group in the U.N. Security Council, many thought he had overplayed his hand. But in his first public comment since the bombing started, the rhetoric was toned down considerably. "I hope these operations are as swift and cause as little bloodshed as possible, and that they do not lead to a humanitarian catastrophe," he said.

China came somewhere in between France and Moscow. The Beijing Foreign Ministry spokesman, Kong Quan, said the United States was "violating the norms of international behavior." He said the "relevant countries" should "stop using force, stop military action" and return to settling the crisis within the U.N. framework.

To the eerie wail of sirens, Kuwaitis went to the shelters established in the basements of public buildings, many people clutching gas masks and watching nervously the broadcasts from the Kuwaiti Ministry of Information on the status of the missile attacks. So far, neither chemical nor biological weapons have been detected and the missiles have, so far, done no damage, although two were reported to have landed in the desert near the vast U.S. military camps north and west of Kuwait City, and Kuwaiti officials claimed that at least two more had been destroyed by Patriot missiles.

The alarms and sirens make it clear that Kuwait City is a war zone, but there is no blackout and the city remains brightly lit. Kuwait civilian airport was still open to flights by Kuwait airlines Thursday, although most international carriers had suspended flights. The center glows with neon and the port is as bright as day under arc lights as troops and dockworkers labor round the clock to get military supplies ashore to feed the vast logistics machine that fuels the attack to the north. The Anglo–American advance needs over a million gallons of fuel a day to keep going.

As midnight came on Kuwait's first day of war, the sirens wailed yet again for the sixth time that day, yet again sending children and frightened mothers trailing down endless stairs to the shelters. The elevators are automatically cut when the alarm goes. Police checkpoints on the major roads remained during the alarms, and the endless convoys of fuel tankers and trucks from the port continued to haul north from the port as the big attack got under way.

Kuwaitis, with bitter personal experience of the Iraqi invasion in 1990 and the subsequent looting and pillage of their city, seem overwhelmingly supportive of the war. The tone was set in a speech to his people by the emir, Sheikh Al-Jaber al-Sabah, in which he said, "Screams coming from those of our people who were tortured, and the wails of the young and old, women and children, still echo loud in our ears."

"Arab and Islamic history have not seen oppression like that we were exposed to by our Arab and Islamic neighbor," the sheikh added. "The state of Kuwait is not sounding the drums of war, but rather that war drums are being sounded by a regime that does not learn from its past experiences."

Dissent

WASHINGTON, March 20 (UPI) — Antiwar demonstrators gathered in front of the White House on a cold and rainy Thursday afternoon to protest the start of a U.S.-led war against Iraq. Chanting, "Bush, we want peace, U.S. out of the Middle East" and "No blood for oil, U.S. off Iraqi soil," fewer than a hundred protesters entered Lafayette Park. The peace group ANSWER, Act Now to Stop War and End Racism, organized the demonstration.

"I feel this is an unjustified war — the U.S. should not commit a pre-emptive strike on Iraq. We should not continue a war on Iraq that has been going on for a long time with sanctions and bombings," said Andrea Scharnau, 41, a museum worker from Arlington, Va.

Margot Brandenburg, 24, a volunteer worker for ANSWER, said she felt the weapons inspections process was halted prematurely.

"I feel strongly against going to war with Iraq. I think it's a mistake to go to war, I don't think it's worth the damage to the Iraqi people and their infrastructure," she said.

ANSWER organized walkouts and protests in Washington and other cities Thursday, including New York, Los Angeles, San Francisco and Boston. Members of the group oppose war with Iraq because, they claim, the Arab nation does not pose a clear and present danger to the United Sates and its allies. "Iraq, a country that has not attacked or threatened the U.S., is now the subject of a state-sponsored terrorist assault as the Bush administration orders cruise missile attacks in Baghdad," said a statement released by the group.

Antiwar protesters frequently have accused the administration of waging a war for the sole purpose of controlling the region's oil supply. Thursday, many activists carried signs that read, "No blood for oil."

Iraq war protests sweep Arab world

CAIRO, March 20 (UPI) — Protests swept the Arab world Thursday following the launch of the U.S. war on Iraq. In Egypt, more than 1,000 people, mainly students from the American University in Cairo, clashed with riot police as they tried to march on the U.S. and British embassies. Thousands of riot police surrounded the protesters, who pelted them with stones in an attempt to break out of the cordon. Police retaliated by beating the protesters with sticks and spraying them with water in an attempt to disperse them. The angry demonstrators burned U.S. and British flags and shouted hostile comments about Arab leaders, describing them as traitors.

Also in Cairo, more then 10,000 Egyptian students, mostly belonging to Muslim fundamentalist groups, demonstrated inside the campuses of Cairo and Kfar al-Sheikh universities and the al-Azhar theological school, calling for an Islamic holy war against the United States.

The protesters shouted that President George W. Bush was the enemy of God and urged Arab leaders to take immediate measures to stop U.S. aggression and to close down all U.S. military bases in Arab countries. Egypt's highest Muslim religious authority, Sheikh Ahmed al-Tayeb, denounced the war on Iraq, which he said would reflect badly on all international organizations, including the United Nations and the Arab League. But Osama Baz, political adviser to President Hosni Mubarak, held the Iraqi regime responsible for the war, noting that "Cairo deployed tremendous efforts to promote a peaceful settlement, but the Iraqi response was late."

Mubarak said in a statement Wednesday that the Iraqi leadership was responsible for the deterioration of security in the Persian Gulf by committing terrible mistakes, including the 1990 invasion of Kuwait, which touched off security fears among regional countries and slammed the door open for foreign interference in the region. In Jordan, lawyers staged a sit-in at the law courts in Amman Thursday, shouting slogans hostile to the United States and causing the suspension of trials.

A member of the lawyers syndicate, Samih Khreiss, told United Press International that some 500 lawyers tried to march to the Iraqi Embassy to show solidarity with Iraq, but were banned by riot police and internal security forces from reaching it. In Morocco, schools and universities suspended classes Thursday as tens of thousands of protesting students took to the streets. Riot police kept the demonstrators from marching in the main streets in Rabat, Casablanca, Fez, Marrakesh and Tetouan.

In the first official reaction to the start of the war, King Mohamed VI Thursday stressed the need to preserve Iraq's sovereignty, independence and territorial integrity. The government spokesman, Nabil bin Abdullah, said Morocco regretted and was disappointed by the resort to force to settle the Iraqi crisis. "Morocco stands on the side of the Iraqi people to alleviate its sufferings and preserve the unity of its country," he added.

Sudan's government strongly denounced the war as thousands of protesters demonstrated in the streets of Khartoum. President Mohammed Taha condemned the U.S. attack, stressing that "the Arab nation was fully capable of resisting and confronting aggression and injustice." Riot police roamed the streets, but no clashes were reported with the demonstrators who marched on the U.S. Embassy.

In Libya, hundreds of angry demonstrators took to the streets of the main cities, including the capital Tripoli, calling for jihad against the United States and brandished placards reading, "No to war. Yes to peace" and "Get your hands off Iraq."

A meeting of the Arab League at its headquarters in Cairo was marred by recriminations between the Iraqi and Kuwaiti representatives.

Kuwait's Khaled Kleib denounced what he called Iraq's aggression, accusing it of firing banned Scud missiles into the emirate.

Iraq's Mohsen Khalil denied the accusation and claimed the firing came from inside Kuwait.

"It is a sad day for all the Arabs when an Arab country and an Arab people are subject to a military strike that does not take into consideration civilians," said League Secretary-General Amr Moussa. "We are deeply angry and sorry."

Voices of dissent: Richard Reeves

LOU MARANO

WASHINGTON, March 23 (UPI) — The U.S. attack on Iraq sets a bad precedent that will make conflict more likely and the world a more dangerous place, a presidential biographer and syndicated columnist said Sunday.

"I am very, very uncomfortable with the whole concept of pre-emptive war," said Richard Reeves in a phone interview. "I think it will lead to things like India attacking Pakistan, China attacking Taiwan."

Reeves predicted that any major regional power would adopt the American model when it suits its interests to do so. "Australia and Indonesia, one or the other," he said. If the United States claims the moral right to attack a country that could be a threat in five or 10 years, others will follow its example in many parts of the world, he told United Press International.

Reeves said he is among those who believe war was unnecessary to achieve U.S. objectives, at least as those objectives were articulated by the Bush administration.

"American citizens were not threatened in any way by Iraq," he said. "As soon as the war began, even (Israeli Prime Minister Ariel) Sharon said that he didn't think that Israel was threatened by Iraq."

Reeves was asked if he saw the need to prevent the possibility of nuclear blackmail as a legitimate casus belli. "People are vulnerable to nuclear blackmail everywhere in the world, and we are one of the blackmailers," he answered. "Israel is one of the blackmailers. North Korea is one of the blackmailers. We wouldn't stand for a minute with American soldiers under the guns of North Korea if they [the U.S. soldiers] didn't have nuclear weapons. ... There are people who threaten us with nuclear blackmail in one way or another, and we're going to have to figure out some way to deal with them. But for the moment at least, we seem to have concluded — wisely, I think — that invasion is not one of those ways."

Reeves was asked if he was referring to North Korea.

"To North Korea," he replied. "We may have to face a showdown with Pakistan sometime in the future. Iran — Nonproliferation seems to have run its course as a policy, though it was generally effective."

Reeves said that at first, nonproliferation meant that only the United States would have nuclear weapons. "And many countries went along with that. And nuclear weapons have not been used since 1945. Part of that is to the credit of the policy, but that policy now seems to have broken down in places like Korea."

Reeves said he lived in Pakistan in the 1980s, "and if you lived in places like Pakistan, you came to understand that in the modern world, possession of nuclear weapons was the badge of adulthood.

"There are two kinds of countries in this world: those that have them and those that don't," the author said. "And those that have them are better protected, whether they intend to use them or not, because of issues like nuclear blackmail. And it may be that the world — and the United States, too — has to take a different tack as medium powers like Turkey, Brazil and Japan try to determine whether they are safer with or without nuclear weapons.

"Unfortunately, North Korea with nuclear weapons would be treated quite differently than without them."

Reeves was asked if it is not true that nuclear-armed countries led by calculating or capricious dictators present greater dangers than other nuclear powers.

"It's one of the reasons why you want democracies," he said. "Democracies tend to be more rational than dictatorships."

But he returned to the example of such countries as Pakistan.

"Remember, Pakistan has never had a peaceful change of government in its history. If it uses nuclear weapons, it will be against India. And if India decides on a pre-emptive strategy, which it will one day, it is those nuclear weapons that it will go after. And it will claim the blessing of American thinking in doing that.

"We are not talking about Minnesota. In a place like Pakistan, the government today could be quite different from the government tomorrow. How close is Pakistan to becoming Afghanistan? We don't know. What kind of government is China going to have in the future? We don't know. Today's madman could be tomorrow's Jefferson, and today's Jefferson may be tomorrow's madman."

Reeves said he disagrees with what appears to be the Bush administration's larger strategy — that the United States can control events in such places as the Middle East.

"We can't remake the Middle East in our image," he said. "The West has gone down that trail many times, and it never seems to lead where we want it to lead. I don't claim to know why that's the case, but it historically is the case. ... The British created the situation we are now trying to rectify or recreate."

After World War I, Britain administered the part of the defeated Ottoman Empire that became Iraq, which had been known as the province of Mesopotamia, under a League of Nations mandate. A revolt broke out in 1920. An Anglo–Iraqi treaty was signed in 1922, with full independence coming 10 years later.

Iraq has been called an artificial state whose borders were drawn by foreigners who forced hostile Kurds, Sunnis and Shiites into the same political unit.

"I think Saddam Hussein is being used as a window of opportunity to try to remake the Middle East in the way we remade Europe or Japan after World War II," Reeves said. "I think a lot of people in our leadership now feel that we blew an opportunity to do that after World War II. I don't think that's an accurate reading of history, but I think the people who read it that way are sincere."

Reeves is author of *President Kennedy: Profile of Power* (1993) and *President Nixon: Alone in the White House* (2001) and has made a number of documentary films.

Voices of dissent: Thomas Fleming

LOU MARANO

WASHINGTON, March 22 (UPI) — A conservative critic of the Bush administration's war policy said much of the hostility and resentment in the diplomatic sphere could have been avoided by a more honest approach. Top administration officials "had made up their minds a long time ago for a war with Iraq," said Thomas Fleming, editor of *Chronicles* magazine and president of the Illinois-based Rockford Institute. "Going to the U.N. when your mind is already made up is a mistake," he said in a phone interview with United Press International. "It looks manipulative. So the Russians, the French, the Chinese are sucked into a process, and when it turns out that they've got the votes and we don't, we then say: 'Well, we don't accept the conclusion.'

"We shouldn't have entered into it if we weren't going to accept the conclusion. And I don't think there was any way — for good or evil, no matter what your stand — that we were not going to war."

Fleming said that although he joined in the general praise of Secretary of State Colin Powell for persuading President Bush to go to the United Nations, he didn't realize at the time that war was a foregone conclusion. "Under those circumstances, it would have been better just to declare to the world: 'We believe we are right. We are going ahead. Join us if you will. Otherwise, it's been good to know you," he told UPI.

Fleming also said Congress has been evading its constitutionally mandated responsibility to decide matters of war and peace. He said, well before the November elections, the president should have declared where he stood. During the campaign, congressional candidates would have been forced to explain to their constituents how they would vote on the war. Congress' evasion, Fleming said, came "because when the president of the dominant party wants a war, then all the members of his party feel obliged to give it to him, but the members of the opposing party — especially when it's Democrats — are often afraid to appear unpatriotic or disloyal. "And that's not what they're elected for. ... On the big issues, I think elections should be referendums on where people stand."

Fleming said he doesn't like to see a lot of irrational and emotional argument breaking out in America during a period of crisis, and people should not take sides on the basis of political ideology or party. He called Senate Minority Leader Tom Daschle's recent criticisms of the president "stupid."

"As the congressional leader of a party that had given President Bush the power to go to war, it's a little late to start complaining," he said. "It was pure politics, and very bad. ... When a country is at crisis, we should try to keep the rhetorical level as low as possible."

Fleming termed his own position on the war "rather complex" and "a hard sell."

Pre-emptive wars are morally wrong and violate international law, he said. Therefore, he would have voted against the war resolution if he had been a member of Congress, even though it will be good to get rid of Saddam Hussein.

ABOARD THE USS HARRY S. TRUMAN, eastern Mediterranean, March 21 (UPI) — Lt. Mike Picciano (*left*) and Lt. Marc Fryman of squadron VF 32 get into their flight gear prior to launching a night strike into Iraq from the aircraft carrier USS Harry S. Truman on Friday, March 21, 2003, in the eastern Mediterranean. The squadron flies F-14 Tomcats. (John Gillis, UPI)

Day 2 — Friday, March 21

"(T)he 'shock and awe' attack of aerial bombing exploded onto TV screens around the world . . . "

MARTIN WALKER

KUWAIT CITY, The first whiffs of burning oil wells began drifting south into Kuwait Friday as American armored units raced north for the bridges across the Euphrates on the way to Baghdad. British and U.S. Marines ground on against stiffening resistance to take Iraq's main port of Umm Qasr and the Rumaila oil fields. It was as though two entirely different battles were under way, one fast and daring, the other steady and deliberate, reflecting the dual objectives of the allied commanders.

But as well as the two strategic targets of Baghdad and the southern oil fields, there were other actions under way Friday. British, Australian and U.S. Special Forces were spearheading attacks on the western Iraqi airfields near the Jordanian border. And in the north, U.S. and British strikes were bombing targets around the city of Kirkuk, but Turkey's refusal to allow the 4th Infantry Division to use Turkish territory to open a major northern front meant that allied capabilities in this region were limited.

On Friday night, the "shock and awe" attack of aerial bombing exploded onto TV screens around the world as the all-out air attack launching 3,000 missiles and smart bombs on Iraqi targets simultaneously sought to stun and cow the Iraqi military command into shocked immobility.

"While it has to be a terribly unpleasant circumstance, (the residents of Baghdad) will have an opportunity to see the precision with which we're going about this task, and that the targets are military targets, and that this is not an attack on the Iraqi people," Defense Secretary Donald Rumsfeld said. "It is an enormous impressive effort, humane (targeting) effort to do what is necessary to reduce this threat against our country and that region, and to eliminate a regime that has killed hundreds of thousands of human beings." ... "The confusion of Iraqi officials is growing. Their ability to see what is happening on the battlefield, to communicate with their forces and to control their country is slipping away. They're beginning to realize, I suspect, that the regime is history," Rumsfeld said.

Iraqi Information Minister Mohammed Saeed al-Sahhaf told reporters in Baghdad that Saddam's family house was hit but "God protected his family." He strongly denied that the U.S.–British forces entered the area of Umm Qasr, saying it is "silly and a lie" and that he had just called the Umm Qasr governor, who rebutted the U.S. claims. "It's an attack and retreat battle. How would they enter Baghdad? It will be their crematory," he said. "Iraq's territories are vast and one or two tanks could enter and be filmed. The Iraqi army will fight them and will kill them in the land of Iraq."

To those watching the flowering of those terrible blossoms of fire in the mammoth air strikes on Baghdad, the attack looked almost biblical in its devastation, like the wrath of God being visited upon the Iraqi capital. But it was not. It was the wrath of man, directed in a new form of war, and remarkably precise in its visitation. Iraq's minister of information, who had no reason to minimize the casualty list, claimed 207 wounded civilians — in a city where electricity and water supplies continued to function. "The lights stayed on in Baghdad," said British Defense Minister Geoffrey Hoon. "It is the institutions of tyranny that are collapsing."

There has never been a bombing campaign like this before in history. Strategic bombing

marched into the pantheon of human horror with the random slaughter of civilians. Even before Oppenheimer's scientists brought forth Hiroshima, the cities of Guernica and Coventry, Hamburg and Dresden were milestones on the march of slaughter in modern, industrialized war. Now strategic bombing has become exactly what its original advocates once intended. It hits at will and with precision the legitimate targets of war. It attacks an enemy's leadership and command, Its communications and crucial logistics, in order to break Its will and capacity to fight. And because the civilians may now retreat mercifully back behind the front line of combat, where the 20th-century mode of warfare so memorably put them, this represents a civilizing advance in the military arts.

But the real outcome of this war may depend on how many people can be persuaded of this. The millions of people across the world who marched and demonstrated against this war Saturday — and some of the largest crowds were in the core coalition cities of London and New York — are unlikely to believe it. And why should they, when the pictures were so stunningly, so pyrotechnically good? The wars of modern advanced democracies hinge on the complexities of public opinion. And it is remarkable that Tony Blair, one of the most astute political salesman of our day, should have found it so tough to clamber his way back to 50 percent support for this war.

Public opinion in Britain and the United States, where critics can, after all, freely organize demonstrations and political campaigns to effect regime change in London and Washington, constitute only one part of the audience. The public opinion of the Islamic world, where there are few such democratic safety valves, have only the evidence of their own eyes and the twisted reports of their own media. For example, one reporter for the Qatar-based al-Jazeera TV channel, widely watched throughout the Arab world, reported from Baghdad during the bombing that the American bombers were "using weapons of mass destruction against Baghdad." Newspapers throughout the Islamic world are parroting the accusations of Baghdad's own propagandists that Bush and Blair are guilty of war crimes against the innocent civilians of

Baghdad — the very claim that made U.N. sanctions against Iraq so unpopular.

Outside Baghdad, the main battles were being conducted by the 230,000 American and British troops based in Kuwait. The battle for Umm Qasr was a two-pronged assault. British Commando troops and U.S. Marines launched an amphibious assault on the Faw peninsula while British armored forces and U.S. Marines surged overland through the Iraqi frontier to attack the port from the rear and seize the Umm Qasr airport. They had three main objectives. The troops were tasked to take the port intact as a new logistics route, particularly for humanitarian supplies; to clear the ground from which short-range Iraqi missiles had been launched against Kuwait; and to secure the hundreds of wellheads of the vast Rumaila oil field.

Thirty wellheads were on fire, British Defense Minister Geoffrey Hoon said Friday, and allied sources in Kuwait said they believed that four small oil refineries had been fired. But the oil facilities on the Faw facilities were taken intact, and U.S. Marines managed to secure at least three of the giant gas–oil separation plants, a major objective of the mission.

Allied patrols were heading north toward Basra, Iraq's second city, occupied mainly by Shia Muslims who have long suffered at Saddam Hussein's hands. British and U.S. psy-ops teams were close behind the forward troops, hoping that Basra could provide the politically needed scenes of Iraqis welcoming allied troops and their liberators.

The second battle, the bold thrust north to the Euphrates bridges and toward Baghdad, was by Friday morning New York time almost 100 miles deep into Iraq and meeting little resistance. Led by the U.S. 7th Cavalry, the armored brigades and mechanized infantry of the 3rd Infantry Division — close to 10,000 vehicles and nearly 20,000 troops — raced north throughout the night and into the day. They stopped only to refuel and to clean their air and oil filters.

Led by the Bradley fighting vehicles with M-1 Abrams tanks close behind and Apache helicopters scouting ahead, the advance was described by military sources back in Kuwait as "a classic cavalry operation — taking strategic ground fast." On the way, specialized units

stopped off to secure Iraqi airfields and get them back into sufficient working order to act as refueling and service points for combat and cargo helicopters bringing forward the vital fuel supplies. Plowing through clouds of dust thrown up by the armored vehicles, the race for the bridges across the Euphrates River would open the way to Baghdad — and to the probably decisive confrontation with the heavy armored units of the Iraqi Republican Guard.

To the southeast, and spearheading the push toward Iraq's second city of Basra, the Royal Irish Regiment found itself led by a sudden superstar back home in the United Kingdom Lt. Col. Tim Collins, commander of the RIR's 1st Battalion, made his entrance to the voracious British media Thursday via a "cool" photograph of him standing in the Kuwaiti desert wearing Ray-Ban-type sunglasses, cropped hair and puffing on a small cigar. He completed the picture by giving a brilliant, low-key eve-of-battle speech to his troops that stood in massive contrast to the hoo-ah! style of a U.S. admiral to his Marines at the same time.

Within a few hours the two allies would be fighting as brothers-in-arms, as they had done since World War I, and indeed would soon be the first to die together — in a helicopter accident that killed eight British Marines and four Americans. But what Collins told his troops was uniquely British, in a style that echoed Shakespeare's Henry V before the Battle of Agincourt.

"The enemy should be in no doubt that we are bringing about his rightful destruction," Collins told his assembled troops. "There are many regional commanders who have stains on their souls and they are stoking the fires of hell for (Iraqi leader) Saddam (Hussein). He and his forces will be destroyed by this coalition for what they have done. As they die they will know that their deeds have brought them to this place. Show them no pity."

Wearing a big curve-bladed *kukri* knife from the Nepali Gurkha company of his battalion, Collins also spoke of some of those among him who might not see the end of the campaign but would be "put in their sleeping bags and sent home. There will be no time for sorrow." And he explained in biblical terms his men's moral duties in the country they came to liberate, not conquer.

"I know of men who have taken life needlessly in other conflicts," he said. "I can assure you they live with the mark of Cain upon them. If someone surrenders to you, then remember they have that right in international law and ensure that one day they can go home to their family. The ones who wish to fight, well, we aim to please."

He spoke of the shame to the regiment and the nation of overenthusiasm in killing, and warned that they were entering a deeply historic land — the site of the Garden of Eden, of the Great Flood and the birthplace of Abraham.

"You will see things that no man could pay to see and you will have to go a long way to find a more decent, generous and upright people than the Iraqis. You will be embarrassed by their hospitality even though they have nothing. Don't treat them as refugees, for they are in their own country. Their children will be poor. In years to come they will know that the light of liberation in their lives was brought by you.

"If there are casualties of war, then remember that when they woke up in the morning they did not plan to die this day. Allow them dignity in death. Bury them properly and mark their graves. … As for ourselves, let's bring everyone home and leave Iraq a better place for us having been there. Our business now is north."

British military commanders rarely talk like this, especially at a time of deep division about the rightness of this war at home. Traditionally, British commanders say things like: "Well, chaps, this is it. We jolly well have to pull our socks up and get going on this one." Daily Telegraph columnist William Deedes, whose first foreign report for that paper was of the Abyssinia War in 1936, wrote Friday that British commanders rarely, if ever, talked of death, and breaking that specter broke a long military tradition.

But Collins is the new face of the British military: age 42, born and raised in Belfast, married with four children, a man with "a gift of the gab," according to a fellow officer. Despite a family history in the British army dating to 1857, Collins is thoroughly modern, with a toughness honed as a member of the legendary SAS (Special Air Service). He has turned the Northern Ireland–based Royal Irish Regiment — 40 percent of them Catholics from the Irish Republic — into a "special operations capable" infantry battalion that works closely alongside two battalions of the famed Red Beret Parachute Regiment.

Hours after he spoke, the RIR went into action with the 16 Air Assault Brigade, seizing oil wells in the Basra area before the Iraqis could blow them up. Friday, Adm. Michael Boyce, chief of the Defense Staff, said only seven oil heads had been set on fire by the Iraqis out of hundreds that remained intact.

Collins and the Royal Irish are part of the reason why, for all their relatively small size, the British military punches well above its weight of 45,000 troops in the Gulf, compared to 250,000 U.S. troops. While the U.S. Marine Corps alone outnumbers the size and power of the entire British army, U.S. Central Command chief Gen. Tommy Franks appears to have had no problem in assigning British forces lead roles in the opening phase of Operation Iraqi Freedom, or in placing 2,000 U.S. Marines of the 1st Marine Expeditionary Force under direct British command, the first time since World War II. Indeed, half of the armored strength of the 1st MEF is provided by 120 Challenger II tanks of the British Desert Rats 7th Armored Brigade. Covered by the tanks and by British artillery, the U.S. Marines entered the port of Umm Qasr and took it after a fight. It was a British commander, echoing the sentiments of Collins, that ordered the Marines to remove their victorious Stars and Stripes and Marine Corps flags from atop their seized objective. Britain, of course, has been here before, not only in 1918, as League of Nations mandated rulerafter the collapse of the Ottoman Empire, but as a principal builder of Iraq's civil service and military infrastructure. Indeed, the old port of Umm Qasr was built by the British, and so were such airfields as Shaibah and Habbaniyah, soon to be reoccupied by the allies.

In 2003, the British know they can only be number 2 to the American superpower, and have to struggle to keep up technologically. In their rush to Kuwait, they revealed their deficiencies in logistics such as boots, desert uniforms and even food supplies, compared to the laid-on showers and Burger Kings for the U.S. Army. Smart U.S. commanders, however, know better than to underestimate British forces. Franks has particularly involved the

British SAS and SBS (Special Boat Squadron) in major special operations.

A War for Oil?

Sam Vaknin

If the looming war was all about oil, Iraq would be invaded by the European Union, or Japan, whose dependence on Middle Eastern oil is far greater than that of the United States. The United States would probably have taken over Venezuela, a much larger and closer supplier with its own emerging tyrant to boot. At any rate, the United States refrained from occupying Iraq when it easily could have, in 1991. Why the current American determination to conquer the desert country and subject it to direct rule, at least initially?

There is another explanation, insist keen-eyed analysts. Sept. 11 shredded the American sense of invulnerability. That the hijackers were all citizens of ostensible allies — such as Egypt and Saudi Arabia — exposed the tenuous and ephemeral status of U.S. forces in the Gulf. So, is the war about transporting American military presence from increasingly hostile Saudis to soon-to-be subjugated Iraqis? But this is a tautology. If America's reliance on Middle Eastern oil is nonexistent, why would it want to risk lives and squander resources in the region at all? Why would it drive up the price of oil it consumes with its belligerent talk and coalition-building? Why would it fritter away the unprecedented upswell of goodwill that followed the atrocities in September 2001? Back to oil. According to British Petroleum's *Statistical Review of World Energy 2002,* the United States voraciously — and wastefully — consumes one of every four barrels extracted worldwide. It imports about three-fifths of its needs. In less than 11 years' time, its reserves depleted, it will be forced to import all of its soaring requirements.

Middle Eastern oil accounts for one-quarter of U.S. imports, Iraqi crude for less than one-tenth. A back-of-the-envelope calculation reveals that Iraq quenches less than 6 percent of

America's "black gold" cravings. Compared with Canada (15 percent of American oil imports) or Mexico (12 percent), Iraq is a minor supplier. Furthermore, the current oil production of the United States is merely 23 percent of its 1985 peak — about 2.4 million barrels per day, a 50-year nadir.

During the first 11 months of 2002, the United States imported an average of 9,000 bpd from Iraq. In January 2003, with Venezuela in disarray, approximately 1.2 million bpd of Iraqi oil went to the Americas, up from 910,000 bpd in December 2002 and 515,000 bpd in November. It would seem that $200 billion — the costs of war and postbellum reconstruction — would be better spent on America's domestic oil industry. Securing the flow of Iraqi crude is simply too insignificant to warrant such an exertion.

Much is made of Iraq's known oil reserves, pegged by the U.S. Department of Energy at 112 billion barrels, or five times the United States' — not to mention its 110 trillion cubic feet of natural gas. Even at 3 million bpd — said to be the realistically immediate target of the occupying forces and almost 50 percent above the current level — this subterranean stash stands to last for more than a century. Add to that the proven reserves of its neighbors — Kuwait, Saudi Arabia, the United Arab Emirates — and there is no question that the oil industries of these countries will far outlive their competitors'. Genteel French and Russian oilmen ask: Couldn't this be what the rapacious Americans are after? After all, British and American companies controlled three-quarters of Iraq's mineral wealth until 1972, when nationalization denuded them.

Alas, this "explanation" equally deflates upon closer inspection. Known — or imagined — reserves require investments in exploration, development and drilling. Nine-tenths of Iraq's soil is unexplored, including up to 100 billion barrels of deep oil-bearing formations located mainly in the vast western desert. Of the 73 fields discovered, only 15 have been developed.

Iraqi Oil Minister Amir Rashid admitted in early 2002 that only 24 Iraqi oil fields were producing. The country has almost no deep wells, unlike Iran, where they abound. The cost of production is around $1.00 to $1.50 per barrel, one-tenth the cost elsewhere. Texas boasts 1 million drilled wells; Iraq barely has 2,000. The Department of Energy's report about Iraq concludes: "Iraq generally has not had access to the latest, state-of-the-art oil industry technology (i.e., 3-D seismic surveys), sufficient spare parts and investment in general throughout most of the 1990s." Iraq reportedly has been utilizing questionable engineering techniques such as overpumping, water injection and old technology to maintain production. The quality of Iraqi oil deteriorated considerably in the past decade. Its average American Petroleum Institute gravity declined by more than 10 percent, its water cut (intrusion of water into oil reservoirs) increased and its sulfur content shot up by one-third. Iraq's oil fields date back to the 1920s and 1930s and were subjected to abusive methods of extraction. Thus, if torched during a Götterdämmerung, they might well be abandoned altogether.

According to a report published by the United Nations two years ago, Iraqi oil production is poised to fall off a cliff unless billions are invested in addressing technical and infrastructure problems. Even chaotic Iraq forks out $1.2 billion annually on repairing oil facilities. The Council of Foreign Relations and the Baker Institute last December estimated that the "Costs of repairing existing (Iraqi) oil export installations alone would be around $5 billion, while restoring Iraqi oil production to pre-1990 levels would cost an additional $5 billion, plus $3 billion per year in annual operating costs." Not to mention the legal quagmire created by the plethora of agreements signed by the soon-to-be-deposed regime with European, Indian, Turkish and Chinese oil behemoths. It would be years before Iraqi crude hits the markets in meaningful quantities and then only after tens of billions of dollars have been literally sunk into the ground. Not a very convincing business plan.

Conspiracy theorists dismiss such contravening facts impatiently. While the costs, they expound wearily, will accrue to the American taxpayer, the benefits will be reaped by the oil giants, the true sponsors of President George W. Bush, his father, his vice president and his secretary of defense. In short, the battle in Iraq has been spun by a cabal of sinister white males

out to attain self-enrichment through the spoils of war.

The case for the prosecution is that, cornered by plummeting prices, the oil industry in America has spent the last 10 years defensively merging and acquiring in a frantic pace. America's 22 major energy companies reported overall net income of $7 billion on revenues of $141 billion during the second quarter of last year. Only 45 percent of their profits resulted from domestic upstream oil and natural gas production operations. Tellingly, foreign upstream oil and natural gas production operations yielded 40 percent of net income, and worldwide downstream natural gas and power operations made up the rest. Stagnant domestic refining capacity forces U.S. firms to joint venture with outsiders to refine and market products. Moreover, according to the energy consultant John S. Herold, replacement costs — of finding new reserves — soared in 2001 to more than $5 per barrel, except in the Gulf, where oil is sometimes 1,000 feet deep and swathes of land are immersed in it. In short: American oil majors are looking abroad for their long-term survival; Iraq always featured high on their list.

This stratagem was subverted by the affair between Saddam Hussein and non-American oil companies. American players shudder at the thought of being excluded from Iraq by Saddam and his dynasty and thus rendered second-tier participants. According to the conspiracy-minded, the oil companies coaxed the White House first to apply sanctions to the country in order to freeze its growing amity with foreign competitors — and, now, to retake by force that which was confiscated from them by law. Development and production contracts with Russian and French companies, signed by Saddam's regime, are likely to be "reviewed" — that is, scrapped altogether — by whoever next rules over Baghdad.

An added bonus: the demise of the Organization of Petroleum Exporting Countries (OPEC). A United States in control of the Iraqi spigot can break the back of any oil cartel and hold sway over impertinent and obdurate polities such as France. How the ensuing plunge in prices would help the alleged instigators of the war — the oil mafia — remains unclear. Still, James Paul propounded the following exercise in the Global Policy Forum this past December:

"(Assume) the level of Iraqi reserves at 250 billion barrels and recovery rates at 50 percent (both very conservative estimates). Under those conditions, recoverable Iraqi oil would be worth altogether about $3.125 trillion. Assuming production costs of $1.50 a barrel (a high-end figure), total costs would be $188 billion, leaving a balance of $2.937 trillion as the difference between costs and sales revenues. Assuming a 50-50 split with the government and further assuming a production period of 50 years, the company profits per year would run to $29 billion. That huge sum is two-thirds of the $44 billion total profits earned by the world's five major oil companies combined in 2001. If higher assumptions are used, annual profits might soar to as much as $50 billion per year."

The energy behemoths on both sides of the pond are not oblivious to this bonanza. The Financial Times reported a flurry of meetings in recent days between British Petroleum and Shell and Downing Street and Whitehall functionaries. Senior figures in the ramshackle exile Iraqi National Congress opposition have been openly consorting with American oil leviathans and expressly promising to hand postwar production exclusively to them.

But the question is: even if true, so what? What war in human history was not partly motivated by a desire for plunder? What occupier did not seek to commercially leverage its temporary monopoly on power? When were moral causes utterly divorced from realpolitik? Granted, there is a thin line separating investment from exploitation, order from tyranny, vision from fantasy. The United States should — having disposed of Saddam and his coterie — establish a level playing field and refrain from giving Iraq a raw deal. It should use this tormented country's natural endowments to reconstruct it and make it flourish. It should encourage good governance, including transparent procurement and international tendering and invite the United Nations to oversee Iraq's reconstruction. It should induce other countries of the world to view Iraq as a preferred destination of foreign direct investment and trade. If, in the process, reasonable profits accrue to business, all for the better. Only the global private sector can guarantee the long-term prosperity of Iraq. Many judge the future conduct of the United States on the basis of speculative scenarios and fears that it is on the verge of attaining global dominance by way of ruthlessly applying its military might. This may possibly be so. But to judge it on this flimsy basis alone is to render verdict both prematurely and unjustly.

ABOARD THE USS HARRY S. TRUMAN, eastern Mediterranean, March 22 (UPI) — An F-14 Tomcat launches from the flight deck of the aircraft carrier USS Harry S. Truman to strike targets in Iraq, Saturday, March 22, 2003, in the eastern Mediterranean Sea.   (John Gillis, UPI)

Day 3 — Saturday, March 22

"Iraqi officials have placed troops and equipment in civilian areas, attempting to use innocent men, women and children as shields for the dictator's army. I want Americans and all the world to know that coalition forces will make every effort to spare innocent civilians from harm." — President George W. Bush

MARTIN WALKER

As the column of the U.S. Marines Expeditionary Force raced across the Iraqi desert Saturday day toward objectives deeper in the Iraqi heartland, it stretched along the highway as far as the eye could see. Armored attack vehicles, troop carriers and trucks loaded with supplies and ammunition raced past small villages. The column stopped occasionally to search buildings and people before the Marines continued on their journey. As the Marines rolled by, they occasionally encountered clumps of people walking down the road. They waved as the Marines went by, but otherwise appeared almost unconcerned at the invasion force in their country. The Marines pulled out of a gas and oil separation plant they captured in fighting Thursday night and Friday, handing the facility over to the British Royal Irish Regiment. They also turned over more than 300 prisoners, among them a lieutenant colonel who had been in charge of the Iraqi defenses at the plant. The entire operation at the plant was conducted in the darkness before dawn; the moon was blotted out by dust and only the eerie fires left from the bombing illuminated the field. Shortly after the battle, Marines approached a ditch where more than 30 Iraqi bodies lay. One Iraqi in his last moments of life was questioned. All he would say was, "Why did you do this?"

Some of the Iraqis in the ditch were killed as the Marines went through trenches routing out the enemy after aircraft swooped down, bombing the artillery battery and infantry company guarding the gas–oil plant. After the battle, the gas portion of the plant was on fire, either damaged in the fighting or set afire by the Iraqis. British engineers moved in to dispose of unexploded ordnance and to check the plant for hidden explosive charges.

The Marines spent most of Saturday moving across the desert, heading deeper into the country. At stops, troops formed tight security around their vehicles and several were detailed to search houses for weapons. The chief concern was that there might be occasional sniping, but none occurred. Along the route at various bridges, small two-man antiaircraft guns could be seen, abandoned like many of the homes along the way. In the distance, occasional plumes of smoke could be seen from burning oil wells. The lead vehicle of the column belonged to Bravo Company. On the hood was a child's toy alligator, nicknamed Crazy. The 26-ton armored amphibious vehicle, which carries troops into battle, had painted on its turret its own nickname: "the Porkchop Express." Lt. Anthony Sousa from Maine, commander of the vehicle, quipped that to be politically correct in a country where pork is not eaten, he had placed a sandbag to cover the word *pork*. Looking down at the baggy suit he wore to protect against possible chemical or biological weapons, he said, "Oops, I kind of looked like Snoop Doggy Dog. Does anyone have any tape to flatten it down?" He then broke into an improvisational rap about crossing the Iraqi desert.

For most of the Marines in the regiment, this is their first taste of war. Many of the senior noncommissioned officers, however, had taken part in Gulf War I in 1991 and also had served in Somalia in 1993. Younger Marines remained boisterous among themselves and full of bravado. But the older, experienced men retained a more sober mien and cautioned against overconfidence as America's force to topple Saddam Hussein moved deeper into

Mesopotamia, where the prospect of resistance increased.

As the Marines headed north toward Kut and Amara along the Shatt al-Arab route, the tanks of the 3rd Division seized the first key crossing over the Euphrates River at Nasiriyah, a city that was to become famous over the coming week as the Iraqis launched ambushes and raids from the urban area against the long and vulnerable U.S. supply lines. Poorly organized and armed with light weapons like machine guns and rocket-propelled grenades, and moving in 4-by-4 vehicles and pickup trucks, the Iraqi guerillas made little impression on the forward troops with their heavy armor. Some of their desperate attacks to challenge the U.S. troops holding the Nasiriyah bridges were almost suicide charges. But they were a constant menace to the supply trucks and tankers on which the whole advance depended.

The commander of the U.S.-led war, Gen. Tommy Franks, said Saturday from his headquarters in Doha, Qatar, that coalition forces had reached Nasiriyah and swept beyond the farthest point of penetration in the 1991 Gulf War in one-quarter the amount of time, a performance he described as "magnificent."

"We have operations ongoing in the north, in the west, in the south, and in and around Baghdad," he said. "Our troops are performing as we would expect — magnificently. And, indeed, the outcome is not in doubt. There may well be tough days ahead. But the forces on the field will achieve the objectives that have been set out by the governments of this coalition."

Franks appeared with British, Australian, Dutch and Danish military commanders in his first news briefing since the war began early Thursday. He said military operations were under way across Iraq, including in and around the capital, Baghdad, insisting the Iraq campaign was "unlike any other in history." He said Iraqi forces in Basra continued to resist U.S. and British troops fighting on the outskirts of the southern Iraqi city. Coalition forces were avoiding heavy city fighting, Franks said. Instead, he said, forces were surrounding the city, trying to arrange for Iraqi surrenders or ascertain that the forces there did not pose a threat to their logistics line before moving north to Baghdad.

"Our intent is not to move through and create military confrontations in that city. Rather, we expect that we will work with Basra and the citizens in Basra, the same way I believe has been widely reported in Umm Qasr," Franks said.

As darkness fell Saturday night across the region, sporadic but steady explosions were heard in Baghdad and the northern Iraqi cities of Mosul and Kirkuk, two oil-rich centers on the periphery of the Kurdish enclave. The United States is particularly anxious to secure them after retreating Iraqi soldiers set fire to several oil wells in the southern oil fields. Meanwhile, 13 U.S. servicemen from the Army's 101st Airborne Division were wounded in a grenade attack in the tents of Camp Pennsylvania in Kuwait, U.S. Central Command confirmed. One civilian witness told United Press International that two grenades were thrown into two tents in what were believed to be staff quarters of one of the brigades in the division, and that at least four soldiers were seriously wounded at the closely guarded base, some 15 miles outside Kuwait City. A U.S. soldier was taken into custody as a suspect.

President George W. Bush monitored the war against Iraq from the Camp David presidential retreat Saturday, meeting with his war council, speaking with British Prime Minister Tony Blair and telling the nation in his weekly radio address that it cannot "live at the mercy of an outlaw regime that threatens the peace with weapons of mass murder. We will accept no outcome but victory."

On the third full day since U.S. and British forces began their march toward Baghdad, the president began the day with an intelligence briefing and then convened his war council, which included Vice President Richard Cheney, Chief of Staff Andrew Card, National Security Adviser Condoleezza Rice, Defense Secretary Donald Rumsfeld, Joint Chiefs of Staff Chairman Gen. Richard Myers and Central Intelligence Agency Director George Tenet. Saturday, Bush said American and coalition forces would face enemies "who have no regard for the conventions of war or rules of morality. ... Iraqi officials have placed troops and equipment in civilian areas, attempting to use innocent men, women and children as shields for the dictator's army. I want Americans and all the world to know that coalition forces will make every effort to spare innocent civilians from harm."

Of the many demonstrations held worldwide against the Iraq war Saturday, the largest was in New York City, where an estimated 200,000 people marched up Broadway. At least 14 people were arrested during the largely nonviolent and dignified protests. An even larger number marched against the war in London, but opinion polls reported that public support was swinging heavily behind Blair, an instinctive rallying behind the troops once the shooting started.

On the northern front, U.S. Special Forces and Pesh Merga fighters of the Patriotic Union of Kurdistan were coordinating with U.S. forces against Ansar al-Islam, an Islamist group in the Kurdish enclave in northern Iraq. Ansar al-Islam, an extremist group containing some "Arab Afghans" who had fought alongside Osama bin Laden in the Afghan war against the Soviet Union, has been linked to the al-Qaida terrorist movement. Thought to number fewer than 1,000 fighters, its small enclave included what Kurdish officials said was "a terrorist training camp." Battle damage reconnaissance photos reviewed by UPI show that the Ansar al-Islam camp was almost destroyed by a Tomahawk cruise missile barrage Saturday. Before and after photos showed at least 17 bomb craters and destroyed buildings.

For the first time Saturday, as the British troops halted outside Basra and the U.S. 3rd Division consolidated its hold on the Euphrates bridges at Nasiriyah, it began to look as if the war might not be an easy and barely contested charge to Baghdad. Americans had been told to brace themselves for military operations of a speed and ferocity unprecedented in modern war. And while some retired military men voiced concern that the U.S. armed forces may have been going to war too light, without enough armored forces and ground combat power, most media analysts expected a quick and easy victory.

There have certainly been positive developments. The 3rd Infantry Division (Mechanized) has been able to advance almost 100 miles into Iraq with little resistance. The vital Rumaila oil fields have been taken more or less intact. Meanwhile, the British Royal Marines have captured the al-Faw peninsula, a major oil storage site. Its seizure prevented the Iraqis from setting the stored oil ablaze or releasing it into the sea. About 30 miles to the west, U.S. Marines under British command took Umm Qasr, Iraq's only major seaport. In the western corner of Iraq, special operations forces seized H-2 and H-3 airfields. In the last Gulf War, the airfields and the surrounding area had been the launch site of most of the Scuds fired at Israel. The capture of this key terrain has made Scud firings against Israel far less likely.

Overall, however, ground operations have fallen somewhat short of expectations. Before the war, some Pentagon officials warned the media not to compare the coming war with the Gulf War of 1991. This offensive, they said, would be much more violent and much more ruthlessly executed. So far, that claim has not panned out on the ground. Certainly, the bombing campaign has been much more intense. There were 288 Tomahawk missiles fired in the first Gulf War. In this one, almost twice as many have been fired already. However, with far less ground combat power than was available in 1991, the coalition's ground operations have been far less violently prosecuted. At this point in the ground phase of the last Gulf War, coalition forces had completely destroyed 15 Iraqi divisions and had taken tens of thousands of prisoners. In this war, two Iraqi divisions have been more or less neutralized, which is to say bottled up or cowed into passivity. No Iraqi divisions have been destroyed, and so far only 2,000 Iraqis have been taken prisoner.

An officer claiming to be the commander of the Iraqi 51st Mechanized Division's commander surrendered his division outside Basra, but he turned out to be a more junior battalion commander and brought fewer than 800 prisoners with him. The bulk of the 51st continued to fight, and coalition forces in and around Basra ran into pockets of stiff resistance from small units within the division. This included a small tank battle on the western approaches of the city. The division was nevertheless bottled up in Basra and unable to interfere with coalition operations.

The 11th Infantry Division seems to be in a similar state in and around the town of Nasiriyah and is apparently being bypassed by the 3rd Infantry Division. There is cause for concern, however. The 11th Infantry Division, made up largely of overage men (aged 30 to 50), had been expected to fold like a house of cards, but at a bridge on the approach to Nasiriyah, one of its units was able to hold the 3rd Infantry Division's cavalry squadron for hours. The fact that these ill-trained, poorly fed, overage soldiers seemed neither shocked nor awed sobered some in the Pentagon as American forces close on Baghdad and the Republican Guard. But the technological overmatch between the Abrams tank and the T-72s of the Republican Guard was almost insuperable. The gun of a T-72 tank cannot penetrate the frontal armor of an Abrams at any range. The most the Iraqis could hope to do was to disable an American tank. But the Abrams tanks could kill a T-72 at ranges up to two miles.

Paradise Lost — The Marsh Arabs

Dan Whipple

Most of the thousands of American soldiers crossing the desert of southeastern Iraq on their way toward Baghdad probably don't know they are crossing the location of the biblical Garden of Eden — and the site of a present-day environmental tragedy. As soon as the war ends and humanitarian relief begins, a band of scientists and environmentalists is poised to attempt to save a priceless ecosystem and a treasure of human history.

Mesopotamia — literally, the "Land Between the (Tigris and Euphrates) Rivers" — is the cradle of civilization. The area is thought by archaeologists to be the spot where agriculture was first practiced, allowing humans to abandon hazardous hunting and gathering for the more stable pursuit of farming. As far as scholars can tell, it is the traditional land where Adam and Eve dwelt.

The area of southern Iraq bordering Iran — the Fertile Crescent, as it is known still — was not always the trackless desert waste now seen on TV and described in news reports. In fact, as recently as 1991, according to the U.N.

Environmental Program, the marshlands extended over their original area of 15,000 to 20,000 square kilometers (5,800 to 7,700 square miles).

"When the soldiers crossed the bridge at Nasiriyah 15 years ago, you would have seen an endless sea of water, green and blue," Suzie Alwash, project director of the Eden Again Project of the Iraq Foundation, told United Press International. "On TV today, you see an endless sea of desert. It's heartbreaking."

Extensive damming by Iran and, especially, by Iraqi dictator Saddam Hussein has led to the drying of over 90 percent of these ancient marshes, leading to what UNEP has described as "one of the world's greatest environmental disasters." It has also been a human disaster for the Ma'dan, the "Marsh Arabs," who have lived in these wetlands for centuries.

The organization's executive director, Klaus Toepfer, said UNEP has a unit ready to aid Iraq with marsh restoration efforts as soon as the coalition military commanders permit it. But while the U.S. State Department has supported some studies on the marsh region, the United Nations role in postwar Iraq remains unclear, given the tensions between the United States and that international body.

In a written statement, Toepfer said UNEP's Post Conflict Assessment Unit, which has carried out successful environmental studies and drawn up action plans for the Balkans and, more recently, Afghanistan and the occupied Palestinian territories, stands ready to assist in any project to restore the wetlands. U.S. State Department officials were not available to comment on the future of the marsh restoration.

"The loss of the Mesopotamian marshlands is one of the world's worst human-engineered environmental disasters," Adlai Amor, spokesman for the World Resources Institute, told UPI. "This was historically what biblical scholars looked at as the likely site of the garden of Eden."

The marshlands were the home to the Marsh Arabs — the Ma'dan group of tribes — inheritors of a culture that stretches back more than 5,000 years toward the dawn of human history. In addition to the millennia-old culture, the marshlands are critical habitat for numerous endangered and threatened species. Yet a UNEP study released at the World Water Forum on March 22 in Kyoto said 3 percent

of the marshes have disappeared in the last two years. They actually are composed of three marsh systems — al-Hammer marsh, Central marsh and al-Hawizeh marsh. According to satellite images, only a small portion of al-Hawizeh marsh, which straddles the Iran–Iraq border, remains and it could disappear completely within five years, according to UNEP.

WRI's Amor said wildlife experts fear three species native to the area have gone extinct: a subspecies of the smooth-coated otter, the bandicoot rat and the gunther. Threatened by the decline are the African darter and sacred ibis, the only populations in the Mideast, along with the Iraqi populations of the pygmy cormorant and goliath heron.

"Since the marshes are important as a staging and wintering area for migratory birds on the Western Siberia–Caspian–Nile flyway from the Arctic to southern Africa," Amor told UPI, "it has put at risk at least 66 species of birds. The global population of the endemic Iraq babbler, the endemic Basra reed babbler and the Dalmatian pelican may have already crashed."

Other wildlife threatened by the war include the cheetah, ferruginous duck, spotted eagle, imperial eagle and Euphrates soft shell turtle.

Draining the marshes has been under way since at least the 1950s as the upper basin nations — primarily Turkey, Iran and Iraq — have dammed the tributaries for water and power. But the problem reached crisis proportions after the 1991 Gulf War. When U.S. forces withdrew, President George H.W. Bush urged local dissidents to rebel against Saddam Hussein. The Marsh Arabs did. When Bush failed to follow through on his promise of assistance, they were brutally crushed by the regime and the desertification of their homeland began in earnest.

According to Human Rights Watch, "Numbering some 250,000 people as recently as 1991, the Marsh Arabs today are believed to number fewer than 40,000 in their ancestral homeland. Many have been arrested, 'disappeared,' or executed. Most have become refugees abroad or are internally displaced in Iraq as a result of Iraqi oppression. The population and culture of the Marsh Arabs, who have resided continuously in the marshlands for more than 5,000 years, are being eradicated."

Alwash's Eden Again Project is dedicated to restoring the Mesopotamian marshes in a post-Saddam Iraq. But she said this means doing more than simply flooding the area again. The group has convened a number of wetlands experts to consider the problem. They have developed a plan for "the first couple of years," she said. "First, we need to make it safe for humans," she told UPI. "There are going to be ordnance and poisons and toxins that have been introduced into the marshlands," some deliberately and some because the rivers have served as an open sewer for the past 15 years.

"Some former lakes have turned into salt pans and there may be a two-foot-thick salt crust," Alwash continued. "If you put water back in there, you're just creating a saline lake that nothing can live in. And some (lakes) have been desiccated for over a decade and may not react properly when they are rehydrated." In addition, there will not be enough water available, because of upstream damming, to return the area to its original state. That poses an interesting philosophical question: What, exactly, constitutes the "original state" of a 5,000-year-old culture that stemmed from Eden?

ABOARD THE USS ABRAHAM LINCOLN, The Arabian Gulf, March 23 (UPI) — An aviation ordnanceman tightens the tip of precision-guided ordnance aboard the USS Abraham Lincoln on March 23, 2003. The Lincoln is deployed to the Arabian Gulf in support of Operation Iraqi Freedom, the multinational coalition effort to liberate the Iraqi people, eliminate Iraq's weapons of mass destruction and end the regime of Saddam Hussein. (Tyler J. Clements, U.S. Navy photo)

Day 4 — Sunday, March 23

"[T]he day the war turned sour for the coalition."

MARTIN WALKER

This was the day the war turned sour for the coalition, as the twin-pronged U.S. advances up the Tigris and Euphrates Rivers each stalled after running into well-planned Iraqi ambushes, and al-Jazeera television screened the first pictures of U.S. battle dead. The Pentagon confirmed that 12 U.S. soldiers were missing, and U.S. prisoners — one of them a woman — were paraded before the TV cameras in Baghdad — a breach of the Geneva Convention on the treatment of prisoners of war.

Irregular Iraqi forces ambushed an unprotected convoy of U.S. supply vehicles in southern Iraq when it apparently took a wrong turn. A Marine combat unit arrived at the end of the battle, rescuing the "remnants of the convoy" and fighting off the remaining Iraqi forces. The ambush left six vehicles demolished. Four soldiers who survived the ambush were evacuated for medical treatment, confirmed Lt. Gen. John Abizaid, deputy commander of coalition forces in Iraq.

An undisclosed number of U.S. soldiers were taken prisoner. Twelve were unaccounted for and some may have been executed, according to Pentagon officials and gruesome video and photographs released by the Iraqi government. The pictures showed approximately six dead soldiers on the floor of a building. At least one American soldier was shot through the forehead. The wound was pictured in a close-range photo. The Pentagon asked news organizations Sunday not to use the images or identify the soldiers involved until their families had been notified.

Stunned Marines in Kuwait spoke darkly to reporters of "one outfit taking 86 casualties in a fire sack," for which there was no immediate official confirmation. But it was confirmed that the 1st battalion, 2nd Marines, had run into a heavy artillery barrage after crossing the Euphrates at Nasiriyah. The U.S. 7th Cavalry, further north at Euphrates crossings near Najaf, also ran into heavy artillery fire, as did a U.S. military convoy bringing supplies to the 3rd Division. An Iraqi military unit Sunday faked a surrender to the Marine battalion but then opened fire as it approached near Nasiriyah, just one fight in a day of pitched battles marked by what military officials called "ruses" on the part of Iraqi forces. "As our forces moved to receive this surrender in an honorable way, they were attacked and sustained casualties," said Brig. Gen. Vincent Brooks, deputy operations officer at Central Command.

The Marines' Task Force Tarawa arrived Sunday to take control of the area and seize two bridges on the eastern side of Nasiriyah. The two bridges lay along the same road and were crucial to moving U.S. forces north of the Euphrates. Iraqi regular army units pounded approaching Marines with tank and artillery fire. The Marines responded with tank and artillery fire of their own. They then called in close air support from F/A-18 Hornet fighter jets, AV-8 Harrier jets, A-10 "Warthogs" and AH-1 Cobra attack helicopters. Fighting subsided after six hours of bombing. Fewer than 10 Marines were reported to have died in the battle. An unspecified number of others were wounded. Embedded news crews said as many as 50 Marines were wounded. The Marines destroyed eight tanks, some antiaircraft batteries along with many Iraqi infantry soldiers.

"The Marines were successful; they defeated the enemy," Abizaid said. "It was one of the few times we've seen regular forces fight. Suffice it to say it was a very sharp engagement." The fake surrender was one of several incidents "in which there were types of behavior I can only describe as ruses," Abizaid added. In one incident, Iraqi troops raised a flag of surrender but then launched an artillery attack. In another, troops disguised in civilian clothes appeared to welcome U.S. forces and then ambushed them.

"Here in the areas that we've been encountering regular Iraqi forces, by far the majority of units have just melted away. We find a substantial amount of abandoned equipment on the field, and in the regular army there is clearly very, very little will to fight," Abizaid added.

Meanwhile, there was scattered fighting outside the largely secured port of Umm Qasr, where the capture of one Republican Guard colonel indicated that some of Iraq's elite troops had been sent to the south to stiffen the resistance. Fleet clearance diving teams and explosive ordnance disposal teams were clearing mines from the port at Umm Qasr and in the Al-Abdullah waterway. Once it is safe, shipments of humanitarian aid will move in and begin distributing food, water and medical supplies. President George W. Bush said Sunday at the White House he expected "massive" amounts of aid to be delivered, starting in the next 36 hours.

The coalition command always expected by then there would be serious fighting as their troops closed on the Republican Guard's main Iraqi defensive positions around Baghdad. The deceptively easy race north from the Kuwaiti border was never going to last. But the hope that the regular Iraqi army would not fight hard has been confounded, even though much of it is manned by Shiite conscripts from a region with little love for the Baghdad regime. The psychological impact of the TV film of U.S. prisoners of war upon the Iraqi troops and population cannot be predicted. But it makes it harder for the coalition's psychological warfare campaign that seeks to convince the Iraqis that theirs is a doomed cause. Moreover, the suggestions from senior Pentagon officials that the Iraqi military's command and control system had been badly disrupted by the bombing of Baghdad looks optimistic. Not only are the Iraqis fighting for their own territory against the invaders, but according to military sources in Kuwait, they appear to be fighting capably and intelligently.

Given the technological superiority and the air power of the coalition, the military outcome can hardly be in doubt. The Bush administration stuck firmly to its assurances Sunday that victory was both near and inevitable. Defense Secretary Donald Rumsfeld said the Iraqi forces should "put down their weapons and put an end any resistance — for it is futile.The regime of Saddam Hussein is gone, it is over, it will not be there in a relatively short period of time." Rumsfeld added. "The outcome of this is certain."

Each time the coalition ground troops run into serious opposition, they call in their big advantage of air power. And combat helicopters and A-10 Warthog ground support warplanes were swiftly on the main battle scenes at Nasiriyah and Najaf. But meteorologists warn that a new storm is brewing to the west, threatening to bring one of this season's regular sand storms to the battlefield — the biggest threat to coalition air power.

The stiffening Iraqi resistance south of Baghdad reflects the scale of the strategic setback suffered by the coalition when Turkey's parliament refused permission for the U.S. to move the 4th Division across its territory to open a second front in northern Iraq. The 4th Division's heavy equipment, after languishing for weeks on ships off the Turkish coast, is in the Suez Canal on its long way round to Kuwait.

This relieved the Iraqi generals of the strategic threat of a heavy, armored punch from the north by American troops. They cannot strip the northern frontier, since Kurdish militia backed up by U.S. Special Forces remain a menace. But it has allowed them to bring their best-equipped and most loyal troops to the south of Baghdad.

As night fell over Iraq Sunday, complicating the work of the U.S. warplanes flying support missions for the ground troops, it was clear that Operation Iraqi Freedom was not going to be a walkover against demoralized and disaffected Iraqi troops.

Iraq: Forces Fighting Back, Awing Allies, Take PoWs

Ghassan al-Kadi

BAGHDAD, Iraq, March 23 (UPI) — Iraqi Vice President Taha Yassin Ramadan said Sunday that Iraqi forces captured a number of U.S. soldiers, denied that coalition forces were near Baghdad and staunchly lashed out at U.N. Secretary-General Kofi Annan for his complicity with Washington. Ramadan, in his first public appearance since U.S. reports claimed he was killed along other Iraqi leaders in the first air strikes on Baghdad, said a number of U.S. soldiers in the region of Souk al-Shiyoukh in southern Iraq were captured, and affirmed that Iraqi TV would soon be broadcasting footage of the prisoners and destroyed tanks and other military vehicles.

"You will see today the U.S. prisoners of war and the U.S. tanks which have been destroyed before they (U.S. forces) pulled back," he told reporters in Baghdad. "Our military operations were proceeding smoothly and in a perfect way." He refuted "as lies" U.S. reports about allied advances in Iraq and the killing of Iraqi leaders. He cited as examples the ongoing fighting in the cities of Umm Qasr and Nasiriyah "while until today, this matter is not finished," he said.

"We hope and wish they (coalition forces) come to Baghdad so that we teach this evil (U.S.) administration and all who are cooperating with it the lesson they deserve," Ramadan said. "Let them advance, mass troops, tanks and Marines and we will not provoke them and will give them all the time they need. But any contact with any Iraqi village or city, they will find (resistance) like in Umm Qasr and Souk al-Shiyoukh."

He said Iraq purposely allowed coalition forces to enter the Iraqi desert without resistance.

He noted that U.S. and British forces based "their strategy and operations on information received from traitors whom they call opposition, and from intelligence services of some Arab countries saying that Iraq is divided in every aspect between families, tribes, provinces, army and people, leadership and leader, (Baath) party and people. In line with this illusion, they believed at first that massing troops and threats of war are enough to achieve their objective of changing the situation and bringing a regime similar to the ones they cooperate with. But they are faced with the wall of Iraq's unity."

Asked about the well-being of Iraqi President Saddam Hussein, Ramadan said Saddam has been appearing on TV every day since the U.S.–British air strikes began four days ago and sometimes "more than once per day." He said that the Iraqi and Arab people all the world will hear from time to time the voice of Saddam, who is running the war operations. "You know, I was among the names they said to have disappeared," he said, adding that the United States was openly calling for assassinating the Iraqi leaders and claiming it was fighting terrorism. "The United States and Britain are terrorist countries of the first degree, and they should be stoned, fought by all the people in the world and be presented as war criminals in a clear and public way."

He rebutted U.S. claims that Iraq possesses weapons of mass destruction and said, "For four days, they have been using all kinds of weapons of mass destruction on Baghdad. I ask you, why then Iraq is hesitating in using those WMD if they are available?"

Ramadan lashed out at U.N. chief Kofi Annan for "fulfilling the wishes of U.S. administration" when he pulled out the U.N. weapons inspectors from Baghdad and the U.N. observers from the demilitarized zone between Iraq and Kuwait, and then halted the U.N. oil-for-food program. "Annan acted as an employee of the U.S. State Department and two days ago presented a draft resolution to the Security Council to modify the oil-for-food program in such a way as to appoint himself general commissioner of Iraq. May he be disappointed in his attempt," he said.

He warned Annan against pursuing his "violations" against the Iraqi people and sovereignty, as he should be "loyal to his mission as U.N. secretary-general and speak on behalf of the majority in the Security Council. Iraq does not need a high commissioner of his sort. He (Annan) speaks as if the United States is his master and he became the military ruler of Iraq," he said, rejecting all of Annan's "suspicious schemes," for "neither him nor his U.S. and British masters can impose anything on the Iraqi people." He called on the Security Council to "prove that it still exists" and "condemn and stop this aggression."

Ramadan denounced some Arab rulers who are either conspiring openly or in secrecy against Iraq as well as supporting the U.S.-led coalition forces in their war on Iraq or preventing the Arab masses from taking to the streets to denounce the aggression. Iraqi forces have taught the U.S. and British invading forces "a lesson they won't forget" by fighting back fiercely and forcing them into a state of shock and then terror, Iraq's information minister claimed Sunday, adding that five coalition warplanes and two helicopters have been so far shot down, while more than 81 Iraqis were killed and nearly 500 people were wounded in the shelling on Basra, Baghdad and other areas.

"The (U.S. and British) mercenaries who advanced last night and at dawn toward Nasiriyah were taught a lesson they won't forget," said Information Minister Mohammed Saeed al-Sahhaf said during a news briefing in Baghdad. "We pushed them in a quagmire from which they will not get out of alive." Al-Sahhaf said the "invaders" were forced to retreat from Najaf after they suffered casualties but said Nayef Shindakh Thamer, head of the Iraqi Baath Party in the city, was killed Saturday night during the clashes. He said the coalition forces began "to enter a state of hysteria" and started to bomb civilian areas, like the neighborhood of Qaddisiya in Baghdad, where a great number of people were injured during "the criminal bombardment."

"If their strategy was shock and awe, it seems that both are on them," he said. "It seems they were shocked (by Iraqi resistance) and will keep them terrified until they are defeated, *inshallah* (God willing), soon. Iraq will be the example to tell those war criminals that their U.S.–Zionist conspiracy will not pass," he said. He pledged that the U.S. and British forces "will face death everywhere. They will see death in the cities and the desert."

Soldiers from the 3rd Infantry Division in firing positions during an enemy approach on their position at objective RAMA, in southern Iraq on March 24, 2003   (Rex Features, UPI)

Day 5 — Monday, March 24

"The war was not supposed to go like this."

MARTIN WALKER

U.S. combat helicopters softening up Iraqi Republican Guard positions at Karbala barely 50 miles from Baghdad ran into a storm of anti-aircraft fire that downed at least one Apache helicopter Monday and badly damaged 17 others as Marines fought to secure the roads north to Baghdad from the communications hub of Nasiriyah. Meanwhile, coalition commanders rushed British troops from Basra back to the Rumaila oil fields near the Kuwaiti border, where Iraqi guerrilla forces had infiltrated to lay ambushes and challenge the coalition for control of the roads north.

There were two kinds of war under way Monday, as the U.S. 3rd Infantry Division closed on Baghdad from the southwest, probing forward from the Euphrates crossing at Najaf toward Karbala. The first was the classic battle of organized armies, where three Republican Guard armored divisions were trying to hold the approaches to Baghdad from the twin-pronged U.S. advances up the Tigris and Euphrates Rivers. In this kind of war, coalition air power and technological superiority should have put the Iraqis at a severe disadvantage. But the air power faltered as the Apaches ran into trouble. The second kind of war, the guerrilla actions being fought by Iraqi militia and irregular forces stiffened by Iraqi special forces, is proving a real challenge for the British and American troops, who are constantly being distracted by the need to rese-cure their communications and supply routes to the rear.

U.S. Marines reacted with outrage Monday to news that some of their comrades had been killed in action against Iraqis and that other U.S. personnel had been captured and shown on televised reports.

"What's the word, captain?" asked 1st Sgt. Bill Leuthe of the 5th Battalion's Bravo Company. "I have Marines f-ing mad and want to kill somebody."

Marines were getting their news through shortwave radio reports, often from the British Broadcasting Corp., as they moved through southern Iraq. The Marines, among the first to enter Iraq last week, are engaged in a long-range penetration into the country. They bypassed Nasiriyah in southeastern Iraq where, on Sunday, some of the fiercest battles of the five-day-old war were fought. The 5th Marines column traveled more than 24 hours non-stop before coming to a brief rest Monday. Food was handed out, vehicles were refueled and the Marines had a welcome chance to stretch. The men had been cramped inside armored vehicles, which were holding as many as 23 men, when 12 is the usual number the vehicles carry.

If the potent armored columns of U.S. tanks and combat helicopters have a weakness, it is their constant reliance on endless supplies of fuel, water and ammunition from the giant logistics dumps in Kuwait, up to 300 miles to their rear. It is these supply lines that the Iraqis are contesting. An ambush Sunday night that killed two British soldiers forced the British to switch armored forces from the outskirts of Basra to clear the Rumaila oil fields all over again. And the U.S. prisoners of war paraded on Iraqi TV Sunday were from a maintenance unit that ran into an ambush. The Iraqis also came up with a counter to the feared U.S. Apache combat helicopters. The success of the Iraqi tactic of mounting "a wall of fire" every time the Apache helicopters approach has star-tled U.S. officers. Every rifle and machine gun in the area opens up in the hope that some of that flying lead will hit an Apache — and 17 Apaches limped home from the first encounter with the Republican Guard Monday, all needing repairs.

The Medina Division, which protects Bagh-dad, was spread out and heavily dug in, requir-ing the attack-and-scout helicopters to engage the forces directly rather than targeting them with long-range munitions that don't put U.S. pilots at risk. By going in close, the Apaches found the Iraqi wall of fire to be alarmingly effective. The attack began with heavy aerial bombardment of the Baghdad, al-Nida, Medina and 10th Armored Divisions. Then, some 30 army tactical missile-system surface-to-surface missiles were fired at Republican Guard com-mand posts and artillery units. ATACMS rock-ets carry 950 half-pound bomblets, which are scattered over an area a quarter mile in diame-ter. Finally, the Medina Division was attacked by 32 Apaches from the 11th Aviation Regi-ment, a German based unit. Coalition planners hoped that the attack would deal the Republi-can Guard a decisive defeat and help persuade other Republican Guard units not to resist. It did neither.

Many pilots said they were forced to aban-don most of their targets and return to base with Hellfire antitank missiles still on their launch racks because of an intense curtain of antiair-craft fire that included heat-seeking missiles. Nearly all of the returning gun ships (31 of 32) sustained damage. One had an engine blown off by a rocket-propelled antiarmor grenade. The damage to the Iraqis was minimal. Report-edly, four or five Iraqi tanks and several light vehicles were destroyed or crippled. To add insult to injury, one Apache was forced by mechanical trouble to land in a farmer's field without firing any of its missiles. Both crew-men were captured.

The use of Apaches in this fashion was unorthodox, a gamble that the Republican Guard was demoralized. Apaches are not designed to be employed against viable, dug-in heavy units with fully operational antiaircraft defenses. In the first Gulf War, attack helicop-ters were a potent complement to the coali-tion's heavy armor, accounting for about 14 percent of all Iraqi armored vehicles destroyed in combat. However, in that war, they were used mostly to attack units that were reeling from an artillery strike or units that were mov-ing. Attacks on dug-in heavy units were usually aided by heavy artillery barrages, usually involving antiarmor bomblets. These barrages knocked the defenders off balance and wiped away most of their antiaircraft weapons, making life much easier for the Apaches. Apaches were also effective when attacking units on the road. When a unit is traveling, its air defenses are usually down, and it can be a sitting duck for an Apache strike. On the other hand, when employed against viable units with potent antiaircraft defenses, an Apache, flying low and slow, can find itself a sitting duck.

The war was not supposed to go like this. While the hard armored battles with the Republican Guard outside Baghdad were expected, the guerrilla war has come as an unpleasant surprise, and strains a coalition force that is considerably smaller than the 600,000-strong allied armies of the first Gulf War. But the guerilla war was the price to be paid for the speed of the main U.S. advance, Gen. Tommy Franks said.

"We have intentionally bypassed enemy formations to include paramilitary and the fedayeen. And so you can expect that our cleanup operations are going to be ongoing across the days in the future. We know that the fedayeen has in fact put himself in a position to mill about, to create difficulties in rear areas, and I can assure you that contact with those forces is not unexpected. We'll fight this on our terms. We'll undertake the sequencing and simultaneity of our operations on a time line that makes sense to us."

Coalition forces are depending on their speed and agility to avoid unnecessary fights with Iraqi ground troops. The fast leading edge of the Army is coming within striking distance of Republican Guard–heavy Baghdad, an intentional strategy to keep forces there off guard. The readiness of some units of the Iraqi regular army and militia — not just the Republican Guard — to fight for their homeland has been another surprise. The Iraqi leadership seems to have planned this resistance. Iraqi President Saddam Hussein's son Qusay organized the fedayeen, the forces dressed in civilian clothes and using pickup trucks to mount the resistance outside the port of Umm Qasr and the guerrilla strikes in the rear of the Basra and Nasiriyah fronts. "Every time the invader has left the desert and come into our homes, they have met resistance," Saddam boasted in his TV address Monday. For once, this was more than vainglorious propaganda.

The built-up areas of Basra, Nasiriyah and Najaf — all occupied mainly by Shiite Arabs with little reason to defend the Sunni-dominated Baghdad regime — have become real problems for the advancing coalition forces. The difficulty for the U.S. and British troops is their reluctance to use their heavy firepower and air strikes against civilian buildings and areas. The reason for this is plain; they wanted to appear to the Iraqi people in general, and to the Shiites of southern Iraq in particular, as liberators, not as destroyers of their homes. The strategy of Qusay's fedayeen guerrillas has been to provoke just such a use of firepower in civilian areas, with worrying political consequences.

The coalition commanders have an ace card up their sleeve: the airborne troops of the 101st Division, highly mobile elite forces with strong helicopter support, largely uncommitted and available for deep strikes to the flanks and rear of the Iraqi defenders around Baghdad. The buildup of U.S. supplies and Special Forces, flying into makeshift airfields in the Kurdish-held districts of northern Iraq, also holds open the prospect of a northern front to threaten the Iraqi rear. But this threat is far, far less potent than it would have been had the Turkish government opened its territory to permit the planned drive of the powerful U.S. 4th Infantry Division.

The military outcome is not in doubt. Heavy U.S. reinforcements are on the way, including the 4th Infantry Division now passing through the Suez Canal, and the 1st Armored and 1st Cavalry Divisions, two armored units that might have been usefully deployed from the beginning. If the military outcome is certain, the political outcome is starting to look problematic as Iraqi resistance mounts and Saddam's appeal to Arab and Islamic support in the world outside Iraq puts intense pressure on other Arab regimes. But the level of Iraqi resistance raises the prospect that the eventual battle for Baghdad may prove tough and destructive indeed, just as the coalition forces start trying to build a post-Saddam administration for the country.

Iraqi leader Saddam Hussein hailed the resistance of his troops and called them mujahedin and the defenders of the whole Arab world in a TV address Monday that was intended to show he was alive and defiant as coalition troops closed in on Baghdad. The speech was packed with references to the weekend fighting in Umm Qasr, Nasiriyah and Basra, as if to confound earlier claims by U.S. officials that his previous television appearance had been taped in advance.

"Every time the invaders leave the desert and attempt to enter our homes they meet our resistance," he said. "The enemy underestimated you — you heroic Iraqis." Dressed in full military uniform and speaking calmly and without histrionics, Saddam spoke over TV from an anonymous room, flanked by an Iraqi flag and a wall plaque depicting an eagle surmounting the national arms of Iraq. Arabic-speaking experts who monitored the broadcast in Kuwait said they believed it was indeed the real Saddam despite earlier suggestions that other TV appearances had been staged by doubles.

The speech was aimed not only at the Iraqi forces and people — "inspired by the spirit of Jihad" — but at a wider Arab and Islamic audience. He closed his 25-minute speech with the words "long live Palestine, long live Iraq" and said Iraqi martyrs would be "rewarded by paradise and by God."

"We will continue our pact with God, and the (Islamic) faithful around the world know we are prepared to sacrifice everything we have to please God and to remind him to humiliate the aggressors and turn their evil upon them," he said. "We are the soldiers of God in our land, after putting our faith in God. The Iraqi mujahedin are causing our enemy to suffer and to lose everything, and as time goes on they will lose more and they will not be able to escape. We will make it as painful as we can for the enemy so they will retreat before our faith, which is endorsed by God. Strike them, strike them, strike evil so that evil will be defeated and that all our mothers will be able to sleep in peace."

The resistance shown by the Iraqis had a strong political effect in the Arab world and spurred them to push hard — and successfully at the United Nations — for a formal debate on the U.S.-led invasion. In closed-door consultations, the U.N. Security Council agreed to the open debate after requests from the Arab Group and the nonaligned movement for all members of the world organization to join in a formal debate on the U.S.-led invasion of Iraq to unseat Saddam.

The green light came hours after U.S. National Security Adviser Condoleezza Rice and U.S. Ambassador John Negroponte met with U.N. Secretary-General Kofi Annan and Deputy Secretary-General Louise Frechette on humanitarian aid to the Iraqi people and a U.N. role in a post-Saddam Iraq. The four met for more than an hour as council members discussed possible revisions in the so-called oil-for-food program in Iraq — just as the humanitarian problem was becoming urgent. The diplomatic complication was that any changing in the wording of the program to allow U.N. aid to be delivered into the war zone was seen by France as a backdoor way to legitimize the U.S.-led war, which France had consistently opposed.

Annan said the United Nations was prepared to do all it could to provide humanitarian assistance to the Iraqi people, but his spokesman added, "However, the United Nations would have limited capacity to do so until security conditions allowed for the safe return of (U.N.) staff to affected areas. Until then, humanitarian assistance would have to be provided by the United States and its coalition partners in those areas under their control, consistent with their overall responsibility under international law."

The Siege of Kuwait

Martin Walker

KUWAIT CITY. March 24 (UPI) — It is an open question which city is the more under siege— Kuwait City or Baghdad. The handful of ineffective missile attacks on Kuwait so far is no match for the relentless bombing campaign against Baghdad. And there is no giant war machine bearing implacably down on Kuwait's approaches. But there is a sense of siege in Kuwait nonetheless. This tiny and prosperous bubble of pro-Western space is afloat in an increasingly hostile Arab and Islamic sea that has been whipped into a furious storm by this war. Kuwaiti students at the Universities of Bahrain, Jordan and Cairo have been told to come home by the Kuwaiti Education Ministry that pays their bills, because of their exposure to attacks and insults by some students in those countries.

"A wave of hate and hostility has been launched against the state of Kuwait," claims Al-Seyasseh columnist Abdul Amir al-Turki. "It has been launched by a number of Arab regimes as a ploy to improve their own image in their own countries by boosting the military effort of Saddam Hussein as a defender of Arab dignity."

The media in the rest of the Arab world outside Kuwait have become so many cheerleaders for the Iraqi resistance. Even when they despise Saddam Hussein as a thug, they hail his fedayeen defenders as the new heroes of the Arab world. And what is striking about the Arab media is that this wave of anti-American solidarity with the Iraqi regime's defenders is not confined to the semiofficial press of the various Arab regimes. Take one sample editorial, from Egypt's best-selling al-Akhbar: "Should the wrongdoers and the oppressive and unjust forces win the war it will only be a fleeting victory. The evil axis and the evil forces will not gain their main political objectives from this war — to crush and occupy the Arab world."

Even the independent Arab media based in London, and the new and relatively free Arab satellite TV channels, are beating this same drum of pan-Arab solidarity. Take al-Arab al-Alamiya, published in London: "America will pay the price sooner than it thinks. There are no limits to American injustice and high-handedness. Despite its power and tyranny America will not win because it has no humanitarian values."

We look back at the first Gulf war of 1991 as the event that made CNN into a global media force. We look back at the Afghan war against the Taliban and the event that catapulted al-Jazeera TV into a similar prominence. But this war on Iraq has been the making of a whole slew of new Arab TV channels. As well as al-Jazeera, based in Qatar, there is now Abu Dhabi TV, based in the emirates. There is al-Arabia, very polished and well-funded by Saudi and Lebanese money and based in Dubai. There is al-Manar, the TV channel run by Lebanon's Hezbollah. What they all have in common is something that looks to a Western viewer, accustomed to the fastidious way Western television tends to shun screening scenes of carnage, like a cult of blood. Their cameras linger endlessly on mangled corpses, on wounds and hospital emergency rooms and pools of blood.

Like generals, television companies tend to be good at fighting the last war. The Western media has organized itself for a replay of Gulf War I. The Arab media has organized itself for a replay of the *intifada*, complete with heroic martyrs, suicide bombers, wicked Crusader invaders and besieged leaders who are hailed for their resistance. On Arab television, Saddam Hussein is turning into Yasser Arafat before our eyes, just as the images of bomb damage in Baghdad and Basra is turning them into Gaza and Rumaila.

Saddam Hussein's propagandists have been trying for years to build this new image of the "Beast of Baghdad," casting him as the modern Saladin, the defiant defender of the Arabs against the Western Crusaders. Finally, under the rain of bombs on Baghdad and the desperate bravery of his fedayeen who charge Abrams tanks with pickup trucks, this campaign is succeeding.

But this is about more than just Saddam Hussein and Iraq. There is a new pan-Arab patriotism being born in this war, an anti-American consciousness that believes in the clash of civilizations and the religious war of Islam against the Christians and Jews. Those of us in the Western media who have covered the Middle East and followed the long, dispiriting tragedy of Arab politics over the past 30 years have never seen anything like this new wave of Arab feeling, just as we have not previously seen television footage of mass demonstrations in Cairo and Amman denouncing those countries' leaders as stooges of the CIA.

Kuwait, the main base of the war against Iraq and a country that well remembers Iraq's brutal occupation 12 years ago, still stands out as a bubble of pro-Western sentiment. But with most of Kuwait's TV screens also tuned to al-Jazeera and Abu Dhabi TV, Kuwait, too, is under siege in a war that now threatens to continue long after the fall of Baghdad.

Al-Jazeera under fire

CLAUDE SALHANI

LONDON, March 27 (UPI) — Amid accusations of what is accurate reporting and what is not, al-Jazeera, the "black sheep" of the "all-war-all-the-time" 24-hour news channels, has found itself the focus of the news once again, instead of simply reporting it.

A British military spokesman, speaking from coalition headquarters in Qatar Thursday, started his briefing by severely criticizing the Arab TV network for showing footage of two British soldiers who were reportedly killed by Iraqi troops. Air Marshal Brian Burridge said al-Jazeera "should take no pride in a film of the bodies of two soldiers lying in a dusty street and two prisoners of war in a room with Iraqis." The British officer called the incident "deplorable."

According to the British Broadcasting Corp., a reporter for al-Jazeera replied to the British accusation by saying the station was independent and determined "to show our audience the truth, even if it is a dirty war."

The Qatar-based satellite network stunned the Arab world with its brazen Western-style reporting. It first attracted the West's attention in the aftermath of the Sept. 11, 2001, attacks on New York and Washington as the only news network maintaining a full-time bureau and correspondent in Taliban-controlled Afghanistan.

Taysir Allouni, a Syrian national, remained in Kabul for al-Jazeera for much of the U.S. bombardments, reporting exclusively on the Taliban and their leaders in ways that often angered and irritated officials in the Bush administration. Secretary of State Colin Powell voiced his displeasure with al-Jazeera's reporting to Sheikh Hamad bin Khalifa al-Thani, Qatar's ruler during a Washington visit, a complaint that was rebuffed by the emir.

During the U.S.-led assault on Afghanistan, al-Jazeera's Kabul offices were destroyed by a U.S. missile. Mohammed Jasim, the network's managing director, was quoted as saying at the time that he would not speculate as to whether the offices were targeted by the Americans, but stressed that the location of the bureau "was widely known by everyone, including the Americans."

The Arab network attracted further controversy in the United States when it aired video- and audiotapes of suspected terrorist mastermind Osama bin Laden urging Muslims to fight against the West in a holy war. In the current war on Iraq, al-Jazeera also exasperated the United States when it aired footage of dead and captured American soldiers, prompting the Pentagon to appeal to U.S. networks not to air the footage. In a strange twist of fate, the network has seen its correspondents banned from covering the New York Stock Exchange, and its Web sites were hacked this week as the West, a longtime critic of government-controlled Arab media, is now enraged by the first independent voice emanating from the Arab world.

"This is yet another unfortunate incident," said Jihad Ballout, communication and media relations manager for the network, to United Press International from Qatar. Commenting on the Wall Street ban, he said al-Jazeera has "urged the authorities to reconsider. Perhaps it wasn't fair to target two al-Jazeera reporters. This will prevent us from doing our job."

Al-Jazeera, which reaches an audience of some 35 million people, complained that freedom of the press must be protected. "This is not restricted only to America, it should be an international effort," Ballout was quoted as saying to ABC Australia.

The United States accused al-Jazeera of breaking the rules of the Geneva Conventions by showing images of prisoners of war. Yet the conventions, adopted after World War II, makes no specific mention of prisoners and television. Article 13 of the conventions states: "Prisoners of war must at all times be humanely treated. … Likewise, prisoners of war must at all times be protected, particularly against acts of violence or intimidation and against insults and public curiosity. Measures of reprisal against prisoners of war are prohibited."

Article 14 stipulates: "Prisoners of war are entitled in all circumstances to respect for their persons and their honor. Women shall be treated with all the regard due to their sex and shall in all cases benefit by treatment as favorable as that granted to men. Prisoners of war shall retain the full civil capacity which they enjoyed at the time of their capture. The

Detaining Power may not restrict the exercise, either within or without its own territory, of the rights such capacity confers except insofar as the captivity requires."

Many people in Europe and the Arab world have accused the United States and Britain of adopting double standards when it comes to the Middle East, and particularly on the issue of prisoners. They cite footage shown on Western televisions of captured Iraqis made to kneel in the sand, being searched while guns are pointed at them and having their hands tied behind their backs as they are made to squat in the desert. Other critics refer to images of suspected al-Qaida members held in Guantanamo, Cuba, which were seen on Western television blindfolded, shackled and caged — images that upset many across the Arab world. Regardless of the outcome of the al-Jazeera debacle, truth, that first casualty of war, will undoubtedly suffer more as the war continues.

Global media onslaught

ARNAUD DE BORCHGRAVE

BEIRUT, Lebanon, March 28 (UPI) — Under the headline "Reaping the Fiascos of Ideological Wild Men," the Beirut Daily Star editorialized Friday, "One would have thought that the current global power in Washington and the former power in London that set out to change the world would know more about how the world feels and works than seems to be the actual case today."

Reflecting dozens of Arab and other foreign editorials and op-ed articles, from Morocco to Malaysia, and from Spain to South Africa, collected by the CIA's Foreign Broadcast Information Service, the Daily Star's front-page editorial added: "It is slightly disingenuous of the attacking forces who have launched an unprovoked and internationally unsanctioned war against an already battered, embargoed and inspected country to point out how some Iraqis are not playing by the rules of war. The first and most serious rule of law that the Anglo–Americans have broken is that you do not launch

a preemptive war for 'regime change' ... when your rationale for war is deemed by virtually all of humanity to be unproven, noncredible, unacceptable, and slightly mythical." The American presence in Iraq, it added, "is certain to generate guerrilla-type resistance that will be reminiscent of the Americans in Vietnam, the Russians in Afghanistan, and the Israelis in south Lebanon — three of the greatest military fiascos in living memory."

All editorials, without exception, also reflect what government officials all over the region are saying, when it writes that the "real fiasco is about a violent, flailing American foreign policy promoted by a small group of ideological hawks and intellectual wild men who have promised a fast, neat, surgical war and have reaped instead — in just one week — a blinding sandstorm of swirling new uncertainties, vulnerabilities, and threats in the night."

The influential Arabic daily al-Dustour used language that is now common throughout the Middle East, including normally pro-American countries: "The U.S. and Britain escalated their brutal aggression against brotherly Iraq and the war operations launched by these two allies took a serious and destructive and bloody turn (when their aerial bombardment) started to target civilian areas and civilian infrastructure that claimed the lives of many."

Richard Perle, a senior fellow at the American Enterprise Institute, who resigned this week as chairman of the Defense Policy Board, is usually credited with being the architect of U.S.–Israeli policies in the Middle East. "Perle," said Bater Warman in al-Dustour, "is one of those in the small circle of oil traders and American owners of military industries, who is a supporter of the Likud party and of those who stand for Israeli interests in the White House and who control American decisions. ... Shame on us, as an Arab nation, to allow a group of Zionists in the White House to determine the future of the Arab world at breakfast tables in Washington."

The editor in chief of the mass-appeal Arabic daily Al-Arab Al-Yawm wrote: "The Bush–Blair war can be called anything but a liberation of the Iraqis. ... What freedom is this that carries within it unspeakable atrocities, and what freedom is this where more than $74 billion are going to be spent on weapons to kill

Iraqis and destroy their cities? A good description of this war is a war of lies. ... It is also illegitimate, criminal, colonialist, brutal, but not as a war for freedom, unless the freedom is to kill Iraqis."

Columnist Mohammad Amayreh wrote in the influential, semiofficial Saudi daily al-Rai, "If the Americans and the British came to liberate the people of Iraq and thought that they would be received with welcoming cheers and flowers, then look at the first eight days of war, which prove otherwise."

Another columnist, Fahd Fanek, in the same paper, said: "Bush's problem lies in his failure to convince the Americans and the world because the justifications given were either not true or true but not new. ... This pushed many to look for the real reasons for the war, finding only the desire to control Iraq's oil and to serve Israel. ... Spreading democracy in the Arab world? Ridiculous, because democracy cannot be imposed from outside."

Most dailies the world over predicted the United States "will ultimately win the war," but, as the Pakistan Observer said, it will be "a long, drawn-out war" or a "quagmire." Both Algerian and Australian newspapers warned that the coalition will have to choose either high coalition casualties from extended street fighting or committing "a crime against humanity, the bombing of civilian areas to make Baghdad a certitude."

Qatar is headquarters for the war and its government is pro-American, but it is also headquarters for al-Jazeera, the immensely popular, anti-American TV satellite network, and its newspapers denounced what al-Raya called America's "haphazard attack" that was "nothing compared to the huge number of Iraqis killed which TV cameras could not reach."

Media in Egypt, Syria, Tunisia, Pakistan and Muslim countries in sub-Sahara Africa denounced the war "as conquest and colonization" and published accounts of "hideous massacres" and "carnage."

Belgium's Het Laatste Nieuws said Bush "never mentioned that the Euphrates River would be colored red by American blood. ... A war in the field appears to be something totally different from the strategic plans designed by the ultra-conservative institutions that appear to have Bush in their grip."

Turkey's mass appeal Hurriyet wrote about "the collapse of the American strategy" and of a United States "on the cusp of a process of internal change."

Meron Benvenisti, in Haaretz, wrote: "Those who initiated the war against Iraq assumed with typical arrogance that there is no such thing as Iraqi patriotism. ... All of the electronic devices and smart bombs cannot conceal the character of this war — it is a colonial war whose conceptual outlook is drawn straight from the early 20th century. Those who wage an anachronistic war should not be surprised by its outcome." Egypt's pro-government al-Akhbar said: "Iraq has seven million strong fighters who are ready to continue the fighting for 13 years continuously. God be with them."

Al-Gomhouriya, also progovernment in Egypt, under the byline of its editor in chief, asked: "What is the difference between Israel's lowly and treacherous crimes against Palestinians and what the American masters are now doing to Iraqis?" What is happening in Baghdad, he continued, "refutes all allegations that the invading troops came to liberate Iraqis."

Taiwan's conservative United Daily News observed that "those Iraqi children who have managed to survive in the besieged Iraqi cities today may possibly turn out to be the 'little bin Ladens,' who will swear to retaliate against U.S. hegemony in the future. Will the United States still feel safe while these orphans of the war are bent on terrorist retaliation against the United States?"

Thailand's pro-opposition Naew Na said: "Cowboy Bush must now be thinking that snatching of oil wells from Iraq is not a piece of cake as he was led to believe. Rather, he is sending his white-skinned children to hell like when a former U.S. leader sent countless GIs to die in Vietnam. ... The longer this war protracts, the more likely it will be curtains for Bush and Blair."

There was not one pro-American editorial in Friday's pickups from the world's leading newspapers outside the United States.

2ND GULF COALITION Royal Marines from 40 Commando based in Taunton, Somerset, on operations in Iraq — March 25.

Day 6 — Tuesday, March 25

"Clearly they are not a beaten force." — Gen. Richard Myers, chairman of the U.S. Joint Chiefs of Staff

The U.S. drive on Baghdad went on hold Tuesday, delayed by a howling sandstorm that cut visibility, grounded the combat helicopters and forced U.S. forces around Najaf to wrap their tanks and vehicles in tarpaulins against the grinding sand. And then came a driving rain that the sand thickened into a liquid mud that obscured windscreens, sealed tank periscopes and blocked the lenses of night vision equipment. One U.S. tank and several Humvees drove into canals. For the Iraqi guerillas, the grim weather provided cover, enabling them to creep close to U.S. lines to launch swift hit-and-run attacks.

"It's a little bit ugly out there today. Weather has had an impact on the battlefield, with high winds, with some rain, with some thunderstorms," said Maj. Gen. Victor "Gene" Renuart, U.S. Central Command's director of operations at a press conference in Qatar.

But the storm did not prevent the constant aerial bombing of Iraqi Republican Guard units around Baghdad by fixed-wing aircraft from bases in Kuwait and Saudi Arabia and aircraft carriers in the Persian Gulf. Some of the air strikes depended on targeting information from British SAS (Special Air Service) and U.S. Special Forces teams on the ground. U.S. forces were supposed to fly some 1,400 sorties over Iraq Tuesday and into Wednesday, but with the sandstorm obscuring visibility on tactical targets like Republican Guard tanks, most of the missions were retargeted to headquarters, communications and fixed positions.

Approximately half of the sorties by coalition air forces were now being flown against the Republican Guard, focusing on the Medina Armored Division and Nebuchadnezzar Infantry Division south of Baghdad. The Medina Division, equipped with Soviet-built T-72 tanks, is seen as the strongest single unit on the Iraqi side. It also has a large contingent of highly mobile ZSU-23 antiaircraft armored vehicles, firing radar-guided quadruple cannons.

British forces Tuesday declared full control of the port city of Umm Qasr and promised that food and water would begin flowing into the city within days. But despairing of the hoped-for welcome by liberated Shiite citizens in Iraq's second city of Basra, British forces declared it a "military target" as they girded for grueling urban warfare against Iraqi irregular forces in civilian clothes.

"We were expecting a lot of hands up from Iraqi soldiers and for the humanitarian operation in Basra to begin fairly quickly behind us, with aid organizations providing food and water to the locals. But it hasn't quite worked out that way," said British military spokesman Capt. Patrick Trueman. "There are significant elements in Basra who are hugely loyal to the regime." We always had the idea that everyone in this area hated Saddam. Clearly, there are a number who don't."

Stiffened by troops from the Iraqi army's special forces brigades, the civilian-garbed guerilla forces in Basra put up a nagging resistance. British troops dubbed the road to the bridge across the Shatt al-Basra canal RPG Alley, after the salvoes of rocket-propelled grenades that came at them through the gray haze and drizzle.

The sandstorm slowed the fighting around the city of Nasiriyah, where U.S. Marines had secured the two bridges across the Euphrates River and the Saddam canal, even though Iraqi forces held out in urban areas nearby. But there were heavy artillery exchanges overnight, and Iraqi forces were using guns concealed in civilian areas. The U.S. Marines pushed on across the Euphrates bridges Tuesday through harassing sniper and mortar fire and prepared to drive north parallel to a second large column of U.S. Marines from the south that was advancing on the central Iraqi city of Kut on the Tigris River. Kut was defended by another Republican

Guard division, the Nebuchadnezzar Mechanized Infantry.

Two other Republican Guard divisions, the Hamurabi Mechanized Infantry and the Baghdad Infantry, were stationed on the outskirts of the Iraqi capital. And a further two divisions, the al-Nida Armored Division and the Adnan Mechanized Infantry, were still located far to the north of Baghdad. The Adnan was moved earlier this month from Kirkuk, near the Kurdish-held zone of the north, to Saddam Hussein's hometown of Tikrit, where it has come under heavy aerial bombing this week.

"Clearly they are not a beaten force," said Gen. Richard Myers, chairman of the U.S. Joint Chiefs of Staff, at a press briefing at the Pentagon.

As the guerilla attacks on their supply lines threatened to take troops from the front lines, coalition commanders Tuesday began considering the need for reinforcements from the 4th Infantry Division, whose heavy equipment was passing through the Suez Canal after spending three weeks waiting in vain off the Turkish coast for permission to land and open a northern front against Iraq.

To sail around the Saudi Arabian peninsula to unload at the port of Kuwait would delay the deployment of the 4th Infantry Division for at least a week. But there may be a possibility of unloading more quickly at Saudi ports on the Red Sea if diplomatic agreement can be secured. The 4th Division's troops are still at Fort Hood, Texas, and will have to fly in to be reunited with their heavy equipment. But as the most sophisticated unit in the U.S. Army, a test bed for high-tech and computerized equipment, the 4th would add a heavy new punch to the coalition's increasingly overstretched forces.

U.S. Marines, who lost nine killed in action near Nasiriyah Sunday, pushed into the city to tackle the bases of the Iraqi guerillas. Earlier Tuesday, Marines from Task Force Tarawa secured a hospital in the city that had been used by paramilitary forces. They took 170 Iraqi soldiers prisoner and confiscated more than 200 weapons, ammunition, 3,000 chemical suits with masks and a T-55 tank that was on the compound. Marines had been fired on from inside the hospital. No civilians were in the hospital when it was seized and no civilians were injured in the operation, according to U.S.

Central Command. The use of the hospital by combat soldiers while it was flying a Red Crescent flag, similar in meaning to a red cross, is a violation of the Geneva Convention, Central Command said.

To prevent the Iraqi regime from shifting forces to the defense of Baghdad, the United States and its Kurdish allies began to open a "northern front line," preparing two quickly upgraded airstrips to handle military cargo aircraft bringing in light armor. A U.S paratroop unit, the 173rd Airborne Brigade, was on alert to fly in from bases in Italy, reinforcing an estimated 50,000 Kurdish Pesh Merga militia.

The U.S. buildup of its forces in northern Iraq is hampered in speed and firepower, the top Kurdistan Democratic Party representative in Turkey told United Press International. The mission of this force will be to try to tie down some 10 divisions of Iraqi troops with the aid of the Kurdish militia, Safeen M. Dizayee told UPI in an interview.

This was the original mission of the U.S. 4th Infantry Division, in a battle plan scotched on March 1 when the Turkish Parliament voted to bar the 62,000-strong American contingent with tanks and heavy equipment that Washington wanted to put on the ground. Since the new force, airborne units, can only be delivered by C-130 aircraft, the big M1A1 tanks and heavy artillery of the 4th will not be available. The "coalition in northern Iraq" as Safeen referred to it, will comprise these Army paratroopers and the 50,000-man, U.S.-trained Kurdish militia, which faces the Iraqis along a twisting border that runs from Syria on the east to Iran on the west.

Kurdish intelligence reckons that some 75,000 Iraqi troops of varying levels of discipline and skill are holding this line, including one Republican Guard division and several well-trained armored and mechanized divisions.

The job of the northern front was to pin those forces down, Safeen said, noting that one unit, the Iraqi 3rd Armored Division, had already been shifted south toward Baghdad because of the delays imposed by the Turkish parliament decision. But the Kurds were determined to maintain a probing pressure on the Iraqi forces, taking ground when possible, because capturing key locations in the north would have a major psychological effect on the defenders of Baghdad. He wanted the Iraqi leadership "to look north and know they are surrounded," Safeen said.

But the U.S. troops have another mission — to restrain the Kurds from complicating the politics of the war by moving too fast and too far and alarming Turkey, which fears an Iraqi collapse and the establishment of a separate Kurdish state. After a 20-year war against Kurdish separatist guerilas in Turkey, the Turkish military has warned that it would feel bound to intervene to prevent the emergence of a Kurdish state that could act as a magnet for its own Kurdish minority.

The Showbiz War

Pat Nason

LOS ANGELES, (UPI) — The Academy Awards celebrated its 75th anniversary in Los Angeles Sunday, but the ceremony was largely preoccupied with controversy over the U.S.-led war in Iraq. Although filmmaker-provocateur Michael Moore's acceptance speech for Best Documentary was the evening's most enduring emblem of Hollywood liberalism, the event offered several moments of reflection on America's invasion and bombing of Iraq — most of them amounting to wishes for the safety of American troops and an early end to the war. When Moore won for his gun culture documentary "Bowling for Columbine," he invited the other documentary nominees to join him on the stage.

"They're here in solidarity with me because we like nonfiction and we live in fictitious times," said Moore. "We live in a time where we have fictitious election results that elect a fictitious president. We have a man who is leading us to war for fictitious reasons."

Up to that point, Moore had enjoyed a standing ovation and energetic applause. But some in the audience began to boo as he went on. "We're against this war, Mr. Bush," he said. "Shame on you, Mr. Bush. Shame on you." Speaking with reporters backstage, Moore was asked whether he was afraid of being blacklisted in Hollywood for his politics. He said he was not. "I don't work in Hollywood," he said. "I'm funded by Canadians and others who don't live here. But it was Hollywood that voted for this award. It was Hollywood that stood and cheered when it was announced."

The audience at the Kodak Theatre in Hollywood and the worldwide TV viewing audience might have heard even more political speeches from the podium, but academy officials insisted that only Oscar winners — not presenters — would have the freedom to speak their minds on the show. Interestingly, telecast producer Gil Cates offered the evening's first denunciation of war — in remarks on the first page of the commemorative program intended to articulate the rationale for holding the awards ceremony while people were dying in a war halfway around then world.

"In times of grim political history it may seem frivolous to some to focus, even for an evening, on an element of our cultural history," said Cates. "Art is no small thing to celebrate, though, and this extraordinarily powerful art form of ours, wielded by men and women of intelligence and human sensibilities, can eventually be a greater force for understanding and tolerance and, yes, peace, than all the bombs and missiles that haunt our globe."

Not all presenters honored the mandate to stick to the script. Gael García Bernal, one of the stars of screenplay nominee "Y tu mamá también," quoted the late artist Frida Kahlo: "Peace is not a dream. It is a necessity." He took it a step further: "If Frida was alive she would be on our side, against the war."

Host Steve Martin largely avoided overtly political humor, engaging in occasionally sly references to Hollywood's image as a haven for the mercenary and the vain. Referring to the questions about whether it was appropriate to hand out the Oscars with the United States at war in Iraq, Martin said, "Proceeds from this Oscar telecast — and I think this is so great — will be divvied up among huge corporations."

Peter O'Toole, who was given an honorary Oscar, told reporters backstage that there is ample justification for handing out Oscars during wartime. "I'm an entertainer," he said. "There are men, women and children — families of soldiers being killed right now. My job is to cheer them up."

The telecast opened with a film clip retrospective of classic moments from Oscar-winning movies over the previous 74 years. It included several segments fondly recalling memorable acceptance speeches and production numbers from past telecasts. A high point of the evening was the appearance onstage of nearly 50 past acting Oscar winners — including Julie Andrews, Olivia de Havilland, Karl Malden, Eva Marie Saint and Denzel Washington. The Academy of Motion Picture Arts and Sciences went all out to make the 75th Anniversary Academy Awards an occasion to remember, despite the competing headlines of war.

The war incited showbiz passions. Some Americans seem so bent on harming the careers of antiwar celebrities they don't care who else gets hurt, as long as their targets pay for speaking freely. Take, for example, the New York Post's Page Six column, which is usually devoted to entertainment gossip. On Wednesday, the column rolled out a list of entertainers who have expressed themselves politically — and suggested that readers boycott their movies, CDs and concerts. The column — which called its targets "Saddam lovers" — seemed to have been inspired by Dixie Chicks singer Natalie Maines. She said in London last week that she was ashamed to be from the same state (Texas) as President George W. Bush.

There have been reports of country stations dropping Dixie Chicks music from their play lists and fans holding ceremonial burnings of Dixie Chicks concert tickets. Maines has apologized for her intemperate comment, but the Rupert Murdoch–owned newspaper (followed by his Fox News channel) persisted in pushing the boycott of Dixie Chicks music. It even saw in the episode an opening to promote economic punishment of several other "appeasement-loving celebs ... who want to stop the liberation of Iraq from mass murderer Saddam Hussein and his rapist henchmen."

The Page Six "quick reference list" of entertainers whose careers readers might wish to harm included Tim Robbins, Sean Penn and Laurence Fishburne — who co-star in the upcoming movie "Mystic River." The paper called it "the mother of all appeasement casts" but did not explain why readers might also wish to harm the careers of others involved in the production. There was no article of particulars alleging insufficient patriotism on the part of "Mystic River" co-stars Marcia Gay Harden or Laura Linney.

One wonders whether the column's writers even bothered to learn that the movie was directed by the reliably conservative Clint Eastwood. By the way, a boycott would harm Eastwood directly in the pocketbook — since he also co-produced the movie through his own production company, Malpaso Productions. It seems not to matter to Page Six that Eastwood and hundreds of others involved in the production could suffer economic losses — as long as Robbins, Penn and Fishburne were made to pay a price for publicly disagreeing with the president on the wisdom of his policies.

The *Post* also suggested that filmgoers stay away from "Basic," the new John Travolta movie that also features Samuel L. Jackson. The paper called Jackson "another Hollywood drone who signed an antiliberation letter to the Bush administration" but did not explain what Travolta or co-star Connie Nielsen did to deserve payback. The paper suggested that viewers shun the Sci-Fi Channel miniseries "Children of Dune" because Susan Sarandon is in it. It seemed not to care that the cast is mainly made up of actors who are still struggling to become bankable — and who see "Dune" as an important step in their career development. Never mind. Sarandon has spoken out of turn and must be punished.

Bear in mind that the Post recommended punishment for statements that celebrities made when the nation was still debating the advisability of invading Iraq. Now that the bombs are falling, of course, there will be different expectations about what celebrities — and politicians and cab drivers and the rest of us — should consider to be the bounds of appropriate dissent. But even so, the "sit-down-and-shut-up" constituency might want to consider that — just as Bush has reminded us all that America doesn't need anyone's permission to defend itself — Americans don't need permission from anyone to say what's on their minds.

And there are plenty of prowar celebrities in Hollywood. Four blocks of a tree-lined Beverly Hills street were bedecked with yellow ribbons, put there by Hollywood celebrities to show support for U.S. troops in Iraq.

Beverly Hills Mayor Tom Levyne and families of men and women serving in Operation Iraqi Freedom took part in the event in Will Rogers Park, organized by entertainer Lorna Luft and actress Alana Stewart. Luft, whose best-selling memoir "Me and My Shadows: Life with Judy Garland" was made into an Emmy-winning TV movie, told United Press International that she and Stewart were concerned that the troops in the field were not seeing enough support from the folks back home.

"My view is that before the boys and women were sent in, if you wanted to protest the war, go ahead, that's your right," said Luft. "Once they're there, it's over. You've got to support them."

Luft said she was also jolted into action when she heard a TV talk show host accuse Hollywood figures of being "backstabbing Americans."

Raquel Welch and Nancy Sinatra also took part in the event, along with Nicolette Sheridan ("Knot's Landing"), Ann Turkel ("Deep Space") and Ed O'Ross ("Six Feet Under"). Lainie Kazan, one of the stars of "My Big Fat Greek Wedding," was scheduled to participate but had to cancel due to illness. Kazan told UPI she supports the troops but remains opposed to the war.

"I don't believe in this war," she said. "I don't believe in any war. I hate the idea that we're over there. But yes, I support the troops. I don't want them to come back and think they were fighting for nothing."

Luft said one of the things that make America great is that people can "hang a yellow ribbon on their home and then go to a peace demonstration." She said the main idea behind the yellow ribbon event was to let the troops and their families know that "we care about them and we want them to come home safe and soon." Before the event was over, said Luft, every tree on both sides of Beverly Drive from Sunset Boulevard to Santa Monica Boulevard had a yellow ribbon tied around it. "I couldn't find any more trees," she said.

Hollywood had another problem with the war — at the box office. American news networks are not just competing against one another for Iraq war scoops — they're also competing with Hollywood for the attention of media consumers. The news business has been cutting into the movie business throughout the war, according to box office analysts. Some show business pros have suggested that grosses have been lackluster because movies haven't been so hot. News executives might not want to see themselves as rivals with Hollywood, but no one can deny that TV news employs show business-style techniques in the increasingly intense battle for ratings supremacy. In a recent behind-the-scenes report on TV coverage of the war, the New York Daily News described a process in which a Fox News artist inserted green plumes of smoke into a 3-D rendering of poison gas.

"Is the gas going to be green? No," said Fox creative director Richard O'Brien. "It will be transparent. We take some liberties so that people can see it." News consumers might be startled to learn that "creative directors" are consciously deciding to distort reality so viewers can see something that is, in reality, invisible.

The Washington Post reported recently that broadcast news consultants have been advising news and talk operations to wear their patriotism on their sleeve. Coverage of war protest has tested poorly among viewers. The time may come when war news of any kind will test poorly in focus groups. Faith Popcorn, founder of the New York–based consulting firm Faith Popcorn's BrainReserve, recently concluded that viewers are tired of watching war news and want more escapist programming.

The competition for the news audience is understandable, given the amount of money that is on the table for media conglomerates. News ratings are up for ABC (Disney), CBS (Viacom) and NBC (General Electric), and up dramatically, historically, for the cable news channels. During the first week of the war, Fox News (News Corp.) averaged 5.6 million

prime-time viewers, CNN (AOL–Time Warner) attracted 4.4 million and MSNBC (General Electric) drew 2.1 million. Those numbers translate into higher ad rates — the better to pay the costs of expensive wartime programming.

Cinny Kennard, assistant professor of journalism at the University of Southern California in Los Angeles, said it's easy to see why media consumers prefer "War TV" — her name for the current trend in war coverage.

"If you have patriotism, flag waving, live reporters, bombs and bullets, why go to the movies?" said Kennard in an interview with United Press International. "It's free in your living room, except for the cable or satellite bill."

Kennard — a former CBS News correspondent who won the Columbia University duPont Award for her coverage of the 1991 Gulf War — said Operation Iraqi Freedom was the most thorough example she has ever seen of entertainment and news merging into one entity. Social and media critics will debate for years the question of whether U.S. media resorted to pandering in their coverage of Operation Iraqi Freedom. But Kennard concluded that it has a serious downside and potentially damaging consequences for the future of American democracy.

"Since when do we tell people how to feel about the news?" said Kennard. "You don't need an American flag, patriotic music for any of this coverage. You don't need to gussy it up with red, white and blue and patriotic songs and statements about how much you love the country."

FORWARD DEPLOYED, SOUTHWEST ASIA, MARCH 26 (UPI) — F-16CJ aircraft sit on a parking ramp during a sandstorm on March 26, 2003. Aircraft move around-the-clock to support Operation Iraqi Freedom at a forward-deployed location in Southwest Asia. (Matthew Hannen, U.S. Air Force)

Day 7 — Wednesday, March 26

"(T)he hardest battle of the war so far."

The second Gulf War began for the first time Wednesday to look like the first, with U.S. forces poised for a massive land attack while U.S. and British warplanes pounded the dug-in Iraqi Republican Guard. But in the first Gulf War of 1991, those air strikes were taking place inside occupied Kuwait. This time, the allied warplanes are flying 300 miles north to strike the Republican Guard lines just 40 miles short of Baghdad. And this time, the U.S. forces of the 3rd Infantry Division around Najaf, and the U.S. Marines at Nasiriyah, have gone through heavy fighting to get to this point.

And the biggest difference of all was the parachute drop of the 173rd Airborne in the Kurdish zone, opening at long last a serious northern front with a threat of an American pincer movement, threatening the Iraqi capital from both north and south.

The 3rd Division Tuesday fought what it called "the hardest battle of the war so far" as it burst through Iraqi defenses trying to seal off the crossings over the Euphrates River. Firing to both sides in a sandstorm that blinded Iraqi gunners, the U.S. 7th Cavalry ran the gauntlet of the Iraqi defenders as U.S. combat engineers under fire battled to deploy bridge-laying equipment after the Iraqis blew up one key bridge.

Three M1A1 Abrams tanks were isolated on the far bank when the temporary bridge collapsed, and U.S. warplanes in atrocious weather conditions battled to fly close air support against

Iraqi units closing in to destroy them. The bridge was relaid, and U.S. patrols swept forward until two more Abrams tanks were put out of action by Iraqi defenses that were then swept away with what the 3rd Division said were up to 750 Iraqi casualties.

The sandstorms and bad weather that held back the U.S. combat helicopters Tuesday cleared somewhat over Najaf Wednesday morning, although visibility was still bad. Apache gunships patrolled the ancient city, an important shrine to Shiite Muslims, and scoured the farmlands ahead on the way to Baghdad. The battle of Najaf has opened the way to Baghdad, but that route still is held by the Medina Armored Division of the Republican Guard, which came under intense aerial bombardment Tuesday from U.S. and British Tornado fighter-bombers. B-52 heavy bombers took off from Royal Air Force bases in Britain early Wednesday to keep up the pounding.

But the precision weapons of the coalition air forces cannot be used with full effect in sandstorm conditions. The "smart bombs" using Global Positioning System navigation coordinates to bomb blind through cloud and smoke and sandstorms depend on the precise geographic location of the target being known in advance. This makes no difference when the targets are buildings, but the tanks and heavy equipment of an armored division can move constantly.

The U.S. forces, with their vast hunger for fuel and supplies, have been fighting for three days to secure the two key crossings over the Euphrates River at Najaf and Nasiriyah, before they can build up the supplies required for the final assault on Baghdad. That process is now virtually complete, and U.S. Marines Wednesday had pushed 25 miles beyond Nasiriyah where they ran into new resistance and called in air support.

A second U.S. Marine column was advancing steadily Wednesday from the captured Iraqi air base of al-Amara on the Tigris River toward the city of Kut, some 80 miles south of Baghdad, held by the Nebuchadnezzar Division of the Republican Guard.

As the worst of the storms passed, a new factor came into play Wednesday — the U.S. 101st Airborne Division, which had moved up west and north of the 3rd Division toward Kar-

bala. Preparing landing ground and forward bases, the 101st set up to open a new front to the west of Baghdad, where its helicopter gunships will also have to stop Republican Guard reinforcements from Tikrit and Falluja moving south to join the Baghdad defenses.

So there are now four U.S. divisions closing on the Baghdad region, the 101st and 3rd to the southwest, and the two U.S. Marine divisions from Nasiriyah and Kut in the south. And U.S. air power continued to dominate the skies, bombing Baghdad and its defenses at will, although early reports from Western reporters still in Baghdad Wednesday said there were many civilian casualties, including a least 14 dead, after one bomb hit a market in the northern part of the city.

Although the U.S. land forces are keeping up the pressure and fighting for positions on the Baghdad approaches, the decisive battle for the city will probably not be joined until the weekend. The tired U.S. troops need resupply and some rest after days of fighting and moving. And there may be reinforcements on the way. Diplomatic sources in Kuwait said they expected the U.S. 4th Division, after passing the Suez Canal, to start unloading tanks and heavy equipment at the Saudi Red Sea port of Yanbu, available to race across the desert to the battle.

Around 1,000 U.S. Army paratroopers landed near the airstrip of Hariri in Kurdish-controlled northern Iraq, the leading edge of what is expected to be the northern front in the war on Saddam Hussein. The airstrip was judged sturdy enough to take U.S. military cargo aircraft carrying Bradley armored vehicles. Armored vehicles were deemed essential if the lightly armed paratroops and Kurdish militia were to be able to punch through the Iraqi defense lines on the hills above the strategic cities of Kirkuf and Mosul, centers of the northern oil fields.

The paratroops joined Special Forces units who have already been operating in northern Iraq since before the war formally began. Tuesday night the Special Forces called in a bombing mission on the ruling Baath Party headquarters in Samawa, destroying it. Wednesday, coalition warplanes stepped up their strikes on Iraqi northern defenses, keeping the Iraqi commanders' focus on the northern threat to deter the shift of forces to the defense of Baghdad. Meanwhile in the South, British troops battled a column of about 100 Iraqi vehicles moving south down the Fao peninsula from Basra toward the port city of Umm Qasr, where the first British aid ship, the Sir Galahad, was due to dock. British tanks and artillery stopped the Iraqi column, and U.S. and British warplanes then attacked it.

The 8,500-ton vessel headed for the single working dock at Umm Qasr, with British and Australian divers and minesweepers checking for mines or obstructions while troops and helicopters watched for any sign of attack from the fanatical fedayeen. Distribution of the aid is considered one of the most important parts of Operation Iraqi Freedom to date. At a time when Iraqis are able to see only invading troops, civilian casualties and vicious fedayeen attempting to ensure they continue to fight, the allies desperately need to show they are there to help them. The allies have prepared a major propaganda effort for the ship's arrival, but the original plan of simply driving the food, medicine and supplies straight to cheering and grateful citizens in Basra, however, is now way behind schedule.

Despite British and American armor almost surrounding it, the city of 1.5 million is far from secure. Hundreds of Iraqi paramilitary soldiers loyal to Saddam continue to cow the population and launch ambush attacks against allied troops. Most of the troops of the 8,000-strong Iraqi 51st Division, which had indicated it was about to surrender on Monday, appear to have melted back into the city. Although engineers from the International Committee of the Red Cross did bravely get into Basra Wednesday to restore power to a vital water pumping station, and British troops were rapidly building a water pipeline to run from Kuwait across the Iraqi border, the British were playing safe, unwilling to get bogged down in a major urban battle with the risk of heavy civilian casualties.

An estimated 1,000 or so of Saddam's "irregulars" are believed still to be holding the citizens of Basra in a grip of terror, according to British officials. But as they are primarily driven by Baath Party functionaries, say the officials, the British plan to dislodge them is to target their headquarters and individual homes and offices by means of "snatch and grab" techniques tried

and tested by the British Army over 30 years in Northern Ireland, Bosnia and Kosovo.

"We have to wait for the right moment or otherwise we put too many civilians at risk," said Lt. Col. David Palteron, commander of the 1st Battalion Royal Regiment of Fusiliers. The plan calls for "aggressive patrolling," which would be done in Warrior infantry fighting vehicles rather than on foot. Section by section, the troops intend to move slowly into the streets, directed by Special Air Service troops and locally supplied intelligence, using their vehicles' turret-mounted 30-caliber Rarden cannons if they come under fire, and deploying sections of seven men at a time to clear houses as necessary.

The army believes its success at nearby Zubayr might be a model for Basra. There, on Tuesday, bombing of the Baath Party headquarters and attacks and arrests of fedayeen appeared to encourage local Iraqis to report on the Baathists. Children led British troops to a school where stacks of ammunition and weapons were piled up in a classroom. Elsewhere, Royal Marines were directed to a house where they took away a colonel, a major and two captains for questioning. In a bid to make themselves more "approachable" to the local populations, British troops in Umm Qasr and Zubayr have started doffing their helmets and wearing their berets.

But the allied propaganda efforts took a heavy blow Wednesday, when TV images from Baghdad claimed a coalition bomb hit a civilian marketplace in the Shahab neighborhood in the city, killing at least 14 people. One British newspaper, the Independent, filled its front page with an account of what it called "a war crime." The Pentagon insisted the residential area has never been targeted since the beginning of the war, but Wednesday U.S. Central Command in Qatar said that it could have hit civilian homes elsewhere in Baghdad when it was bombing nine surface-to-surface missile sites, most of which were placed within 300 feet of private homes. "While the coalition goes to great lengths to avoid injury to civilians and damage to civilian facilities, in some cases such damage is unavoidable when the regime places military weapons near civilian areas," Central Command stated Wednesday. It suggested a more likely scenario was an Iraqi air-defense missile falling back to earth.

"I don't accept the premise that the civilians have been killed by coalition bombs. I just don't accept that. What we have seen over the last several days is Iraqi citizens being marched out in front of irregular formations while they are firing. Iraqi civilians are being killed on the battlefield by Iraqis," said Brig. Gen. Vincent Brooks, Central Command spokesman. The coalition has fired more than 600 Tomahawk cruise missiles and dropped more than 4,300 precision-guided weapons, according to the Pentagon.

The Armchair Critics

The taking of American prisoners of war, the resistance by Iraqi paramilitary forces and the slowing effects of the sandstorm inspired a rising tide of criticism over coalition strategy and Pentagon war planning. On March 24, the Washington Post ran a front-page headline "US Losses Expose Risks, Raise Doubts About Strategy." The New York Times editorial said, "The Marines were bogged down in tough fighting in Nasiriyah." Tom Brokaw, the NBC news anchor, spoke of "high-profile allied blunders" and NBC analyst Gen. Barry McCaffrey said in an interview with the BBC that the coalition could be facing as many as 3,000 casualties.

At coalition headquarters in Doha, Qatar, the Arab correspondent for Abu Dhabi TV asked U.S. Lt. Gen. John Abizaid, "Are you facing a new Vietnam in Iraq or are you victims of over-self-confidence?" The criticism continued, despite the mounting evidence of coalition successes. On March 30, New York Times analyst J.W. Apple (who had suffered much criticism for a premature judgment that the 2001 war against the Taliban in Afghanistan was becoming "a quagmire") wrote, "With every passing day, it is evident that the allies made two gross military misjudgments in concluding that coalition forces could safely bypass Basra and Nasiriyah and that Shiite Muslims in southern Iraq would rise up against Saddam Hussein."

Analysis: Winning both war and peace

PAMELA HESS

WASHINGTON, March 26 (UPI) — Pentagon officials contend that "armchair generals" criticizing conduct of the war in Iraq are failing to grasp the fundamental changes in strategy from earlier conflicts. The changes include accepting more tactical risk to reduce long-term strategic risk; using air dominance to make the battlefield three dimensional; and selecting the least number of critical targets to get the maximum impact on the enemy's will to fight.

Five days into the war, armchair generals, including retired warriors, are calling military reporters to express their concern that there is only one heavy division committed to the battle, that only 250,000 personnel are undertaking the war when more than 500,000 were required to expel Iraq from tiny Kuwait in 1991, that there is not enough artillery, and that there is not yet a northern front to attack the Republican Guard divisions north of Baghdad. Iraq has captured at least two prisoners of war and there may be five more.

The U.S. Army's 3rd Infantry Division is cutting a narrow swath at a breathtaking pace toward Baghdad, bypassing cities and eschewing firefights as it races to meet its quarry — the Republican Guard division protecting the Iraqi capital. As it moves, it is leaving its rear undefended — or at least that's how it looks to those viewing the battlefield through historic lenses. Proof of that vulnerability: A convoy of supply vehicles was ambushed Sunday and 12 lightly defended soldiers went missing.

It is a puzzling strategy to former generals and to an increasingly military savvy public reared on traditional land warfare, where a line on the ground (referred to in the Pentagon as FLOT, or Forward Line Own Troops) is moved forward as the territory behind it is occupied and held.

But senior Pentagon officials explain there is a method to what some consider madness: accept more tactical risk to reduce the long-term strategic risk. The tactical risk is that which troops accept on the battlefield. Certainly they would be safer with more heavy divisions than less, with more artillery than less, with more soldiers than less.

More important to Pentagon and Central Command planners is reducing strategic risk. They do not want to win the war just to lose the peace afterward. Bringing such firepower would run the risk of flattening the country, killing civilians and convincing the Arab world that the United States does indeed intend to "own" Iraq for a long time to come, according to military officials. That approach would undermine the strategic goal for the United States in Iraq, which is not just to topple Saddam Hussein's regime — bombing alone would do that — but to win the hearts of the Iraqi people. The United States has committed to rebuilding Iraq, and the less it has to do, the better. And post-Saddam, it wants in place a government friendly to the United States. To achieve this it needs to convince the Iraqis — and the rest of the Arab world — that the American force is a liberating rather than a conquering one.

It plans to do this with the minimum amount of bombing and the minimum amount of civilian casualties. A U.S. Air Force officer described this a week ago as "effects-based targeting." This approach to bombing uses a hyper-intelligent and culturally sensitive examination of the battlefield to identify and bomb the least number of critical targets to get the maximum impact on the enemy's will to fight, rather than its ability to fight.

Leaving Baghdad largely intact is critical to the long-term peace, even if it ends up drawing out the near-term battle, Pentagon sources say. There are sound tactical "effects-based" reasons for opting for a leaner force on the ground, Pentagon officials insist.

The relatively agile ground force assembled for this fight jumped into Iraq more than 24 hours before the original plan, in part because intelligence revealed the southern oil fields were rigged with explosives, a senior military official said Tuesday. A larger ground force might have slowed down what the Pentagon hopes will be a lighting-fast strike on elite Iraqi units — no less a part of "shock and awe" to undermine the regime than the deafening bombing of Baghdad.

"If I were in Baghdad and I was looking south and I saw a U.S. Army division that is on the outskirts of Baghdad, I think — you know, I don't know that that would be shock, but I'd certainly be a little concerned," Gen. Richard Myers, chairman of the Joint Chiefs of Staff, said at a Pentagon news conference Tuesday.

With its rear exposed on the ground — unheard of in traditional military planning — the 3rd Infantry Division is relying on the Air Force and the Navy to provide cover from the air. A quick-moving land force just has to be faster than the enemy forces behind it. The 3rd Infantry may appear surrounded on the ground, but under a sky firmly controlled by U.S. aircraft, the enemy is actually the one surrounded, military officials suggested. What was once a two-dimensional battlefield is now a three-dimensional one, and one of those dimensions is firmly in American hands with the advent of precision munitions, laser-range finders and Global Positioning System-aided targeting.

"We've got total dominance of the air. It is not air superiority, it's dominance. They have not put an airplane up," U.S. Defense Secretary Donald Rumsfeld said Tuesday. He also launched a spirited defense of the approach at the Pentagon, saying it has the full support of the men charged with carrying it out. "The people who are involved in this ... are very comfortable, as are the Joint Chiefs of Staff," he said. Myers pronounced the plan "brilliant" at the same press conference.

War chief Gen. Tommy Franks' plan employs a stunning, commonsense approach to the hairiest scenario of the battle: urban warfare. He doesn't want his people involved in bloody street fighting — for their own sakes and for the civilians inevitably caught in the crossfire. So he directed the leading edge of the ground forces to largely skirt the cities, focusing their urban fighting on securing roads, bridges, waterways and airfields to allow food and water to be delivered to people increasingly at risk. The plan envisions that any Iraqi fighters remaining in the bypassed cities after the demise of the regime would lose their motivation to fight.

The maneuver has been strained over the last two days, as irregular forces have taken up positions in the cities and harass U.S. Marines and British soldiers' positions on the edges.

But coalition forces reiterated their intentions Tuesday: They will secure the cities for humanitarian aid without occupying them. They are banking on targeted raids to win the day. They refuse to be drawn into a fight not of their own choosing. What remains unclear is what the coalition responsibility will be if humanitarian workers are victimized by Iraqi troops once in the cities. Both Rumsfeld and Myers have a strong interest in seeing this work. Winning the war with a minimum of U.S. and Iraqi civilian casualties will be its own reward. But if the strategy works, it will also bear out a central theme of Rumsfeld's reign in the Pentagon.

Rumsfeld came into office promising transformation — transitioning the services and, especially the Army, to use lighter, faster tanks and weapons, but more important, changing the way the leading edge fights wars. What would be traditionally a lumbering, logistics-heavy forward march is now a speedy, agile sword — all tooth, very little tail, in Pentagon parlance.

It is Rumsfeld's enthusiasm for transformation that has his critics grumbling, charging that his insistence on seeing it realized on this battlefield and his hubris in believing it can be successful puts troops in danger. If the strategy works — if Iraq is "liberated" from Saddam Hussein and a friendly government takes root — the success will be a stunning endorsement of Rumsfeld's leadership and of Franks' tactics. It will be perhaps the first instance of a ground force winning a war without capturing a square inch of enemy territory but moving through it toward its final engagement.

Its success hinges on the belief that the Iraqi people don't really oppose the United States, and instead will just go peacefully about their business. If the forces encounter significant indigenous opposition, it will be a very different outcome, Pentagon officials recognize. The only way the U.S. force will be welcomed is if it inflicts no unnecesary damage, no unnecesary violence. It is a delicate balance and one never achieved by an invader before, Pentagon officials say. It will be made possible by excellent intelligence, precision targeting, and patience.

Rumsfeld is aware of the criticism leveled at him but he is unmoved by it. "I can't manage what people — civilians or retired military — want to say. And if they go on and say it enough, people will begin to believe it. It may not be true, and it may reflect more of a misunderstanding of the situation than an analysis or an assessment of it, but there's no way anyone can affect what people say. We have a free country. In Iraq, they can affect what people say because you get shot if you say something they don't like," Rumsfeld said. "We don't do that."

NORTHERN IRAQ, MARCH 27 (UPI) — Iraqi Kurd Peshi Merga fighters patrol at a Seyed Sadegh checkpoint near Halabja on March 27, 2003. (Ali Khaligh, UPI)

Day 8 — Thursday, March 27

"The enemy we are fighting is different from the one we'd wargamed against." — Lt. Gen. William Wallace, commander of the U.S. Army V Corps

MARTIN WALKER

The sandstorm's enforced slowing of the U.S. drive on Baghdad, along with the damage inflicted by the Iraqi guerilla attacks and international criticism of the civilian bombing casualties in Baghdad, combined to fuel a growing mood of concern back in Washington. Media commentators and ex-military men fretted publicly that the war was not going to plan. New York Times defense analysts reported Thursday, "The air campaign that the Pentagon promised would 'shock and awe' Saddam Hussein's government appears to have done neither."

But the most sobering comment came from the U.S. commander in the field, Lt. Gen. William Wallace, commander of the U.S. Army V Corps, who told the Washington Post: "The enemy we are fighting is different from the one we'd wargamed against. We knew they were there — the paramilitaries — but we didn't know they would fight like this."

Worried that talk of setbacks and crisis could become self-fulfilling, the political and military chiefs in Washington — along with British Prime Minister Tony Blair, who was visiting President Bush as Camp David — resolved to push one simple and reassuring message — that the war plan was on track and going well.

Not quite. But the campaign was looking promising Thursday morning, as coalition commanders scrambled to meet Iraqi counterattacks moving out of Baghdad and south of Basra. The counterattacks were swiftly hammered by coalition air power, recovering from the two days of near blindness imposed by the driving sandstorms. As the dust cleared over the Euphrates River crossings at Najaf and Nasiriyah Thursday, the scale of this tactical U.S. victory became clear. In a defensive battle against Iraqi raids that tried to take advantage of the sandstorm cover that grounded the U.S. helicopter gunships, U.S. troops reported counting "hundreds of Iraqi dead." And south of Basra, where an Iraqi armored column of some 80 tanks and armored personnel carriers was "almost entirely destroyed" by allied guns and air power Wednesday evening, the firepower superiority of the coalition forces was again on display. Thursday morning, the Royal Scots Dragoon Guards outside Basra claimed to have knocked out another 14 Iraqi tanks making what a British military spokesman called "a suicide charge" from the city.

But the U.S. troops were still fighting on two fronts, one against the regular military forces to their front, another against the paramilitaries fighting guerilla-style to their rear and on their flanks. The U.S. Marines took 20 casualties, none fatal, in the defense of Nasiriyah overnight. Thursday morning, the Marines sent loudspeaker trucks into the city of some 200,000 people, telling the civilians to pack up and leave. The initial rules of engagement requiring allied troops to avoid damaging civilian areas appears to have been modified, after the use of civilian cover by Iraqi guerrilla-type fedayeen. The initial plan to bypass the towns and simply use the bridges was no longer viable. The Marines would have to root out the fedayeen in the streets and compounds.

With the weather clear and the gunships flying again, the flat terrain of the fertile plains between the Tigris and Euphrates Rivers became a killing ground for the Republican Guard divisions trying to hold the approaches to Baghdad. But in strategic terms, there was a lot of flexibility — if not change of plan — on display at the coalition command headquarters of U.S. Gen. Tommy Franks in Qatar. Plan A — a two-pronged attack on Iraq from north and south — was ditched when the Turks refused passage to the U.S. 4th Infantry Division. Plan B was the abortive attempt to end the war at a single blow by decapitating the Baghdad regime

with the bombing raid on March 19. Plan C was the swoop on Baghdad, the flanking drive up the west bank of the Euphrates to shock the Iraqis into an acceptance of their defeat.

Not one of those first three plans has fully succeeded, in part because the sandstorms slowed the coalition advance and in part because of the guerilla raids on the long and vulnerable supply lines of the U.S. 3rd Division, which had swept forward almost 300 miles in three days. But the further elaboration of Plan C is now under way. It began with a serious opening of the northern front with the airdrop of 1,000 parachutists from the U.S. 173rd Airborne Brigade on the airstrip at Harir, near the town of Bashur on the Kurdish occupied zone. Once the airfield was secure, C-17 military transports flew in the rest of the brigade and began flying in Bradley armored vehicles and antitank weapons.

The 1st Battalion of the 63rd Armored Brigade (normally based in Germany) was scheduled to be flown into Harir later to provide armored support. The deliberate publicity given to these movements by the allied command suggested that they wanted the Iraqi commanders to know — and worry — about the U.S. forces gathering to their north. The Iraqis will have to think long and hard before taking Republican Guard units from the north to reinforce the defense of Baghdad.

Meanwhile, south and west of Baghdad, the U.S. 3rd Division and the Marines were getting to grips with the main Republican Guard units, the Medina and Baghdad Divisions. Led by the 7th Cavalry, the 3rd Division continued its drive up the west bank of the Euphrates, battling its way through repeated ambushes by lightly armed troops with rocket propelled grenades and by regular army units with dug-in antitank guns. For the first time in the tank's 20-year history, two M1A1 Abrams tanks were knocked out by guns firing at close range, although none of the crewmen was killed. And the Iraqi defense positions were only able to get off one or two shots before they were hit by barrages from the Paladin self-propelled artillery guns or the air cover.

The Marines pushing north from Nasiriyah to Ash-Shatra and al-Amarah fought a series of sharp, tactical battles. One Iraqi armored unit and its accompanying infantry were pummeled with air strikes and artillery fire Thursday after falling for a trap that lured the Iraqis into vacated U.S. positions in central part of the country. The Marines advanced to contact and then pulled back in apparent disarray. Tuesday, the Marines had vacated an area near the main Highway 7, where militia from a nearby training camp had ambushed a Marine column. A U.S. Navy medic was killed by mortar fire while tending a wounded comrade. The militia fought well. "Some of these guys must have gone to Fort Benning (Georgia) at one time or another," said Capt. Jason Smith, commander of Bravo Company, 1st Battalion. "The ambushes are right out of the book — ambush, ambush again as the target either withdraws or moves forward to consolidate. They also have the road boxed in (preset) for the mortars."

As 3rd Battalion Marines repelled the attack and hunkered down for the night, artillery further to the rear pounded enemy positions. Air strikes were not possible because of a raging dust storm that turned day into an eerie twilight world, in which visibility was sometimes reduced to less than 10 feet. A hard rain in the night compacted the dust in the early morning, increasing visibility, but a strong wind continued to blow. Late Tuesday, the wind was blowing at about 45 knots.

"This is miserable. This has got to be the ass end of the world," Lance Cpl. Gregory Moll, from Harrisburg, Pa., commented. "It's so unreal."

The storm was not a sandstorm but a dust storm. Once part of the fertile crescent of Mesopotamia, the area where the Marines were had once been marshland. Saddam began draining it in the late 1970s. The result: a moonscape, covered with inches and inches of soft, fine dust and what was once silt. Senior officers in the column said the attacks by militia included attempts to penetrate Marine defenses with pickup trucks armed with machine guns. About a half dozen Iraqi army T-72 tanks tried to join in the fighting by moving down the highway Tuesday night, but they withdrew after the Marines' 155 mm artillery gave them a deadly welcome.

In a regiment-sized movement, the Marines took to the road and swung toward the airport to the northwest, as if to attack it in force. As hoped, the Iraqi tanks and infantry, which had been turned back Tuesday when they had approached the column farther south, then moved in to exploit what they thought was a situation that would bring them in behind the Marines on the move.

The Iraqi force, a Republican Guard unit equipped with Soviet-made T-72 tanks, was approaching the vacated positions across the open desert when two Navy F-14 aircraft swooped down from a bright, clear sky — the first after three days of vicious dust storms — and released laser-guided missiles and bombs. Cobra helicopter gunships then buzzed in lower, firing Gatling guns and rocket launchers. Plumes of smoke could be seen in the distance from the burning hulks. "It was a feint and they fell for it," Gunnery Sgt. Ron Jenks of Bravo Company, 1st Battalion, told United Press International. "We really lit them up," added Capt. Shawn Basco, an F-18 pilot acting as a forward air controller for the company.

Meanwhile, troops of 2nd Battalion, 5th Marines, were attacking a regional airport about two hours away by slow-moving armored troop carrier. Two Marines were killed by small-arms fire. Word on Iraqi casualties was not immediately available. The fighting Thursday was the culmination of a four-day march from the southern Rumaila oil fields, seized and secured by the Marines in the hours after the 5th Battalion became the first U.S. units to enter Iraq at the start of the ground war to unseat Iraqi leader Saddam Hussein and disarm Iraq of its suspected weapons of mass destruction. Although it has not suffered a chemical-weapon attack in its dash into Iraq, the Marines are in their chemical protection suits, with gas masks in small bags attached to their belts. During the hot days, the suits slowly bake the Marines, but at night offer a bit of help against muscle-cramping cold.

"OK, are we having fun yet? I know it's miserable, but we're all in the same boat. Keep your spirits up, keep your guard up," 1st Sgt. Bill Leuthe of Bravo Company told troops as he moved down the line of armored tracks carrying his charges. "I know it was cold last night, but so what. Heat up for MREs, guys. It will hit the spot."

New Wars, Old Gods in Babylon

John Bloom

NEW YORK, March 24 (UPI) — There's a reason the lower plain, between the Tigris and Euphrates, where all the death is occurring right now, looks like a wasteland.

God wiped it out himself.

"Therefore," said the prophet Jeremiah, "the wild beasts of the desert with the wild beasts of the islands shall dwell there, and the owls shall dwell therein: and it shall be no more inhabited for ever; neither shall it be dwelt in from generation to generation."

It has been dwelt in over the past 25 centuries, but just barely: The dynasties have been short and the settlements sporadic. As the prophet said, it's failed to last "from generation to generation." And yet, under the ground — almost everywhere under the ground — lie the bones of our ancestors.

Every battle takes place where a hundred battles have occurred before. Every missile that penetrates into the ground destroys not just the current occupant of the land, but as many as seven major civilizations below it. Every death, however shocking at the moment, is, from the standpoint of history, a mere jot in the boneyard.

When the 3rd Infantry Division marched up the right bank of the Euphrates, it passed over the ruins of Ur, oldest civilization in the world, older even than Egypt — the newest world literally trampling the oldest, at the place where the sons of Noah are believed to have settled after the Flood. For some this is mere coincidence — that the most powerful nation would go to the oldest battleground at this particular time. But if you watch some of the more fringe evangelists on religious TV, you'll find this war is being monitored with the sort of rapt attention they normally reserve for the proceedings of the state biology textbook committee. By their reckoning it's an entirely spiritual event.

When the second Babylon is destroyed — that would be Iraq — they expect it to be followed by an era of peace during which the whole world will be in harmony. A charismatic leader will emerge from this time of calm, a beloved man — who will turn out to be the Antichrist. He'll then destroy Israel in a fiery cataclysm, and Christ will come again. I'm abridging, of course, but the literalists holding the Book of Revelation in their hands are looking on this war as the beginning of the end, or the beginning of the beginning, depending on how you relate emotionally to the apocalypse.

And why not? We have every reason to believe that this particular patch of land is exactly where God gets his hands dirty. He deposited the sons of Noah there. He called Abraham out of there. And when it suited him, he reduced everything to rubble. That makes the rubble currently being created by the heavy bombing at Mosul especially ironic. Fortunately, most of King Sargon's summer palace, built in 709 B.C., has long since been removed to the Louvre. But the bombing area was the site of Nineveh, a city especially despised by God, where the kings were so terrible that their entire nation had to be destroyed.

But again, it's a tale better left to a prophet — this time Zephaniah: "And He will stretch out his hand against the north, and destroy Assyria; and will make Nineveh a desolation, and dry like a wilderness. And flocks shall lie down in the midst of her, all the beasts of the nations: both the cormorant and the bittern shall lodge in the upper lintels of it; their voice shall sing in the windows; desolation shall be in the thresholds; for he shall uncover the cedar work. This is the rejoicing city that dwelt carelessly, that said in her heart, I am, and there is none beside me: how is she become a desolation, a place for beasts to lie down in! Every one that passeth by her shall hiss, and wag his hand."

The part here that fascinates me is that the sin of Nineveh was that it was a "rejoicing city that dwelt carelessly, that said in her heart, I am, and there is none beside me … I think we can assume that Babylon, where the god Marduk was worshipped in the Tower of Babel, and where the Iraqi 11th Infantry Division was recently turned back, was devastated for similar reasons. But the intriguing thing about the phrase "I am, and there is none beside me," is that it could be the mantra of a homicidal dictator, but it could also be the slogan of any conqueror. It was interesting to see that two days ago an American soldier erected a banner reading "Future Iraq: The Rule of Law" — just a few miles from the capital city of King Hammurabi, who actually *invented* the rule of law: He codified the first legal system around 1800 B.C. "I am, and there is none beside me" is something that every child says — before he understands there are others beside him.

As I write this, American soldiers are pouring into the Aram-naharaim, the "land between the two rivers," and according to the speculation of the rent-a-generals on television, a second American force will move to the north so that Baghdad can be squeezed in a pincer operation. This means the second force would reconnoiter somewhere around the confluence of the Tigris and the Zab. Though they won't realize it, they'll be at Nimrod, one of the first human settlements, called Larissa by Xenophon, who encamped there with the 10,000 Greek warriors during the most famous retreat in military history.

King Nimrod, "the mighty hunter," is the third generation after Noah, and his symbols were enormous winged lions and winged bulls, most of which fortunately now reside in the British Museum. After resting for 2,800 years, they were excavated, loaded onto rafts, shipped 600 miles down the Tigris to Basra, and then onto British ships that carried them 12,000 more miles around the Horn of Africa.

Austen Henry Layard, the British foreign officer who supervised this rather stupendous feat, was approached by a local sheikh as the sculptures were being loaded, and the sheikh asked, "In the name of the Most High, tell me, O Bey, what you are going to do with those stones? So many thousands of purses spent upon such things! Can it be, as you say, that your people learn wisdom from them, or is it, as his reverence, the Cadi, declares, that they are to go to the palace of your Queen, who with the rest of the unbelievers, worships these idols?" Well, as it turns out, there are some of us who learn wisdom from them and some of us who worship them. Unfortunately, I don't think any presidents or generals are numbered among either group. And that makes it dicey for the Army.

This war gives me the creeps. As armored divisions roll past the palaces of Nebuchadnezzar, tramp down the bloody graves of terrorists like Sennacherib, march over the banquet hall of the Sumerian gods, the cities of the Chaldeans, the fortresses of the Kassites and the Elamites, the enemy before them must seem as strange in its way as the fearsome Sirrush, the dragon of Babylon, a long-legged four-footed scaly beast with talons and a snake head on a long neck, topped by a horn on a flat skull. The Sirrush destroyed many an army, and became impotent — according to Daniel — only when it faced "the living God."

There are many gods in Sumeria and Akkad and Iraq, and all of them are broken into shards that lie crumpled on the backs of a million mangled, stabbed, speared, beheaded and murdered people. The very ground consists of their blood and flesh. It's not a place to be taken lightly. If and when we win this war, we should leave quickly, as though from a cursed place, lest we be thought of as a rejoicing people who dwelt carelessly. God doesn't like that.

CENTRAL COMMAND AREA OF RESPON-SIBILITY, KUWAIT, MARCH 28 (UPI) — A pilot of a CH-53 Super Stallion helicopter bends down to gather himself after surviving a crash at an expeditionary airfield station while in support of Operation Iraqi Freedom.   (Lance Cpl. J.T. Spencer, USMC/UPI)

Day 9 — Friday, March 28

"...however long it takes..." — U.S. President George W. Bush

The battle of the Sunni triangle is now fully engaged, and coalition commanders now hope it will continue long enough to secure the destruction of the Republican Guard before they close in on the city of Baghdad. Bounded by the cities of Baghdad, Najaf and Kut, this triangle of some 1,200 square miles is the heartland of the Sunni Muslims and the cradle of the ancient Babylonian civilization.

It is now becoming a killing ground. As the skies clear and the fierce sun of spring burns down, the U.S. combat helicopters and air power have been unleashed upon the Republican Guard and Iraqi army forces who are being constantly reinforced to hold this bleak and flat terrain. In the view of coalition commanders in Qatar, this is a gift. With steady pressure from their own ground troops, they can fix the Iraqi forces in place, where they can be killed from the air. And the more Saddam's loyalists are ground down in this happy hunting ground for U.S. air power, the fewer they will meet in the streets of Baghdad. In the meantime, the U.S. troops can scour the remaining guerilla threats to their supply lines, 300 miles back to Kuwait, and start the "hearts and minds" campaign with humanitarian supplies among the Shiite Muslims of southern Iraq.

Now that they have heard President Bush declare his readiness for a long war — "however long it takes," as he said at Thursday's news conference with British Prime Minister Tony Blair — the coalition commanders feel under no pressure to mount a premature attack on the Iraqi capital. They are repairing the captured Iraqi airbases at Tallil outside Nasiriyah and at al-Amara to base and resupply their own air power. They are securing the Euphrates bridges at Najaf and Nasiriyah, which means clearing the houses and buildings within sniper and mortar range. And U.S. Marines fought a long battle Thursday in Nasiriyah against pro-Saddam fedayeen.

Baghdad's outer defenses have been dubbed the "Red Zone" by Central Command planners, after the last 20 yards before the end zone of a football field. The Red Zone contains between eight and 10 Iraqi divisions. Based around Amarah, between the southeastern city of Basra and Baghdad, is the Regular Army's IV Corps. The IV Corps consists of two weak light infantry divisions and the 10th Armored Division, one of the best in the Iraqi army.

Behind the IV Corps is the Republican Guard's Baghdad Motorized Division, a not particularly good truck-mounted unit. Closer to Baghdad are four Republican Guard Divisions and at least two commando brigades. To the north of the city are the Hammurabi and al-Nida Armored Divisions and the 26th Commando Brigade. To the south are the Medina Armored and Nebuchadnezzar Motorized Divisions. Guarding the southern edge of the city is the 3rd Commando Brigade. Two more solid regular army tank Divisions may also be in the ring.

The 6th Armored Division is unaccounted for. It was supposed to be stationed in the south. However, there have been reports that the division was moved north to defend Baghdad. Aside from a few contacts with rear-guard units, there has been no serious contact between coalition forces and the 6th Armored. There have also been reports that the 3rd Armored Division, usually stationed in the north, across from the Kurdish Autonomous Region, has been moved to Ramadi, on the western approaches to Baghdad.

The question is whether the Iraqi commanders will cooperate with the new American strategy. So far, they have proved capable of delivering some nasty surprises, and Iraqi leaders are now talking openly of fighting a long campaign of attrition against the coalition forces that seems drawn equally from the Soviet defense of Stalingrad in World War II and the Viet Cong guerillas. In a long news conference in Baghdad Thursday, Iraq's defense minister, Sultan Hashim Ahmed, suggested Iraq had its own counterstrategy. He acknowledged that coalition forces might encircle Baghdad within 5 to 10 days, but sooner or later they would have to try to enter the city.

"The enemy must come inside Baghdad, and that will be its grave," he said. "We feel that this war must be prolonged so the enemy pays a high price. God willing, Baghdad will be impregnable. We will fight to the end. The longer the American and British soldiers stay in our country, the more they will pay in lives.

"The enemy can bypass the resistance and go in the desert as far as it wants. In the end, where can he go? He has to enter the city," he said, stressing that this war for which the Iraqi army had been preparing for the last year had barely begun. "It can't be decided in 10 days. It could be decided in a month, two months or more."

Nor was he overawed by U.S. air power, which Iraqi generals had been studying since the first Gulf War. By moving at night and in small groups and using camouflage, Iraqi forces had learned to survive it. "The regular army is well dug-in and soldiers' foxholes are hard to hit accurately," he said. "Our casualties from air power so far have not been heavy."

While the Iraqi capital soaked up U.S. attacks in house-by-house fighting, the Iraqis were determined to keep up the guerilla strikes against the U.S. supply lines.

"They are a snake that is stretched over 500 kilometer, we would like to stretch them even further and then start to chop them up," Iraqi Information Minister Mohammad Saeed al-Sahhaf told Abu Dhabi TV.

In short, the commanders of both sides now think they have found their killing ground. For the Iraqis, it will be the streets of Baghdad and the enemy's stretched and vulnerable lines of communication. For the U.S. and British commanders, the killing ground will be the 1,200 square miles of the Sunni triangle south of Baghdad. This war is becoming a struggle between two differing concepts of the war of attrition — in which the side with the greater political will to take casualties and resist internal dissent has usually won.

Even as they buckled down to a war of defense, the Iraqi regime's offensive capacities were not exhausted. Their missile attacks had hitherto proved almost pointless. Unlike the first Gulf War, no missiles were fired at Israel. And the missiles fired at Kuwait, with its vast civilian target of Kuwait City and the military targets of the vital port of Doha and the sprawling U.S. military camps in the desert, had little effect. The missiles either veered off course into the Persian Gulf or were shot down by the Patriot missile systems. But a large explosion rocked downtown Kuwait City at 2 a.m. local time Saturday, as an Iraqi missile hit the cinema of a deserted seafront shopping mall, within a stone's throw of a Kuwaiti Foreign Ministry building and a residence of the ruling al-Sabah family. The usual radar-triggered air raid alarms did not sound, suggesting the missile was one that came in low, below radar coverage, and the Patriot antimissile defenses did not react. Kuwait International Airport continued to operate as usual, and commercial jets were heard taking off, although the airport is routinely closed during a missile alert. Kuwaiti officials said it was a low trajectory missile, fired from the direction of Basra, Iraq, across the Persian Gulf.

Kuwait City had lost its initial fears of the Iraqi missiles, after 12 missiles had failed to inflict any damage, and many more false alarms inspired many to shrug and ignore the regulations requiring people to head for the shelters. Some Kuwaitis, finding some English writing on the missile that hit the movie theater, believed it was an American Tomahawk that went astray.

In fact it was an Iraqi-made missile, a homemade modification of a Chinese sea-skimming Silkworm cruise missile, fired from the vicinity of Basra. One striking fact of the war was that Iraq fired no Scud missiles, although U.S. intelligence reckoned it had retained as many as 24, despite U.N. orders that they be destroyed.

As well as the Scuds that Iraq claims to have destroyed under U.N. disarmament rules, Iraq has two other locally made missiles that can reach Kuwait. The first is the al-Samoud, whose range U.N. inspectors deemed last month to exceed the 150-kilometer (93-mile) limit imposed on Iraq after the 1991 Gulf War. They ordered those missiles destroyed, which Iraq was in the process of doing when war broke out. The second is the shorter-range al-Fatah missile, with a 130-kilometer (80-mile) range.

Until the Saturday explosion, there had been no air raid warnings and no missiles for 36 hours. U.S. military spokesmen said the threat of missile attack would inevitably recede as coalition forces moved farther north into Iraq, pushing Iraqi forces back out of firing range. The explosion in Kuwait came as the coalition air forces launched another series of heavy bombing raids against Baghdad. Iraqi authorities claimed some 50 more civilians had died in what they called "another war crime" attack on a residential district.

The Lonely Refugee

Arnaud de Borchgrave

RUWEISHAD, Jordan, March 24 (UPI) — The sole Iraqi refugee to make it to the Jordanian border since the beginning of the war is now stuck in a tent in no man's land between the two countries. Mohammad Ali Goufi, 30, told United Press International that he had traveled to the border by bus and was allowed to leave Iraq "to see my dying mother in Yemen." With him on the bus were 22 Palestinians who are bearers of Iraqi and Egyptian travel documents. But the Egyptian Embassy in Amman is unwilling to guarantee their onward journey, and the Iraqi Embassy in the Jordanian capital won't take them back. Goufi said he worked as a car salesman in the duty-free zone outside Amman, but no one recognized his name.

International relief organizations had been expecting hundreds of thousands of Iraqi refugees. So far, however, only a trickle has been reported on all frontiers. Jordanian authorities erected eight tents in the desolate wind- and rain-swept zone between the two countries — some 400 miles from the Iraqi capital, Baghdad, and about 200 miles from Amman. Families occupy seven tents — three per tiny tent — and Goufi has one to himself. The temperature Monday was near freezing. International Red Cross and United Nations refugee agency representatives were on hand when UPI reached them. The media have not been authorized to enter the no man's land. Observers said this was partly because gouger's fees were being charged for taxis and other transport, and partly because Jordan, Turkey and Syria had closed their borders to refugees at least for the moment, as had the Iranians. But, the observers said, Iraqis could well be staying put in anticipation of being liberated by troops of the U.S.-led coalition.

Fattima Saeed, a medical doctor, has a Jordanian passport, but she wants to stay with her Palestinian lawyer-husband and three of her five children (two stayed behind in Baghdad).

None spoke ill of the Saddam Hussein regime: "We left because of the bombing and food shortages." When asked why they thought the United States decided to invade to remove Saddam from power, they looked at each other to see who would speak first. Then the husband said, "We're not involved in politics." They declined to offer their opinions about the Iraqi regime and kept saying, "We're not in politics."

Casablanca 2003 — Everyone goes to Rick's

NICHOLAS M. HORROCK

RUWEISHED, Jordan, April 7 (UPI) — The Abu Saif isn't Rick's, and Muwfaq Syouf doesn't have a white dinner jacket, but just like Rick's mythical café in the 1942 movie "Casablanca," the Abu Saif has been the end of the line for a lot of people in this war.

Ruweished is the last Jordanian town before you enter Iraq, 175 miles from Amman, Jordan, and 530 miles from Baghdad down a road you can get killed on, and is for many who pass through it in either direction the end of a way of life or maybe the beginning of another. The town is a dusty way station in the desert, here to serve the giant oil trucks that for years ran down this road and the army posts of the Jordanian army, which maintains a *cordon militaire* to keep the wanderers 50 miles from the Iraqi border.

North of this village, some 12 miles, are vast refugee camps set up by the U.N. High Commission on Refugees, the International Red Cross, the Red Crescent and a Jordanian charity known as the Hashemite Foundation. The tent cities have a capacity of perhaps 100,000 refugees or more, but as yet only a handful have come, mainly third country nationals fleeing Iraq after the war began. "They come to the border," said Suifan Amar Ahmed al-Hided, a regional disaster manager for the Red Crescent,

by car, bus, van and on foot. "Two Egyptians walked 140 kilometers (90 miles) to get here," he said with some amazement.

But to date the refugee crisis that overwhelmed Jordan in the first Gulf War has not happened, and Suifan sits in a large bus–office waiting. "We are ready," he promises. "We are prepared."

In the 19 days of this war, thousands of people have moved each way across this border who are not claiming refugee status, on such divergent transport as buses, Mercedes Benz limousines, family vans and giant trucks. And those travelers are most likely to stop at the Abu Saif — the name is Arabic for "father of the sword" — a 24-hour restaurant with perhaps 40 seats, a butcher shop, a grocery store and, like Rick's, lazy fans circulating in the ceiling.

This is where the hundreds of Iraqis have had a last supper of peace before returning to Iraq, many vowing to fight for Saddam Hussein, many just wanting to be with their families as they watch their nation being bombarded. This is where the "human shields" stopped for supper on their way to give their bodies to protect humanitarian sites in Baghdad, and this is where many of them of had the first relaxed meal on their way back from the war.

Manager-owner Muwfaq, 44, was wearing a short-sleeved green shirt and slacks on Sunday night, doesn't own a white dinner jacket, and thinks he once saw "Casablanca" in the movies. Like Humphrey Bogart's Rick in "Casablanca," he deplores the war around him. "We don't like war," he told United Press International correspondents as they dined. "It is not good to gain money over war." And clearly war has been, although perhaps unwelcome, a boon to Muwfaq and his brother.

The walls tell the story, with the business cards of his new customers, some famous, some not so famous. Jim Cox of USA Today has apparently eaten there, as have representatives from the Associated Press, a half dozen Japanese television and print organizations, Newsweek photographers and BBC producers and reporters from Brazilian papers.

Never mind the business cards, his café bears the unmistakable atmosphere that Hollywood tried to recreate in the "Casablanca" movie set: desperate people caught up in a war beyond their control and fortunes they can no longer predict.

Sunday, the Abu Saif featured a quite tasty fried chicken and french fries, a Middle East mixed salad, black olives, hummus garnished with olive oil and large flat pieces of a pita bread to be dipped into a delicious sauce of yogurt and garlic. The price of dinner was $8.30 for two, including Arabic coffee and a complementary bottle of water for the trip.

The waiter was an Iraqi. He was afraid to give reporters his name, but in a few days he will return to Iraq, to find out the fate of his mother in Samawa. He has been unable to call her for days. Like most Arabs in this region, the waiter thinks life will never be the same, and like most Arabs in this region, he does not have much faith in the vision that George W. Bush has for his country.

HARIR AIR BASE, IRAQ, MARCH 29 (UPI) — American troops keeping watch March 29, 2003, in northern Iraq during the coalition-led war against Saddam Hussein's regime. (Ali Khaligh, UPI)

Day 10 — Saturday, March 29

The pause

MARTIN WALKER

Back in Washington and London, the armchair pundits called it "the pause," the sudden slackening of the breakneck advance that had taken U.S. forward patrols to within 50 miles of Baghdad as the vast logistics and supply convoys hauled the food and fuel and ammo 200 miles north from the Kuwaiti ports. They had to supply the 90,000 troops inside Iraq with 400,000 gallons of water a day. Maj. Gen. Dennis Jackson, director of logistics for U.S. Central Command, said he thinks of it as enough to fill 20 swimming pools. And the tanks, Humvees, trucks, helicopters and mobile generators for the field hospitals need 15 million gallons of fuel every day. That means 750 giant fuel tankers — with their accompanying security units — heading north each day.

For the troops on the front line, it did not feel like a pause. The security of those logistics convoys, and the lightly armed troops who tried to guard them against Iraqi guerillas attacks, had become a prime concern after the ambushes of recent days. So in the towns of Najaf and Samawa and Nasiriyah, Marines and Airborne troops began the grueling work of urban warfare, clearing the houses and industrial plants and factory compounds within sniper and mortar range of the roads and bridges used by the vulnerable supply convoys.

Suddenly, it was a different kind of war, with civilians in the front line, and new security tasks for the combat troops who found themselves manning roadblocks and checkpoints. It was at such a checkpoint in Najaf that four American soldiers were killed Saturday when a suicide bomber exploded his car while he was stopped for a routine check. The incident reflects the way the conventional military battle U.S. and British forces thought they would face has started to look more like the guerilla war of the Palestinian *intifada* against Israel.

The suicide bomber was dressed as a civilian and approached the checkpoint in a taxi. He signaled for help, and then blew himself and the vehicle up as the soldiers of the U.S. Army's 1st Brigade, 3rd Infantry Division approached. Iraqi officials identitied him as Ali Jaafar Hammad al-Naamani, an army officer, and Iraqi TV screened a film of him swearing on a copy of the Koran to become a martyr. It will not be the last such attack, however, declared Iraqi Deputy President Taha Yassin Ramadan later Saturday, and he claimed that "thousands of volunteers" were arriving in Iraq daily from other Arab countries to join the war against the coalition forces. "This is a beginning. You will hear good news in the few coming days. The Iraqi people will receive them the way those miserable (U.S. – British forces) deserve," he said.

U.S. military officials tried to put a better face on the tactic. The bombing was "a symbol of an organization that's starting to get a little bit desperate," said Maj. Gen. Victor Renuart during a briefing Saturday afternoon at the Combined Forces Command headquarters in Doha, Qatar. "I'd ask, 'Where have we seen those types of events occur?' I think we would all agree that all of them are associated with terrorist events."

Ramadan's comments came as Baghdad residents braced themselves for another night of bombing by the coalition's sea-launched cruise missiles and aircraft bombs. In the two previous days, Iraqi television has shown residential areas the government says were hit by U.S. munitions, killing dozens of men, women and children. Coalition spokesmen, confident of the accuracy of their precision weapons, suggested that the damage had been caused by Iraqi anti-aircraft missiles hidden in residential areas. The booms of explosions have sounded sporadically throughout the Iraqi capital during the daylight hours as well Saturday, suggesting

coalition forces are more confident their bombs are reaching Iraqi antiaircraft facilities.

Traffic in Baghdad has dwindled even during the day and people have been seeking safer havens for their families, away from the deafening blasts that have broken windows and shaken the foundations of their homes. Destruction and death has become a common sight. State and satellite television channels are filled with images of attacks said to have been propagated by American and British forces, showing twisted and bloody bodies and bandaged children in hospital. Neither daytime air raids nor rationing of electric power, water and communications services have kept residents off the streets looking to purchase necessities, however — especially vegetables and meat, which have once again flooded the popular local markets and allowed people to stock up as they did before the outbreak of the war.

Iraqi Information Minister Mohammad Saeed al-Sahhaf declared Saturday that a total of 140 Iraqis were killed and 351 others injured by U.S.–British air strikes on the country since Friday. He said in a daily briefing in the capital that 68 "were martyred only in Baghdad since last night's bombing, and 107 injured."

Scores of Palestinians from refugee camps in south Lebanon have headed to Iraq to battle coalition forces, and Lebanese security services also reported that several other Lebanese and Egyptian volunteers, mostly members of the Arab Baath Socialist Party, have traveled to Iraq in recent days.

"There is not a single (Iraqi) refugee coming out, but six or seven hundred leave every day," a Syrian border officer told United Press International. "Those who are going to Iraq, mostly Iraqis and from various Arab nationalities, outnumber those who are coming."

A Lebanese couple reached al-Tanaf on Friday to look for their only child. Wael Sabah, a 19-year-old university student, left a letter to his parents in Beirut telling them he was heading to Iraq along with four of his friends to pose as human shields. Syrian border officers confirmed that he was already in Iraq. "May God protect him and all his friends and people in Iraq. What more can I say?" Sabah's father said.

Kuwaiti border troops have arrested 11 Iraqi fedayeen infiltrators on a mission to carry out a bombing campaign in Kuwait as they tried to slip across the frontier. The 11 fedayeen were arrested in two separate operations Thursday and Friday near the remote border crossing of Bahar Houshan and have since been under interrogation by Kuwaiti security police.

But as the heavy equipment of the U.S. 4th Division began to unload at Kuwait's port Saturday, security officials in this essential logistics base for the coalition forces were bracing for Iraq's new guerilla tactics to start operations against their small, oil-rich emirate. Although there are no blackouts in Kuwait City at night and the shopping malls are full, there are constant police checkpoints on the roads and heightened security at public buildings. Twelve Iraqi missiles have been fired at Kuwait since the war began, and air raid sirens send people scurrying to their shelters daily.

Many Iraqis, who speak the same language and in many cases have close family links across the border, can pass unnoticed in Kuwait. And with U.S. and British air and military bases in Kuwait, the country is a prime intelligence opportunity for Baghdad. So far, however, Kuwait has been an intelligence objective rather than a target for hostile covert operations, which makes the arrest of the infiltrators so alarming for the emirate. But there is no sign that the new threats to Kuwait, nor the constant attacks on Kuwait's support for the war against Iraq coming from the Arab media, will change the government's policy.

"We have interests as Kuwaitis that the Iraqi regime leader is ousted," said Kuwait defense minister Sheikh Jaber al-Sabah, speaking to reporters on an inspection tour of Kuwaiti naval forces Saturday. "We denounce the methods used by some media outlets and politicians against the stance of Kuwait towards the war in Iraq."

Kuwait is a country of almost 2 million people, but fewer than half of them are Kuwaitis of Arab descent, and a majority of the workforce is composed of immigrants from Palestine, Egypt, Pakistan, India and Bangladesh. Oil wealth provides a highly prosperous per capita income of over $20,000 a year, and it is one of the most democratic of all Arab states. Kuwait has a parliament with a genuine popular mandate, a division of powers, a relatively free speech and press and a written constitution. But with Shiite Muslims (like those of Iran and southern Iraq) furnishing almost half the population, and Sunni Muslims providing another third, and many tribal and family links across the border, Kuwait remains uncomfortably locked into the political fate of neighboring Iraq.

Baghdad Under Bombardment for 10th Day

Ghassan al-Khadi

BAGHDAD, Iraq, March 29 (UPI) — As the U.S.-led invasion of Iraq entered its 10th day Saturday, Iraqis began to feel the dangers their lives faced, particularly after attacks on residential and civilian areas that killed and injured dozens over the past two days. More than 50 civilians are reported to have died Friday, when a missile hit a crowded street in a low-income Baghdad neighborhood. Iraq blamed the raid on the U.S.–British coalition. Coalition forces have consistently denied targeting civilian areas.

Residents of Baghdad began to feel exposed after the missile attacks targeted the impoverished and low-income al-Shaab and al-Shula neighborhoods on Friday. People began to seek safer havens for their families, away from the missiles and rockets, whose deafening noise were particularly terrifying for children. The explosion from the bombing shook the foundations of houses and buildings and broke windows.

On Friday night, a missile hit the Information Ministry in the center of Baghdad, breaking windows of a nearby residential neighborhood. Iraq said the missile was American. Hundreds of Iraqi artists and journalists demonstrated in front of the ministry building, condemning the attack.

Destruction and death has become a common sight in Baghdad. Images of attacks by American and British forces being broadcast on Iraqi television has saddened Iraqis who are convinced that there is no such thing as a "clean war" or one that differentiates between civilians and military. Iraqis are convinced that the missiles and rockets raining down on their heads were far from "smart."

The attacks, combined with the rationing of electric power, water and telecommunications services, has led to a reduction of traffic on the main streets of Baghdad, a city of some 5 million people. Because of the risks involved in moving about the city, traffic has remained at a minimum during the past two days. Air raids carried out during the day on Baghdad have prevented people from going about their daily lives and forced some shops to remain closed. Still, that has not prevented residents of the capital from purchasing food, especially vegetables and meat, which have once again flooded the popular local markets, allowing people to stock up as they did before the outbreak of the war.

Information Minister Mohammed Saeed al-Sahhaf said the bombing of his ministry "will not affect its work and its responsibilities," and accused the British of destroying more than 75,000 tons of foodstuff in a warehouse in Basra, in the south of the country. Sahhaf said there were efforts by Arab and European lawyers to "try George W. Bush and British Prime Minister Tony Blair as war criminals," accusing their forces of killing civilians in southern Iraq on grounds they were soldiers. The air raids continued throughout the day on Baghdad Saturday, but the targets were not clear. The loud sound of explosions could be heard repeatedly around the capital.

Buying the tribes

MARTIN WALKER

KUWAIT CITY, March 29 (UPI) — The striking scenes of Iraqis cheering and welcoming U.S. troops as liberators in the Shiite holy city of Najaf Wednesday came as no surprise to a handful of British and American undercover officials who have for months sought with sweet talk and hard cash to win over the country's traditional tribal sheikhs and chieftains.

"The most important duty of a tribal chief is knowing when to switch sides," one British official with knowledge of the undercover operation told United Press International. "In Najaf, the al-Jaburi tribe understood that Saddam Hussein's time was over."

Afghanistan was the model for the operation, where a handful of CIA agents spent $70 million to buy — or perhaps rent — the loyalties of Afghan tribal chiefs in the campaign against the Taliban in the fall of 2001.

"The Iraqi tribes knew instinctively what was going on," the British official noted. "The week that the Washington Post reported that $70 million had been spent on the Afghans, they all knew that figure — and several said openly that Iraq was a much more important country — and would cost a lot more."

There are about 150 major tribes in Iraq, and close to another 2,000 another smaller tribes or clans, some of them little more than extended families of fewer than 1,000 people. The big traditional tribes such as the al-Jaburi and the Beni Hasan, the Bardosti and Shammari and al-Dulaimi, have been dominant players in the region's tribal mosaic for centuries before the British carved the state of Iraq from the wreckage of the Ottoman Empire 80 years ago. The British also understood the importance of securing the loyalty of the tribal sheikhs. To this day, a prized possession of many tribeswomen, to be worn only at weddings or formal occasions, is a necklace made of British gold sovereigns from the 1920s — relics of another time when Western troops had to navigate the shifting loyalties of the tribes.

Traditionally rural-based, the tribes have managed to survive the process of modernization that turned desert nomads into urban dwellers. Scholars in Kuwait reckon that between a third and a half of the Iraqi population would identify their primary loyalties to their tribes, rather than to the national government in Baghdad. Ironically, Saddam helped this process. Although his Baath Party in the 1960s and 1970s tried to crush the tribes as alternative power bases, he has more recently worked to win them over by restoring judicial authority to the sheikhs and channeling money for public works through them. And despite repeated attempts at land reform, more than half of Iraqi land is "owned" by tribes rather than by individuals.

Three years ago, Saddam's regime tried to transfer land near Basra to some loyalists, and the Beni Hasan tribe rose in outrage. At least 24 Iraqi soldiers were killed, and 14 of the Beni Hasan before Baghdad dropped the plan — largely because other tribal sheikhs warned that they, too, opposed any tampering with tribal land rights. Last week, the abortive uprising against Saddam's forces inside Basra began when a junior sheikh from the Beni Hasan was shot for being lukewarm in his loyalty.

It was the strain of the Iran–Iraq war, which lasted throughout the 1980s, that forced Saddam to woo the tribes. He needed their political support and their men for his army. When the sheikh of the large al-Jaburi tribe died and there was a dispute over which clan leader would succeed him, Saddam saw his chance. He backed the son, Machan al-Jaburi — and once installed, the new sheikh delivered 50,000 men to the Iraqi army for the Iran war. The al-Jaburi became favored and powerful, and public money for roads and schools and housing was steered their way, enhancing the sheikh's influence as he delivered jobs and other favors to his people.

But tribal loyalties can shift fast. Once he suspected the al-Jaburi were becoming too strong, he sacked the two al-Jaburi ministers and cut off the flow of funds. In January 1990, the al-Jaburi tried to mount a military coup with their officers. It failed, but the cautious sheikh was in Paris and later was able to continue running tribal affairs from across the border in Syria. The al-Jaburi officers mounted another coup attempt in 1993 — a desperate last-ditch affair, as Saddam steadily purged the al-Jaburi from the military. Then the Baghdad regime patched up relations with a newly installed sheikh. The tribal vendetta continued — three years ago, al-Jaburi officers in the Republican Guard were shot after another coup attempt.

Governments in Baghdad come and go, but the tribes go on forever. Saddam, who has faced revolts from the al-Jaburi, the al-Dumaini, the Bani Hajam and the Beni Hasan, knows they cannot be crushed, but only bought, cowed or accommodated. Now the Americans and British are playing at the same game. "This is not just about toppling Saddam with briefcases full of cash or telling their people it is time to welcome the coalition troops," notes the British official. "The tribes play a long game. For them, the real currency is not just money but privileges and the promise of roles and influence in the post-Saddam government, whatever the United Nations or the Iraqi exile groups may say."

AL FAIR, Iraq, March 30 (UPI) — Marines prepare to destroy the 120mm mortars found in an Iraqi military truck that was halted by 3rd Battalion, 1st Marine Regiment, Regimental Combat Team 1 in Fajr, Iraq, on March 30, 2003. Marines and sailors of RCT1 are conducting operations in support of Operation Iraqi Freedom. (Mace M. Gratz, U.S. Marine Corps/UPI)

Day 11 — Sunday, March 30

"We are on plan. And where we stand today is not only acceptable, it is remarkable." — Gen. Tommy Franks, commander, U.S. forces

A confident U.S. Army Gen. Tommy Franks, the overall U.S. commander in the Iraq war, insisted Sunday that the campaign was going according to his plan and those who seek to find a wedge between him and his political chiefs back in Washington would be unable to do so.

Moments before Franks spoke at Central Command headquarters in Qatar, a truck was driven into a line of U.S. troops outside a military store in Kuwait, injuring several people. Coming a day after four U.S. troops were killed by a suicide bomber in Iraq, the attack in Kuwait sparked fears of a widening guerrilla onslaught against U.S. troops wherever they could be found and targeted.

"It is not at all remarkable that a dying regime should resort to such suicide bombing tactics," Franks said. "We see the regime in Baghdad claming credit for the suicide attack — I'm reminded of what we heard at the United Nations of the connections between terrorism and this regime."

"Of course it's a threat," he said, referring to the Iraqi guerrilla tactics. "We see them occupying centers of cities and in a position to terrorize the inhabitants and to move out in an attempt to interdict our supplies. They have not been able to do so. These bands of thugs face more and more of our capability every day. And every day we see more and better connections between Iraqis and our forces in those cities."

Franks, who seldom gives the daily briefing at the Central Command headquarters, appeared Sunday intent of squashing reports of any pause in military operations, of any interruption in supplies to the troops and of any rift between him and his Pentagon chiefs over the timing and forces available for the war. Back in the United States, TV pundits were warning not just of pauses but of setbacks and delays. "New Yorker" magazine ran a long article quoting serving officers who claimed that Defense Secretary Donald Rumsfeld had pressured Franks to attack with too few forces too soon.

"It is simply not the case that there is any operational pause. There is a continuity of operations in this plan," Franks declared. "We are on plan. And where we stand today is not only acceptable, it is remarkable."

But Franks' subordinate, V Corps commander Lt. Gen. William Wallace, already had told journalists in an interview at his forward command post Thursday that constant guerilla attacks on the supply lines had depleted the 3rd Division's stocks of fuel, water and ammunition, and forced it to rein back in order to amass a 10-day supply. And embedded reporters could see the unorthodox measures the U.S. Army was taking to meet the logistical challenge, pressing captured Iraqi fuel tankers and hired Kuwaiti civilian trucks into service. At any given time, logistics convoys up to 30-mile long are moving through Iraq, feeding the vast hunger of the coalition forces, whose Abrams tanks each consume 300 gallons of fuel every eight hours.

Iraqi officials have charged that the coalition forces were shocked and dismayed because of the intensity of Iraqi resistance. Franks, however, ticked off a list of operational successes, from the seizure of the southern Iraqi oilfields to prevent their demolition to Saturday's occupation of what he called a "massive terrorist camp" in northern Iraq. He said that the ground troops closing on Baghdad were in fine fighting shape, with a combat readiness of more than "90 percent."

He added that coalition warplanes were operating from captured Iraqi airbases and that the coalition had effective control of western Iraq to inhibit "the use of weapons of mass destruction against neighbors and allies" — a reference to the threat of Scud missiles being fired against Israel. Significantly, he went on, British forces in Basra and U.S. forces in Nasiriyah were now "working with local Iraqis, who are helping us with records on the Baath Party." The U.S. commander also dismissed fears that the heavy bombing of Baghdad and the shelling of other Iraqi cities might lose the campaign to win over the Iraqi population. "I think there is an appreciation inside Baghdad and across the Iraqi population that this is an incredibly precise military operation," Franks said. "The people of Iraq will welcome their liberation."

Franks had little time for the commentators and retired military pundits who suggested that Defense Secretary Donald Rumsfeld had kept his force too small, too weak in armor and too dependent on political decision-making in Washington. It was simply untrue, he said, that Rumsfeld had insisted the attack go ahead despite Franks's desire for more time after the Turkish government refused to let the U.S. 4th Division use Turkish territory to open a northern front against Iraq.

"It was important strategically and operationally to have the force (the 4th Division) where it was until the day it moved," Franks said, implying that its presence aboard ship off the Turkish coast forced the Iraqi commanders to keep troops in the north against the potential

attack. Moreover, Franks went on, there was now a northern front after the landing of the 173rd Airborne Brigade at airfields in Kurdish-held northern Iraq, with armored support being flown in from the 63rd Armored Brigade in Germany. This was "a very capable force, with enormous leverage in air power," he said.

Sunday saw a further flood of U.S. press reports that alleged or documented discord within the Pentagon and bitter recriminations over a war already turned sour after less than two weeks. The New York Times led its influential "Week in Review" section, with an article by Vietnam vet and respected author James Webb entitled "The War in Iraq Turns Ugly: That's What Wars Do." And the Washington Post carried a report Sunday by Vernon Loeb accusing Rumsfeld and his lieutenants of having "micromanaged" the deployment plan out of mistrust of the generals and an attempt to prove their own theory that a light maneuverable force could handily defeat Iraqi President Saddam Hussein. "More than a dozen officers interviewed, including a senior army officer in Iraq, said Rumsfeld took significant risks by leaving key units in the United States and Germany at the start of the war," Loeb reported. "That resulted in an invasion force that is too small, strung out, underprotected, undersupplied, and awaiting tens of thousands of reinforcements who will not get there for weeks."

Rumsfeld, under pressure on the TV interview shows Sunday morning, acknowledged that coalition troops had faced "quite stiff resistance. The most dangerous and difficult days are still ahead of us." But while the guerilla-style attacks and ambushes were a challenge, the Iraqi army and Republican Guard had yet to mount any significant military operation against the coalition troops. A handful of scattered armored thrusts had not been coordinated with artillery and infantry support, and the coalition's total command of the air made it difficult for them to do so. Nightly attacks by Iraqi forces on a key bridge at Kifl, 15 miles north of Najaf, were described as "suicide missions" by the defending U.S. troops.

For once, the system of "embedding" reporters with combat units served to embarrass the U.S. military, as they reported back that their units were not moving, and in some instances, were running so short of supplies that Marines were down to one meal a day. What the embedded reporters could not see was the broader strategic picture, in which far to their front, U.S. air power was relentlessly hammering the dug-in Republican Guard units to destroy them before the U.S. troops rolled forward to meet them.

U.S. and British warplanes flew a total of 800 missions Sunday, almost 500 of them against the Republican Guard positions south of Baghdad. Air Force Gen. Richard Myers, chairman of the Joint Chiefs of Staff at the Pentagon, said that the Republican Guard units had been degraded "to less than 50 percent of their prewar strength."

U.S.–U.K. Alliance Shows Strains

Roland Flamini

WASHINGTON, March 30 (UPI) — It looked cozy enough in the television news — roaring fire, big chintz-covered armchairs, both leaders coatless. No different, in fact, from Tony Blair's previous sleepovers at Camp David, President George W. Bush's retreat in Maryland. But this week's visit was both the same and also different. Despite the fire, well-informed diplomatic sources said, there was an unprecedented hint of coolness as the remarkable Bush–Blair partnership faces the dual strains of a war not going according to plan, and looming differences over how to reshape postconflict Iraq.

The widely held perception in Washington that all the consortium's troops had to do was kick the door in and Saddam Hussein's regime would collapse has turned out to be wishful thinking. The war is turning out to be a much bigger challenge than anticipated. Every day more military experts have been predicting a tougher, wider conflict, with every inch of the way gained at human cost. Instead of the "cakewalk" and the "collapse after the first whiff of gunpowder" that administration officials and gung-ho conservative advisers were predicting, Bush's new mantra is that the war will last, "However long it takes to win."

A few days before Blair's departure for Washington, Gordon Brown, the British chancellor of the exchequer (and Blair's rival for the Labor Party leadership), was forced to double Britain's war budget. But with more than 40,000 of Britain's best troops in action in Iraq, the British patriotic sense has kicked in, giving Blair's position at home a much-needed boost. Two weeks ago, only 19 percent of Britons approved of going to war without a U.N. mandate. On Saturday it was close to 60 percent. Still, the political reality remains the same: Short war plus low casualty rate equals success; long war plus high casualty rate equals Blair is toast — and possibly Bush as well.

At Camp David, Bush and Blair reviewed the rules of engagement, and the diplomatic sources said they gave their approval to raising the level of military pressure, defined by increasing the number of troops, opening a northern front and intensifying the bombing on Baghdad targets.

The Bush–Blair news conference in Washington Thursday offered several glimpses of Blair doing his now familiar political balancing act between loyal support for Washington and Britain's role and obligations in Europe.

He repeated his impassioned conviction that the U.S.-led war against Saddam was right, but there was more than a hint of conciliation with the war's European opponents. Answering the question "Why haven't you got (French, German and Turkish) support?" Blair replied, "There's no point in denying it. ... There is a part of Europe that disagrees with what we are doing. ... We believed that we had to act. Others disagreed. At some point, we will have to come back and we'll have to discuss how the disagreement arose."

Bush, on the other hand, dodged the question entirely. "We've got a huge coalition," he said, and there was no attempt to echo Blair's more conciliatory approach.

Ahead loom larger differences over the question of who will govern post-Saddam Iraq. Both called for the resumption of the U.N.'s food-for-oil program, and Friday the Security Council voted to extend by 45 days U.N. Secretary-General Kofi Annan's authority to dispense humanitarian aid from the program.

But the gap in understanding between Washington and London widens when it comes to U.S. plans for governing Iraq once Saddam has been removed. As explained by Secretary of State Colin Powell on Capitol Hill, "the center of gravity" will remain "the coalition, military and civilian." This is Powell-speak for a military administration run by a U.S. general to restore a measure of normalcy. Eventually, a government of Iraqi civilians will take over, but there is no confirmed official time frame for the change.

Informed observers say Blair shares other European leaders' distaste for a formula that installs a U.S. military administration because it makes the whole thing look more like occupation than liberation. "It is important. ... that the United Nations is involved, and that any postconflict administration in Iraq is endorsed by it," Blair said in Washington. But the Bush administration, still harboring resentment at the Security Council's failure to support the U.S.-led military action against Saddam, has no plans currently to give the United Nations a major role, beyond the humanitarian effort, in post-Saddam Iraq.

Compare Blair's view of how the reconstruction should proceed with Powell's testimony on the Hill last week. "We didn't take on the huge burden with our coalition partners not to be able to have significant dominating control over how it unfolds in the future," Powell declared. "(The United States) would not support handing everything over to the U.N., or someone designated by the U.N. to suddenly become in charge of the whole operation."

Blair would find it difficult to explain to his party why Britain was either a part of, or at least accepted, a de facto U.S. military occupation. The Downing Street view, as British commentators point out, is that a U.N.-governed reconstruction program, shared and under the authority of the United Nations, would be a good way of healing differences in the international community. It would also make a start in repairing relations between the United States and Europe. Can Blair use his special relationship with Bush to cobble up a compromise plan?

France and Russia threaten to veto any U.N. resolution giving the United States a major role in the reconstruction, ostensibly because that would retroactively bestow legitimacy on the U.S.-led war, which many nations regard as illegal. But another reason is that Paris and Moscow don't want U.S. firms to monopolize the huge contracts for reconstruction that are already being handed out. The United States would prefer to steer clear of the never-never land of Security Council resolutions. A White House nightmare involves the United States having to accept a U.N.-appointed French civilian as administrator for Iraq.

Blair hinted at differences of approach over how to put Iraq together again once Humpty Hussein had his great fall. But having identified the problem, he said, "There are a huge amount of details as to exactly how it is to be implemented that have to be a matter of discussion" — a tactic known in diplomacy as "kicking the can down the road," when an issue is raised but no solution offered.

Blair also pressed Bush for action on the Middle East peace process. European leaders — Blair included — believe the groundswell of world opposition to the war, and in particular Arab opposition, could be reduced if the Bush administration were to move forward now on the "road map" for peace between Israelis and Palestinians, fathered jointly by the United States, the European Union, the United Nations and Russia.

The road map has yet to be released in detail, but is known to consist of a series of steps, such as the end of attacks on Israelis by Palestinian militants, and on the Israeli side a halt to building new settlements in the West Bank and Gaza. The road map will lead to the establishment of a Palestinian state by 2005. As recently as March 14, Bush promised to unveil the plan once a Palestinian prime minister took office. Mahmoud Abbas, more widely known as Abu Mazen, became the Palestinians' first prime minister earlier this month and is holding talks to form a Cabinet.

Blair pressed Bush to stick to his word. There is wide belief — even in Washington — that the Bush administration will drag its feet on the peace effort until the Iraq war is resolved. But Blair argues that tackling the war and seeking an end to the Arab–Israeli conflict simultaneously will demonstrate that the alliance is "evenhanded."

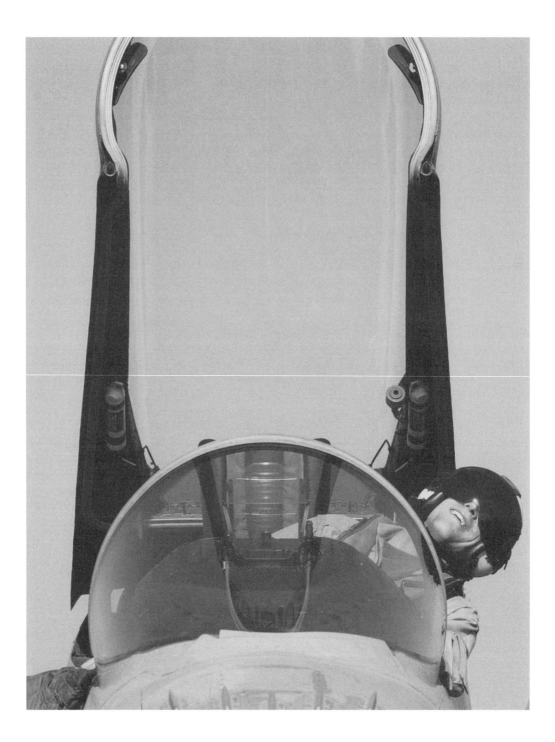

ABOARD THE USS HARRY S. TRUMAN, Eastern Mediterranean, March 31 (UPI) — A pilot of an F-18 Hornet from Squadron VMFA-115 shows his relief after returning to the aircraft carrier USS Harry S. Truman following a mission over Iraq in support of Operation Iraqi Freedom on March 31, 2003. (John Gillis, UPI)

Day 12 — Monday, March 31

"We are beginning to rat them out." — Gen. John F. Kelley, deputy commander of the Marine Expeditionary Force

MARTIN WALKER

This week will see the decisive battle for the approaches to Baghdad, as U.S. troops took the upper hand on their offensive against the Iraqi guerrilla-style forces attacking their supply lines and Gen. Tommy Franks launched combined air and land attacks against Baghdad's Republican Guard defenders.

After intense discussions over the weekend among coalition command staff and with Washington, United Press International has learned that Gen. Franks has decided to go for Baghdad without the full reinforcements of the 4th Infantry Division, to beat the arrival of the intense heat of a desert summer.

Despite widespread reports of an "operational pause," coalition forces advanced Monday beyond the city of Hilla, within 30 miles of Baghdad's outskirts, as the Republican Guard's Medina Division began to crumble under the weight of air and artillery strikes. Forced out of their bunkers and forced to give away their concealed firing positions to tackle ground probes from the 2nd Brigade of the U.S. 3rd Infantry Division, the Republican Guard became prey from the prowling U.S. fighter bombers and combat helicopters. "This is classic combined arms tactics," a coalition staff officer in Kuwait told UPI. "The ground forces winkle them out from their cover and the air power then hits them."

Coalition spokesmen estimate that half the fighting power of the Medina Division, the best equipped of the Republican Guard elite force, has been destroyed and that its command-and-control has been so reduced that commanders were forced to communicate by unciphered radio, easy to monitor by coalition intelligence teams. The Iraqis continued, however, to reinforce their front-line units by night from Baghdad and the north, running the gantlet of U.S. air power.

The full might of the U.S. Air Force was deployed Monday against the dug-in Republican Guard divisions, with B-1, B-2 and B-52 bombers pounding their bunkers and the small farms and villages where the Republican Guard had hidden their remaining tanks. Western reporters in Baghdad said they could hear the intense air bombardment from more than 30 miles away. But the Iraqi tactic of deploying their artillery inside towns and civilian areas was protecting their guns from the allied warplanes, under firm orders to minimize civilian casualties.

With the U.S. 101st and 82nd Airborne units taking over the battle to guard the supply lines and reduce Iraqi pockets in Najaf and Nasiriyah, the 3rd Division was free to open the "crumbling" battle against the Republican

103

Guard units at Karbala and Hilla, as they advanced on the city of Al Musayyib, the gateway to Baghdad.

There were two separate kinds of warfare under way in central Iraq Monday. In addition to the 3rd Division's conventional air–land battle against the Republican Guard south of Baghdad, other units were fighting a messy guerrilla war along the coalition's supply lines. Rather like the battle the British have been fighting in Basra for the last week, the U.S. airborne troops and Marines have been fighting to secure their supply lines against Iraqi guerrilla attacks and reduce the Iraqi pockets in the cities. This is an urban and counterguerrilla battle that the British understand from their experience in Northern Ireland, and British officers have been flown in to captured Iraqi bases near Najaf and Nasiriyah to advise their U.S. allies on tactics. "I can assure you that U.S. forces have leaned heavily on their British counterparts," Gen. Richard Myers, U.S. chairman of the Joint Chiefs of Staff, said in Washington Sunday. "The British in Basra have been absolutely magnificent."

Copying British tactics refined in Northern Ireland, U.S. Marines Monday sent "snatch squads" into the town of Shatra, north of Nasiriyah, hunting Saddam Hussein's cousin Ali Hassan. Known as "Chemical Ali" from his role in the use of chemical weapons against Iraqi Kurds, Ali Hassan is supposedly in command of the urban resistance in southern Iraq (although he was earlier supposed to have been killed in the "decapitation" bombing attack on Baghdad that launched the war). "We are beginning to rat them out," the deputy commander of the Marine Expeditionary Force, Gen. John F. Kelley, told reporters.

A brigade of the 82nd Airborne used similar "snatch squad" tactics against Iraqi resistance command posts in the cities of Samawah and Diwaniyah Monday. Intense work by military intelligence units in the field, monitoring Iraqi radio and other communications, convinced coalition commanders that these two cities held the main command bases of the Iraqi fedayeen and Special Forces who have been organizing the militia attacks.

Meanwhile, in Iraq's second city Basra, British troops have been waging what looks like a dress rehearsal for the eventual siege of Baghdad, combining "hearts and minds" tactics to win over the population with targeted strikes against Iraqi military and political command centers. Sunday, British Royal Marines staged a dawn raid on the outlying village of Abu al-Khanib, seizing 200 prisoners of war and five senior officers believed to have been organizing the city's defense.

Coalition forces said Monday that total battle casualties so far were 45 U.S. and 29 British deaths in combat. Iraqi officials in Baghdad claimed that 589 civilians had been killed and 4,582 wounded in the coalition bombing.

Meanwhile, in the north, the first two trucks carrying U.N. relief supplies, since the war began 11 days ago, arrived in northern Iraq from Turkey Monday under the oil-for-food program, U.N. spokesman Michael Bociurkiw told United Press International. A bigger convoy of 40 trucks is expected to arrive in the next few days. "There is $4 million worth of supplies waiting at the Turkish port Mersin," he said, "and another 10 million in the pipeline."

RICHARD TOMKINS

WITH THE 5TH MARINES, Iraq, March 31 (UPI) — Three Marines were slightly injured in central Iraq Monday by the explosion of a bomb cluster from a U.S. shell that went off as they were digging defensive positions. One man received a shell fragment in the back of the head, another to the neck and the third man received leg wounds, but none of the injuries was considered serious and the injured were treated on the spot. The incident came just a few hours after Iraqis attempted to fire mortars on positions held by Bravo Company, 1st Battalion, 5th Marines, who at the start of the war had captured gas and oil facilities in the oil fields of southern Iraq. The mortar fire fell far short of the Marines' position, and U.S. 155 mm cannons replied, lighting up the pre-dawn sky. The mortars were not heard from again. The mortar attack came about three days after the 5th Marines stopped its advance and hunkered down for resupply.

"Operation Standstill," "Operation Do-Nothing," some Marines said of the break in advance. "I wish we'd get moving. The sooner we get to Baghdad, the sooner I get home," said Cpl. Jason Malley, from Buffalo, N.Y.

Fixed in the minds of the Marines living in harsh conditions, Baghdad is the symbol for a ticket home. Malley's wife is expecting their first child in early June.

Later Monday the regiment resumed its march toward a destination and an Iraqi army unit, the details of which could not be disclosed. The deeper into central Iraq the regiment penetrated, the more green the countryside appeared, with large swathes of palm trees and brush along the deserts and small canals. As the regiment's convoy — which stretched all the way to the horizon — passed villages, people stood by their doors to watch. They did not wave but watched silently as the vehicles crept by. Much of the convoy consisted of 26-ton amphibious assault vehicles that move at about 15 mph. The vehicles, depending on model, get gas mileage of between 1.5 and 3 miles per gallon. The Marines faced wide-ranging weather conditions. It is freezing cold and damp at night while the days are hot — a situation exacerbated by the wearing of full-body chemical-weapons protection suits.

The Top Enlisted Man

Martin Walker

CAMP DOHA, Kuwait, March 31 (UPI) — Command Sgt. Maj. John Sparks, 41, is a 25-year U.S. Army veteran and a native of Detroit and as the senior enlisted man in the Iraq theater of war, finds the early summer climate in Kuwait pleasantly cool.

"I have never been as hot as we were at the National Training Center in California last August. It was 112, maybe 113 degrees, and we were dressed up in chemical warfare protection suits and body armor," Sparks told United Press International in an interview.

"It was uncomfortable, and it made operations harder, absolutely. No question about it. But we could deal with it. With proper training and proper water management, we could function. And since we have been here in theater, we have not had a heat problem yet."

Training, Sparks maintains, is the key to military efficiency. "We train for it to be as hard as it can possibly be," he says. What he does not say is that despite his seniority, he sees it as his duty to go through the trials that the troops will suffer. That's part of his job. Constantly at the side of the ground force commander Lt. Gen. David D. McKiernan, he has made five helicopter trips to the front lines so far. After our conversation in his office, he was leaving on another mission. "I have been as far forward as we have had soldiers," he said. "I have seen every force, visited every major unit."

As the senior enlisted man, Sparks says it is his role to represent the views of all the enlisted men, whether in the U.S. or British Army or U.S. Marines, Air Force or Special Forces, to the command staff. "My job is that when Gen. McKiernan tells me what he's worried about, I try to fix it. And when the troops tell me something I think the general ought to hear, I see that he does. If they are concerned about mail or ammunition supply or whatever, I get on to it." He continued, "The only real worry I have heard so far from the troops up forward is something I heard from a sergeant major in V Corps when we were up there a couple of days ago. He asked what about the humanitarian supplies for the Iraqis — the troops see a need for that."

Asked about reports about hiccups in the U.S. logistics that left some Marines with only one meal a day, Sparks shook his head. "I have not found any incident where any soldier is eating just one meal a day. I'm not saying it couldn't happen or hasn't happened. It's quite possible that due to the tempo of the operation, they may only be eating once a day until the mission is accomplished. But one thing I'm sure of — if it was an issue, they would share it with me.

"We expend a lot of time and energy to ensure that doesn't happen," he went on. "The planning that goes into an operation like this is unbelievable — including the training. We try to train for everything, to replicate just about very kind of enemy contact — including checkpoint procedures."

His next trip will be to talk to the individual soldiers involved in the tragic Najaf checkpoint incident, when seven civilians died when they failed to stop. But Sparks is not making a personal investigation so much as checking that the Army is doing things right. "I don't know if they were trained in checkpoint procedures, or were they surprised or did they handle it as they should. I don't know. There will be an inquiry that asks, 'Was the training right; are the Rules of Engagement appropriate for the preservation of the force?' "

There's a military saying that goes back to the Roman legionnaires that claims any army is only as good as its noncommissioned officers. A great deal of the force morale, as well as small-unit leadership, depends upon these long-service veterans who also embody an army's institutional memory and much of its tradition.

Like many other senior NCOs, Sparks has served throughout the U.S. Army, as a cavalryman with the tanks of the 1st Cavalry Division, and as a mechanized infantryman in the 3rd Division. He has served in Korea and Germany as well as the Persian Gulf, and keeps on his office wall pictures of 19th century U.S. cavalry troopers in the American West. Tough and trim with a brisk military haircut, Sparks is not a sentimental man — until he talks about "his" soldiers.

"It's very uplifting when you talk to soldiers who are forward," he said. "Mostly they don't ask about themselves, but ask how they are doing, how does command see it. They want to know if they are doing as well as they think they are. I just tell them they have covered more ground in less time than any force in history. At one unit that had been sitting in the same place for eight hours, they just asked me when they could start moving again.

"It's the same when I visit the wounded in hospital. One Marine, both his eyes bandaged, didn't want to know when he was to be shipped out. He just wanted to know how other Marines in his unit were doing. I looked through the flap of one tent, and there was a young soldier unconscious. And the nurse — she didn't know I was there — she was stroking his head and talking to him. He could not have heard a thing, but that's the kind of commitment these soldiers have, all of them."

———————

IRAQ, April 1 (UPI) — Private Matereti Vere, 25, originally from Fiji, now serving with the 1st Battalion, the Black Watch, shares a laugh on April 1, 2003, with some of the children of Azubayr, a town captured by the British soldiers in Iraq. It was decided to patrol through the streets without body armor or helmets to show a softer and less agressive side in order to win over hearts and minds during Operation Telic. (Giles Penfound, Rex Features/UPI)

Day 13 — Tuesday, April 1

"They are moving into a killing ground ... "

The war entered its decisive phase Tuesday as midday temperatures in central Iraq soared toward 100 degrees and U.S. forces advanced north from Najaf into Iraq's so-called Red Zone around Baghdad, where local commanders may have authority to use chemical weapons. The best of Iraq's conventional forces, five Republican Guard divisions, have now been identified gathering south of Baghdad for what looks to be the decisive battle of the war. Coalition military intelligence sources add that a sixth Republican Guard division, the al-Adnan, is also reported moving south from Saddam Hussein's hometown of Tikrit to join them.

They are moving into a killing ground, the flood plain of the Tigris and Euphrates Rivers south of Baghdad. It is a relatively confined battlefield where allied warplanes and combat helicopters now hover like predatory hawks to swoop on any target that shows itself. The clear weather conditions and the coming of the heat of a desert summer suggest that coalition commanders are pressing on to Baghdad without waiting for the expected reinforcement of the U.S. 4th Infantry Division.

Although no Iraqi chemical or biological weapons have yet been deployed or found, chemical alert and response units were close behind the forward U.S. troops Tuesday just in case. Large numbers of Iraqi gas masks and other protective gear have been found by advancing coalition forces, suggesting that Iraqi units are ready for chemical warfare.

The airstrikes against the dug-in RG units were backed up by the artillery from the U.S. 3rd Division, their shells now able to range up to 10 miles from Baghdad itself. Units of the 3rd Division hooked to the west around the key town of Karbala and established firing positions and pushed forward observation posts to bring direct fire only on Iraqi defensive positions.

To the east, driving in two vast columns up the Tigris valley and the plains between the two rivers, the U.S. Marines fought a pitched battle with elements of the Republican Guard Baghdad Division to secure a key bridge over the river Tigris near Kut. No Marines of Bravo Company, 1st Battalion — who bore the brunt of the battle — were injured. Known Iraqi casualties came up to seven killed in action, with 33 taken prisoner.

"One down, one down," the radio in an armored vehicle crackled, shortly after the Marine column began receiving small arms fire and the Marines replied with machine guns. Members of 1st Battalion poured out of their vehicles along a berm and immediately began returning fire as Cobra helicopter gunships swooped down to help them.

"Mortars up! Mortars up!" someone yelled.

Staff Sgt. Mario Lockett and his men quickly set up their tubes and began a rhythmic firing of 60mm shells at the Iraqi positions. When ammunition started running low, various Marines ran back to the armored vehicles to grab shells for Lockett and his men. Throughout the small-arms fire and incoming mortar and rocket-propelled grenade rounds, Lockett, from East St. Louis, Ill., remained calm and moved between his mortar positions encouraging his men.

At one point an RPG came within 150 feet of the mortar unit — and United Press International reporter Richard Tomkins, embedded with the Marines — but no one was injured. At another point a 120mm Iraqi mortar shell landed within 20 feet of a platoon, but again, everyone miraculously escaped injury.

After fighting died down, Marines moved stealthily between berms rooting out Iraqi troops, at one point shooting and killing two who raised their weapons to fire instead of dropping them. It was reported that Iraqi troops flying a white flag as they approached Marines were bait for an ambush. Marines spotted other Iraqis nearby in the bushes waiting to open fire on whoever came close. At the end of the battle, the prisoners were placed flat on the ground along the road, their weapons stacked nearby along with personal possessions, including wads of Iraqi money, wallets, boom boxes and sports bags. The prisoners did not seem relieved they were out of the fight. Their hard, bitter stares contrasted sharply with the looks of relief of prisoners taken during fighting in southern Iraq. In the distance, meanwhile, a horrendous rolling sound of numerous explosions could be heard. A B-52 was doing its work on an Iraqi artillery position.

The five Republican Guard divisions are anchored on the Medina Armored Division, the strongest of all, which began the war with 20,000 troops and 270 of Iraq's most advanced Soviet-built T-72 tanks. They are outmatched by the U.S. M1A1 Abrams tanks, which can pick them off at a distance while remaining out of rage of the T-72 guns — if the visibility is clear enough.

Gen. Richard Myers, chairman of the Joint Chiefs of Staff, said Tuesday that the RG Medina and Baghdad Divisions have been degraded by about half after a week of strikes with artillery, aircraft and helicopters to "pretty low percentages of combat capability, below fifty percent in, I think, at least two cases, and we continue to work on them."

Myers said he has not seen the Iraqi divisions retreating but rearranging their forces and taking defensive positions — digging in and attempting to hide tanks and armored vehicles from aircraft.

"We haven't seen a retreat. We've seen dispersals. I think we showed some pictures of them dispersing into neighborhoods and things like that. We've seen reinforcements, and we continue to work away at them both from the ground and from the air," Myers said.

Two of the other RG divisions south of Baghdad, the Hammurabi and the Al-Nida, are armored units but equipped with 1960s vintage T-62 tanks and thought to number not much more than 10,000 troops each. The Baghdad Mechanized Infantry Division, already worn down by a series of defensive battles against advancing U.S. Marines in the south, has been reinforced by other RG units brought down from Tikrit over the last week.

The objective of coalition commanders is to destroy these RG divisions where they stand, rather than let them fall back into Baghdad to stiffen the city's defenses. Once inside the city, where they can take cover from coalition air power, they could be much more difficult to tackle than they are now on the relatively open ground south of Baghdad.

Coalition military sources said the advances on Baghdad, and the first ground war clashes with the Republican Guard, decisively refuted the media suggestions over the weekend of a pause in operations. They dismissed suggestions of a "race for Baghdad" between the two prongs of the U.S. advance, the Marines from the south and the 3rd Infantry Division from the southwest, noting that one of the key breakthroughs to the town of Hindiya was achieved by the 101st Airborne.

"The 101st sent small reconnaissance teams by helicopter deep into Iraqi lines, where they spotted and targeted Iraqi positions and then called in artillery and air strikes," a military source told UPI. "So when the main assault went in, the Iraqis had very little left to stop it."

The capture Monday of the bridge over the Euphrates at Hindiya means that the two advancing U.S. columns can now communicate directly, and coalition commanders can use it to seize tactical opportunities and push reinforcements from one front to the other. Meanwhile, in southern Iraq, British troops took the final bridge around Basra, virtually sealing off the city except for a small land route up the eastern bank of the Tigris. The British are still deliberately holding back from a full-scale assault on the city, but nibbling at its edges and raiding and bombing the buildings from which Saddam Hussein's loyalists try to maintain their grip.

British Marines stepped up their patrols around Basra after two Iraqi Seersucker missiles, Russian-based projectiles modified from antiship missiles, were fired overnight. One landed close to the British prisoner of war camp outside Umm Qasr, where over 3,000 Iraqi prisoners are held. The other struck close to a site previously occupied by the headquarters of the Royal Marine Commandos.

On the northern front, the immediate challenge was political, as U.S Secretary of State Colin Powell traveled to Ankara Tuesday to begin restoring the long-standing alliance with Turkey. To intense U.S. frustration, the new parliament in the predominantly Muslim but secular country voted down a government proposal to let the U.S. 4th Division transit through Turkey to open a northern front against Iraq. And Powell's new mission was to keep his Turkish and Kurdish allies apart. Turkish generals have vowed to block any attempt to establish an independent Kurdish state from the wreckage of Iraq — by force, if necessary.

The Human Shields

Nicholas M. Horrock

The cruise missiles, he said, made a "shushing sound" as they came in, and the explosion sent a shock wave "and you feel pressure on your chest, like the signs of a heart attack."

Tom Cahill, 66, a grandfather from the northern California coastal town of Fort Bragg, was describing in the Jordanian capital the 10 days he spent as a so-called human shield around a water treatment plant in Baghdad, enduring what U.S. military analysts called a "shock and awe" bombardment from the perspective of the bombarded.

Cahill is one of several busloads of volunteer human shields who went to Baghdad to deter coalition attacks from humanitarian institutions, schools, hospitals, electrical power generators and, in his case, a water purification facility. Last week several shields returned to Amman by bus. Many others are still in Iraq, Cahill said.

"We would go out and watch the attacks start," Cahill said, "and in my conscious mind, I was not afraid, but I realized later that in my subconscious mind, I was terrified." As the bombing continued, chronic back pains that he had defeated years before came back. "I could feel my back tightening up."

"When I started to leave Baghdad my back was ok," as it is ok now, that he is back alive and unscarred and trying to tell his story in Amman and wherever people will listen.

Cahill is a photographer and one-time journalist as well as an activist for "peace and justice" virtually all his adult life. He has worked on labor issues, been jailed in San Antonio, Texas, as a result of his peace activities and, along with his sister, been the target of an FBI "COINTELPRO" operation in 1968, which he charges resulted in his imprisonment in a Texas jail and his brutal attack there by inmates.

In the Saraya Hotel — the name means "palace" — a neat, if not palatial 50-room hotel in Amman's working-class district, Tom Cahill talked about the anger that brought him from retirement along California's beautiful north coast and a town that grew from a 1850s military post on the Mendocino Indian Reservation.

"This war is George W. Bush out to control the world," he argued, and arises "from America's greed." He stopped to point out that half the world's billionaires live in the United States. "The U.S. needs to be cut down. The world doesn't need a superpower," he argued, "but an effective world organization."

Convinced that even if the war removed a dictator, it would terribly punish the Iraqi people, Cahill saw a notice on the Internet calling for human shields. He decided to go to London and volunteer. He didn't tell any of his friends for fear they would dissuade him.

He flew to London in February and joined the group brought together by Uzma Bashir, who is still in Baghdad. After staying with her mother for several days, a group was put together, the second wave to go, and flew to Amman. They entered Baghdad by bus on Feb. 20 on a special visa. He had wanted to be a human shield at a children's hospital, but those slots were already taken. His shield group worked with an Iraqi "committee on friendship, peace and solidarity," which gave out assignments. Cahill had seen a documentary about the 1991 war, which showed the terrible disease and difficulties of the loss of a water treatment plant, and that was his second choice.

In the weeks before the war, the group lived two to a room at the Palestine Hotel, where journalists are housed. They could go downtown alone in a new car provided for their use. They were taken on trips to southern Iraq to hospitals where children were suffering from leukemia and other problems.

But when the bombing started, things changed. They took up their posts at the water plant, men and women living together in a dormitory. They had "minders," as the journalists do, and were told not to walk on the street without them. One shield who did was set upon and beaten by police.

Through Cahill's time there, they were warned they were being electronically eavesdropped on. He said they devised a code name for talking about Saddam Hussein, calling him Fred when they wanted to mention him. There so many photos, paintings and sculptures of Saddam, Cahill concluded that he posed so much that he couldn't have time to govern.

There were no military activities at the water treatment plant, he said, but it was near old military barracks and they could see other military facilities in the area. The plant was not damaged, but glass in nearby buildings was. He personally saw no civilian casualties, but he said two Belgian doctors described horrendous injuries at a children's hospital where they worked.

After 10 days, the smoke from oil fires and bombings began to acutely affect many of the older shields, and about a dozen or so left. "It is strange. I was willing to give my life, but not my health," Cahill said.

They were roaring down the highway to Amman when they were stopped by a group of long-haired, armed men in desert uniforms. They all sat frightened in the bus until one shield, a woman from Australia, jumped up and ran out to talk to the soldiers. He could hear her say, "G'day." She had seen the patches. They were Australian special operations soldiers.

Cahill, who served in Air Force intelligence from 1954 to 1958, said it made him angry. "That's the U.S. Air Force up there. If you go to Baghdad angry, you come back angrier."

Charles Litkey lay in the al-Wadah water treatment plant in the darkness listening to the B-52s, and his mind drifted back to Vietnam and to the night when he had lain in the darkness listening to the giant bombers blast the ground.

"It took me back to Vietnam in a big way, to feel the rumbling of the ground and the horrific noise. I began to feel sorry for the Iraqi soldiers beneath all of that," he said. Later, as the U.S. Marines entered Baghdad, a firefight raged around the water plant. He heard the familiar sounds of machine guns and mortars and the unmistakable sound of a bullet passing his ear.

Litkey knows about firefights. He won the Medal of Honor 35 years ago as an Army chaplain when a platoon of the 199th Light Infantry Brigade on a routine patrol in South Vietnam stumbled across 500 North Vietnamese soldiers. When the battle ended they found that Litkey, despite being wounded, had carried 23 wounded men to safety.

Now 70, still with a piece shrapnel in his foot, Litkey spent 20 days living at the Baghdad water plant under the coalition bombardment because "it seemed the place to be." Litkey long ago became a committed peace activist and sent his Medal of Honor back to President Reagan because Reagan supported CIA wars in Central America.

The outriders of the American peace movement here — like Litkey and Kathy Kelly — are a trifle tattered and worn after years of risking their lives, their fortunes and sometimes their freedom to end what they see as the vociferous U.S. appetite for conquest. This particular group, Voices in the Wilderness, first arrived in Iraq almost a decade ago trying to tell America of the terrible human suffering being caused by international sanctions. They often were under suspicion by Saddam Hussein's regime and minded by his secret police operatives.

However, they formed friendships, documented leukemia cases, allegedly stemming from U.S. ammunition in the first Gulf War, and reported on the medical difficulties that resulted from the embargo on selling medical drugs and equipment to Iraq. In the decade since Litkey left the Army and the priesthood and became a devoted opponent of war, the peace movement slipped from the American consciousness, making him and others quite as their name described them, Voices in the Wilderness.

Now in the lobby of the al-Sanar Tower Hotel — with no electricity, occasional water, bomb-blasted windows and falling plaster — these veterans congregate a few hundred yards from U.S. Marines. They are trying to understand where the peace movement goes from here but never in doubt of why they go forward.

Last December, as the war against Iraq became more and more a reality, Litkey flew home to San Francisco disheartened at the seeming inevitability of military action against Iraq. He was lifted up by the peace movements around the world and in the United States that had succeeded in informing people of their views. The organization has every sort of member, from Buddhist to atheist. Kelly and Litkey grew up as serious and committed Catholics. Litkey was ordained in 1960 in the Mission Services of Holy Trinity and with roots in the Catholic church and the military. He was born in Washington and his father was a naval officer. He said he went to Vietnam with all the commitment that he sees in the young U.S. Marines now guarding Baghdad's streets. But when then Secretary of Defense Robert MacNamara ordered the "body count system," Litkey became convinced that it was "nothing but a bounty."

Litkey met a young soldier who had earned a three-day pass to a Vietnamese beach by killing three Viet Cong soldiers. He complained, taking his complaint all the way to Gen. Creighton Abrams, the commander in Vietnam. Abrams couldn't end the body count system, but he ended the rewards for soldiers who killed the enemy. This incident began Litkey's metamorphosis to peace activist. He has served two prison terms for demonstrating against the School of the Americas — the U.S. Army training facility at Fort Benning, Ga., that trained Latin American military officers accused of repressive practices in their home countries.

Kathy Kelly, a Chicago native, was a student at the Catholic Hyde Park Jesuit School of Theology, as remote, she said, "as Brigadoon in the mist" from issues of war and peace, when she volunteered at a northside Chicago soup kitchen. She said she found herself. "Everything fell into place; it was easy. I did not have to go to my sisters' Tupperware parties anymore." In 1991, she came to Baghdad to try and stop the first Gulf War and was in the city during the bombing. At the end of that conflict, she demonstrated against other war issues, but it wasn't until 1996 that she says she came to realize how deadly the U.N. sanctions were for the Iraqi people. She and others wrote a letter to U.S. Attorney General Janet Reno, saying they were going to knowingly violate the embargo. They came back and forth from Iraq carrying teddy bears and antibiotics — both violations of the law. In 1998, Kelly and others were fined

$10,000 each and the group was fined another $10,000. The fines have never been collected. Kelly's passport was also seized, but several years later she was allowed to apply for a new one.

So last October, she and other group members, 40 strong at one point, came to Iraq again to try and end the sanctions and end the war. They believe that you have to risk your life and fight for peace as hard as you'll fight in a war. Most of them remained here throughout the bombing, and one activist died in an accident as they went to the Kuwait border to demonstrate against the U.S.-led coalition's invasion. Now they are regrouping to return to the United States and change the political forces they see committing the nation to endless wars.

———

RUMAILA OIL FIELDS, Iraq, April 2 (UPI) — A soldier from the Army helps to guard the Rumaila oil fields in southern Iraq as firefighters prepare massive water lagoons in the desert to extinguish the last two fires at oil wells sabotaged by the fleeing Iraqi army on April 2, 2003. Teams from Boots & Coots International Well Control and the Kuwait Oil Co. failed to put out the blazes earlier this week, using water from smaller storage tanks. (Chris Corder, UPI)

Day 14 — Wednesday, April 2

"The (Republican Guard) faces a terrible choice. They can stay where they are and get pounded by our air and artillery and die where they stand. Or they can try to fall back along the roads and get killed as they retreat."
— A coalition staff officer

MARTIN WALKER

Coalition forces were on the brink of a stunning military victory in the battle of Baghdad Wednesday, as U.S. troops drove forward from the southeast and southwest against slackening Iraqi resistance. American troops were pushing hard on two fronts to outflank the five Iraqi Republican Guard divisions south of Baghdad and cut them off from the city in a classic encirclement battle that would force the surrounded Iraqi elite troops to surrender before they could fall back into the city.

U.S. Marines advancing from Kut captured "the last big bridge we need" across the Tigris River early Wednesday and pushed on toward Baghdad through the collapsing defenses of the Republican Guard Baghdad Division. Meanwhile, the tanks of the 7th Cavalry of the U.S. 3rd Division drove on to the north of Karbala as combat helicopters and A-10 "tank-buster" warplanes, operating from nearby captured Iraqi airfields, cleared the path for their advance through the shattered Republican Guard Medina Division.

"I would say that the Medina and Baghdad Divisions are no longer credible forces," Maj. Gen. Stanley McChrystal, Joint Chiefs of Staff vice director of operations, told a Pentagon briefing.

The new focus of the battle was the twin towns of Mahmudiya and Musayyib, 10 and 20 miles south of Baghdad, respectively, on the main highway south from the capital toward Karbala and Najaf. Taking these two towns, which requires seizing new crossings across the Euphrates River south of Fallujah, will cut the Republican Guard's line of retreat into the capital. Even if the two towns hold out but come under coalition artillery fire, they could become an impassable bottleneck for the 60,000 RG troops if they try to retreat from their defensive lines to the south. The struggle for these two towns is shaping up to be the last stand of the Republican Guard.

"The RG faces a terrible choice," a coalition staff officer told United Press International Wednesday. "They can stay where they are and get pounded by our air and artillery and die where they stand. Or they can try to fall back along the roads and get killed as they retreat."

The prospect of victory was clouded for the U.S. troops by the constant threat the Iraqi defenders might, in desperation, resort to chemical and biological weapons.

For the U.S. forces, a stunning victory now beckons that would silence the critics inside and outside the Pentagon and vindicate the battle plan of coalition commander Gen. Tommy Franks. The defeat of the Republican Guard outside Baghdad would deprive the city of its best-trained potential defenders. This could have a dramatic impact on the much feared siege of the city, with its grim prospects of high civilian and U.S. casualties in Stalingrad-style street fighting.

"The mystery is why the Iraqis left the Republican Guard in defensive positions so far south of Baghdad," a British staff officer in Kuwait told UPI. "They must have known from Desert Storm what our air power could do. I can only assume that Saddam Hussein was worried about the loyalty of the guard if he pulled them back into the city. His priority has always been the survival of his own regime rather than the survival of his troops."

The key breakthrough into the Karbala gap came in two days of fighting Monday and

Tuesday as the 3rd Division and the 101st Airborne worked together to thrust deep inside the Republican Guard Medina Division between Karbala and Hilla. Small teams of Airborne troops were helicoptered forward, behind enemy lines, to spot targets and call in air strikes before the main assaults began.

A host of other battles along the way made the breakthrough possible. The 7th Cavalry of the 3rd Division mounted a classic left hook, sweeping to the west of the city of Karbala, taking the risk of forcing a passage through a narrow neck of land between the city and Lake Razzara. It could have been what Soviet military doctrine calls a fire sack, a predefined patch of important ground covered by prepared artillery with its rounds already zeroed in on target. But the 7th Cavalry got through without loss, Karbala was bypassed, and the Republican Guard now faced an unexpected attack from the north and west.

A crucial element in the breakthrough was the capture of Iraqi airfields at Hilla and Karbala, and the ability of U.S. engineers and support troops to get them working and supplied again. These forward airfields meant that the ground troops were given nonstop support by airborne fire power, as the combat helicopters could refuel and reload just minutes from the battlefield.

Another important factor was the ability of the U.S. troops at Nasiriyah and Najaf to fight off the Iraqi guerrilla attacks on the stretched supply lines, guaranteeing an endless flow of fuel, ammunition, food and water to the troops far ahead. Those grinding battles for the Euphrates bridges, which encouraged the Iraqi commanders to keep their RG divisions forward rather than pulling them back into Baghdad, were the essential precondition for the battle of Baghdad.

The U.S. commanders also launched a preventive strike to ensure that the Iraqi regime could not breach the dams on the Euphrates River to flood the approaches to Baghdad, a desperate measure to hold off the U.S. advance. A Special Forces team seized Hadithah Dam Monday, a dam that could potentially flood the area of Karbala, where U.S. troops are pushing northward.

In another preventive strike, this time aimed at destroying the military supplies available to a potential defense of Baghdad, U.S. aircraft bombed an Iraqi storage facility with 40, 2,000-pound, satellite-guided bombs Wednesday in the al-Karkh district of Baghdad. The military storage site is used by the Special Security Organization and the Special Republican Guard, charged by Saddam Hussein with the city's defense.

Despite the scale of the U.S. success in ground taken, there were few prisoners — but many abandoned military boots and helmets to be seen by the U.S. troops driving north. The Pentagon had expected many more prisoners, as in the first Gulf War. But this time, fighting inside their own country, the Iraqis apparently preferred to ditch their uniforms, adopt civilian clothes and head for home.

"We are seeing some surrender, but not in tremendous numbers. We are essentially able to move through. It's unclear what is happening to some of those elements," McChrystal said. "As people melt away, it's very difficult to stop very small groups of people."

Coalition command spokesman Brig. Gen. Vincent Brooks said that an in-depth inquiry had found no evidence that coalition action was responsible for the bombing of a market in northern Baghdad that reportedly killed 14 civilians on March 25.

"We have examined our flights, our weapon systems that were used in the period of time associated with the explosion in the market. We've also examined imagery that we can get available to us, the best we can do to try to determine the size of some of the craters, the direction where some of the blast went, as indicated by surrounding buildings and what have you. And there's absolutely nothing that joins that to coalition action," Brooks said.

It could be significant, coalition officials added, that Iraq's air defense commander in Baghdad had been replaced, and they suggested Iraq's own surface-to-air missiles, and antiaircraft artillery falling back to earth could be the cause of some of the reported civilian casualties.

Tuesday night saw the debut of a new antiarmor cluster munition called the Sensor Fuzed Weapon. Each of the six 1,000-pound bomb canisters dropped carried 10 bomblets, each with four independently targeted nonexplosive projectiles that track infrared signatures to destroy "soft" and armored vehicles. Coalition forces have fired more than 700 cruise missiles and used more than 10,000 precision-guided munitions since the war began two weeks ago.

Against defeatism

John O'Sullivan

WASHINGTON, April 1 (UPI) — No sensible pundit makes predictions at the best of times — and April Fools' Day is certainly not the best of times. But the current elite media epidemic of doubt and defeatism about the course of the war in Iraq sorely tempts me to stick out my neck and state firmly that Iraqi resistance will soon crack — and crack so completely that, as at the fall of Kabul, we will be astonished at the gloomy forecasts of "quagmire" and "endless" guerrilla warfare that preceded the collapse.

One reason for believing this is the dramatic progress of the Anglo–American forces in only 11 days campaigning. In every engagement thus far — including the largest British tank battle since El Alamein — the allies have defeated Iraqi forces and inflicted heavy losses in men and equipment. They have secured the southern oilfields without significant environmental damage. They control vast areas of both southern and northern Iraq, and have persuaded the Turks not to intervene against the Kurdish-controlled north. It took them less than a week to reach the gates of Baghdad — perhaps the quickest advance of a heavily armored column in military history. And these extraordinary gains have been achieved with the loss of about 60 American and British lives, and of approximately 40 other soldiers either captured or missing in action. These figures represent a tragedy for 100 families, but they prefigure a military triumph rather than a disaster.

Critics argue, however, that they are short-term gains in contrast to the long-term disasters foreshadowed by two other developments: first, that there is stronger Iraqi military resistance than expected and, second, that ordinary Iraqis have failed to welcome the invading allies as liberators with flowers and kisses. What these setbacks allegedly foreshadow is a long-running guerrilla warfare campaign against the allies that will continue long after Baghdad has fallen and Saddam Hussein has been dispatched to enjoy his 70 virgins. What we face, in the jargon, is a "quagmire."

What should be first said is that this stronger-than-expected Iraqi resistance is still not very strong. It consists of irregular soldiers, generally disguised as civilians, harrying the armored column and picking off the occasional straggler. It manifestly failed to halt the allied advance and, if it delayed that advance slightly, it still failed to prevent the allies from setting a new world record in seizing enemy territory. This falls several notches below the defense of Stalingrad on any scale of heroic resistance.

Such resistance would be even less effective if the allies had embarked on a conventional strategy of merely defeating the enemy by the unconstrained use of superior firepower and the destruction of the enemy's infrastructure. But the novel strategy, adopted by the allegedly ruthless figure of Defense Secretary Donald Rumsfeld, consists of defeating the enemy while safeguarding civilian lives, protecting his ordinary civil and economic infrastructure and even minimizing those enemy casualties that are not strictly necessary to gain military objectives.

Fighting a war in this "compassionate conservative" way has its drawbacks: it takes longer; it may suggest that the allies lack the necessary toughness to carry them through to victory; and it may encourage the other side to keep fighting. That would be an additional explanation for the Iraqi resistance. On the other hand, it reduces the likelihood of a future "quagmire" by minimizing the harm and destruction that might otherwise stimulate a desire for revenge among the Iraqis. At present, the "Arab street" outside Iraq, which sees the air attacks on Baghdad through the distorting lens of al-Jazeera, seems more likely to harbor resentment and revenge than the city's inhabitants, who know just how precise the targeting has been. Still, together with the fact that ordinary Iraqis have not generally welcomed the allies, Iraq's continued military resistance requires some explanation. Why has Iraq not yet cracked?

The conventional explanation — advanced to CNN by any passing Arab ambassador — is that the Iraqis are inspired by nationalism. However much they hate Saddam, they prefer him to an invader and will fight to defend their land. But the evidence for this explanation is very thin. It is either circular logic — nationalism is inspiring their resistance. What is nationalism? It is what inspires people to resist — or it rests on patriotic public statements made to television cameras by Iraqi civilians.

But what happens when the cameras are switched off? Here is what a journalist from Arab News, Saudi Arabia's English daily, discovered when he took aside a young Iraqi man who had been chanting, "With our blood, with our souls, we will die for you, Saddam" to television crews filming a Red Cross handout of food in an area under allied control. The young man later explained in private: "There are people from Baath here reporting everything that goes on. There are cameras here recording our faces. If the Americans were to withdraw and everything were to return to the way it was before, we want to make sure that we survive the massacre that would follow. ... In public we always pledge our allegiance to Saddam, but in our hearts we feel something else."

Iraqi "resistance" can be similarly explained. Iraq's regular forces are stiffened by the special security forces, in reality licensed thugs, that Saddam has recruited to sustain his regime against both popular discontent and military mutiny. Ordinary soldiers, not excluding officers, are forced into battle either with a gun at their backs or by threats to their family at home if they should fail to fight. In these circumstances, surrendering may require more courage than advancing against a militarily superior enemy. As the Arab News reporter concluded: "The people of Iraq are terrified of Saddam Hussein." And that includes the ordinary Iraqi soldier.

Those who predicted that resistance would collapse and the allies be welcomed as liberators, as I did, made the reasonable assumption that this universal fear would dissipate when allied tanks came into view. But Saddam had reached exactly the same conclusion and, as the months of U.N. diplomacy dragged on, he set in place a structure of repression that would survive the mere arrival of the U.S. and British armies. He instilled in the Iraqi people a fear, rooted in the memory of how the first President

Bush betrayed the Shiite uprising in Basra immediately after the Gulf War, that the liberation would be strictly temporary. He persuaded them in advance that the allies were mere birds of passage who, after an interval, would fly off and leave them to the ruthless revenge of a returning Baath Party. He made them passive and suspicious of their own hopes.

It may seem odd that this should work in the face of overwhelming allied power. But it is an inventive variation on two established totalitarian practices. All totalitarian parties — and Saddam's Baath Party is a blend of fascism and communism — rely on politicized security units to enforce their will. That is especially so when their power is dying and the regular troops can no longer be relied on.

It was true of the Vichy regime that in its last days it recruited the ideological paramilitaries of the Milice to crush the Resistance; it was true of Hitler, whose bunker was defended against the Russians by non-German fascist volunteers of the Charlemagne division of the SS; it was true even of the Soviet regime, which as late as the perestroika period used the thuggish "special forces" of the Soviet Interior Ministry against the Baltics. Such forces tend to be recruited from the dregs of society who enjoy not only the perquisites of power but power itself — the more brutal the better. Or as Orwell described the totalitarian ambition: "A boot stamping on a human face forever."

Power itself is their ideology, justification and drug. As long as they can exercise it, they are loyal to the only kind of regime that would ever give them authority. Once it is removed from them, they lose all motivation. The reverse of the power wielded by such creatures is the fear of everyone else. And such fear lasts as long as the paramilitaries are a visible presence wielding power.

Saddam's variation on these themes was to realize that the paramilitaries could continue to inflict fear — and thus to uphold his regime's power — even in the territory occupied by the invading Anglo–Americans. But for how long? And will the paramilitaries remain a terrorist threat after the coalition establishes its rule clearly and without doubt?

History has some lessons to teach us here. In 1945, Germany resisted the allied advance to the bitter end, relying on the fanaticism of the SS and calling up elderly men and 14-year-old Hitler Youth, despite the deep war-weariness of the German people. There were even plans for a campaign of guerrilla resistance — the so-called "Werewolves" — after a formal German surrender. The wartime allies took this threat very seriously.

With Hitler's death, however, the Nazi myth of totalitarian power evaporated and the entire apparatus of terror collapsed. Those who had acted from Nazi conviction — like Saddam's thugs — vanished into the shadows, deprived of the drug of power that had sustained them in their wickedness. Those who had acted from fear — like ordinary Iraqis today — were suddenly released from a living nightmare. Not a single Werewolf emerged from his lair. And the allies, who had arrived as conquerors, not liberators, soon found themselves handing out food parcels to a grateful German population.

That will happen in Iraq too. When? That no one can predict with certainty. But happen it will — and not long after the battle of Baghdad is joined.

———————

BASRA, Iraq — A soldier serving with No. 1 Company, 1st Battalion, the Irish Guards looks for possible Iraqi enemy positions as Royal Engineer technicians prepare to cap one of the burning oil wells within the city of Basra, Iraq, on April 3, 2003. In a dawn raid on a university–factory complex within sight of their patrol base at Bridge Four on the outskirts of Basra, the Irish Guards attacked and cleared the base after coming under fire from small-arms mortars and surface-to-air missile systems, which were fired from Iraqi positions at a British Lynx helicopter supporting the Irish Guards. (Giles Penfound, Rex Features/UPI)

Day 15 — Thursday, April 3

"We have the Baghdad skyline in sight."

MARTIN WALKER

Outmatched, outflanked and outgunned, troops of the Iraqi regular army and Republican Guard fought on with clumsy desperation Thursday as the jaws of the two U.S. armored thrusts closed around them and the U.S. 3rd Division reported, "We have the Baghdad skyline in sight." By Thursday morning, the U.S. 3rd Division's multiple-launch rocket systems were firing directly into Baghdad's international airport and defensive positions in the city's western sub-urbs. By nightfall, the airport was in U.S. hands.

Iraq's 4th Army Corps, anchored by its 10th Armored Division, which has fought better than many Republican Guard units, was cut off and surrounded by U.S. troops, and U.S. artillery and warplanes pounded the escape routes back into Baghdad for the remainder of the Iraqi forces.

But not all the Iraqi troops have been caught outside the capital. The Adnan Republican Guard Mechanized Infantry Division, recently moved south from the northern cities of Mosul and Tikrit, was digging in to defend Baghdad's western suburbs after it failed to hold Saddam International Airport. Elements of the al-Nida Republican Guard armored division, also for-merly north of Baghdad, were also reported moving into Baghdad, coalition military sources said.

Hard fighting lies ahead for the coalition forces, and a crucial decision that may have to be taken in Washington rather than by coalition commanders on the ground or at the Qatar headquarters. The question is what to do about Baghdad.

Coalition officials in the region prefer, United Press International has learned, to copy the "softly softly" British tactics in Iraq's second city of Basra. The British have now spent 12 days running a gentle siege that never sealed off the city, allows civilians and food to come and go after being searched and worked to restore water and power supplies. At the same time, with raids and targeted air and artillery strikes, the British picked away at the command posts and headquarters of the Baath Party, the fedayeen and the remaining military forces inside the city.

"We are deliberately not taking the city yet, but we are not destroying it either, and we are starting to get more and more support and information from the civilian population," said British spokesman Group Capt. Al Lockwood. "In the end, they are what this war is all about."

The alternative to the British method is for a full-scale assault on Baghdad "on the run," as the Marines and 3rd Infantry use the momentum of the stunning advances in the past 48 hours and take advantage of Iraqi disorganization. This option is apparently being urged by Pentagon officials. The decision, which must be taken soon, may hinge on the intelligence estimates of the power structure inside Baghdad. If Saddam Hussein and his general staff remain alive and in command of their defenses, a full-scale assault could be slow, bloody and costly in civilian casualties.

There is as yet no certainty about Saddam's health or location, though Kuwait is filled with rumors that high-ranking Iraqis, including members of Saddam's family, have been seen in the neighboring Syrian capital of Damascus. Coalition intelligence officers maintain, however, they see little sign of a coherent Iraqi command system. The siege-or-assault decision, which also implies important political decisions in Washington about whether or not to establish an interim governing authority for Iraq outside a besieged capital, cannot be delayed long.

On the western side of Baghdad, advance units of the U.S. 3rd Division pushed to within artillery range of the Iraqi capital Thursday morning, after seizing a key double bridge across the Euphrates south of Fallujah Wednesday. One span of the double bridge, carrying the main six-lane auto route west from Baghdad toward Jordan and Syria, was destroyed, but the other span withstood desperate Iraqi artillery fire, and U.S. combat engineers crossed the river under fire in rubber boats to dismantle the demolition wires. That left the 3rd Division with a three-lane highway to Baghdad.

On the eastern side of Baghdad, the Marines advancing up the Tigris were less than 30 miles from Baghdad after capturing a key bridge at al-Numaniya, about 15 miles north of Kut. By Thursday morning, U.S. combat helicopters were operating from the captured al-Numaniya air base. So the battle *for* Baghdad is over. The battle *of* Baghdad is about to begin.

The overnight capture of Saddam International airport, some 10 miles from the center of the Iraqi capital, brings to an end a stunning victory in two weeks of mobile warfare that reinforces the lessons of the first Gulf War and of Kosovo. The U.S. military machine is unstoppable — and looks set to continue the kind of global dominance that the British enjoyed in the century after their decisive defeat of France's naval power in 1805.

A technological generation ahead of any other military on earth, the U.S. armed forces have built on the lessons of the German blitzkrieg of 1940 to pioneer a new style of war. The German panzer divisions integrated tanks, artillery, mobile infantry and close air support with radio communications — and consistently defeated larger armies.

The Germans lost for three main reasons. First, they never understood sea power, and modern America does — having also learned the lesson of British naval dominance. Second, German logistics were poor. Most of their divisions in 1940 depended on horses to haul their guns, and their logistics failed miserably in the Russian campaign when German troops froze to death in their light summer uniforms at the gates of Moscow. Third, the German military failed to nurture the national technological and industrial base on which military superiority depended. They produced magnificent weapons, but never enough of them.

None of these weaknesses applies to the current U.S. armed forces, which have long learned the importance of sea and air power. But the real genius of the modern American way of war is the way they have combined their logistics with the best of civilian technology, from communications to information technology. It is one thing to marvel at the way the V Corps post office in Kuwait delivers 100 tons of incoming mail a day, quite another to see the massed ranks of PCs in the giant hangars at Camp Doha, with GIs e-mailing home and surfing the Web to see what al-Jazeera or the British media has to say about their war.

The supply systems are stupendous because the U.S. military has applied the technologies of commercial companies, such as FedEx and Wal-Mart, to track the use of equipment, locate spare parts through bar codes, and start shipping them forward to the combat troops even before they ask for them. German troops froze for months in their Russian campaigns. American troops outside Nasiriyah were able to take hot showers less than 48 hours after they reached the place — despite the worst sandstorm in a decade.

As a result, the U.S. armed forces defeated the best army in the Arab world with one hand tied behind their back. The U.S. Army did not even field its first team. The 4th Division, the most technologically advanced of all, with a computer in every vehicle and a TV camera on the helmet of every squad leader, sending real-time images back to headquarters, never even arrived on the battlefield.

The tank-heavy Iraqis, trained and equipped according to the Soviet theories of armored warfare, were defeated by an outnumbered U.S. force that did not even contain an armored division. They were beaten by one U.S. mechanized infantry division (the 3rd), one Airborne division (the 101st) and a Marine expeditionary force fighting further from shore than any Marine unit before them. They had the backing, on a secondary front, of one reinforced British armored brigade.

This has been a campaign for the history books, an example of modern blitzkrieg that will convince every other military on Earth that there is no future in taking on the Americans.

As a result, they will have to think in terms of asymmetric warfare, in ways to achieve their political goals by avoiding an all-out military confrontation.

They will look for an equalizer — like nuclear weapons. North Korea's salesmen are going to become very popular. They will look very hard at deniable terrorist surrogates. And they will study carefully the guerrilla attacks the Iraqi paramilitary staged against U.S. supply lines to work out how and why it went wrong. They will work at information warfare to see if those awesome American communications networks and computer-dependent logistics can be disrupted.

Above all, they will study the new campaign that is about to take place in the battle *of* Baghdad, the first time in its history that the U.S. armed forces have taken on a contested city of 5 million people. The U.S. commanders know what the cities of Leningrad and Stalingrad did to the blitzkrieg experts of 1940. To avoid that fate, and demonstrate flexibility in the face of new challenges that really test an army's mettle, the victors of Blitzkrieg 2003 have to learn some asymmetric tactics of their own.

The Rescue of Jessica Lynch

It was for the Americans the worst moment of the war, when the supply convoy of the 507th Ordnance Maintenance Company took a wrong turn as it headed north past the city of Nasiriyah and ran into an ambush of heavy machine guns, mortars and rocket-propelled grenades (RPGs). They weren't combat troops, but cooks and supply clerks and mechanics. And they fought back hard, even though the first volley of RPGs sent two Humvees flipping over onto their sides. In the 15 minutes of fighting, nine Americans died and six were taken prisoner. Pfc. Jessica Lynch, 19, was thrown from her vehicle, breaking an arm and a leg. She fought on despite her injuries as her comrades died beside her, shooting until she ran out of ammunition.

"It wasn't a small ambush," Sgt. James Riley, 31, a bachelor from Pennsauken, N.J., recalled as he flew back to the United States after the prisoners' eventual rescue. "It was a whole city. And we were getting shot from all different directions as we were going down the road — front, rear, left, right. We were like Custer. We were surrounded. We had no working weapons. We couldn't even make a bayonet charge — we would have been mowed down. We didn't have a choice, sir."

Exhilarated at taking prisoners, the Iraqis took them to Baghdad and paraded them — and the dead — before the TV cameras. But Lynch, her wounds too serious to travel, was taken to a local hospital in Nasiriyah, which was also being used as a fedayeen command post. An Iraqi nurse helped look after Lynch and told her husband — a local lawyer who is still known only as Mohammed — that she was being slapped and beaten by the black-clad fedayeen. Mohammed went to the hospital to see for himself and slipped into her room with a doctor friend to warn her that she would be fine. And then he walked to the nearest U.S. Marine checkpoint, his arms up, to alert the Americans that one of their own was in trouble.

The Marines needed more information. With remarkable bravery, Mohammed went back twice to the hospital, checking on the numbers of fedayeen, the size of the courtyard, the location of strong points — and Lynch. The second time, the fedayeen grew suspicious and searched his house. Mohammed sent his wife away to stay with relatives.

Ten days after the ambush that made Lynch a prisoner, Black Hawk helicopters dropped into the hospital courtyard at dead of night. While Marines on the outskirts of the city staged a diversionary attack, Special Forces commandos, including Rangers and Navy SEALs, stormed what they called "the hospital fortress."

Resistance to the rescue team was "light," according to a U.S. Special Operations Command official, but there was a gun battle outside the building while the rescue mission was getting both in and out. A second team that remained behind recovered 11 bodies — two from the hospital morgue and nine in a gravesite in town — that are being tested to determine their identities. Lacking shovels, the commandos dug the bodies from the shallow graves with their bare hands. The rescue team also found ammunition, mortars, maps, a terrain model, military documents "and other

things that make it very clear that it was being used as a military command post," a military spokesman said.

"And they wanted to do that very rapidly so that they could race the sun and be off the site before the sun came up, a great testament to the will and desire of coalition forces to bring their own home," Maj. Gen. Victor Renuart, U.S. Central Command's director of operations, told reporters. "After completing the excavation and ensuring there were none left behind, the force recovered all bodies and transported them back to the staging location and moved those back with the rest of the assault force."

Two teams raced to the hospital itself, one to rescue Lynch and the other to exploit the site for information. As the hospital had been used as a command and control site, Renuart said, the rescue mission also gave the forces an opportunity to collect intelligence on the Iraqi operation.

The assault force entered the hospital and, according to Renuart, "persuaded a local physician to lead them to Pvt. Lynch's location." The doctor also volunteered information about remains of other U.S. military personnel in the morgue or buried nearby, he said. "As the team entered the hospital room, they found Pvt. Lynch in a hospital bed. The first man approached the door and came in and called her name. She had been scared, had the sheet up over her head because she didn't know what was happening. She lowered the sheet from her head. She didn't really respond yet because I think she was probably pretty scared," Renuart said.

The soldier said again, "Jessica Lynch, we're the United States soldiers and we're here to protect you and take you home," according to Renuart. The soldier approached her bed and took off his helmet. Lynch "looked up to him and said, 'I'm an American soldier, too,'" according to Renuart.

The rescue team strapped Lynch to a stretcher and carried her down a stairwell to a waiting helicopter. As she was loaded, Lynch grabbed the hand of her American doctor — a U.S. Army Ranger — and held it for the entire flight.

The Pentagon Saturday identified nine of the 11 bodies exhumed as Americans and released the names of eight. They are soldiers who went missing with Lynch on March 23, when their maintenance convoy was ambushed in southern Iraq. At least five others of the team are thought to be prisoners, and two others were killed in the attack.

Lynch is suffering from two broken legs, a broken arm, ankle and foot, and a back injury, according to Centcom. Her family left West Virginia Saturday to the U.S. military hospital in Landstuhl, Germany, where she has been undergoing surgery and treatment.

The Embedded Media: Embedding as Bonding

Claude Salhani

LONDON, April 2 (UPI) — Whoever came up with the inspiration of "embedding" journalists into fighting units deserves the military equivalent of an Academy Award. Without a doubt, they should be given the "Oscar for Best Advance Planning of the Year." From the Pentagon's perspective, this is the best darn idea to emerge from the minds of war planners since the "Bouncing Betty" came into existence. If the initiative was a civilian's, he (or she) should be given a big fat raise. If it's someone in uniform, they deserve a promotion, a cigar and a special toast in the officer's mess.

Think about it for a moment. There are hardly two more dissimilar sets of minds than the military, and the media. In the military, when someone shouts, "Jump," soldiers are trained to reply, "Sir, yes, sir. How high, sir?" But should someone ask a member of the media to jump, chances are they will mouth back, "Who should jump? What are they jumping over? Where is this jump to take place? When is it scheduled for? How exactly will this jump happen? Why is there a jump in the first place? And if I may be allowed a follow-up question, is there a precedent for such a jump?"

Then they will then try to figure out how to turn the jump into a $150 lunch that can be passed off on expenses.

Yet once embedded, the situation changes dramatically. They change. The two become joined at the hip. They eat together, sleep together, travel together and go through the dangers of the battlefield together. Deep bonds are formed. The two become old friends, battle buddies. They start to jump.

When the U.S. Marines landed in Beirut in 1982 as part of a multinational peacekeeping force, a few of us who shared foxholes, frights, bad food and the occasional beer became good friends. We experienced some of what they were going through. We felt their fears, frustrations and anger. Twenty years later some of us are still friends and remain in touch via e-mail, the odd greeting card and even the occasional reunion.

Invited to join up, as they have in the Iraq campaign, the media became far more manageable for the generals and the Pentagon suits. It was far better than having several hundred uncontrollable hacks running around the battlefield reporting on whatever they want, including much of what the military would not want reported. Once embedded, they report — or rather do not report — information that headquarters deems harmful. The "embed" became the ideal way to control the flow of information emanating from the front. Since the war in Iraq started, how many times have we heard embedded correspondents reporting from somewhere in southern Iraq say, "We cannot tell you exactly where we are for 'operational reasons'"?

Operational reasons became the key word. This would hardly be the case with "independent journalists," who are not obligated to abide by the same set of ground rules imposed by the Pentagon and who do not feel the same burden of camaraderie with frontline troops as their embedded colleagues. While most responsible journalists remain deeply concerned with safeguarding human life — and reporting on troop movements can certainly endanger life — their reporting would not be subject to the same strict self-imposed censorship. The "operational rules" change. On the other hand, independent journalists would never have the access offered to embedded hacks.

Rather than have to fight the media, as they did during the first Gulf War and previous wars, the Pentagon has simply recruited them. The old maxim "If you can't beat them, join them," has been masterfully turned into "If you can't beat them, make them join you."

Who says military intelligence is an oxymoron?

———

Embedded or not, we're with the boys

MARTIN WALKER

BASRA, Iraq, April 8 (UPI) — Something fundamental has happened to the British and U.S. media during this war. Those who have spent time on the front lines with the coalition troops, whether embedded with individual units or traveling independently through liberated Iraq, have learned to love the military. Time after time, they saved our necks. They put our soft-skinned vehicles behind their armor when the shells came in. They told us when to duck and when it was safe to move. They shared their food and water with us and were embarrassingly grateful when we let them use our satellite phones to call home. We were embarrassed that it was all we could do for them.

We saw how hard they tried to avoid civilian casualties and the risks they took by their self-restraint. We began to understand their quiet pride in their skills, and the plain decency of the men and women who follow the profession of arms. When we got lost, U.S. Marines went out of their way to put us right, and British officers sketched "safe" areas on a map. They are kind to one another and considerate to civilians like us.

"Thank God for the British army," said grinning United Press International photographer Chris Corder (an American) as we tucked in behind the comforting bulk of a Warrior armored infantry vehicle of the Royal Scots Dragoon Guards one night outside Basra, and were offered a cup of tea.

Above all, they are no longer "the military." They have become individuals that we have come to know, like little Robert, who to his regret is too short to stand guard outside Buckingham Palace and has to remain behind doing stores duty.

There is Paul, from Northern Ireland, who is genuinely upset at the poverty of the Iraqi people he sees and fills his pockets with biscuits and candy to give to the children. There is Sarge, who grumbles that this war is all about oil and is far from sure he likes it. There is Chris, a volunteer from Zimbabwe, whose dream is to play his bagpipes for the queen and who hesitantly asks if we can find out if Manchester United won its match.

With the British troops and the U.S. 3rd Division, with the 101st Airborne and the Marines, with the gunners and the medics and the Air Force and aboard ships, there are hundreds of journalists learning the same lessons, getting to know the same kinds of troops, and realizing that we in the media had better rethink the way we do our work.

One of the consequences of the way the British and Americans have dropped conscription and now use professional armies is that the media and the broader population have become disconnected from their troops. The military has become a private club, and one that has learned to distrust most of the media, who know little of the people who fight in their country's name. The legacy of wars in dubious causes like Vietnam or some of the British colonial wars has widened the gulf of mutual ignorance and mistrust.

This still happens. At one of the daily briefings at coalition command headquarters in Qatar (about 300 miles behind the lines), a large and skeptical media corps became restive at what they saw as military stonewalling or weasel words about responsibility for civilian casualties in the Baghdad bombing. Journalists on the front lines took a very different view of the need for operational security. We did not even complain when we were ordered to turn off our satellite phones because the Iraqi guns seemed to be able to zero in on their transmissions, or when we were asked not to report something.

"Screw the nut on it, mate," a British SAS Special Forces trooper told me when I came across him questioning one of his Iraqi agents inside Basra. "No photos, and not a word until Basra falls. All right?"

Of course it was all right. Forget journalistic objectivity. There were armed men across the road trying to kill me, and my protection depended on these British troops, many of whom I knew by their first names. There was no question which side I was on.

In the same way, those of us in the field knew that those gloomy armchair pundit accounts from London and Washington of setbacks and "pauses" were missing the point. We learned to understand the painstaking way the British were gathering intelligence in Basra and steadily separating the Saddam loyalists from the bulk of the population — so the place finally fell like a house of cards. Air Marshal Brian Burridge, the British commander, suggested that the hundreds of journalists "who have learned a new understanding of the military could change the way the media covers war." I really hope so.

While expressing admiration for the reporters who shared the dangers with front-line troops, Burridge had nothing but contempt for the media back home, with their reports of setbacks, Iraqi resistance and civilian casualties.

"The U.K. media has lost the plot. You stand for nothing, you support nothing, you criticize, you drip. It's a spectator sport to criticize anybody or anything, and what the media says fuels public opinion. It may sound harsh, but that's the way it feels from where I sit."

The media wimp out

JOE BOB BRIGGS

Apparently the new media catch phrase is "In Harm's Way." Normally, movie stars would wear $2 million diamond necklaces to the Oscars, but that would be inappropriate when troops are In Harm's Way.

Everyone has the right to his opinion — this is what people say when they despise your opinion — but protests should be muted when our boys are In Harm's Way.

Normally we would be interviewing militantly anti-war French intellectuals on this channel, but, you know, IN HARM'S WAY.

When did the media become such WIMPS?

When a war starts, *everybody* is In Harm's Way. It's kind of part of the definition of the word "war."

Just a month ago I attended a conference where ABC News correspondent Sam Donaldson defended the airing of footage showing American troops being dragged through the streets of Mogadishu by Somali rebels. "Images like that are where policy becomes real," he said.

So what was up with the general refusal to air the footage of the five American prisoners of war? From all accounts, and from the grainy images reproduced in the New York Daily News, this video was about a dozen times *less* graphic than the Mogadishu footage.

Is this the same media that once aired images of a Vietnamese officer executing a civilian with a gunshot to the head? When war gets nasty and graphic and deadly, that's exactly when we *need* a dose of reality. And you know why?

Because people are IN HARM'S WAY. People on both sides.

Even the *idea* of two sides — normally held sacred by the proud American media — goes out the window in these modern lopsided wars of a technological army swooping down on an army of the 19th century. The press becomes nationalistic, jingoistic and blind to the point of view of "the enemy." To a real journalist, there would *be* no enemy, only combatants.

Once again, repeating the whole Afghanistan experience, we have to go to the foreign press for information. (Interestingly, the British newspapers apparently don't have this "In Harm's Way" moratorium on bad news, even though their soldiers are just as involved as our own.) Al-Jazeera has footage, our own networks do not. European and Arab journalists hit the ground running in Baghdad, toting up the civilian dead — our own journalists do not.

Even within the relatively safe confines of New York City, the press seems to work for the war information ministry. Widely covered on Saturday was a pro-war demonstration on Times

Square. There were 1,500 people there, and it was *more* ballyhooed than the previous demonstration of 200,000 people *against* the war.

The tough anti-U.S. speeches of Russian President Vladimir Putin and French President Jacques Chirac are not aired. The White House is not pressed on the oil issue. (Since most of the world believes we're engaged in an oil grab, one way to rehabilitate our image would be to bar American oil companies from participating in post-war contracts. Other countries have already called for this.) And every day, bleating from CNN, Fox, MSNBC and all the other networks, are sentimental features about "family" (our own families, of course, never Iraqi families) and the agony of the professional soldier's loved ones. Yet these are men and women who have signed up for combat duty, all volunteers, and it's not clear to me how they're so different from families of, say, Vietnamese soldiers, or those who fought in Korea.

The other strange thread running through American coverage is the certain assumption that there will be democracy in Iraq. No one has considered that the Iraqis might not cotton to democracy. They might prefer a strongman system. They wouldn't be the first culture to do so. Giving them self-determination could result in several forms of government, including an Islamic theocracy or some version of the Late Roman–style dictatorship they have today.

There was a time when our newspapers and networks were neither pro-war nor anti-war, neither pro-America nor anti-America, neither overly sentimental nor overly hard-boiled. The phrase "yellow journalism" itself dates from an era when a newspaper publisher agitated for war and then crusaded for the troops who fought it. For years it was used as a slur. The press considered it a dark forgotten chapter in its otherwise illustrious history.

That was, of course, before we all landed In Harm's Way — of the media's pandering.

KHAZER, Iraq, April 4 (UPI) — American troops hold a position near the northern Iraqi town of Khazer, about 20 miles from Mosul, on April 4, 2003. Skirmishes continue as the U.S. military consolidates its position. (Ali Khaligh, UPI)

Day 16 — Friday, April 4

"What really matters is not whether or not (Saddam)'s dead or alive, but the fact that whoever is left in this regime, whatever is left of the regime leadership, got up today and realized they have less and less control of their country." — Pentagon spokeswoman Victoria Clarke

MARTIN WALKER

As U.S. 3rd Division troops consolidated their hold on Saddam International Airport, newly released TV footage of a jovial Saddam Hussein walking amid cheering Iraqis was hailed by coalition commanders as good news: that he, or his regime, feels sufficiently shaken to have to make such a bold show.

"What really matters is not whether or not he's dead or alive, but the fact that whoever is left in this regime, whatever is left of the regime leadership, got up today and realized they have less and less control of their country," Pentagon spokeswoman Victoria Clarke told a Pentagon news briefing Friday.

U.S. forces had secured the Saddam International Airport by dawn Friday and renamed it Baghdad International Airport. It sits on the southwest side of the Iraqi capital, about 10 miles (16 kilometers) from the center of the city. Patrols discovered tunnels and underground facilities at the airport, and started the long job to search and clear them as combat engineers cleared burned aircraft from the runways and taxiways and began preparing the field for allied aircraft. The 3rd Division fought off a series of attacks trying to recover the airport in the early hours of Saturday and called in air support to help defeat a strong armored probe.

The Iraqi information minister warned Friday that "an unconventional" attack would be launched against the airport overnight. The announcement followed a suicide car bombing earlier Friday near a military checkpoint in western Iraq. The bombing, the second since the U.S.-led war began March 20, killed three coalition troops, U.S. Central Command said. The driver and a pregnant woman who jumped from the car were also killed. The pan-Arab satellite channel al-Jazeera showed two women later Friday, one of them dedicating herself and her unborn child to the defense of Islamic land, that it said were responsible for the attack.

But U.S. forces are ready for such tactics, insisted Joint Chiefs of Staff Vice Director of Operations Maj. Gen. Stanley McChrystal: "We went into this operation expecting the unexpected, and from car bombings to the potential use of weapons of mass destruction, we've had to stay postured for sort of anything that the regime is capable of using. So at this point, we are just postured for that. We have no particular threat that we consider more than another."

While the Iraqi minister indicated chemical or biological weapons would not be used, McChrystal said the troops are prepared for such a scenario: "Logically, now that we are at Baghdad Airport, they wouldn't use chemical and biological weapons because we are right amongst their populations. But they have not fought logically from the beginning."

In the first real sign that the Iranian capital was coming under siege from the ground as well as repeated bombing attacks from the air, Baghdad's electricity supply was cut Friday night.

"We didn't do it. It's as simple as that," Brig. Gen. Vincent Brooks said. "We tried to do a number of things to protect the people of Baghdad. Electrical power in Baghdad also relates to water in Baghdad. Electrical power in Baghdad also relates to power in hospitals in Baghdad. That's not part of the coalition design at this point, so I wouldn't characterize it … as fortuitous. It's a matter of concern at this point in time for the population that's inside of Baghdad."

Outside the city, the fighting went on, with the Marines advancing from the southwest meeting pockets of determined resistance from guns and armored vehicles dug into small farming villages. The Marines also had to watch their right flank against the possibility that Iraqi troops still stationed along the Iranian border, 150 miles east of Baghdad, might yet brave the gantlet of coalition air power and try to intervene.

To the rear of the 3rd Division troops at the airport, other units mopped up along the 30-mile swathe the armored units had cut to reach the Iraqi capital. Soldiers from the 3rd Brigade Combat Team of the Army's 5th Corps rendered more than 30 Iraqi armored weapon systems inoperable in a military compound in the Karbala Gap, southwest of Baghdad.

The 101st Airborne Division "completed the isolation" of Najaf, cutting off access to the city by the paramilitary forces that have so dogged the American troops. The division enlisted the help of a local cleric to begin distributing supplies to the townspeople, according to U.S. Central Command. The 82nd Airborne attacked paramilitary and Iraqi intelligence service facilities near As Samawah, taking up positions to defend coalition supply routes, Central Command said.

The prospect of a stiff battle for the city of Baghdad still lay ahead, but Iraqi commanders had extracted few trained troops to fight it from the killing ground where the coalition air and artillery had ground down the Republican Guard. Coalition spokesmen in Qatar said the Baghdad and Medina divisions of the Republican Guard outside Baghdad had been completely destroyed and the remaining four divisions had been significantly degraded.

U.S. forces still have not discovered definitive evidence of Saddam's so-called weapons of mass destruction program, one of the primary reasons for the entering the war. Brooks said further examination of a possible chemical weapons operations site discovered by special operations forces in Mudaysis has turned up less than was initially thought.

"We think that there may have been an explanation for this as an NBC (nuclear, biological and chemical) training school, not an operational facility. We think now it was probably an NBC training school," Brooks said. "We don't have any further investigation we're going to do on that site. And so our conclusion at this point is that it was not a WMD (weapons of mass destruction) site per se. In this case, it proves to be something far less than that. It doesn't mean they're not out there."

Meanwhile, back in Washington, the U.S. Congress approved President Bush's war budget, granting nearly $80 billion to the conflict in Iraq in an overwhelming show of support. The House passed the measure 414-12; the Senate 93-0.

Lawmakers, however, curbed Bush's request that the administration have total control over the funds for the war. The House gave Bush flexibility over $25.4 billion of the defense money, but asked the Pentagon to notify Congress seven days before any money was spent. The Senate cut that figure to $11 billion. Bush had wanted $59.9 billion of the $62.6 billion in his bill for the Pentagon placed in a large discretionary fund, which would have given Defense Secretary Donald Rumsfeld latitude in the war in Iraq and on terrorism.

The House also passed by a voice vote a proposal to block Germany, France, Russia and Syria from post-war reconstruction contracts, but U.S. subsidiaries of companies from those countries could still compete for contracts. In the Senate, however, the Bush administration pressured Sen. John Ensign, R-Nev., to withdraw an amendment that would have barred any of the plan's nearly $2.5 billion for rebuilding Iraq from going to French and German companies because they opposed the war.

"If America is going to become an arrogant nation and do things only our way, this is a good way to begin," said Dianne Feinstein, D-Calif., who opposed the amendment.

Besides domestic security funds, both bills contained more than $62 billion for the Pentagon and roughly $8 billion for aid to countries supporting U.S. efforts overseas. Included was money for replacing satellite-guided munitions, setting up a tribunal to try Saddam for alleged war crimes and letting state and local agencies bolster security at home.

The international aid funds would go toward rebuilding Iraq and for U.S. allies in the war on terrorism — Turkey, Pakistan, Israel, Jordan, Afghanistan and other countries. The issue of funds for Turkey was a contentious one. Some conservatives wanted to kill $1 billion in aid for Turkey because of its resistance to letting the United States use its bases for the war on Iraq. But the White House fought hard to prevent that from happening.

"Despite recent difficulties, the president is devoted to maintaining the strategic partnership" with Turkey, said National Security Adviser Condoleezza Rice. In a letter to Congress, Richard Armitage, deputy secretary of state, said it would be "particularly damaging to our diplomacy" to strip the funds Bush requested for Turkey.

The House voted 315-110 to reject the bid to kill aid for Ankara. All the money would come from growing federal deficits, which could approach $400 billion this year and in 2004.

Saddam Tours Baghdad Neighborhood

Ghassan al-Khadi

BAGHDAD, Iraq, April 4 (UPI) — A self-composed and defiant Saddam Hussein apparently made his first public appearance Friday since U.S. forces bombed his bunker March 20. Iraqi TV showed pictures of him walking the streets of a Baghdad neighborhood, where a throng of jubilant and enthusiastic residents greeted him.

The appearance was the culmination of several efforts Friday by the Iraqi president to rally his people against coalition troops poised just outside the Iraqi capital. The date of his actual visit was not definitive, however — some nearby buildings showed possible bomb damage.

The television pictures showed a smiling Saddam in military uniform and black beret surrounded by people in what was said to be the al-Mansour area, a target of coalition bombardment.

"With soul, with blood, we redeem you Saddam," shouted dozens of bystanders. Women ululated while some of the men pushed through to kiss their leader's hand or cheeks. "May God protect you," shouted one man as more joined the crowd.

Saddam, his military men and armed bodyguards in a cluster around him, was then seen checking military reinforcements in the city and chatting with residents. Afterward, he stood to overlook the crowd and raised his fist to salute them. The television then showed pictures from a driving car, allegedly with Saddam aboard, of many streets in Baghdad. Smoke clouds were seen in these pictures.

It was one of the very rare public appearances of Saddam. Mideast commentator Moustapha Maher, a retired Egyptian general, called it "a courageous step by Saddam, since he was not heavily guarded." He told al-Jazeera that the tour did not look prearranged "or else we would have seen a much bigger crowd." The appearance seemed intended to raise the morale of the Iraqi people, "especially at this time with reports of American troops near the city."

The broadcast of his visit came less than two hours after he appeared on television to read a statement urging Iraqis to resist what he called the U.S. and British "invasion" of Iraq and to "hit them hard."

The date of the recording of the brief statement was also unclear, but Saddam did make mention of an Iraqi farmer who purportedly shot down a U.S. Apache helicopter last week. It was the first time during several recent appearances on television that Saddam made a definitive reference to an event after March 20, when some 40 cruise missiles and F-117A bombs were dropped on a bunker in which Western intelligence analysts said Saddam and other senior leaders were staying. U.S. officials have not yet declared definitively whether or not they believe he survived the attack, but have suggested he was at least wounded.

"Come to jihad," said Saddam, according to a CNN translation. "Their dead are in hell and their living in humiliation. Our dead will be in paradise and our living in dignity."

He declared, "Whenever they approach you and try to attack you, depend on God and hold close to your principles. ... Dignity belongs to God and victory belongs to Iraq."

The traditionally secular leader has invoked religious tones in recent years and particularly in recent days, trying to unify the factions within his country and Muslims in general against the U.S.-led forces. Iraqi Foreign Minister Naji Sabri told the British Broadcasting Corp. Friday that the Iraqi leader was, in fact, alive. Indeed, Saddam appeared to be in good health in both appearances, but in the past, U.S. intelligence officials have noted that he has many look-alikes and doubles.

Large sections of Baghdad lost electricity Thursday as coalition forces drew within 20 kilometers (12 miles) of the Iraqi capital and captured its airport. Nevertheless, Iraqi Information Minister Mohammed Saeed al-Sahhaf launched a verbal offensive on Iraqi television by Friday morning, reading what he said was a message from Saddam. The message said Iraqis were determined to defeat and destroy the "invaders" at the gates of Baghdad and in "the land of Islam." It also called on the Iraqis to "fight them and hit them day and night, and make the land of Islam a crematorium's fire under the feet of the invaders and their faces wherever they pass."

Al-Sahhaf also warned U.S. forces at Baghdad's international airport that "unconventional weapons" would be used against them within hours. He later clarified the term, saying the unconventional weapons would be suicide bombers. The United States has long claimed that Iraq posses chemical and biological weapons, an accusation the Iraqis have denied.

"We are determined with God's will to defeat and destroy them at the walls of our cities as much as we are determined to smash their miserable armies and defeat them in every part of the land of Islam, the land of Iraq," the message said.

Al-Sahhaf concluded the message in the same fashion as previous ones attributed to Saddam: "*Allah Akbar* (God is Great). Glory for the struggling Iraqis and shame on the enemies of God and humanity. Long live Iraq … Long live Palestine!"

Has Saddam mellowed?

ANWAR IQBAL

WASHINGTON, April 3 (UPI) — Saddam Hussein has written a letter to his niece, Thurayya, according to the Iraqi government. Read on television across the Arab world on Wednesday, the letter gives interesting insight into the thinking of the man or men running

Baghdad. The urge to write to someone close in the family is natural. But not the need to have it read on the national television. Those who decided to release the letter knew that it would be broadcast across the world. Perhaps that's why the letter tries to answer all the concerns Saddam's loyalists may be having about their besieged leader.

The first point the letter attempts to prove is that Saddam is not only alive but is well enough to receive letters from his family and write back. This, of course, is intended to take care of the reports that he might have been killed or wounded in the daily pounding that Baghdad has been receiving since coalition forces launched their military offensive in the region 14 days ago.

By releasing the letter, the Iraqi regime is also sending the message that it is very much in control of Baghdad and its leader is so relaxed that he can read letters from his family and respond. The letter also tries to present a humane image of a man who has so far tried to rule with a heavy hand, killing and hounding out his own family members when they dared to challenge his authority.

It reads:

My dear Thurayya, I received your letter saying that even if the enemy reached Baghdad, you will fight as God has ordered you to do like any good Muslim. God bless us all, and that includes you and your sister Ahlam. May the enemy be defeated! We have thousands of fighters defending this land of prophets, this sacred land of ours. These young men will fight the enemies until they're defeated. God is great. Long live our people. Long live our country, and long live the spirit of Thurayya in every Iraqi citizen.

The first sentence carries two messages: Here is a man, fighting his enemies with the blessings and prayers of his family and his people. And by saying that she is doing only what "any good Muslim" will do, the letter links his niece's pledge to fight for her uncle with the religious injunction that all good Muslims should fight the invading forces if a Muslim land is invaded.

This has been Saddam's refrain since the first Gulf War in 1991. The defeat in 1991 had

turned Saddam — who until then was a declared non-believer and an Arab nationalist and who killed many Muslims for following their creed — supposedly religious. Disappointed by Arab nationalists forces that did not come to his help, he has been attempting to exploit religious feelings of the Iraqis and other Muslims since 1991, albeit without much success.

But since the beginning of the second Gulf War, the Iraqi regime has increased its efforts to coerce into action those thousands of Iraqis and other Muslims who do not necessarily like Saddam but are willing to fight the coalition forces for invading a Muslim country. Rather innocently in tone, the letter also informs Saddam's worrying niece that her uncle still has the support of "thousands of fighters" who would fight the enemies until they are defeated, if not for Saddam, for "this land of prophets, this scared land of ours." He ends the letter with his usual chants, "God is great! Long live this country," but not before adding a new chant: "… long live the spirit of Thurayya in every Iraqi citizen." This obviously is an attempt to show that all Iraqis share the spirit of Saddam's niece in defending Iraq.

This carefully crafted letter would, perhaps, have a much greater impact on Arabs in general, and the Iraqis in particular, than the diatribes broadcast daily by the official Iraqi television. It is brief. It sounds humane and sentimental. But coming from a man who did not hesitate to kill his own sons-in-law when they dared to defy him, it looks rather crafty.

The power struggle has become more intimate and more vicious during the last 20 years. In the early 1980s, the entire extended family was in power, with Saddam's half brothers, cousins and clan members part of the ruling structure. Gradually after 1988, when the Iran–Iraq war ended, Saddam began to get rid of a lot of the members of the extended family to ensure that his sons, and not another relative, inherited his throne after him.

The process accelerated after the first Gulf War, and by 1993 it became clear that the only three people who had real power in Iraq were Saddam and his two sons, Uday and Qusay. In the process, a large number of Saddam's relatives have effectively been removed from the power circle, some also from this world. And the visible signs of this exclusion came when

Saddam and his sons clashed with Saddam's brothers. In 1995, when Saddam's brothers were in charge of security and the interior ministry, they were kicked out of office and in a very dramatic way came to blows with Saddam's sons. Uday shot one of them in the leg.

But the most dramatic incident was the defection to Jordan of two of his sons-in-law, Hussein Kamel and Saddam Kamel, with their wives, Raghad and Rana, in August 1995. In February 1996, they foolishly returned home after receiving what they believed was a pardon. Within 72 hours both men were dead, gunned down and killed in their houses. Their wives, Saddam's daughters, are believed to be alive but haven't been seen in public since. Even Saddam's first wife and the mother of his two sons could not escape Saddam's wrath. She was reported to be under house arrest. She is believed to be unhappy with the regime because she blames it for making her two daughters widows.

BASRA, Iraq, April 5 (UPI) — Christopher Muzvuru of the Irish Guards, part of the elite British 7th Armored Brigade also known as the Desert Rats, mans the road to Basra, Iraq, on April 5, 2003. British troops have moved just outside the city of Basra and have been conducting raids on resistance groups in Iraq's second largest city. (Chris Corder, UPI)

Day 17 — Saturday, April 5

"We'll soon be home drinking beer." — A U.S. Marine

MARTIN WALKER

U.S. soldiers made a daring and dangerous raid into the center of Baghdad Saturday during the day, an operation carried out less to gain terrain than to prove to the Iraqis — and to a global TV audience — that they could. The fight for Baghdad was a two-front war, as American troops battled both to control the streets and to control the Iraqi and international perceptions of the battle, as Iraq's information minister maintained to Arab TV cameras that the American claims were false and the film of their invasion of the city was fabricated.

The heavily armored raid was conducted by two task forces of the 3rd Infantry Division. They began south of the city, then preceeded north to the Tigris River that bisects Baghdad, and then swung west out to the airport.

Bradley fighting vehicles and Abrams tanks battled Republican Guard, Special Republican Guard and irregular forces, fighting from infantry positions, with rocket propelled grenades and 23mm and 57mm anti-aircraft guns firing on the American force. There were moments of "intense fighting" against the convoy in some areas of the city, but elsewhere people were standing on the sidewalks waving at the American convoy.

"I think that it was very clear to the people of Baghdad that coalition forces were in the city," said U.S. Central Command Director of Operations Maj. Gen. Victor Renuart. "That

image is important, and so I think being in the daytime was a very clear — it was a very clear statement to the Iraqi regime as well that we can move at times and places of our choosing, even into their capital city."

Similar probes are likely to continue, as the U.S. military tried to walk the careful line between routing the Iraqi forces from the city and being drawn into all out urban combat. Urban fighting carries with it the possibility of massive casualties, on both sides and among Iraqi civilians, as well as tremendous damage to building and streets. A critical part of the U.S. strategy is to leave Baghdad intact and cause as few civilian casualties as possible, both of which will ease the way for a new U.S.-led interim government.

Renuart admitted the United States has had difficulty denying the Saddam Hussein regime access to the airwaves, a critical piece of the strategy to convince Baghdad the dictator's reign is finished. The longer Saddam is able to show his image on television, the longer it will take to convince the people he is gone and to switch their loyalty to the American invaders. The U.S. government is trying to find a way to prevent Iraq from getting access to satellite services.

"I can say that it appears that there are a number of satellite companies who have sold broadcast time to Iraqi National Television, and so we're trying to work in some way to encourage that not to happen," Renuart said.

The U.S. military was already invading the Iraqi airwaves, broadcasting on Iraqi Channel 3.

"We're trying to expand our ability for Iraqis (who support the United States) to broadcast on satellite television. And as we try to improve that capability and expand that capability, we will do so," Renuart said. "We're beginning to see many more leaders in the communities of Basra and An Nasiriyah, As Samawah, Najaf, even now towards Karbala, become much more supportive, openly supportive of the coalition forces as they see the threat from these other irregular troops go away. And some have expressed interest in helping to get that message out." American F-15 and A-10 "Warthog" and British Tornado warplanes circled overhead, continuously circling Baghdad on call to provide urban combat bombing support for American soldiers. Some of the aircraft were equipped with precision 500-pound "inert" bombs of concrete, which can be targeted at individual buildings without inflicting much collateral damage on surrounding areas because they do not explode. The advanced U.S. base at the airport was secured and in use by combat helicopters. One of the runways was destroyed by U.S. bombs to prevent Iraqi leadership from fleeing, but a second, civilian airstrip was found intact, albeit covered in mounds of dirt. The airport's condition is an indication that the quick feint by the 3rd Infantry Division to the airfield, rather than attacking Iraqi forces in Karbala, was successful in gaining the edge of surprise.

"It appears the rest of the infrastructure on the airport was intact, and I think the — well, the Iraqi government still today says we're not there, so clearly they weren't expecting us, so they left the airfield in a fairly operable condition," Renuart said. He could not confirm reports there had been a suicide bomb attack at the airport.

Marines and Army forces launched attacks across central Iraq, seizing a vast munitions cache in Diwaniya, about 100 miles south of Baghdad, and attacking Karbala to the southwest of the capital. They took the headquarters of the Republican Guard's Medina Division, a unit the U.S. military declared largely destroyed on Thursday. With the Army entrenched on the west side of Baghdad, Marine units are operat-

ing on the east side of the city. Renuart said the Marines have been engaged in challenging combat for the last 36 hours, some of it hand-to-hand combat with Iraqi forces.

"But that's basically infantry moving through positions on the battlefield. So I am certain that they probably had some very difficult engagements in that area," he said.

RICHARD TOMKINS

WITH THE 5TH MARINES OUTSIDE BAGHDAD, Iraq, April 5 (UPI) — U.S. Marine artillery pounded the defenders of Baghdad into Saturday morning as the 5th Marine regiment took up positions outside the city to control access into and out of the Iraqi capital. The explosions of the 155mm artillery shells repeatedly lit up the night sky, and as dawn approached Saturday the sound of helicopter gunships going about their business could also be heard.

"It topped it off just like a zit," Capt. Shawn Basco said, viewing an Iraqi armored personnel carrier destroyed by a Hellfire missile. "We're giving them a real beating. I'll bet they aren't going to be sleeping well tonight."

Basco, from Cleveland, is an F-18 pilot acting as the forward air controller for Bravo Company, 1st Battalion, 5th Marines.

As of Saturday morning the Marines were on the southeast outskirts of Baghdad, within 20 kilometers (12.4 miles) of the city's center. No immediate move was apparent to advance farther into the city. The positioning of the Marines, the exact details of which could not be disclosed for operational security reasons, coincided with the Army's 3rd Infantry Division capturing Baghdad International Airport on the southwest side of the city.

The Marines and Army have been running a two-pronged advance on the Iraqi capital. The final push up to the outskirts of Baghdad began Friday morning after the Marines had crossed over the Tigris River, late Thursday, in the dark. Although not much could be seen crossing the river, the Marines were greeted with the unmistakable smell of flowers as they did so.

The long road to Baghdad had been littered with burned out Iraqi tanks and trucks, destroyed by U.S. helicopters and jets. Also littering the road were piles of uniforms Iraqi soldiers had stripped off as they fled.

The object of the Marine artillery was the Iraqi al-Nida army division, which had been an objective since the Marines crossed the border at the start of the ground war. That division fled their billeting area as the Marines approached but were still hitting the advancing column with periodic mortar fire, small-arms ambushes and rocket-propelled grenade attacks. There were also unconfirmed reports of extremists (said to be non-Iraqis) attempting to attack vehicles in the convoy using explosives-laden pickup trucks.

"Thirty-six kilometers, 36 kilometers," one Marine yelled out earlier Friday. "We're that much closer to home. We'll soon be home drinking beer."

The sentiment was understandable, but given continued Iraqi resistance and uncertainty about what will happen when troops enter the city itself, they could just be a pipe dream.

As dawn broke Saturday, the sky toward Baghdad was dark at the lower levels of the horizon. The telltale signature of burning vehicles was the indication the artillery was doing its job. For the 5th Marines, the periodic ambushes were sporadic while the pounding of artillery was steady. There were reports of one or two suicide dashes by the small pickup trucks favored by the paramilitary forces. In all, the Marine column is composed of about 3,000 vehicles of one sort or another. The Marines heard of the capture of Baghdad International Airport through the rumor mill, after someone heard the news on a shortwave radio.

Temperatures have begun escalating, making the "MOPP" anti-chemical suits the troops have to wear very uncomfortable, particularly at the oven-like temperatures inside armored assault vehicles, where drivers can wait for hours at a time. Iraqis encountered along the road near Baghdad have seemed far more solicitous of the U.S. troops than at earlier points, waving and shouting. But the troops, unable to measure the sincerity of the gestures, remained wary. Some young male Iraqis appear too fit to be ordinary civilians, but unless they display hostile intent, they are being ignored. All vehicles have to clear Marine checkpoints.

In the distance, the bombing of Baghdad could be seen, occasionally lighting up the night sky while planes and helicopter gunships are heard clearly. The battlefield remains a constantly busy place.

A Night at the Front Line

MARTIN WALKER

We drove into the outskirts of Basra late Saturday afternoon, down the main four-lane highway from Baghdad, littered with wrecked Iraqi T-55 tanks and BMP armored cars from the initial coalition attacks. It was an edgy drive for this United Press International reporter and UPI photographer Chris Corder, along this road where two British reporters had been killed a week ago, a road still described by the British troops as "bandit country."

The sky was dark with thick plumes of greasy smoke from the oil-filled trenches the Iraqis had lit to blind the British troops, and the air tasted thick and sour. The land was flat sand, carved into nightmarish bunkers by the tank treads. Iraqi women sat by the side of the road, offering fresh tomatoes for sale from crates and buckets, on a desolate empty road that had no customers.

We were waved through one British checkpoint, where a small knot of Iraqis was being body-searched, and then past another, guarded by a British Warrior armored infantry vehicle. We drove on, past the first of the smoking trenches of burning oil, and suddenly realized that there were no more British troops in sight. We made a hasty U-turn and raced back to the British checkpoint, where an Irish Guards sergeant with a bushy red moustache was searching an Iraqi pickup truck while the rest of his squad kept watchful guard with machine guns from their foxholes.

"Any more British checkpoints ahead?" we asked him.

"No, this is it. The front line," he said. "You don't want to go past us unless you're a tank."

We parked the jeep and began interviewing the troops, who were dug in behind berms of sand, pushed up by the combat bulldozers of the Royal Engineers to provide cover. They had been taking intermittent sniper fire and the occasional mortar round throughout the day. From inside the protection of a Warrior armored vehicle, one squad with rich Belfast accents offered us a cup of tea. One of them had another accent altogether, and a big toothy grin that lit up his dusky face. Guardsman Isoa Nagera comes from the South Pacific island of Fiji, one of more than 700 who have volunteered to serve with British forces.

"It was a bit scary at first, coming under fire," he told UPI, as he lay behind the sand berm, only his helmet and the barrel of his Minimi machine gun poking above. "But I'm getting used to it. It's so great when the fire comes in and nothing hits you."

Their forward position, the furthest into Iraq's second city that coalition forces had advanced, was on the road just ahead of a badly damaged compound. A sign, perforated by bullet holes, identified it as the Basra Technical College. The ornamental gateway had been holed by a tank round, and there were smoke-blackened holes in the roofs of the workshops and garages from mortar attacks. For the British troops, this had been home for the previous 36 hours. As darkness fell, we asked if we could take cover there for the night, and they told us to park beside a Warrior armored vehicle.

Once inside, the compound was enormous — and devastated. It had been taken after hard fighting, including an air attack by Cobra helicopter gunships, and every building was damaged. But every building was full. Over 600 troops, 14 heavy tanks and 18 Warriors were camping within, without electricity or running water. Some took an hour or so to clear a room of broken glass and wreckage to lay down their sleeping bags; others just slept on the ground.

"We still call it 'Target One' because that was its name when we took the place," explained Guardsman Craig Marshal, from Liverpool. This was the temporary headquarters of the Royal Scots Dragoon Guards battle group, with their heavy Challenger-2 tanks. Attached to them were the armored infantry of the Irish Guards and the armored bulldozers of a squadron of Royal Engineers. They all had trained together at their bases in Germany to fight as a unit.

The engineers have had some of the most dangerous fighting, laying temporary bridges under fire and dousing the flames of the oil-fed trenches. The crew of "Penndragon," one of the giant armored bulldozers, showed me the scorched and charred side of their vehicle, with its melted equipment, where the fires briefly took hold as they shoveled tons of sand onto the flames.

"Don't think you're safe just because you're in here with us," grinned Cpl. Peter Chilton of Penndragon, who comes from Ashendon in Northumberland. "We get some incoming here every day. It's sniping and mortars, not very accurate, but they dart out in pickup trucks with mortars loaded on the back, fire off a few rounds, and then reverse back under cover."

Once night fell, just after 7 P.M., we were under blackout conditions. Twice, sudden alarms provoked a salvo of illumination rounds, phosphorous flares that light the sky and sink slowly to earth on their parachutes. The heavy guns fired sporadically throughout the night, and there were a few scattered shots from snipers that only served to make the silences hang more heavily.

Then it was time for patrol change, and the Challengers and Warriors reversed noisily in and out of the shattered gateway, taking up advanced guard positions. Some of the soldiers slept through it all, despite the deafening clamor of a 61-ton tank revving up 10 feet away.

We shared another brew of tea with the Irish Guards from the water heater in the back of their Warrior vehicle. Cut off from news of home, they wanted to know if the British opinion polls were still against the war (far from it!) and whether the Americans had captured Baghdad yet. And they wanted to grumble. A foul-up in the British supply system meant that only desert boots of size 8 and size 12 had arrived for them. The rest either arranged for families back home to buy some and ship them out or had to wear the heavy black leather combat boots they wore in Europe — intolerably hot in Iraq.

"And look at me bum hanging out of me cammies," said one Guardsman, who had better not be identified, who bent over to show where the material of his desert camouflage had worn away. They have only been issued with one set of camouflage clothing each — and joke that the Iraqis stay away because they smell so bad.

But life looked up this week when a British Army mobile bath unit started supplying hot showers at Basra airport — although few of the combat troops have been able to make the trip there yet.

There was a mood of suppressed excitement, some bad jokes about Army food and a lot of forced laughter and talk of home, because they all knew that a big raid was being prepared to go into Basra at dawn the next day. So far, the unit had suffered no combat deaths, although they cheerfully showed us the scar on the back of their Warrior where rocket-propelled grenades had struck with serious damage.

Each Warrior carries a driver, a commander and seven soldiers, who become a very tight-knit team despite the remarkable spread of nationalities among the troops. One platoon contained men from Northern Ireland, southern Ireland, Scotland, England, Fiji, Gambia and Zimbabwe, all volunteers and all united by a passion for the Manchester United soccer team, whose banner fluttered proudly from the back of their Warrior. They were also all members of the regiment's bagpipe and drum band.

At dawn, as they prepared to launch the attack that would capture Basra, Guardsman Christopher Muzvuru from Zimbabwe took out his chanter, a small pipe that bagpipe players use for practice, and played some Irish tunes.

"I always wanted to learn the bagpipes," he explained. "When we take Basra and all this is over, it's my dearest ambition to play before the queen."

Then the orders came. The dregs of tea were tossed aside, the chanter put away, the guns opened up and the battle group of the Royal Scots and the Irish Guards went in, driving hard for Basra.

━━━━━━━━━━━

BASRA, Iraq, April 6 (UPI) — The rear door of a Warrior armored personnel carrier from the Royal Scots Dragoon Guards, 7th Armored Brigade, aka Desert Rats, displays a little door art as the crew rests just outside a former technical school and Baath Party headquarters they had taken control of only days previous, during a dawn raid on Basra on April 6, 2003. British forces faced fierce resistance inside the city of Basra but kept driving forward, taking over control of most of Iraq's second largest city after days of fighting.   (Chris Corder, UPI)

Day 18 — Sunday, April 6

"There's no army, no organized resistance. This place is going to fall." — Guardsman Paul Caughers from Newtonnards, Northern Ireland

MARTIN WALKER

BASRA — Coalition troops took effective control of two of Iraq's largest cities Sunday amid reports of two friendly-fire incidents in the north of the country and an attack on a Russian diplomatic convoy leaving the Arab state. In Baghdad, U.S. troops faced intact Republican Guard forces north of the city and irregulars who maintained a scattered but determined resistance inside. Coalition planes dropped thousands of leaflets on the city, imploring citizens to stay inside their homes while U.S. 155mm artillery shells were lobbed into Iraqi strong points in the southeastern suburbs.

Iraqi authorities imposed an entry-exit ban into Baghdad between 6 p.m. and 6 a.m., but it was not clear what the warning would accomplish, as coalition forces extended their own control over all the southern routes of entry and U.S. Marine and armored units raced north to encircle the capital.

More explosions were heard in Baghdad earlier Sunday, several hours after a column of about 30 tanks and armored vehicles made a brief Saturday foray into the center of Iraq's capital, killing more than 2,000 defenders in the process. U.S. forces, Army on one side of the city and

Marines on the other, continued to advance and the newly captured suburban airport was the center of a widening circle of U.S. control.

Iraqi irregulars were patrolling Baghdad streets in the absence of regular army or Republican Guard troops, which U.S. Central Command officials said had been "obliterated" in the approaches to the city. United Press International's Martin Walker reported Sunday that Basra, the second-largest city, was falling after nearly two weeks of siege. He watched British tanks, backed by U.S. Cobra helicopter gunships, launch the biggest raid so far into the city, and after meeting light resistance, dig in to hold their new positions.

"It's only a few militia still fighting for Saddam Hussein now," Guardsman Paul Caughers from Newtonnards, Northern Ireland, told UPI. "There's no army, no organized resistance. This place is going to fall."

The battle for the city has raged for two weeks. Over that time, a series of raids and precise artillery barrages targeted the command posts and known positions of the Iraqi militia leading the defense. The British plan was to try to separate Saddam's loyalists from the bulk of the population. By the time Sunday's attack was launched, the defenders had been isolated and ground down. The route and targets of the Sunday morning assault were plotted overnight after reports from anti-Saddam Iraqis to the battle group intelligence officer, Capt. Paddy Truelove of the Royal Scots.

The British intelligence operation inside Basra has been closely coordinated with its humanitarian effort in the local towns and villages, and with attached SAS Special Forces units that have been conducting their own missions into the city. Local Iraqis have been providing crucial intelligence about the locations and weapons of regime loyalists like the Baath Party and the fedayeen.

Just 10 miles from the center of Baghdad, the 3rd Marines reached the southern end of the 500-feet-long bridge over the Diyala River, running wide and slow before it joins the Tigris, and ran into their toughest battle of the war. The Marines' battle for the Diyala bridge, its supports too damaged to take the weight of tanks, was to last over 48 hours. The Iraqis, Republican Guard troops backed up by fedayeen, and with strong artillery support from 122mm guns hidden

away in suburban buildings that knocked out Marine armored vehicles, fought tenaciously.

The Marines finally took the bridge in a classic infantry charge, covered by smoke and an artillery barrage, before closing with Iraqis in their trenches and bunkers.

"Blue-collar warfare," Lt. Col. Bryan McCoy called it. Hand-to-hand combat. And then another long day fighting off the suicide charges of pickup trucks with mortars and .50-calibre machine guns mounted on the rear as the Iraqis tried to push the Marines back across the river. The day before they reached the bridge, the Marines had lost a M1 Abrams heavy tank when a suicide bomber drove alongside it with a truck filled with explosives. After that, the Marines did not want to let anyone get close.

In Moscow, Russia's Foreign Ministry summoned U.S. Ambassador Alexander Vershbow and his Iraqi counterpart, Abbas Khalaf, Sunday to demand explanations for the shooting incident near Baghdad that left at least five people wounded as a group of Russian diplomats, including the envoy, and journalists headed for Syria.

Twenty-three people, including Ambassador Vladimir Titarenko, were traveling in the convoy that came under fire twice, 8 and 15 miles from Baghdad, respectively, en route to the Iraqi–Syrian border. The motorcade left Baghdad at 10:30 a.m. Sunday and traveled along a previously agreed route that had been relayed to U.S. officials, along with the license plate numbers of the cars, Russia's state-controlled RTR television network reported. The U.S. military in turn was expected to provide the so-called "green corridor," ensuring safety of the convoy on its way toward Syria.

However, the convoy was attacked by a group of soldiers suspected to be members of a U.S. intelligence platoon that apparently knew nothing about the travel, RTR reported. At least five people — all diplomats — were wounded. None of the eight journalists was injured as they traveled at the back of the convoy.

The Russians bandaged the wounded, abandoned a damaged car and kept going. Then, around 15 kilometers from Baghdad, they came upon a jeep convoy, stopped and sent a car ahead with a flag to show who they were. Then the Russians came under fire again. One of the rounds apparently hit the Russian ambassador's armored limousine and the wrecked car was left behind on the road as the convoy proceeded farther on.

Central Command in Qatar denied responsibilty, insisting that no coalition forces were operating in the area. The attack came as U.S. National Security Adviser Condoleezza Rice was flying to Moscow for talks with Russian officials Monday. The Russian media erupted with conspiracy theories about the attack, mostly suggesting that the convoy contained top-secret Iraqi documents concerning a Russian arms deal, or senior Iraqi figures, possibly including Saddam.

Centcom also said "coalition aircraft may have engaged" special operations and friendly Kurdish ground forces some 30 miles southeast of Mosul, in the vicinity of Kalak. At least one civilian and one U.S. soldier were killed in yet another of the friendly fire incidents that have marred the otherwise glittering coalition military achievement. A Kurdish soldier and four civilians were wounded, Centom said. Kurdish sources said at least 12 Peshmerga fighters and U.S. Special Forces were killed. In another friendly fire incident, Centcom said three U.S. servicemen were killed and five others wounded in an incident "involving an F-15E Strike Eagle and coalition ground forces."

In other developments, U.S. Brig. Gen. Vincent Brooks told reporters in Doha, Qatar, that U.S. Marines attacked what he said appeared to be a training camp for non-Iraqi fighters in Salman Pak, southeast of Baghdad, after being told of its existence by some captured fighters. Reports of such a training camp at that location had circulated as long ago as June.

Iraqi Information Minister Mohammed Saeed al-Sahhaf, in a Sunday afternoon news conference, said Iraqi forces killed 50 U.S. soldiers and shot down two Apache helicopters in the Baghdad area. He repeated Saturday's claim, that Iraqi forces had recaptured the Baghdad airport. He also acknowledged coalition forces were in fact in Baghdad but were only using an escape route from the airport. Iraq's Information Ministry earlier took reporters on an extensive tour of Baghdad to show there was no sign of U.S. troops. However, the tour was ended when gunfire was heard in the distance.

Looking ahead to the post-war situation, Deputy Defense Secretary Paul Wolfowitz said Sunday it would take more than six months to set up a government in Iraq after Saddam's regime is toppled. Until then, the Arab nation will be in the hands of the U.S.-led coalition.

"Six months is what happened in northern Iraq," he told Fox News Sunday. "This is a more complicated situation. It will take more than that." (Kurds began governing northern Iraq in 1991 after the first Gulf war ended.) The U.S.-led coalition will run the country until then, he said, adding he does not favor a U.N.-led government in Iraq.

"It's not a model we want to follow, of a sort of permanent international administration," he told CBS TV's "Face the Nation."

The United Nations operated such a government in Kosovo, and while wanting to curb any future role for the international body, Wolfowitz said he believed the United Nations could help in bringing humanitarian assistance to Iraqis.

"The U.N. can be a mechanism for bringing that assistance to the Iraqi people ... but our goal has to be to transfer authority and operations of a government as quickly as possible, not to some other external authority but to the Iraqi people," he said.

The Battle of Basra

Martin Walker

BASRA, April 6 (UPI) — British troops occupied the Baath Party headquarters Sunday, center of the remaining resistance in Iraq's second city, after an initial heavy raid turned into an assault on all fronts — and Iraqis welcomed them by kissing the dusty armor of their tanks.

The first two-pronged assault at dawn by the famed Desert Rats, the 7th Armored Brigade, went so well that shortly after midday British commanders ordered a third attack by the Royal Marines in the south. Then from the north came another attack from the paratroops of the Air Assault Brigade — and the full weight of the British land forces in Iraq was engaged.

Iraqi civilians braved the artillery bombardment and small-arms fire to come into the open to cheer the British troops and cry, "*Marhaba*" — greetings. They gave thumbs up to the Irish Guards' infantry rolling past in their Warrior armored vehicles. Others began looting, carrying off typewriters and furniture from offices. One group gleefully rolled away a broken down Iraqi military jeep. The Baath Party headquarters was hit by well-aimed fire by the Royal Horse Artillery, and then the infantry rushed out from their armored vehicles and took the building and its surrounding complex by storm. They kicked down doors and threw grenades inside before darting inside, their guns firing.

The Iraqi resistance was described as "weak and scattered," and no British casualties were immediately reported. But the Iraqi fire was heavy enough to force one Cobra helicopter gunship to make a forced landing outside the city. And late Sunday, sniper fire was still coming from a power station on the outskirts of the city.

The British carefully kept one Western exit from the city open, hoping the remnants of Saddam Hussein's loyalists would take their chance to flee and allow the rest of the city to be occupied without further violence. The decision to launch the attack came after British military intelligence learned that the governor of Basra province, the mayor, and the military chief of staff had all fled the city in the previous 48 hours.

Acting again on intelligence from local Iraqis obtained by the Special Air Service, the British launched a separate air strike on a building believed to be used by the remaining Iraqi southern front commander, Saddam's cousin Ali Hassan. Better known as "Chemical Ali" for his role in the use of chemical weapons against the Iraqi Kurdish village of Halabja in 1989, he has been a prime target of the coalition command. His personal bodyguard was found dead in the wreckage of the building by British troops later Sunday.

"Chemical Ali has war crimes to answer for and we are very keen to see him stand trial," British forces' spokesman Group Capt. Al Lockwood said Sunday.

Earlier, British tanks backed by U.S. Cobra helicopter gunships launched a massive raid on the city after nearly two weeks of besieging it. They met only light resistance before reaching the heart of Iraq's second city and then decided the time was ripe to take Basra.

This United Press International reporter and photographer Chris Corder spent the night on the front line with the assault troops and rose to join them before dawn for the successful attack that saw Iraqi civilians cheering the advancing British troops by the end of the morning's battle. A dark pall of greasy smoke hung over the first rays of the rising sun as the tanks of the Royal Scots Dragoon Guards stormed past the pools and trenches of burning oil. The Warrior armored infantry vehicles of the Irish Guards followed them in support as they charged directly for nearly 3 miles into the heart of the city.

The flat, slamming coughs of British artillery fire had been heard throughout the night, but at 5.30 A.M. as the tanks went in the gunfire became a barrage that ignited blossoming fireballs by the key traffic intersection known as Gate of Basra. Then the armored infantry drove through, the thudding of their 30mm cannons sounding harsh above the noisy clamor of the tank treads and interspersed with the higher burping pitch of the infantry assault weapons.

Guns supporting tanks, and tanks supporting infantry in a classic combined arms assault, the British battle group destroyed the fedayeen command post that had been their initial target and pushed on through small-arms fire and volleys of rocket-propelled grenades to the grounds of Basra University. The RPG shots bounced off the heavy armor of the Challenger tanks — one of them has, so far, taken seven hits without damage. Taking a carefully planned route to minimize civilian damage and casualties, the British fought their way with steady determination through a suburban industrial area of small factories and walled compounds, with few civilian areas.

"This is what I joined up for," grinned Guardsman Craig Marshall, from Liverpool.

As the tanks of the Royal Scots and the Irish Guards launched their assault along the main road from Baghdad, another British column to the north, spearheaded by the Black Watch regiment, launched a second attack that caught the defending Iraqis between two fires. At 6.30 A.M., after an hour of ground fighting, two U.S. Cobra gunships, on standby for the British call, flew low and fast over the wrecked technical college where we had spent the night with the assault forces, circled twice to verify targets and then swooped down from the north to fire three precise missile volleys into the last Iraqi strongholds. The British drove on, calling in artillery support as scattered small-arms fire continued to harass their advance. The Challenger-2 tanks, at 61 tons the heaviest weapon in the allied armory, pushed on to the edge of Basra old town.

"Resistance light and scattered," the advance tanks reported back by radio to the Irish Guards' forward command post.

"Hold your positions," came the reply, as the planned raid turned into a solid advance, and by midday came the words "Positions secured."

"It's only a few militia still fighting for Saddam Hussein now," Guardsman Paul Caughers from Newtonnards, Northern Ireland, told UPI. "There's no army, no organized resistance. This place is going to fall."

The battle of Basra has been a classic example of strategic patience, to take the city with the minimum of friendly and civilian casualties. Over the past two weeks, a series of raids and precise artillery barrages targeted the command posts and known positions of the Iraqi militia who were leading the defense. The British plan was to try to separate Saddam's loyalists from the bulk of the population. By the time Sunday's attack was launched, the defenders had been isolated and ground down.

The route and targets of the Sunday morning assault had been plotted overnight after reports from anti-Saddam Iraqis to the battle group intelligence officer, Capt. Paddy Truelove of the Royal Scots. The British intelligence operation inside Basra has been closely coordinated with its humanitarian effort in the local towns and villages, and with attached SAS Special Forces units that have been conducting their own missions into the city. Local Iraqis have been providing crucial intelligence about the locations and weapons of regime loyalists like the Baath Party and the fedayeen.

"A week ago, the Iraqis wouldn't even look at you," Caughers added. "Now they are cheering and waving at us."

The crowd of Iraqi civilians standing back far behind the start line of the attack, jostling with their bicycles and donkey carts and battered pickup trucks filled with fresh tomatoes to sell in the city, finally surged forward as the Irish Guards lifted their roadblock once the position was reported secure, but not before they had each been handed a leaflet in Arabic by the British troops, an advertisement asking any civilians who were interested in working for and helping the coalition forces to contact the headquarters later in the day.

Senior Airmen Greg Pelletier and Phil Soares, both security forces journeymen deployed from the 157th Security Forces Squadron, Pease Air Reserve Guard, N.H., to the 363rd Expeditionary Security Forces Squadron, authorize a vehicle to proceed through an entry control point during a sandstorm on April 7, 2003. The 363rd ESFS members work around-the-clock performing force protection measures, air base defense, and protecting personnel in support of Operation Iraqi Freedom at a forward deployed location in Southwest Asia.   (Matthew Hannen, UPI)

Day 19 — Monday, April 7

President Saddam Hussein "no longer runs much of Iraq" regardless of whether he is alive or dead. — U.S. Defense Secretary Donald Rumsfeld

MARTIN WALKER

President George W. Bush flew to Belfast, Northern Ireland, for what became a victory meeting with his closest ally, British Prime Minister Tony Blair, as Iraqis pressed kisses on the dusty British tanks in Basra and American tanks rolled along the western embankment of the river Tigris in the heart of Baghdad.

Behind the tanks, the 2nd Brigade of the 3rd Infantry Division was setting up a new command post in the new presidential palace. Journalists in Baghdad's Palestine Hotel watched U.S. infantry patrols cautiously probing the riverbank, shooting at Iraqi soldiers who had stripped to their shorts and dived into the river to escape.

Further back along the 6-mile stretch that brought Highway 8 into the capital, furious fighting erupted at three separate intersections, known to the Americans as Curly, Larry and Moe, after the comedy trio the Three Stooges. But there was nothing funny about the daring advance into the city ordered by the 2nd Brigade commander, Col. David Perkins. For him, it was the crucial battle of Baghdad.

"It was a pretty ambitious plan to come in with one brigade and take the whole city," he told reporters after the battle. "I knew that if we could stay that night, we would own Baghdad. That was the key to quickly collapsing the regime." Perkins sent his two tank battalions, the 1st and 4th of the 64th Armored Regiment, punching up Highway 8 from Objective Curly, the intersection with the Dawrah Expressway, through Objective Larry to Objective Moe, the Umm Attuboul mosque. Hundreds of Iraqi defenders let the tanks pass and then opened a furious fire on the supporting U.S. mechanized infantry from the 3rd Battalion in their Bradley fighting vehicles. At Objective Larry, where the intersection led to the Al-Jadriyah bridge across the Tigris, the 3rd Battalion came under attack from three sides. Almost every vehicle was hit by rocket-propelled grenade rounds.

Two American soldiers were killed and 12 more needed medical evacuation after the fighting along Highway 8. The defenders, a mix of Republican Guards, fedayeen and Syrian volunteers, lost over 400 killed, some of them in suicide attacks as pickup trucks packed with explosives tried to drive close to the U.S. vehicles. At times during the 18 hours of close fighting, with fuel and ammunition running out, the American troops were close to being overrun. One American fuel truck ignited after an ammunition truck beside it exploded. At Objective Curly, the enemy came so close that U.S. troops called in artillery fire so close to their own positions that two of them were wounded. But the Americans held their ground, fought off the desperate counter-attacks, and by establishing themselves firmly in the heart of the city, broke the back of the defense.

In New York, U.N. Secretary-General Kofi Annan called in members of the Security Council to discuss "developments on the ground and the post-conflict situation in Iraq" — a sign that the international community felt the war was almost over. President Saddam Hussein "no longer runs much of Iraq" regardless of whether he is alive or dead, said U.S. Defense Secretary Donald Rumsfeld as U.S. tanks and armored vehicles fought their way along Highway 8 early Monday, while Marines moved to close the noose on the city to the north and a fierce battle raged near one of Saddam's presidential palaces on the bank of the Tigris River.

The value of the palaces is both tactical and symbolic: They could yield important intelligence documents about the location of any hidden caches of chemical or biological weapons, and at the same time contribute to the perception that Saddam's regime is done ruling Iraq.

"We've secured Baghdad International Airport and have begun using it for coalition missions," Joint Chiefs of Staff Chairman Gen. Richard Myers said Monday, adding that more than 125,000 coalition troops are now inside Iraq and that a total of 340,000 are in the region.

"We've secured most of the major roads into and out of Baghdad. We've visited two of Saddam's presidential palaces. Republican Guard divisions have only been able to conduct sporadic attacks on our forces. Of the 800-plus tanks they began with, all but a couple of dozen have been destroyed or abandoned. We have more than 7,000 enemy prisoners of war. We are restoring power to cities throughout southern Iraq. And we're delivering a growing amount of humanitarian relief to the Iraqi people in various locations," Myers said.

By contrast, Iraqi Information Minister Mohammed Saeed al-Sahhaf declared that Iraqi forces had "destroyed" U.S. forces that entered Baghdad overnight and swore to "slaughter the invading troops." U.S. forces "learned a lesson last night they will never forget," he said, and insisted that Baghdad was "secure and great."

British military officials, meanwhile, confirmed that Gen. Ali Hassan al-Majid was killed in an air raid late Saturday on his home near Basra in southern Iraq. Al-Majid, also known as Chemical Ali, reportedly ordered the use of chemical weapons against Kurds in northern Iraq in 1998. He was also Saddam's cousin.

Far to the south, they cheered, they waved, they kissed the tanks. The people of Basra gave the British troops, and their political masters back in Washington and London, the TV images they needed to buttress their case that this was a war of liberation. But the scenes of unfeigned delight among the inhabitants of Iraq's second city, while gratifying and important, were not entirely what they seemed. Of all the freedoms now promised the Iraqis, the one uppermost in their minds was the fear of imminent death from the war that had descended upon their homes.

"It's over. That's what I'm so happy about," Abel Rahman al-Gazwieni told United Press International as he waited for the British troops to lift the security cordon and let him and a host of others rejoin their families inside the city. "That is why we are all happy now. No more bombs, no more shelling."

He broke off to give a thumbs up to a passing British tank. A science teacher, he said the most important things now were to get the water back on and the schools reopened, and for life to return to normal.

"But what about my money?" he wanted to know, bringing out a thick wad of Iraqi dinars, adorned with the head of Iraqi leader Saddam Hussein. "I hear the money is no longer good."

The money, in fact, has not been all that good for some time. Once, in the fat and oil rich days before Saddam launched wars against Iran and then against Kuwait, the official rate of exchange was $3 to 1 Iraqi dinar. Lately it has been more like 3,000 dinars to the dollar and few people now expect the Saddam banknotes to be in use for long.

The big problem for Abel Rahman and many other Iraqis now that the fighting is over is the threat of a dead economy and no more jobs. The curious feature of this war that many thought would degenerate into urban warfare was that house-to-house fighting was relatively rare. At Basra, and to an extent at Najaf and Nasiriyah, most of the fighting took place in the industrial areas on city outskirts, in factories and plants where the defenders had room to park their vehicles under cover.

Once stuck inside these sprawling compounds, where the militia and military commanders liked to keep their troops so that it would be harder for them to run away, they tended to get stuck there by the coalition air power. The result is that a lot of industrial plants have been damaged in the cities that saw the main fighting — which means the jobs have gone, too.

So as Basra fell and the cheerful looting began, and reports came in of Baath Party officials being lynched by the people they had misruled, other Iraqis clustered around any obvious American or European. In broken English or sign language, or clamoring for English speakers like Abel Rahman to translate, they all said they had heard the British were hiring drivers for water trucks and paying them in

U.S. dollars. Where were these wondrous jobs to be found?

It was true. Down in the border town of Umm Qasr, which depended on daily deliveries of water from Baghdad 30 miles away, the British army's civil affairs officers had indeed hired six drivers to put a tanker on every street corner at least once a day.

On the barren patch of scraped desert grit that Umm Qasr calls a sports field, the British and U.S. civil affairs units have managed to reopen the soccer field, and the first game was played on Sunday afternoon. U.S. Marines in their green camouflage smocks, body armor and helmets and guns at the ready, stood guard and smiled despite the fierce heat of the day.

Behind the soccer field, there was a sudden splash of color, neon pinks and greens and bright royal blue amid the dull, mud-brown uniformity of the Arab town. It was a plastic playground for children, with swings and slides and rockers. The Marines had brought it in, sunk the railway sleepers around it, shipped in soft sand, and installed the first and brightest-colored playground the children of Umm Qasr had ever seen.

But there were few takers, as most of them clustered around any visiting car to plead for water. It must have been sheer habit, since the water trucks were trundling down the street behind them and other kids were wheeling disused oil barrels filled with water back home on rickety homemade trolleys.

The fact is that apart from the casualties of war and overburdened hospitals there is no real humanitarian crisis in Iraq, at least in the traditional sense of famine or epidemic. The country was dependent on the U.N. food-for-oil program, but it was well organized and large stocks of food are still on hand. U.N. officials in Umm Qasr said six to eight weeks of food stocks were on hand, and that seemed to be the case elsewhere in Iraq.

Nor have there been any great floods of refugees to neighboring countries. People left the cities of Baghdad and Basra when the bombing became heavy, and regional cities that saw serious fighting, like Najaf and Nasiriyah. But when the fighting died down and people saw that the damage was limited, the British civil affairs staff say, they went home.

The real emergency now in Iraq is for medical supplies, said Dr. Dimitrius Mognie, formerly with Doctors Without Borders, who left Baghdad after making a survey of medical needs for the World Health Organization. He reported a desperate shortage of most pharmaceuticals, including anesthetics.

"They don't have drugs," he said. "I saw it myself when I visited the hospitals. I went around and checked the drug cabinets."

RICHARD TOMKINS

WITH THE 5TH MARINES OUTSIDE BAGHDAD, Iraq, April 6 (UPI) — U.S. Marine artillery pounded the defenders of Baghdad early Monday as U.S. forces neared completion of their encirclement of the Iraqi capital. The bombardment by 155mm artillery shells began Sunday evening. The explosions of shells could be heard by troops of the 5th Marine regiment, and bright flashes lit up the sky from secondary explosions. While the artillery hammered away at Iraqi positions, U.S. warplanes joined in the operation by dropping laser-guided munitions. At least three B-52 strikes could be heard in the distance — ominous multiple explosions indicating carpet bombing.

Earlier on Sunday, Marines searched a large field, once used by Iraq's Republican Guard, that contained armored vehicles, supply trucks and artillery pieces. In one abandoned armored vehicle, Marines found the remains of an MRE pack — the food rations known as Meals Ready to Eat that are given to U.S. troops.

"This is a crazy war," Capt. Shawn Basco said. "They come to us in civilian clothes, see what we've got, get some food, go back to their own vehicles and then decide not to fight."

Basco, from Cleveland, is an F-18 pilot acting as the forward air controller for Bravo Company, 1st Battalion, 5th Marines.

Iraqis in civilian clothing often walk by U.S. positions but are not challenged unless they appear to show hostile intent. Apparently some are Iraqi troops, who check things out and decide whether or not to return to their units.

It started with the kids. Somehow it always does — curiosity elbowing aside shyness of strangers and parents' admonitions for caution.

"Ameericaah?" a little girl asked a Marine who had entered her village and taken a defensive position as others began to search homes. The streets were deserted. People peered around their gates.

The Marine smiled, wiggled his fingers in the girl's direction and her fear — and that of the rest of the townspeople — melted. Within minutes people had left their houses and began to shake hands with the Marines. Liberation from the strictures of the regime of Iraqi leader Saddam Hussein had come for a nameless village just a few miles from downtown Baghdad.

Marines had visited the village in force to hunt for the people who fired two mortar rounds at them earlier in the day. An Iraqi soldier was quickly caught on the roof without a fight and taken away. Townspeople led Marines to the Baath Party headquarters where two mortars, ammunition and rocket-propelled grenades were stored. As the men of the village were questioned individually through an interpreter, the Marines searched about 100 adobe-style homes. They knocked on doors before they entered and spoke firmly but politely to the residents, relatively gentle behavior from men bearing weapons that the villagers had not seen before. Later a Marine spoke to the crowd and asked the name of the local party official. People looked sheepish and did not give it.

"I know you think Saddam Hussein may not be finished, but I'm telling you he is," said the soldier, who requested anonymity. "I know you are afraid. Look at the soldiers behind me. We've all come to rid you of Saddam. You don't need to be afraid any more."

The crowd of about 100 people immediately broke into applause. It was obvious they had learned in the past to cheer anything any official said. The response had been automatic, almost perfunctory. But the expressions of joy later when the Marines handed out food, picked up children and hugged them and passed out the furnishings of the party office led to genuine expressions of gratitude.

Later a man with two young children approached me. He looked embarrassed and through sign language indicated people were still afraid of Saddam and his party officials. He pointed to the party headquarters, pointed to himself and with one hand indicated a talking mouth, and then he brought home the message: With his thumb he drew a line across his throat and then the throats of his children.

Analysis: Saddam's Sense of Scale

MARTIN SIEFF

WASHINGTON, April 9 (UPI) — Saddam Hussein has only himself to blame for his failure to turn the city of Baghdad into a gigantic Stalingrad to confound, trap and slaughter thousands of American soldiers. It was not just that too few people were prepared to fight for him; it was also the architecture.

Had Saddam been content with the city he inherited as formal No. 2 and real strongman of the second Baathist regime in Iraq 35 years ago, he could have done it. For, as prominent Iraqi democratic dissident Kanaan Makiya, writing under the nom de plume Samir al-Khalil, noted in his 1991 classic study of Iraqi totalitarian architecture, "The Monument," Baghdad in 1968, with a quarter its current population of 5 million people, was a "much maligned, anarchic and crumbling cosmopolitan city."

It still retained large areas of "old" Baghdad "with its sectarian and ethnically divided neighborhoods, its colorful souks, its horizontal skyline punctuated with pretty vertical minarets, its inward-looking houses and shaded narrow alleyways." In other words, the perfect kind of environment in which to fight a bloody, last-ditch guerrilla war. But Saddam did not leave it that way.

As Makiya wrote, "Baghdad first began to metamorphose into its present form in the late 1970s. ... Overnight Baghdad became a giant construction site: new and wider roads, redevelopment zones ... and many new monuments — all were put in hand."

"New and wider roads ... many new monuments" — and all the new monuments had wide, magnificent arterial roads leading to them.

They all proved perfect for the armed forces of the U.S. 3rd Mechanized Infantry Division to punch into the heart of the city, demoralize its defenders and fragment their forces in a matter of only four days. There are many other reasons, many of them predicted by United Press International military analyst Thomas Houlahan, as to why Saddam failed to turn his capital into an urban stronghold to inflict significant, let alone massive, losses on the invading U.S. forces. But this one should rate highly too. The architecture of fear that he imposed upon his own city led directly to his downfall.

There is a consistent pattern to this kind of irony. Dictators have always loved monumental architecture and long, immensely broad, endless boulevards that crush the individual human being's sense of significance and worth with their overwhelming scale. But, more often than not, their boundless, megalomaniac arrogance backfires on them and they fall, plagued by their own pride and vices.

The Emperor Napoleon III of France transformed Paris into a magnificent city of glorious boulevards in the mid-19th century, giving it a splendor it retains to this day. But his real purpose was to fragment the city and allow loyal military forces recruited from the provinces to move about it easily without being stymied by urban barricades in its ancient narrow streets. His visionary scheme was meant to end the succession of urban revolutions and riots that had plagued the city for three-quarters of a century since the French Revolution, as shown in the hit musical "Les Miserables." But it failed to prevent the bloodiest insurrection of all, the rising of the Paris Commune that succeeded his own failed Second Empire in 1870. And after that was crushed, it was the democratic Third, Fourth and Fifth Republics that enjoyed the urban tranquility and magnificent architecture Louis Napoleon had wrongly imagined would perpetuate his own glory.

Adolf Hitler discovered the hard way how amazing road systems, designed to facilitate the easy conquest of his neighbors, instead ended up facilitating the destruction of his own Third Reich. Germany's national autobahn system, built in the 1930s, was a full 20 years ahead of even America's fabled interstate highway system. It greatly aided the massing of the German army for its early victorious campaigns against Poland, France and Russia from 1939 to

1941. But in 1945, the forces of the U.S. 12th Army Group driving across the Rhine to encircle Field Marshal Walter Model's armies in the Rhur instead found it a fast track into the heart of Germany, annihilating Hitler's last fading hopes of survival. In 1989, the grandiloquent scale of communist urban architecture and street planning backfired on brutal dictatorships at opposite ends of the Eurasian land mass.

First, more than a million students and their supporters demanding Western-style democracy flooded into Tiananmen Square, the colossal central staging area of Beijing in front of the ancient Forbidden City of the Old Emperors. Mao Zedong, founding father of the Chinese communist state, had razed the heart of Beijing to make Tiananmen Square a worthy city for the monumental mass spectacles that totalitarian regimes are so obsessed with holding. Instead, it became the natural focus for anti-communist revolution. And although the demonstrations were brutally crushed with the slaughter of thousands of students, Tiananmen Square's most lasting association was no longer with the supposed glory of Mao and his successors, but with the ever-reviving, uncrushable immortal human impulse to be free.

That same year, down in the Balkans, one of the endless popular demonstrations that Romania's communist dictator Nicolae Ceausescu had summoned in central Bucharest to celebrate his own genius and endless rhetorical powers finally turned on the murderous, grandiloquent old blowhard. Popular revolution spread like wildfire and Ceausescu — popularly known among his adoring subjects as "Draculescu" and "the Antichrist" — faced a firing squad on Christmas Day.

Now Saddam has joined the long and no doubt ever-growing list of monstrous tyrants who raised supposedly magnificent superhighways and monuments to their own glory, only to see them become symbols and instruments of their own ruin. The 40-foot high statue he raised to himself in the heart of Baghdad will instead be indelibly remembered by future generations of Iraqis — and the whole world — for being torn down with a noose around its neck, and its severed head then joyously passed in a spontaneous frenzied freedom ritual among a rejoicing crowd.

The other battle of Baghdad

ROLAND FLAMINI

In Iraq, the battle for Baghdad is under way, but so is the other battle for Baghdad fought on battlefields from Washington to Brussels, and from Paris to the United Nations in New York. The preferred weapons are statements, reports and memoranda; the land mines are leaks to the media.

This is the battle for who controls post-Saddam Iraq, and it is shaping up as a confrontation between the United States and virtually everybody else, ranging from faithful coalition members to opponents of the war. Like any good general, U.S. Secretary of State Colin Powell was in Brussels Thursday to reconnoiter "enemy" positions. From all accounts, he found them dug in and determined.

At NATO headquarters, where Powell discussed the Bush administration's post-war plans with fellow foreign ministers of the Atlantic alliance, spokesman Yves Brodeur said, "They did not meet to decide anything — just to get an idea of the views of different member countries." There is little question what the Europeans think. British Prime Minister Tony Blair in Washington told President George W. Bush, "There's no doubt at all that the United Nations has got to be closely involved in this process. That's not just right, it's in everyone's interest that it happens."

Following Thursday's meeting with Powell, French Foreign Minister Dominique de Villepin put it more succinctly. The United Nations, he said, "must have the central role" in the political and economic reconstruction of Iraq.

A large swathe of U.N. members has coalesced around proposals based on the Afghanistan model, a senior European official in Washington said Friday. These include a U.S.-sponsored conference of interested parties on Iraq to be held soon, bringing together representatives from exiled political groups and leading figures from inside Iraq itself. The conference will appoint an all-party interim government. Its main tasks will be to organize urgent humanitarian relief, make changes to the

Iraqi constitution, and prepare for democratic elections, the official said. The interim government will be headed by a civilian administrator appointed by the United Nations. At the same time, a peacekeeping force that could be provided by NATO will take over security duties from U.S.-led coalition forces.

Last week, the Bush administration agreed to a Security Council vote, extending the oil-for-food program for 45 days under U.N. supervision so that urgent humanitarian needs could be met. But beyond that function the U.N.'s role in putting together Iraq remains in doubt. Powell told NATO allies Thursday that the world body will not be shut out, but Washington and London should "play the leading role in determining the way forward." Powell argued that the coalition was paying for the war not just politically and financially, "but at the expense of lives as well," and therefore believed that the leadership role should be theirs.

Powell also hinted he might be willing to go part of the way and agree to a U.N. conference, and to the appointment of a U.N. liaison with the same functions that Lakhdar Brahimi has in Afghanistan. But the Bush administration is sharply divided over how much U.N. involvement is tolerable in the emergent Iraq, and some observers are not at all sure Powell will be able to get White House approval even for this minimal role without a struggle.

Based on recent developments, it looks as though the Pentagon and not the State Department has the lead in shaping Iraq's postwar political and economic future. Secretary Donald Rumsfeld and the phalanx of hard-line conservative civilians that surrounds him have cobbled up an interim administration that combines U.S. and coalition military control with some Iraqi political participation. In a beach-house outside Kuwait City, retired Lt. Gen. Jay Garner, the U.S.-appointed administrator for Iraq, and his team are putting the finishing touches to their plans for taking over in Baghdad, buttressed by American and British troops, as soon as the Saddam Hussein regime collapses.

Garner will report directly to Gen. Tommy Franks, commander of coalition forces in Iraq. But according to a report in Friday's Washington Post, Rumsfeld has now proposed the immediate formation of an interim civilian administration drawn from among Iraqi political exiles, as well as from Iraq itself. Its probable leader will be Ahmed Chalabi, head of the Iraqi National Council, and one of the leading personalities in the Iraqi opposition. Rumsfeld's move is seen by observers as an attempt to limit any action by supporters of a U.N. involvement. Chalabi — a somewhat controversial figure — also has his enemies in Washington, notably in the State Department and in the Central Intelligence Agency. But administration sources say Rumsfeld's plan already has Bush's approval in principle.

There are several reasons why involving the United Nations in reconstructing Iraq makes sense, including its experience in countries like Camdodia and East Timor. But the most compelling for the Bush administration is how politically damaging excluding the world body will be for its allies.

As news of the Rumsfeld plan crosses the Atlantic, the unease in Europe grows. One problem is that the Garner administration is open-ended, and there are reports that it could remain in place for at least 18 months. When Blair makes the case to Bush for a more-than-nominal U.N. role at their scheduled meeting in Ireland next week, he will be speaking for other European leaders — U.S. allies and adversaries alike. Having survived the war politically, Blair would face fresh problems at home if a Pentagon-run administration were installed in Baghdad for any length of time — even one that includes British troops.

In Spain, Prime Minister Jose Maria Aznar, another ally, faces punishing anti-war sentiment. With crucial provincial elections scheduled for the end of this month, his popularity rating is a disastrous 20 percent. Concerned by opposition to the war that continues to grow, Italian Prime Minister Silvio Berlusconi has recently toned down his support for the war, and a senior administration official complained last week that "Berlusconi has failed to step up to the plate." He was conspicuously absent from last month's coalition leaders' war summit in the Azores bringing together the leaders of the United States, Britain, Spain and Portugal.

In the Arab world, the presence of U.S. soldiers in the streets of Baghdad long after the conflict is sure to aggravate public sentiment, already incensed by the war. "Prolonged American military rule in Baghdad could also antagonize Iraq's neighbors, especially Turkey and Iran," the Saudi Arabian paper Arab News commented. "Both can cause a nuisance and endanger Iraq's territorial integrity and national sovereignty. ... There is no evidence that a majority of Iraqis will welcome American rule even for 18 months. An army of liberation can turn into an army of occupation almost instantly."

BASRA, Iraq, April 8 (UPI) — A burnt out Iraqi 155 tank on the southern road to Basra, Iraq, on April 8, 2003. Members of the 40 Commando Royal Marines look on. (Rex Features/UPI)

Day 20 — Tuesday, April 8

"It was really something, the children just streamed out of the gates and their parents just started to embrace us." — Lt. Col. Padilla, commander of the First Battalion, U.S. Marines

MARTIN WALKER

American tanks ranged almost at will through central Baghdad Tuesday, dominating the bridges across the Tigris and consolidating their hold on the heart of the vast and sprawling city of 5 million people against scattered but stubborn resistance from rooftops, mosques, ministry buildings and street ambushes.

Alerted by undercover agents that Saddam Hussein had been seen entering a restaurant in an apartment building in the al-Mansour district of Baghdad, a B-1 bomber was able to drop four 2,000-pound, bunker-penetrating bombs on the place within 45 minutes of the sighting. The building was destroyed, but military officials warned it may be sometime before it can be determined who was at the location in what they called a "target of opportunity."

In the day's confused fighting, at least three journalists were killed and six others injured Tuesday in incidents that destroyed the al-Jazeera television bureau in Baghdad and damaged the hotel used by more than 300 foreign journalists in the Iraqi capital. Al-Jazeera said two U.S. missiles struck its office Tuesday, killing correspondent Tariq Ayoub, 34, a Jordanian national. A cameraman, Zuheir Iraqi, was slightly injured in the attack. Just before he was hit, his camera filmed a spray of empty cartridges being ejected from an automatic rifle being fired from a balcony immediately below him.

Both journalists were standing on the roof preparing for a live broadcast amid intensifying bombardment of Baghdad when two missiles struck the building, the network said. Shortly after the bombing of al-Jazeera's office, Abu Dhabi Television's offices were hit by a missile. The network said no one was injured.

Later Tuesday, a tank shell apparently struck the 15th floor of the Palestine Hotel, killing two journalists and wounding at least three others. Reuters cameraman Taras Protsyuk, 35, and Spanish cameraman Jose Couso, 37, were killed. A Japanese cameraman working for Fuji TV was also injured.

Iraqi Information Minister Mohammed Saeed al-Sahhaf described the U.S. attack on the hotel as a "desperate attempt to weaken the capital."

Al-Jazeera correspondent Majed Abdul Haidi accused the U.S. military of "intentionally targeting" the two Arabic-language channels' offices in Baghdad. He said: "The first missile could have been excused as a mistake, but when the second one landed, and then our colleagues at Abu Dhabi were hit, it became clear the bombing is intentional."

In a statement, U.S. Central Command said coalition troops received fire from both locations and "consistent with the inherent right of self-defense, coalition forces returned fire. Unfortunately, both of these buildings were being used by journalists reporting on the war."

Despite outbreaks of looting that the British troops seemed unable or unwilling to control, the situation was starting to stabilize in the southern city of Basra. British military commanders in Basra reached an agreement with a local sheikh from the Beni Hassan tribe to establish a provisional civilian administration in the region, as the breakdown of law and order unleashed a spate of looting in the city.

"This is still a dangerous environment for our troops, and we simply do not have the time and resources to try and run the city and bring life back to normal," said Col. Chris Vernon, British military spokesman. "This is a temporary agreement with the local tribal authorities, but we think it important to demonstrate that we are not here to run the place but to let Iraqis run their own affairs."

The local leader was not named and has been given full rein to set up an administrative committee. Vernon said the sheikh offered his services and a check determined that he had authority with area tribal leaders. (The agreement did not last. The sheikh, a former Iraqi general and Baath Party official, was replaced before the end of the week, after other local citizens claimed he was too linked to the former regime.) Basra remains dangerous, with some opposition remaining despite the broad public welcome for the British troops. Two British soldiers were killed Tuesday morning, apparently as they slept. Three British soldiers were killed in the assault on the city Sunday, one by a booby trap.

British troops were moving freely through all parts of Iraq's second city by Monday evening, after the parachute regiment had moved through the narrow streets and winding alleys of the old town, where armored vehicles could not penetrate. Saddam's ornate "winter palace," with its bathroom fittings of gold and well-tended gardens, had become a base and rest center for British troops, who installed showers on the grounds once the water was restored.

Even as the fighting continued in Baghdad, the job of cleaning up was starting in the rest of the country. British Royal Engineers were clearing mines from the edges of the roads into Basra and destroying Iraqi ammunition dumps. Most of the mines were hastily laid and easily cleared, but the engineers went cautiously, wary of the kind of booby trap that had killed one of its comrades two days ago.

Just outside Najaf and east of Nasiriyah, U.S. troops mounted a series of forays into regions where they believed they might find some groups of the most dangerous remaining enemy, the Arab volunteers from other countries who came to fight for Saddam and now have nowhere to go. U.S. troops had been steered toward the area by local Iraqis who claimed the "Arab volunteers" had been stealing food from nearby farms.

"Combat operations continue east of Karbala," U.S. military spokesman Brig. Gen. Vincent Brooks said Tuesday. "The mission is increasing security and hunting down remaining hostile elements."

British troops, who claim to have "pacified" most of the region around Basra and along the main road to Kuwait, the essential supply route for the British Army and for humanitarian supplies, are organizing "sweep squads" to start hunting down the remaining pro-Saddam loyalists who fled the city of Baghdad.

RICHARD TOMKINS

WITH THE FIFTH MARINES, Iraq, April 8 (UPI) — U.S. Marines rolled into northeastern suburbs of Baghdad Tuesday, where thousands of cheering Iraqis yelled, "America, America, America," and "Bush, Bush, Bush." The Marines, led by Bravo Company, 1st Battalion, entered the area after fording a tributary of the Tigris River.

Iraqis held up children, waved white flags and showed no hostile intent. The sincerity of their emotions was unquestionable. The crescendo of welcome increased as an Iraqi woman led the Marines to a children's prison, where than more than 160 youngsters were freed.

"It was really something, the children just streamed out of the gates and their parents just started to embrace us," said Lt. Col. Fred Padilla, commander of the 1st Battalion.

Further into the suburb, at a large Baath Party headquarters, the Marines had to push people back who wanted to welcome them. The crowd had been busy looting the headquarters of everything that wasn't nailed down. At a nearby agricultural research factory and facility, scenes of people tearing away things were repeated. Again, there were cheers for the Marines.

"I feel really good today," said 1st Sgt. Bill Leuthe of Bravo Company. "I think we all do."

The suburb is definitely a poor section of the city, with open sewers and garbage strewn everywhere. Later a patrol of Marines went deeper into the suburb without incident. More such patrols were planned.

There was an incident that marred the entrance. At a village on the approach to the suburb, a man in civilian clothes jumped a wall and ran toward the lead vehicle, nicknamed the "Pork Chop Express." Three Marines in another vehicle gunned him down when he put a rocket-propelled grenade launcher to his shoulder, preparing to fire.

The arrival in the suburb culminates a long journey for the 1st Battalion from the Kuwaiti border that began March 20 and further tightens the noose around Saddam Hussein and his Baath Party lieutenants.

Civilian Rule and Its Problems: CIA Report Slams Pentagon's Favorite Iraqi

Eli J. Lake

WASHINGTON, April 7 (UPI) — The Central Intelligence Agency issued a report last week claiming that the opposition leader airlifted by the Pentagon to Iraq over the weekend, Ahmed Chalabi, would not be an effective leader to replace Saddam Hussein because many Iraqis do not like him. In a classified report distributed widely within the U.S. government, the CIA argues that Chalabi, a favorite of Pentagon civilian officials, and Mohammed Baqr al-Hakim, the leader of the Tehran-based Supreme Council for the Islamic Revolution in Iraq, have little popular support among Iraqis on the ground. Critics of the agency have questioned the report's timing and motives.

"The CIA has been bad-mouthing Chalabi and the INC (Iraqi National Congress) for years. What is surprising is that they are still devoting resources to their character assassination effort instead of other more obvious missions," said Randy Scheunemann, a longtime adviser to Chalabi and now president of the Committee to Liberate Iraq, a lobbying group formed last year to support ending Saddam's regime. "Whatever the stories the agency may be spreading, it's clear Centcom Commander Tommy Franks thinks the INC has an important role to play."

The report comes at a critical time for U.S. policy as coalition forces enter Baghdad. While publicly senior American officials have said they plan to include both Iraqi opposition leaders and leaders culled from inside the country in the next government in Baghdad, behind the scenes, hawks and doves in the administration are fighting a nasty battle over the leadership of the transition authority that replaces Saddam's regime. Chalabi has long been supported by a leading hawk, Deputy Defense Secretary Paul Wolfowitz and other advocates of regime change in Iraq.

Last week, congressional appropriators voted to funnel $2.5 billion to the State Department for reconstructing the country even though the White House originally requested the money go to the Pentagon. Senior State Department officials deny lobbying for the money. Secretary of State Colin Powell, according to two State Department officials, called the White House from his plane returning from Brussels last week to complain about a policy memo from Secretary of Defense Donald Rumsfeld calling on the White House to name the transition authority for Iraq sooner than expected.

A U.S. official familiar with the CIA report told United Press International Monday: "This is about the Iraqi interim authority. It discusses the factors likely to affect the legitimacy and acceptability of an Iraqi transitional authority in the eyes of the Iraqi public. In part it looks at Iraqi attitudes toward the Iraqi opposition and how the INC is viewed on the inside."

A former U.S. intelligence official familiar with the report said, "They basically say that every time you mention Chalabi's name to an Iraqi, they want to puke." This official, however, questioned how accurate the CIA's assessment of Iraqi politics could be given the fluidity of events on the ground there.

"I think that nobody has any idea who is popular on the ground inside Iraq," Danielle Pletka, the American Enterprise Institute's vice president for foreign and defense policy studies, told UPI. "People who say that they do, including agencies of the U.S. government, are saying so to further a political agenda."

When asked about the CIA report on CBS' "60 Minutes" Sunday evening, Chalabi said it seemed to him the agency "is more focused on me than on Saddam."

The CIA has long considered Chalabi an unsuitable leader for the government that replaces Saddam. In 1992, while the agency

supported Chalabi and an open strategy to spark a rebellion against Baghdad from the north, they also pursued a palace coup strategy without telling him. The agency has also held Chalabi accountable for compromising a coup attempt in 1995, when Saddam's men rounded up disloyal military officers the agency had hoped would kill the Iraqi leader.

Last year, the agency released an assessment of intelligence that Chalabi's organization provided to the U.S. government, concluding that approximately 30 percent of it was accurate. However, one key piece of intelligence from Chalabi's operation was firmed up over the weekend when Marines raided a terrorist training facility outside of Baghdad in Salman Pak. Defectors slipped out of the country over a year ago by Chalabi's Iraqi National Congress said the facility trained numerous al-Qaida fighters. A spokesman for U.S. Central Command said over the weekend the U.S. military had concluded the facility was being used for terrorist training.

The agency has also blamed Chalabi for predicting Iraqis would welcome American troops in the initial phases of the war, though recent reporting from Najaf and Basra suggests that the opposition leader's optimism may not have been as misplaced as at first thought.

Analysis: Coalition loses a key ally

ELI J. LAKE

WASHINGTON, April 11 (UPI) — The United States and the Iraqi people lost a valuable conciliator Thursday with the slaying of Seyyed Abdul Majid al-Khoie, scion of one of Shiism's most revered clerical families and an Iraqi leader willing to embrace Americans as liberators.

Al-Khoie was stabbed to death outside of the shrine of Imam Ali, son-in-law of the Prophet Mohammad and the first Islamic martyr. Imam Ali is the founder of the Shiite Islamic sect, to which 60 percent of Iraqis belong. Al-Khoie was in the process of giving the key to the mosque to Haider al-Kadar, a longtime ally of Saddam Hussein and widely hated in Najaf for usurping the temple's spiritual leadership.

Accounts of the killing vary, but it's thought that Al-Khoie — who had just returned to his native Iraq from exile in London — was killed by the mob because he was mistakenly associated with al-Kadar, who was also killed. Some report that Al-Khoie fired a gun inside the mosque after a disagreement with al-Kadar, an official with Saddam's Ministry of Religious Affairs. But both clerics were then hacked to death by a crowd outside the building.

The Najaf clerics had come to symbolize the Saddam regime's persecution of the country's Shiite community. Twice in the past 20 years, Saddam's men killed the grand ayatollah of Najaf, leaving the city leaderless. In 1999, Ayatollah Mohammad Sadeq al-Sadr, the leading Shiite religious authority in the world, was slain with two of his sons. Less than a year before, Al-Sadr had begun speaking out against Saddam. It is not clear what Al-Khoie was doing with Kadar or why he had given him the key. Some U.S. officials argue that Al-Khoie should not have had the key in the first place, but rather the slain ayatollah's living descendant Muqtadah.

"It was a great risk he took going to Najaf. But that was not his key to give to anyone. Particularly someone like Kadar, who was hated," one U.S. official said.

Al-Khoie's decision to allow the U.S. military to transport him from Kuwait to Najaf was also controversial. The week he left, a leading Iranian-based cleric, Ayatollah Mohammed Baqr al-Hakim, criticized the decision publicly.

"He was a very brave guy," says Dr. Mowaffak al-Rubaie, a neurologist in London who was working with Al-Khoie to form a moderate Muslim political party for Iraq. "He is by nature a high risk taker. He wanted to do something with the coalition and to help them in Najaf and Karbala without a lot of fighting."

Arriving in Najaf, one of the first things he did was to calm the crowds and urge them not to attack American military men.

In London, Al-Khoie had been consulted by Prime Minister Tony Blair on aspects of the post-Saddam reconstruction. He had also been working discreetly with the United States on the State Department's "Future of Iraq Taskforce," a committee consisting of Iraqi dissidents that discuss a wide range of issues germane to rebuilding their country. Al-Khoie was a member of the task forces on local governance and civil society. He was an early critic of the attacks on Sept. 11, 2001. On Oct. 4, 2001, he wrote in Al-Hayat, the most respected Arab language newspaper, "What happened on 11 September … was a criminal and barbaric action totally remote from moral values and religious and human principles." His foundation was instrumental in setting up Shiite mosques throughout the world.

Representatives of six Iraqi opposition groups are to meet on Tuesday in Nasiriyah. Al-Khoie's presence will no doubt be missed.

Iraq's vanished middle class

SAM VAKNIN

Iraq had no middle class to speak of until the oil boom of the 1960s and 1970s. At the turn of the previous century, Baghdad sprawled across a mere tenth of its current area. However, since then and as late as 1987, the Iraqi capital was renowned throughout the Arab realm for its superior infrastructure, functioning services, splendor, conspicuous consumption and educated populace. "Baghdadi," in many Arab dialects, meant "big spender."

Two-thirds of all Iraqi children attended secondary school, thousands studied abroad, and women actively participated in the workforce. The oil wealth attracted hundreds of thousands of menial laborers from Africa and Asia.

It was Saddam Hussein, the country's tyrant, who rattled the moribund and tradition-bound entrenched interests and ratcheted up living standards by imposing land reform, increasing the minimum wage and expanding health care.

Even the Iran-Iraq war, which decimated tens of thousands of intellectuals and professionals, barely dented this existence. Rather, the middle class — mostly Sunni — was done in by the sanctions imposed on Iraq, the aggressor in the first Gulf War, after 1991. Iraq's relatively affluent and well-traveled urban denizens had access to all the amenities and consumer goods — now proffered by the impoverished owners in improvised curb markets. As wages and the dinar plummeted, once-proud Iraqis were reduced to agonizing, humiliating and sometimes life-threatening penury.

Prostitution, street kids and homelessness have flourished. Divorce and crime rates are sharply up. Young couples cannot afford to marry, so promiscuity and abortions are in vogue. At the other extreme, Islam — both moderate and fundamentalist — is making headway into a hitherto devoutly secular society. Head-scarved women no longer are a rarity.

Official unemployment is about 20 percent but, in reality, it is at least double that. Polyglot professionals with impressive resumes drive taxis, moonlight as waiters or sell vegetables from rickety stalls.

According to Humam al-Shamaa, professor of economy and finance at Baghdad University, quoted by the Asia Times, one in every two Iraqis are employed in agriculture — most of it subsistence farming, raising cattle and poultry. Many an urbane urbanite now tends to tiny plots, trying to eke a living out of the fertile banks of the two rivers — the Euphrates and the Tigris.

Industry — cement and petrochemicals — is at a standstill due to the dearth of raw materials and spare parts delayed or banned by the ponderous sanctions committee. The currency collapsed from $3 to the dinar to 3,000 dinars to the dollar. Iraqi Airlines pilots saw their monthly earnings plunge from $1,500 to $2.50. Malnutrition and disease prey on the traumatized and destitute remnants of the bourgeoisie, the erstwhile nobility of the Arab world. The virtual elimination of the purchasing power of one of the richest Middle Eastern countries has had a profound impact on neighbors and trade partners across the region.

The U.N. Human Development Index has chronicled the precipitous decline of Iraq's ranking to its 127th rung. The New York-based Center for Economic and Social Rights says that "Iraqis have been extremely isolated from the outside world for 12 years. The mental, physical and educational development of an entire generation has been affected adversely by the extraordinary trauma of war and sanctions."

Public services — from primary healthcare through electricity generation to drinking water — were roughly halved in the past 12 years. Quality has also suffered. Gross domestic product plunged by four-fifths. With infectious diseases on the rampage and a debilitating stress load, life expectancy dropped — men now survive to the ripe old age of 57. Infant mortality, at 93 in 1,000 live births, soared. Three-fifths of the population depend on an efficient system of government handouts. An exit tax of more than $350 virtually fenced in all but the most well-heeled Iraqis. The U.S. administration, in the throes of preparations for the reconstruction of a postbellum Iraq, acknowledges that the rehabilitation of the war-torn country's middle class is the cornerstone of any hoped-for economic revival.

But income inequality and a criminalized regime led to huge wealth disparities. The tiny, fabulously rich elite beholden to Saddam (the "war rats") is removed from the indigent masses. They make the bulk of their ill-gotten gains by maintaining Saddam-blessed import monopolies on every manner of contraband, from building materials and machine spare parts to cars, televisions and beauty products.

Bush administration officials estimate that the dictator and his close, clannish circle have secreted away more than $6 billion in illicit commissions on oil sales alone. But the proceeds of smuggling and intellectual property piracy have trickled down to a growing circle of traders and merchants. So has the $30 billion influx from the oil-for-food scheme, now in its eighth year — though, as Hans von Sponeck, head of the program between 1998 and 2000, observed in the Toronto Globe and Mail: "Until May of 2002, the total value of all food, medicines, education, sanitation, agricultural and infrastructure supplies that have arrived in Iraq has amounted to $175 per person a year, or less than 49 cents a day."

This has made postwar reconstruction impossible, and ensured mass unemployment and continuing deterioration of schools, health centers and transportation. "Smuggled" oil revenues represent only a small fraction of oil-for-food funds. Even here, an estimated three-quarters of these funds have been directed to social services.

Still, the economy has been partly remonetized and is less insulated than in 1996. Even the Baghdad stock exchange has revived. Whatever the length of the war, its outcome is said to be guaranteed — the ignominious demise of the hideous terror regime of Saddam. Then, the scenario goes, U.S. and British "liberators" will switch from regime-change mode to the nation-building phase. Iraq will once again become the economic locomotive of the entire region, prosperous and secure.

But the bombed and starved denizens of Iraq may be holding a different viewpoint. Quoted in The Californian, Terry Burke and Alan Richards, professors at the University of California, Santa Cruz, noted that "the invasion and air attacks are forging intense hatred against the United States that will undermine any hope of gracefully replacing Saddam Hussein's dictatorship."

It would be instructive to remember that the 1958 overthrow of the monarchy by the Free Officers, followed by the Baath Party in 1968 and, later on, by Saddam, represented the interests of the lower-middle class and petty bourgeoisie: shopkeepers, low- and mid-ranking officials and graduates of training schools, law schools and military academies.

The most important economic policies in the past four decades — agrarian reform and nationalization of oil — catered to the needs and aspirations of these socio-economic strata. The backbone of Saddam's regime is comprised of bureaucrats and technocrats — not of raving rapists and torture-hungry sadists, as Western propaganda has it.

Saddam's days might well be numbered, but the levers of power — based on tribal affiliation, regional location, religious denomination and sectarian interests — will survive intact. If the West really aspires to resuscitate a stable Iraq, it has no choice but to collaborate with the social structures spawned by the country's long and erratic history. The Ottomans did, the British did — the Americans will too.

NORTHERN IRAQ, April 9 (UPI) — Airman 1st Class Edward Grofoot, 100th Security Forces Squadron, Midenhall Air Base, 86th Expeditionary Contingency Response Group, greets local children during patrol on April 9 in support of Operation Iraqi Freedom. Children and adults in this region have been supportive and friendly to the coalition forces here. Operation Iraqi Freedom is the multinational coalition effort to liberate the Iraqi people, eliminate Iraqi's weapons of mass destruction and end the regime of Saddam Hussein. (Tech. Sgt. Rich Pucket, U.S. Air Force, UPI)

Day 21 — Wednesday, April 9

"The game is over." — Mohammed al-Douri, Iraq's ambassador to the United Nations

MARTIN WALKER

Jubilant crowds took to the streets in Baghdad Wednesday, looting and celebrating the apparent demise of the Iraqi regime and enthusiastically accepted the help of an American tank to topple a giant statue of Saddam Hussein. Draped briefly in an American and then an Iraqi flag, the statue's fall was a moment of high symbolism that seemed to signal the war's end, although the White House urged "utmost caution" as sporadic resistance continued throughout the city. A full-blown firefight erupted between coalition troops and Iraqis near Baghdad University.

When the tank finally pulled the 50-foot statue to the ground, the people in the town square rushed to dance atop it. They then separated its head and dragged it through the streets of Baghdad, some slapping it, others kicking it. Other symbols of Saddam's rule, including giant portraits, were defaced and beaten with footwear, a symbol of denigration. These acts were previously punishable with death.

As Iraqis and a wider Arab audience sought to comprehend the implications of the defeat of what had once been the leading military power of the Arab world, Abu Dhabi TV analyst, Marwan Bishara, a Palestinian, said what happened in the Iraqi capital Wednesday was typical of the Arab status: "We either live under foreign occupation or under dictatorships and tyrannical regimes." He said it was time the Arabs began learning lessons from their "miserable history."

In Basra and Baghdad, other symbols of the regime were on display, as Iraqis led Western TV crews into the torture chambers and prisons of the Baath regime, and British and American soldiers poked through the wreckage of the many shattered palaces of Saddam, his sons and cronies. Among their findings, $100 bills charred at the edges, where Saddam's son Uday had used them to light his cigars.

Advancing U.S. troops met little or no resistance from Iraqi forces and paramilitary units. There was no sign of members of Saddam's ruling Baath Party, and the daily news briefing with Iraq's Information Minister Mohammed al-Sahhaf was canceled because the man Western audiences have begun to recognize as Iraq's face of the war did not turn up. City police were also absent.

Iraq's ambassador to the United Nations, Mohammed al-Douri, told reporters in New York, "The game is over," while diplomatic sources said Iraq's ambassador to Egypt, Mohsen Khalil, demanded political asylum in Yemen and in Moscow.

In the northern city of Erbil, jubilant Kurds — victims of Saddam's weapons of mass destruction in 1987 in Halabja — took to the streets to celebrate. Similar scenes were seen in Shiite population centers to the South. But the evident collapse of the regime was paralleled on the northern front, where Kurdish militia backed by U.S. Special Forces followed up retreating Iraqi troops to the gates of the main northern cities of Kirkuk and Mosul.

The Kurdish advance alarmed Turkey, which has long feared the emergence of a de facto independent Kurdish state as a magnet for its own dissident Kurdish minority, despite the protestations of Kurdish leaders that they would stick to their agreement with the United States to accept autonomy within an integral Iraqi

state. Arabs imported into the northern cities by Saddam to strengthen the regime's demographic hold on the north began to flee southward, and local Iraqi military commanders were reported to be negotiating for a cease-fire. The prime U.S. demand was for any explosives in the northern oil fields to be dismantled.

"I think we are at a degree of a tipping point for the population that recognizes that the regime is gone," said coalition command spokesman Brig. Gen. Vincent Brooks.

Gen. Richard Myers, chairman of the Joint Chiefs of Staff, warned that coalition forces still had to contend with Iraq's special security organization — the Special Republican Guard — death squads and Baath Party members.

"In terms of regular army, there are about 10-plus regular army divisions left in the north, and perhaps as much as one brigade of a Republican Guards division up there, an infantry division, that we think is still left in the north," he said. For the U.S. and British military, the imperative of protecting their own forces had a far higher priority than restraining looters or protecting the hospitals, banks and museums, which began to fall prey to the breakdown of law and order.

On the humanitarian front, U.N. agencies warned that civil disorder and looting in Iraq were blocking relief for hospitals and thousands of injured and sick Iraqis. They called on the "belligerents" to restore civil order as soon as possible so relief supplies could arrive from Jordan and Kuwait and critical supplies could be delivered to hospitals. An interim U.S. administration, led by retired Lt. Gen. Jay Garner, had already begun working on humanitarian operations from its base in Kuwait and was preparing to move to Baghdad once the city was fully secured. A meeting of Iraqi notables, including tribal leaders and exile figures, was planned to meet in the southern city of Nasiriyah. U.S. Army engineers had already begun trying to restore Baghdad's electricity supply, and the vast work of cleaning up and restarting something like normal life for Iraq began. But already there were signs that the United States was eyeing another potential target.

"I've accurately observed that they (Syria) would be well advised to not provide military capabilities to Iraq. They seem to have made a conscious to decision to ignore that," said U.S.

Defense Secretary Donald Rumsfeld at his daily Pentagon news briefing. "Senior regime people are moving out of Iraq into Syria, and Syria is continuing to send things into Iraq. We find it notably unhelpful."

In an interview with Spain's El Pais newspaper, chief U.N. weapons inspector Hans Blix criticized Washington's decision to go to war in Iraq. More inspections could have resolved the impasse, he argued, and noted that after 21 days of war and widening occupation, no evidence of chemical, biological or nuclear weaponry had been found.

It was not quite over. United Press International's Rick Tomkins, embedded with the 5th Marines, filed this report from the capital on the day after the city's liberation.

RICHARD TOMKINS

WITH THE FIFTH MARINES, Iraq, April 10 (UPI) — Marines in Baghdad were hunkering down for an expected tense night Thursday at the Al-Azimiyah palace compound following fierce fighting earlier in the day against Iraqi soldiers and other gunmen. The fighting began before dawn as the 1st Battalion, 5th Marines, rolled down highways and streets in eastern Baghdad toward the 17-acre compound. One Marine was killed and 35 others were wounded in street battles against Iraqis firing automatic weapons and rocket-propelled grenades from bridges, rooftops, balconies and alleyways near the palace on the east bank of the Tigris River.

The exact number of attackers killed was not immediately available, but more than a dozen bodies were seen on the streets. The attackers appeared to be a mixed bag of forces — men in army green, others wearing all black, and some in civilian clothes. Marine intelligence sources told United Press International that about a half dozen Syrians, Jordanians and Algerians had been detained Wednesday and were suspected of heading to Iraq to fight.

The presidential palace, built for the former Iraqi leader Saddam Hussein, is an ornate two-story structure that had been badly damaged by coalition airstrikes and was deserted. But as the Marines entered the 17-acre compound they came under fire from Iraqi gunmen. Intense gunfire and rocketry lasted 4 1/2 hours before becoming sporadic.

As the Marines reached the palace, rocket-propelled grenades began to rain down on their convoy. Three Marines were wounded when a grenade struck their armored vehicle while they were firing at Iraqi forces. Another grenade struck the company's command vehicle, but no one was injured.

"Hang in there, kid. Keep thinking of your daughter that is about to be born," Capt. Jason Smith, commander of Bravo Company, told one of his Marines who had been severely wounded.

While the more seriously injured Marines were evacuated, Marines not seriously wounded rejoined the fight around the high-walled compound.

"This is the lousiest birthday I've ever had," said Capt. Shawn Basco, an F-18 pilot attached to Bravo Company as a forward air controller. "Happy birthday to me. Where's my cake?"

Basco, from Cleveland, braved enemy fire throughout the day and coordinated miracle evacuation flights while carrying the wounded to a grassy area near the compound's riverside swimming pool. The area was being used as a helicopter loading area. Only after the fighting died down did Basco notice the blood on his pants leg and the pain from a shrapnel wound. Basco was not evacuated.

By late afternoon, Marines were establishing a perimeter defense and said they expected mortar and RPG attacks during the night.

Saddam's Jester

Roland Flamini

To millions of Western viewers, Iraqi Information Minister Mohammed Saeed al-Sahhaf is the comic relief in the Iraqi tragedy. He is the porter in "Macbeth"; the grave digger in

"Hamlet." His comments provide a backdrop of gallows humor as the Saddam Hussein regime unravels before a disbelieving world public on television. Al-Sahhaf's version of developments has added a touch of the bizarre to the battle for Baghdad. Some examples from Sunday's U.S. incursion into the center of the city:

> With U.S. heavy armor grouped around Saddam's main palace and the crump of artillery reverberating through the city, he insisted that there was "no presence of the American villains in the city," because their advance has been defeated.

> As U.S. military C-130 transporters thundered down the runway of Baghdad airport Sunday, al-Sahhaf was still saying that the airport was not in American hands. He also said large numbers of U.S. troops had been "poisoned" as they attempted to approach Baghdad. At one point — surrounded by Arab and Western journalists — he again denied that there were U.S. troops in the streets. Someone asked him what all the firing in the streets was about. Those are our soldiers chasing the Americans out of town, he replied.

In the Arab world, however, al-Sahhaf's daily TV appearances, carried on Arab channels and often without the reality check of CNN or another Western channel, have made him a star. In an extremely unpopular war, he tells Arabs from the Atlantic to the Gulf what they want to hear.

Television images showing the U.S.-led military presence in parts of Baghdad and inside presidential palaces in the capital and Basra in the past days were hard to dispute. But al-Sahhaf is not imparting information, he is engaged in psychological warfare. He is playing on a particular Arab trait of clinging to fantasy in the face of stark reality.

To some degree, people everywhere believe what they want to believe. In the Arab world this trait is embedded in culture; it is often life itself.

On Monday, Arabs were stunned by the early morning images of American soldiers and tanks apparently wandering freely through the streets of Baghdad. But the appearance of al-Sahhaf vigorously denying the evidence of their very eyes cheered them up. Tanks? What

tanks? U.S. soldiers were "committing suicide against the walls of Baghdad," etc., etc.

This time al-Sahhaf had to go to the Palestine Hotel, where journalists have been staying since they evacuated Al-Rasheed and the Mansour Melia hotels. The usual venue was the Ministry of Information, but that was "a dangerous zone." Actually, U.S. troops claimed to have temporarily entered it, along with the Al-Rasheed Hotel.

Al-Sahhaf wore his usual military styled fatigue and black beret. The usual self-assured smirk was a little out of focus and the bulbous nose sweated a little in the camera lights. That and the occasional anxious sidelong glance at the camera were dead giveaways that Baghdad's voice of truth was a little nervous. But the rhetoric poured out with its rapid-fire automobile-salesman delivery. There was nobody in the presidential palace. Iraqi forces had "destroyed" the American soldiers. His invitation to the journalists to go and see the bodies of the dead Americans in the streets was rhetorical, since journalists appeared still not to be allowed to move about freely in Baghdad and had to wait for organized tours by the Iraqi Foreign Ministry for their own "safety."

Arabs are also fascinated by al-Sahhaf's use of the Arabic language. Even Arab journalists had to check their dictionaries — sometimes unsuccessfully — for a correct translation of some word or expression he used. He can get vitriolic when describing the coalition forces, particularly President George W. Bush and British Prime Minister Tony Blair. His preferred word for U.S. and British soldiers is "Oulouj," which in the dictionary means infidels, but al-Sahhaf once explained to a Lebanese satellite TV station that he meant "leeches."

Al-Sahhaf's early accounts of ongoing battles in the first two weeks of the conflict turned out to contain more than a grain of truth as the U.S. and coalition forces took casualties and suffered some setbacks, though he has never discussed Iraqi military casualties — only civilian victims. But as the coalition has moved into Baghdad, his statements have become increasingly surreal to Westerners. To the wider Arab world, what he says is less important than the fact that his appearances mean the Iraqi government has not been toppled. But while al-Sahhaf promises resistance and the defeat of coalition forces in Baghdad, a rapid process of corrosion is leading inexorably to an Iraqi defeat. The Arabs will miss him.

Also, it seems, will many Westerners. In the U.K. press, his bombastic optimism quickly earned the nickname "Comical Ali," an echo of "Chemical Ali," the nickname of the Iraqi general who ordered the 1988 gassing of the Kurds.

Western entrepreneurs swiftly saw an opportunity. The first product on sale in London and New York was a talking "Disinformation Minister" doll featuring some of al-Sahhaf's choicest quotes. The online auctioneers, eBay, features al-Sahhaf mugs and recorded compilations of his finest performances.

The Web site www.welovetheiraqiinformationminister.com puts him at the scene of great historic moments like the 1815 battle of Waterloo between the British and the French, where Comical Ali insists that Napoleon is winning all along. And T-shirts with al-Sahhaf's face alongside the caption "We are in control" have become collectors' items.

"We've sold over 5,000 of that one," said Elizabeth Ryan of Rivals Digital Media. "It's interesting that it went global as soon as all the press interest started. It was in quite a lot of the U.K. national press, and we've had interest from CNN in New York and a couple of South African radio stations, and even the Indian press and also France. So it's kind of gone all over the place. Sky News and the BBC also bought some for their news teams as a bit of a joke."

The Observer, a British Sunday paper, found al-Sahhaf's most devoted fan — his son Osama. He said his father is a "good man ... a very friendly guy."

To the surprise of many who had come to see al-Sahhaf as the public face of the Saddam Hussein regime, he was not featured on the U.S. list of the Baghdad regime's 55 most-wanted men — largely because there is no evidence that the veteran journalist was directly responsible for any atrocities.

But al-Sahhaf's old colleagues in the Iraqi media of the 1960s have few warm memories. Kamran al-Karadaghi of Radio Free Iraq, who worked with al-Sahhaf at Iraq National Radio, recalled: "He used to walk with this stick and he used it sometimes on people if he didn't like something. Then when he became the general director he used to beat a lot of people with it. Sometimes even some artists, for example. I remember I used to work at the radio at the time in the Russian service. We would sometimes hear people screaming in the courtyard, and then we'd look through the windows and see al-Sahhaf chasing somebody and beating them with a stick."

Iranian newspapers carried reports this week that al-Sahhaf had committed suicide, hanging himself as the U.S. troops got so close that he even he could not deny that Baghdad had finally fallen.

CHAPTER 4
AFTERMATH

INCIRLIK AIR BASE, Turkey, April 14 (UPI) — 39th Security Forces members Senior Airman Michael D. Vuyancih and Airman Ist Class Aaron L. Kuckovic plot traffic control points during a security forces exercise at Incirlik Air Base, Turkey. (Joseph Thompson, U.S. Air Force/UPI)

The Anglo-American alliance wins again

MARTIN WALKER

BASRA, Iraq, April 7 (UPI) — The rule of Saddam Hussein is over. Iraq's capital of Baghdad awoke Monday to find American tanks on the grounds of the presidential palace and the second city of Basra thrilled to its first full day of freedom from Saddam's Baathist regime.

This double triumph of American and British military machines could hardly have been better timed, as U.S. President George W. Bush and Britain's Prime Minister Tony Blair prepared for their summit in Belfast, Northern Ireland. Their war plan vindicated, their critics at least briefly silenced, the two English-speaking leaders who had defied so much of world opinion and conventional wisdom enjoyed another extraordinary bonus as their predictions of a liberator's welcome by the Iraqi people finally came true.

Confounding the Arab media and the pundits who had talked darkly of a new spirit of Iraqi patriotism resisting the invaders, the people of Basra braved gunfire to dance in the streets and cheer for the British troops who finally broke the grip that Saddam's dreadful regime had exerted on Iraq for so long. This reporter saw one Basra citizen even kiss a British tank.

Iraq, the Middle East and — if they so choose — a new world order is now for Bush and Blair to define. The world's enduring, and only reliable military alliance has done it again.

Or rather, the world's two best militaries delivered the outcome their political masters ordained, and did so with minimal friendly and civilian casualties.

But as Bush and Blair hail the magnificent achievements of their troops Monday, there are some small and familiar but ominous clouds on the horizon. Each man will have been delivered briefing books by his respective staff on the new post-war challenges. There will be fat tomes on relations with Russia's prickly President Putin, with France and Germany and that curiously named entity the European Union, a body that seems designed to illustrate that traditional Texan description "all hat and no cattle."

The two men also have to agree on the governance of postwar Iraq and the role of the United Nations, the body that reacted to its first real post-Cold War crisis by reverting to Cold War-style division and immobility.

All of these issues boil down to one overwhelming question: What does the Anglo-American alliance now do with a world that so dislikes what is good for it?

It is very odd. The Americans and British stand for a world based on a handful of principles that have stood the tests of time: representative and democratic government, free speech and free press, free economies, free trade, human rights and the rule of law.

The verdict of our times is already in. Those countries and regions that have embraced these core principles, from Japan to Western Europe, from South Korea to India, have seen their people prosper beyond any dreams possible in the wreckage of 1945. Middle Eastern countries that try the same medicine may in the not so distant future look back on this seedbed year of 2003 with a similar complacency.

Yet so many of the beneficiaries of the Anglo-American principles that defined, protected and enriched the West after 1945 evidently resent their benefactors. Throughout the grim diplomatic weeks before the Iraqi war began, the United Nations became a conspiracy of anti-Anglophones, conspiring to frustrate the best efforts of Washington and London to make U.N. resolutions actually mean something. There are two big questions for Bush and Blair to tackle in Belfast Monday. Why should this be? And does it matter?

There is one simple answer: Stick to the Anglo-American principles that have worked. If other countries and institutions want to cooperate for their own good, fine. They deserve all the help and support that the world's only two serious powers can provide. If they don't, that is their problem. The Anglo-American principles are too proven in their success to be compromised for any passing diplomatic comfort or advantage.

Also, build on success. The Anglo-American alliance, based on principles, political will, and a mutual loyalty and trust unique among nations, has once more proved its value. Strengthen it further by allowing British and American — and Australian — citizens to live and work and study and trade in one another's countries at will. In everything that matters, they comprise a single culture, and Blair and Britain should be rethinking their "European vocation" with that plain fact firmly in mind.

If Bush and Blair should mark one small regret about the double liberation of Baghdad and Basra, it is the seizure by U.S. tanks of the Ministry of Information in Baghdad. The end of the daily antics of the Minister, Mohammed Saeed al-Sahhaf, the "Baghdad Blowhard," is a sad loss. He provided comic relief throughout the 19-day war. Silence may now befall the man who produced a timeless comic masterpiece in his wondrous response to the capture of Baghdad airport — "We have them where we want them — surrounded and doomed."

War crimes trials permitting, this man has a future on Comedy Central — or maybe Madison Avenue. After all, one of the many things that Anglo-American alliance has in common, to the bafflement of much of the rest of the world, is a sense of humor.

After Saddam, Osama?

MARTIN WALKER

KUWAIT CITY, April 9 (UPI) — Pro-Western reformers in the Arab world have long been gripped by the nagging worry that the arrival of democracy would not install a happy new era of freedom and prosperity. They fear it could elect a series of fundamentalist Islamic governments. And at some point in the next year or so, Iraq now looks likely to put that fear to the test.

The Belfast summit between President George W. Bush and his trusted ally, British Prime Minister Tony Blair, agreed on one key principle for Iraq's future — that it should be run by the Iraqis themselves. It was "a false choice," Blair insisted, to debate whether the United Nations or the American and British forces in place should run the interim government.

"It will be run by the Iraqi people," Blair insisted.

"From day one, we have that the Iraqi people are capable of running their own country," stressed Bush.

It is too often forgotten that Iraq has some experience of democracy. From 1931, when the British handed the reins of government to the constitutional monarchy of their World War I ally King Feisal, until Gen. Abd al-Karim Qasim's coup of 1958, Iraq had elected parliaments, the rule of law and separation of powers. The British kept two military bases in the country, and considerable influence.

The period was in many ways a success. Under British tutelage, public health and education blossomed, and the ancient canal and irrigation systems were restored. Iraq had the liveliest and most free press in the Arab world, and Baghdad became a vibrant cultural center.

But like the British before him, King Feisal and his successors, and the longest serving prime minister, Nuri Said, relied heavily on the Sunni minority to run the bureaucracy and the officer corps, to the resentment of the Shiite majority of the south and the Kurds of the north. They also depended on the traditional tribal leaders as a counterweight to the labor and communist movements in the fast-growing towns and cities. The monarchy was staunchly pro-Western, which proved a major factor in its overthrow by a pan-Arabist military coup.

The lessons here for the future are clear. The post-Saddam government will have a federalist structure, with wide autonomy for the Kurds and Shiites. It will need to keep a tight rein on its army. It will probably need to demonstrate that it is not a pawn of Western interests, particularly the American and British oil giants.

It will have to come to an accommodation with the tribes, which remain a powerful force of identity for at least half the population. And the tribal sheikhs, wooed with cash and promises in recent months by undercover British and U.S. agents, are already reasserting their authority as the collapse of Saddam's Baath Party leaves a vacuum of power.

In Basra this week, the British agreed with a leader of the Beni Hasan tribe that he would assemble and chair a new interim local administration, to clear the garbage, open the schools, handle food distribution and to start rebuilding a police force. In Najaf, tribal leaders and local teachers and doctors are working with the U.S. troops to reopen the schools and hospitals. Facts are being created on the ground, and the new government will have to tread carefully.

But there is a worrying new factor that the old Iraqi monarchy never had to worry much about — fundamentalist Islam. Saddam tried to repress it, even as he began parroting Islamic slogans and building massive mosques. He failed, even among the Sunni, where the venerable Muslim Brotherhood has undergone a revival. Islamic parties have won around 20 percent of the vote in Kurdish elections. One of the most influential exile groups, the Supreme Council for the Islamic Revolution in Iraq, the leading opposition force among the Shiites, has been based in Tehran and absorbed many of the theocratic Islamic principles of the ayatollahs.

The fear that an Arab state brave enough to experiment with democracy would be overtaken by Islamic fundamentalism has worried Arab reformers since the Algerian elections of 1992, when the army stepped in to block an Islamic victory at the polls. The remedy may have been worse than the cure; the subsequent civil war has claimed an estimated 150,000 lives.

Egypt's Hala Mustafa, a reformer who edits the pioneering quarterly journal "Democracy," argues that democracy is too great a shock for the demoralized and impoverished Arab world, and that the ground must be carefully prepared through education, the media and the deliberate cultivation of civil society, public debate, political parties, an independent judiciary and public interest groups.

"In this country (Egypt), if you say 'Have free elections,' the next day you'll have the Islamists in power. No doubt about it. So you must first modernize and secularize to predispose society to democracy," she says.

In Iraq, faced with the immediate tasks of rebuilding and international clamor for a U.N. role and a swift end to Anglo–American military rule, there may not be time for such careful preparations. And 30 years of brutal Baathist rule is not the best preparation for the instant plunge into democracy. The worst outcome of all would be for Saddam to be replaced, with an electoral mandate, by someone whose real loyalty is to Osama bin Laden.

Baghdad, the stricken city

NICHOLAS M. HORROCK

BAGHDAD, Iraq, April 17 (UPI) — The waiter in this small hotel by the Tigris has been kind to me, finding me tea when there is none and a bowl of soup after it is all gone. He is a dignified man, 53, once an engineer, with a trim mustache, wire eyeglasses and a gentle manner.

It is not easy in the hotel, packed with journalists, peace activists, homeless Iraqi families, working without electricity, walking miles to work and facing a complete body search by U.S. Marines each time he comes to work or leaves. Early Thursday morning he looks stricken and I ask him what is wrong. "My country," he says, "it has been destroyed. It is no more."

Perhaps, perhaps not. But certainly he and his country and its people are the victims of our time, able to vie now for misery with the Cambodians after the Khmer Rouge or Sarajevans after the siege. They survived a relentless medieval war with Iran in the 1980s in which thousands of their sons died in hopeless battle and thousands have never been found. They have been bombed in the 1991 Gulf War and

trodden down by a decade of sanctions that embargoed not only arms for Saddam Hussein, but a million necessities, from drugs to surgical supplies. One French surgeon who came here, and stayed during the bombing, said instruments and clothes in his hospital were so worn and damaged from overuse that he wondered if they had been through all the wars.

In late March and April, they were subject to a bombing perhaps as surgical as the coalition forces could make it but with enough collateral damage to kill and injure still uncounted numbers of people and traumatize a generation of children. Baghdad and other major cities may have been conquered with what counts as ease in the annals of war, but it was not easy if you were lying in the darkness, covering your child's body and praying to Allah that the crossfire would not rip your family to shreds — as it all too often did.

They were conquered by a force too limited to quickly enforce order, and so for weeks the conquered cities have been ripped apart by civil chaos, still more people killed by looters or looters killed by people defending their homes and shops. If you drive around Baghdad in any direction, you realize that terrible final indignity of anarchy was more damaging than the bombing. Hospitals, museums, shops and homes have been looted. If the looters took nothing, they destroyed anything else they found, mindlessly tearing apart both the history of one of the first great civilizations on Earth and the history of individual families. In the litter of looting you persistently find family photos, a child's toy, a music school's violin, a family antique.

Animals, some family pets, run wild throughout the city, crazed by fear and hunger. Along the Tigris banks at night, packs of literally dozens of dogs race crazily about, howling for hours in a search for food. Others find food in cemeteries, angrily growling at interlopers who come to search gravestones. After one of Saddam's son's homes was searched by Marines this week, they found an Arabian stallion racing loose and a family of tigers. At the city's zoo, animals were not so lucky and many died of thirst or starvation locked in their cages when zoo workers fled, according to Iraqis who finally broke the zoo's gates.

As late as Tuesday, human bodies were still unburied on downtown streets. It was Wednesday before any firefighters in Baghdad returned to work, and until then the hundreds of fires set by the looters or by exploding ordinance simply burned out of control. It was also Wednesday that Baghdad police began trickling back to duty, but any notion of order suggested by the television pictures of a few men getting back into their cars was likely premature. Before the war this city of 4.5 million people was policed by a force of 40,000 men, but it is a relatively painstaking job for the Marines to cull out the ones who handled the squalid tasks of Saddam's repression from the ones who were enforcing law and order. By Thursday morning there were fewer than 200 men actually on duty.

Streets are literally awash with raw sewage and garbage quickly attacked at night by rats. Until late this week thousands of workers in different jobs here were afraid to come to work, so nothing is cleaned, little is washed and if it is, it was washed with dirty water. Insects abound, crawling over the garbage and up the walls of houses.

On Saturday, the coalition command began to try to get the water department, electric department and sanitation employees back to work. Perhaps their work is more crucial than that of the police. It is hard to say which of those services is the most vital. Water certainly is vital. Thousands of families have been drawing their water from outside pipes, and not all of it is drinkable. Electricity is the second most vital, for it operates machines that can purify the water, light hospital treatment rooms, run fire alarms. By Wednesday night, several grids in central Baghdad had light, but much of the city seen from the 16th floor of one hotel was dark.

Medical services are crippled, not only in the near future, but in the longer term. On the immediate level there is no electricity, several major hospitals were stripped by looters and there is no clean water — a fundamental element in medical care. Important drugs were in barely sufficient supply during the war, according to a team from the charity Doctors Without Borders, who were here to assist in medical care and remained throughout the bombing, but now medicine is running short. One visiting surgeon, Dr. Mario Del Vecchis of Bologna, Italy, said in a sense the whole system is breaking down.

"Iraq has many well-trained doctors, but many of them are afraid to come to hospitals because of revenge for being favored by the Saddam Hussein regime, others are afraid of harm, others no longer can get to work," he told United Press International. But others he said are "simply at a loss" what to do. "This was a rigid system run by the government, they have never administered a hospital or decided what to do."

He said the administrators, often appointed by the regime, are gone and "a whole new structure will have to be formed," deciding who runs hospitals, where doctors should work and what types of patients should be served. In addition to seven major hospitals, Baghdad was served with 40 smaller ones that must be reorganized, he said.

Communications, or the lack of them, is another perhaps little-noticed factor of this chaos. There are no telephones, either local, long distance or international lines. Thousands of people in Baghdad seek out anyone who has a satellite telephone, begging for a just a minute to reassure a loved one that they are safe. Sometimes they can cadge a call from a sympathetic news reporter or international worker, but it has also given rise to a cruel escalating sales game where a few seconds can be bought for $20 — a small fortune in Iraq, where the local currency is being devalued by the hour.

There is no Iraqi television left, and so unless a Baghdad family has a satellite dish, which is unlikely, the only television station they can pick up is Iranian one that has a news broadcast that every half hour runs several minutes of photos of Iraqi children injured by bombs and coalition soldiers.

The question is not the coalition forces on duty in Baghdad. In the center city, they are primarily young Marines who have been carrying out a Herculean task with enormous patience, good humor and judgment. They body search literally thousands of human beings every day, as demeaning a function for the searcher as for the searched. One young private jokes with English-speaking people that this is the cheapest massage in town, but it's no laughing matter in a nation where people's bodies and the exposure of its women to a male outside the family can be an explosive issue.

Day or night they have to guess the intentions of the drivers as cars full of people hurtle towards checkpoints, wondering whether the passengers are among the 10,000 alleged terrorist and dangerous elements the coalition says are left in Baghdad or simply a family trying to get to a hospital.

Meanwhile, they search for ammunition dumps, brave occasional gunfire exchanges, and shepherd important Iraqis who might help the new government through sometimes hostile crowds. They live for days as they did in the field — in their armored vehicles with no more water or comfort than many in Baghdad.

The Bush administration has persisted in blaming Saddam's repressive regime for most of these woes, but in Baghdad these past weeks that explanation sounded trite. Persistently, people ask an American reporter: Why did you come and do this to us? So whether Bush is right is becoming immaterial. Saddam has disappeared, and the object of blame for all misfortune is fast becoming the United States.

The incoherence of doctors who cannot function without an authoritarian regime is a metaphor for the whole country. Iraq is no Afghanistan, Iraqis tell you. It has a well-educated cadre of engineers, doctors, lawyers, and government administrators. It had an art and music community of some world note and a cultured upper middle class. But tribal loyalties are still strong, and the country is deeply divided by religious and ethnic differences.

Revenge killings, coalition forces report, are on the rise, but many cultured Arabs will tell you that that is not simply a function of the freedom of repression from Saddam, but something still deeply ingrained in the tribalism of the region. There is public justice and there is family justice — even in the orderliness of nearby Jordan a man who kills someone who has defiled his daughter can still escape a Jordanian court.

All kinds of international and coalition spokesman assure reporters in Baghdad and abroad that help is on the way, but Iraqis quickly notice that it is not coming as fast the bombers did. It was only Thursday that the first major World Food Program convoy from Amman came to Baghdad, and there is still so much else that needs to be done.

Family reunion in Iraq

NICHOLAS M. HORROCK

BAGHDAD, Iraq, April 16 (UPI) — We are standing in the hot sun this Wednesday in a graveyard, actually a secret graveyard walled off from the vast acres of the Islamic Karch cemetery, six miles southwest of Baghdad, with Abdul Hadi and Salim Abid. There are no gravestones here, no statues, simply row upon row of small aging yellow markers with numbers on them: 307, 992, 468. The numbers make no rhyme or reason, and Hadi and Abid are waiting for a man who knows what is below these markers.

This is one of a score of burial places in and around Baghdad used by Saddam Hussein's secret police force to bury its victims. Both Hadi and Abed lost relatives nearly two decades ago, two of thousands who under Saddam simply disappeared. Hadi's brother was taken on his wedding night in 1980 for what the translator said was "praying too much," but might have been for being an Islamic fundamentalist in Saddam's secular Iraq. Abed's brother-in-law went missing in 1983 for crimes even more vague and confused. The missing man's mother, now 65, had long lost hope of knowing his fate.

Now, under the watchful eye of a pack of wild, growling graveyard dogs that had been feeding here, they wait for a man to tell them which grave markers might be their relatives. Even learning this much was a stroke of luck, one of those things that are happening in this topsy-turvy city. Four days after the end of the war, a man connected with the secret police that lives in their neighborhood brought them files taken from police headquarters. They said it was a gesture of someone who wanted to avoid revenge. The files contain all kinds of family records — interrogation reports by investigators and reports on how many family members could be turned into secret police informers. All this was laid out in neat Arabic handwriting on tissuelike paper inside a cheap binder. The picture of the family's elder male member was pinned to the sheet. But in it also were execution notices and notices that the body had been brought here for burial. Other nearby graves are empty; families have already come and recovered the remains of their loved ones. The area is strewn with human bones and bits of clothing as well. So we wait for the man who has the map of this ugly place, but finally after an hour he doesn't come and they and several other families go home to try and locate him.

Col. Ehssan Kahtan of the Baghdad police, a man you would not like to be interrogated by, stands in front of his former police station with a half dozen other police officers of the Saddam regime. They are here, they say, to clean up and protect the police precinct. It is too late to protect it. Every window is smashed, files are strewn around and one room has been completely burned.

"What was there?" we asked the colonel.

"Files of criminals," he said. "Everything we knew about them."

These men do not talk about the crimes of Saddam; instead, they tell a group of reporters that U.S. Marines roughed them up while looking for $36 million in missing Saddam money.

"They put my head in the ground and stepped on it," one said.

Another policeman said Marines put pistols to his head and threatened to shoot.

"Did the Marines actually shoot anyone?" we ask.

"No."

Later they were joking with four young Marines posted outside the station.

The traffic in the city is totally out of control — street after street blocked by total gridlock. There are no streetlights, few police officers, and no motorists with patience. There is an abundance, however, of aging, rusting Volkswagen Passats made in Brazil. They came from the Iran–Iraq war when Saddam awarded one to any family whose firstborn son died in the fighting. As the deaths mounted the regime ended the program, but it left Baghdad awash in 1980s Passats. Southeast of the city, in the direction of Karbala, a herd of dairy cows were caught in the crossfire of a firefight, slaughtered where they stood. For days they lay in the open, but finally this week, coalition forces began to bulldoze them under. Nevertheless, raw sewage and often decomposed human bodies can be seen in many areas, and doctors say the health risks from sewage are increasing. There are unconfirmed reports of cholera outbreaks in the southern suburbs of the city. Coalition forces are checking.

Cash on the line

RICHARD TOMKINS

WITH THE 5TH MARINES, BAGHDAD, Iraq, April 18 (UPI) — Nearly 40 years ago, U.S. troops began America's military buildup in Vietnam to "I Walk the Line," a tune by country singer Johnny Cash about a man walking a straight-and-narrow out of love for his woman.

Lt. Carey Cash, great-nephew of the singing legend, is walking the line today in Iraq for God and country. Cash, 32, is a Navy chaplain, and his parishioners are the front-line grunts of the 1st Battalion, 5th Marine Regimental Combat Team, which has been involved in some of the fiercest battles of the war to topple the dictatorship of Saddam Hussein.

"At the same time God was calling me into the ministry I felt a call to minister to the military," he said. "My father was a 30-year veteran of the Air Force, so military people were the people I knew. I knew their lifestyle, their worries, the transience of the community. I was a product of it."

Cash was first brought to this reporter's attention by Marines of Bravo Company, 1st Battalion, who would troop en masse to Cash's Sunday services in what was called the LSA, or Life Support Area, in northern Kuwait, close to the Iraqi border. The chapel in the Kuwaiti desert for the staging Marines was a mess tent with chairs hastily positioned around a makeshift altar.

It was soon apparent why he was so popular. He spoke directly and compassionately to the Marines' anxieties about impending war, family separation, the righteousness of ending repression, the firm belief that they were not alone in life and, yes, possible death and what awaited beyond. Forty-eight Marines asked for and received baptism from Cash before crossing into Iraq. The 49th received the sacrament on Palm Sunday in a bombed out palace of Saddam. The Sunday before crossing into Iraq in late March, he concentrated on the 23rd Psalm, and Romans 8, which affirms that nothing will separate believers from the love of God. "For I am convinced that neither death nor life, neither angels not demons, neither the present nor the future, nor any powers, neither height nor depth, nor anything else in creation, will be able to separate us from the love of God that is in Jesus Christ our Lord," it says.

"The main concern of these kids is 'What's going to happen to me if I die?' and urgency to have an assurance of heaven," he said.

The Sunday before the battle for the Saddam Hussein Canal in central Iraq, he led the dog-tired Marines in hymns and prayers, calling for God's protection and asking they honor their maker throughout their lives. As the battle raged around Marines besieged by foreign extremists at and near the al-Amiziyah Palace in eastern Baghdad this month, he brought solace, comfort and hope to the wounded, braving gunfire and rocket attacks as he did so. The fight for the palace and a nearby mosque is spoken about in tones of hushed awe by those who were not there. The Marines ran a gantlet of rocket-propelled grenades while approaching the 17-acre complex, which sat on the eastern edge of the Tigris River. For nearly six hours, with their backs to the river, advance elements fought fiercely against attackers who fired at them from nearby rooftops, balconies and streets in an unrelenting barrage. At one point, ammunition was running desperately low and supply trucks were unable to reach the Americans. An almost miraculous lull of just a few minutes allowed helicopters to quickly drop off the needed supplies.

"Lucky? It wasn't luck," a Marine was overheard to say to another after the fight. "Go talk to the chaplain, he'll tell you."

A glib remark? A clichéd response to their escape? Perhaps. But to many, the author of that luck was clear. Despite numerous direct enemy rocket hits on armored vehicles, and the thousands and thousands of rounds of ammunition expended by foreign extremists and Baath Party diehards, the Marines suffered just one death and 35 wounded that day.

"It's natural for people to turn to God in war, especially after near escapes," Cash said. "I try to emphasize that God is always near, in good times as well as bad."

When not walking the lines visiting with Marines and conducting services, Cash holds well-attended Bible study groups. He calls them Head, Heart and Feet sessions — learning about God and His love, committing your life to God and following the teachings of Christ in life's journey. They may be in a tent, or a few feet distant from an artillery position, or around a patch of foxholes.

Informal counseling is also a staple, especially for Marines — some still in their teens — who have had to take life. That came within the first hours of the 1st Battalion crossing into Iraq and seizing a gas and oil separation plant in the Rumaila oil fields. More than 30 Iraqis were killed in the first frenzy of fighting. So too a Marine lieutenant, hit by a bullet in the side, just under the protective cover of his flack jacket.

Cash is a Southern Baptist from Memphis. He says he is not complacent about his efforts to help bring Marines to God and walk with Him. Nor does he ever feel helpless, because "I can pray for help and guidance."

"But I guess that when I'm separated for some reason from the (Marine) companies, I don't feel as if I'm doing all I can."

Cash travels in his own special Humvee, adorned with a cross on the side doors.

Singer Johnny Cash is the chaplain's great-uncle, his grandfather's brother. Although Cash says singing is no great passion for him, he is one of the few pastors I've met who cannot only hold a tune without musical accompaniment, but also do the hymn justice.

"My mom and dad both sing a lot, and the whole family sang together when I was growing up," he said, "but it's not a particular passion of mine."

Cash was commissioned in the Navy in 1995 and received his chaplainship in 1998. He's married and has five children, ages 2 to 8.

This Sunday, Easter, his sermon to Marines will of course be about "Hope and the Resurrection," he said, but he'll also touch on the risen Christ meeting two men on a road after His crucifixion who did not recognize him.

"God is all around us," Cash said. "You just need to look for him, to recognize him."

What to do with the oil

MARTIN HUTCHINSON

WASHINGTON, March 24 (UPI) — Once Saddam Hussein is defeated, the U.S.-led coalition that has defeated him will have its most difficult economic decision: what to do with Iraq's oil revenues, to ensure that they benefit the Iraqi people as a whole, rather than simply fueling a destructive and greedy government machine. It's a difficult problem. Of all large-scale revenue sources, oil has proved itself the most destructive to the quality of local governments and the welfare of local peoples.

Examples abound. Venezuela, in spite of being a democracy and relatively well off, has been appallingly run since the 1950s, completely failing to develop a viable non-oil economy. Mexico, one of the world's wealthier countries in 1945, declined into an orgy of corruption owing to its oil wealth, with the worst corruption coming during the 1970–82 period, when oil was at its most valuable. Indonesia, while a dictatorship, was a beacon of Asian success until President Suharto's last years, but has descended into a mire of corruption since the middle 1990s. Since Suharto's departure in 1998, none of his three democratically elected successors has shown any ability to make the Indonesian economy work. And then there's Nigeria.

There aren't a lot of favorable counter-examples. Tiny countries like Kuwait, Dubai and Qatar do OK, proving that if you have *enough* oil wealth — say $100,000 per annum per head of population — you can manage to avoid dissipating it. Even Saudi Arabia, the world's oil-wealthiest country, saw its per capita gross domestic product decline from $25,000 to $7,000 from 1980 to 2000, proving that in spite of the Suharto example, autocracy is no cure for oil-financed corruption. Britain,

Norway and Russia have shown that oil wealth in modest quantities can be a boom, but all three countries had strong non-oil economies before the oil wealth appeared (in the case of Britain and Norway) or a huge non-oil sector that coexisted alongside it (Russia). Therefore, it is pretty clear that simply removing Saddam and installing a democratic government will not ensure good government in Iraq. Since the country has the world's second-largest oil reserves and only a weak non-oil economy, there is no chance that it will follow the path of Britain, Norway and Russia, and every likelihood that even a democratic Iraq will become a second Venezuela or Nigeria, failing to enrich its people and squandering the money in worthless government projects and unbounded corruption. And, of course, there remains the possibility that such an Iraq will continue at some level to sponsor terrorist activity.

So what are the alternatives? Until last Monday, under the 1995 "oil-for-food" program, Iraq's oil revenues were handled by the United Nations. This rendered a large portion of the Iraqi population — some 14 million out of the country's population of 24 million — dependent on handouts from the U.N.'s relief administrators. A pure handout program of this kind, in a society that has a high poverty level and considerable social dislocation, simply creates dependence and reduces economic activity. Naturally, the "oil for food" program has also done nothing for Iraq's agriculture. While possibly a necessary (if ineffectual) remedy at a time Iraq was subject to international sanctions, the U.N. administration of Iraq's principal source of foreign exchange earnings is bound to cause huge political and economic trouble going forward.

Another possibility would be for the oil revenues to be administered by the World Bank or the International Monetary Fund, which would use them to pursue a carefully thought-out development strategy, according to the governing policies of the international institution concerned. This has two problems. First, it would be perceived in Iraq as an exercise in U.S. imperialism, since the World Bank and IMF are perceived in the Third World, rightly or wrongly, as instruments of U.S. policy. Second, it would provide no tangible benefits for the Iraqi population itself (other than by U.N.-type handouts, which have the problems outlined above), but would simply provide a huge "gravy train" for the international institutions and their associated consultants, by which the money will be wasted on ineffectual projects, while the true needs of the population go unmet.

If you think I'm exaggerating, consider Bosnia, a relatively prosperous country with a good education system before 1991, into which tens of billions of dollars of international aid have been poured, without any sign of having created a viable economy. The reason for this is quite simple: The international aid agencies, bound by their own agendas, paid little attention to the needs of the Bosnians themselves. In every other country that broke away from the former Yugoslavia, one of the first orders of business was to provide a mechanism to restore to the populace their foreign currency savings, which had been expropriated by the Yugoslav National Bank in 1991 and used to fund the Serbian war machine. Once this had been done, new business formation and the restoration of a functioning economy were once again possible, since these savings were of course the main source of small business financing. In Bosnia, the problem was ignored by the aid agencies and the government they controlled, and the small business sector is consequently notably absent from the current Bosnian economic scene.

The central problem in all the above schemes for spending Iraq's oil revenues is that they depend on a central Marxist fallacy: that the oil under a country, and the oil production issuing from the country, are rightfully the property of that country's government. This is equivalent to nationalizing the U.S. semiconductor industry on the grounds that the U.S. government had provided for the education of William Shockley and his successors who invested in the various devices involved. The principle makes no sense economically; still more does it make no sense morally.

In economic reality, there are two groups of people who have a right to the revenues from Iraq's oil industry: the oil companies that developed it and the owners of the land under which the oil was discovered. In the event that private property rights were undeveloped in the region when the oil was found, the latter ownership devolves, not on the Iraqi government, but on the Iraqi people themselves.

The majority of Iraq's oilfields were developed by the Iraq Petroleum Corp., a consortium founded in 1925 and owned by British Petroleum (23.75 percent), Shell (23.75 percent), Compagnie Francaise des Petroles (23.75 percent), ExxonMobil (23.7 percent, between the two constituent companies) and the late Nubar Gulbenkian, the famous "Mr. Five Percent" wheeler-dealer, owner of that percentage of the company. IPC was partially expropriated in 1964 and fully nationalized in 1972, the latter by a government of which Saddam was already the guiding figure.

There would thus seem no reason to recognize the expropriation, and every reason to return the operation of the oil fields to the British, Anglo–Dutch, French, U.S. and Portuguese (the Gulbenkian Foundation, domiciled in Lisbon) entities whose rights were so brutally overruled by Saddam's thugs. The Iraq National Oil Company, a corrupt tool of the Saddam regime, can legitimately be cut out of the business. It is also clear, however, through examination of current operating agreements in the oil industry, that the great majority of the oil revenues, perhaps 75 to 80 percent, should accrue to the landholders, in this case (subject to any well-founded title claims by individuals on particular oil fields) to the Iraqi people as a whole — *not* to the government. By ensuring that oil revenues accrue to individual Iraqis, not to their government, the coalition can provide the Iraqi people with a huge tangible benefit from the invasion and spread the money widely enough so that any funding for terrorism or a military machine is insignificant. Therefore, the requirement is for a fund that holds the money and that contains individual accounts in the name of the Iraqi people, who derive benefit from their holdings and have at least some degree of control over the way the money is invested. Fortunately, there is an excellent model for such an entity: Singapore's Central Provident Fund, with currently 2.9 million members and assets of $45 billion.

The CPF was set up initially in 1955, but its growth dates from 1968, when by a provision of Singapore law a percentage of every employee's salary (currently 20 percent paid by the employee plus 16 percent paid by the employer) up to SGD 6,000 ($3,000) per month is paid into the fund, to accrue in solid investments and pay for the employee's future retirement, health and later housing needs (by means of home mortgage withdrawal). The fund's investments are managed by trustees who provide "a fair market return at minimal risk," which is linked to bank deposit rates. However, fund members may also choose their own investment vehicles from an approved list for their accrued fund balances.

Iraq's short-term potential oil production is around 2.5 million barrels per day, with the possibility of an increase to 3.5 billion barrels per day within three to five years from investment in new fields. At an oil price of $25 per barrel, with 80 percent of oil revenues devoted to the fund, an Iraqi CPF would have initial revenues of $18.25 billion per annum, or $760.42 for every Iraqi man, woman and child. In addition, going forward, a portion of employed Iraqi's earnings, maybe 10 percent, could be added to his or her account in the fund.

Over a period of years, as the fund's revenues and assets grow, this should prove sufficient to provide the Iraqi people with basic retirement, health and unemployment benefit needs, as well as educational services for Iraq's children. It would best be managed by the staff of Singapore's CPF, who have 35 years experience in running this type of scheme, and are as far as humanly possible incorruptible (Singapore ranked fifth lowest in the world, after three Scandinavian countries and New Zealand, in Transparency International's most recent annual corruption rankings.)

By instituting an Iraqi CPF, with individual accounts, funded by the oil revenues and managed by staff of the Singapore CPF, the coalition would over a two- to three-year period allow the Iraqi people to develop an asset over which they had (if they wished) individual investment control, which would fund their basic social program needs. The new Iraqi government, in turn, would have to depend on non-oil sources, such as sales and income taxes on the Iraqi people for its revenues. It would thus be relatively impoverished, but would also have no need to provide basic social security, health or education services for its people. With at most 10 percent of Iraq's gross domestic product under its control, it would be unable to afford expensive military adventures, would have very limited control over the Iraqi economy, and would have relatively few and minor avenues for serious corruption.

An Iraqi people who had their basic social security, health and education needs taken care of by a Central Provident Fund managed by incorruptible and capable Singaporeans, and whose government was modest and not very corrupt, would be the happiest polity in the unhappy Middle East. That, at least, is something worth fighting for.

No more easy enemies

MARTIN WALKER

WASHINGTON, April 20 (UPI) — If a man can be judged by the enemies he keeps, then President George W. Bush has picked some beauties. Osama bin Laden and Saddam Hussein are as foul a pair as current humanity has to offer.

The Taliban and Baathist Iraq were two of the most dreadful regimes on the planet. North Korea, with its gulag and famine, may be even worse. Baathist Syria, which seems to be graduating into the ranks of the axis of evil after its sly support for Saddam Hussein, is defined to this day by the ruthless brutality with which it crushed the rebellion in the town of Hama just 20 years ago. Bombarded into ruin by massed artillery, the rubble and some 20,000 civilians were then ground into flatness by bulldozers and the vast tomb sealed with cement.

These are desirable enemies, not simply because they rest on state terror and institutionalized cruelty, but because they are breathtakingly incompetent. Regimes that rule with such viciousness tend to be very much better at maintaining domestic power than at exporting their power abroad. Secret policemen make poor generals, and armies whose main job is to intimidate and mow down their own civilians are seldom good at fighting well-armed opponents.

America's two Presidents Bush could hardly have had a more cooperative enemy than Saddam Hussein. His use of chemical weapons against his own people and his invasion of neighboring Kuwait defined him as a regional menace. His military skills, unlike his rather skillful diplomacy, were pitiful. In the first Gulf War, he kept his armies dug into the sands of Kuwait and southern Iraq, where they could be devastated by nearby U.S. air power. In the second Gulf War, he watched his forces destroyed again from the air in the great killing fields south of Baghdad, between Karbala and Kut.

The problem now is that the Bush administration may be running out of such incompetent and cooperative adversaries. It is too soon to say how America's current diplomatic intimidation of Syria will unfold, or how North Korea might be talked and threatened and sanctioned into closing down its nuclear workshops and its ballistic missile assembly lines.

But neither Pyongyang nor Damascus looks likely to emulate Saddam Hussein's folly in giving the United States such plausible excuses for military action. They are not going to invade the neighbors. Syria, which has a seat on the Security Council, will make a point of keeping on the right side of the United Nations. North Korea will do whatever it must to maintain at least some Chinese protection; Pyongyang only agreed to the talks with China and the United States after China closed the oil pipeline across the Yalu River for "technical reasons." The even tougher enemy for Bush will be Iran, a charter member of Bush's axis of evil, and now appreciably closer to becoming a nuclear power than it was when that phrase was coined in January 2002.

Iran remains a considerable irritant, and perhaps even a threat in the Middle East. Its agents appear to be fomenting Shiite opposition to the U.S. presence in Iraq. It backs terrorist organizations like Hezbollah and Hamas with arms, cash and diplomatic support. (Iran long denied direct support for Hamas, but a raid on the Hamas offices in Amman by Jordanian security police in October 1999 found documents that spelled out the relationship in great detail.) And yet Iran has played it smart, and not just in the secret talks with the United States this spring on subtle ways to cooperate with Bush's war on Iraq. Despite the incipient state of civil war between the elected "moderate" government of President Mohammed Khatami and the hard-line ayatollahs who run the military, the judiciary and the secret police, Iran is a tough and prickly challenge for the United States.

To outsiders, Iran's incipient civil war can look like a hard cop–soft cop routine. Try to condemn the ayatollahs, and Khatami's silky diplomats are on the phone to their friends in London and Paris. Criticize their support for Hamas and Hezbollah, and the entire Arab world rallies behind these "resistance" groups against Israel. Raise the issue of Iran's nuclear ambitions, and suddenly the ayatollahs cooperate with the Afghan war on the Taliban or offer to let the United States use their airspace to rescue pilots downed over Iraq.

The problem for the Bush administration, apparently invincible and dominant after its stunning victory in Iraq, is that there are no more such palpably wicked and incompetent enemies. In fact, the future of American power is likely to be shaped by the emergence of smart enemies like Iran. And behind Iran lurk the new soft enemies like France and Russia, who will snipe and criticize and use their diplomatic strength to block U.S. policies without ever giving the United States an excuse to do much but grumble.

War reflection: With the Marines in Iraq

RICHARD TOMKINS

WASHINGTON, April 21 (UPI) — What's the face of the Iraq war? Is it a scene of physical destruction people see on their televisions and in their newspapers? Is it a glimpse of sullen — more often relieved — Iraqi prisoners or celebrating civilians? Or is it the wave of camouflaged U.S. troops routing an enemy, and in typical American fashion, then embracing the children of a foe vanquished?

It's all that and more.

For journalists embedded with U.S. forces, the dominant feature of Operation Iraqi Freedom is, and always will be, the faces of the individual Marines, soldiers, airmen or sailors with whom they lived, sweated and feared during the long slog to Baghdad. There is, for example, the unidentified Marine with his mouth set in a grimace from the bullet that passed through his knee. He tried to wave off comrades who eventually carried him to cover during the heaviest fighting for al-Azimiyah Palace in eastern Baghdad. While being carried he continued to fire his weapon at the enemy until his ammunition ran out.

There is Marine Pvt. Aaron Davis, a jovial and slightly pudgy kid from California, who moved with unbelievable speed and abandon, braving explosions and flying fragments from rocket-propelled grenades to help carry wounded to an evacuation.

There is Capt. Shawn Basco, a forward air controller, who handed out candy from Meals Ready to Eat packs to village children, and food to their parents, with the same personal sense of mission that earlier had saved scores American lives and snuffed out many an Iraqi one when calling in air strikes.

"You hear about the World War II generation being 'the Greatest Generation,'" Lt. Col. Fred Padilla, commander of the 1st Battalion, 5th Marines, told this correspondent. "In a sense that's true — we're certainly living off the equity they earned. But this generation — call it Generation X or whatever — is also every bit as extraordinary. They measure up."

For 36 days this correspondent was in a unique position to gauge that sentiment. As part of Pentagon policy for media coverage of the war, I was embedded with Bravo Company, 1st Battalion, 5th Marines, or simply Bravo 1/5.

Bravo 1/5 was one of the first two units to cross into Iraq from Kuwait at the start of the land war (we would have been first, but Alpha Company broke the line of march and moved ahead of us). Bravo 1/5 captured a gas and oil separation plant in the Rumaila oil field in southern Iraq, routed Iraqi defenders while capturing a key bridge over the Saddam Hussein Canal in central Iraq, liberated village after village and a children's prison, fought its way into Baghdad through a gantlet of rocket-propelled grenade fire, and seized and held Saddam's 17-acre complex on the Tigris River despite a five-hour onslaught from Baath Party gunmen and foreign extremists.

It was one of the heaviest battles of the Iraq conflict, with the besieged Marines nearly run-

ning out of ammunition. Thirty-five Marines were wounded that morning and one killed. Luckily for Bravo, only three of the wounded came from its ranks.

In battle, the men of Bravo 1/5 fought with tenacious courage. In liberating a people long cowed by the repression of dictatorship, they acted with great compassion, and in many cases a great tenderness. Operation Iraqi Freedom, a name they initially greeted with scorn and expletive, gained poignant currency as the Marines viewed the plight of the Iraqi people — lives in unbelievable squalor — and their explosions of joy at being set free from the grip of fear.

Earlier mutterings that the war to topple Saddam Hussein should be called Operation Sandstorm because of the weather, or Operation Stand Still for the delays in the march to allow logistics vehicles to catch up with advancing front line units, were quickly forgotten.

"I feel pretty good today," 1st Sgt. Bill Leuthe of California said after liberating a town near Baghdad and a prison for children, where charges were reportedly beaten every morning simply for being there. "I think we all do."

Leuthe, Davis, Shevlin, Washburn, Malley, Lockett, Jones, Moll, Lyon, Bishop, Avilos, Nolan, Lockett, Meldoza, Craft, George — the list of names of the men who did themselves proud, the Marines proud and their nation proud is too long to recite. There were more than 180 in the company; more than 200 when you add in attachments, such as armored vehicle crews and additional Navy corpsmen.

They were a cross-section of America. There were whites, blacks, Hispanics, Asians, American Indians and every hue and mixture in between. Pvt. Dustin Pangelinann, 23, was from Saipan in the U.S. Commonwealth of the Marianas. Fifteen members of Bravo Company were not U.S. citizens and represented the newest wave of immigrants to our country. Some were from Mexico and one was from Haiti. There were also several from Russia and Ukraine. Some came from poor backgrounds, others were solidly middle class. One Marine, who didn't need to work because of a family fortune, enlisted in his late 20s in the aftermath of the terrorist attacks of Sept. 11, 2001. And, yes, some even had had youthful brushes with the law.

But they all shared two things. They were Marines and "Devil Dogs." Not hyphenated Marines, just Marines — the "Few and the Proud," carrying on the tradition of courage their regimental forebears showed at Bellieu Wood and the Argonne, at Guadalcanal and Okinawa, at the Chosen Reservoir and Inchon, and at Hue.

"None of you had to be here," company commander Capt. Jason Smith told his men before crossing the border berm into Iraq from Kuwait. "You all chose to be here by becoming Marines, by doing something good for the world.

"Take a look around you. We are all different. … what other military force or country in the world can say that? The fact that we are all different and live with each other and focus together under adverse circumstances tells me and the world a lot."

This group of men, this collection of Marines, he said, comes from a nation that "is going to war to defend an idea" of freedom, rule of law and human dignity. "We're going to war to make the world a better place because we don't want to happen again what happened on Sept. 11."

It's difficult to convey the rich texture of the men who make up Bravo 1/5 and the special camaraderie among them. Words just aren't adequate enough. But they are truly a band of brothers. Even the company oddball, the Marine who somehow never seemed to fit in or pull his own weight, was looked out for and protected with the concern of that of a big brother looking out for an awkward sibling.

Bravo 1/5, in a sense, proves two truisms this correspondent has discovered in 30 years of reporting, much of it in war zones: Sharing a foxhole is the ultimate bonding experience, and the word "cliché" needs a new definition.

According to the American Heritage College Dictionary, "cliché" is "a trite or overused expression or idea" or stereotype. All too often it is used with a negative cast. Yet clichéd characters and generalizations are based on truths. Take the characters in any war movie you've ever seen. There is the jokester, the screw-up, the smart mouth, the lothario, the kindhearted sergeant with a tough-as-nails exterior, the good-natured medic and the caring-but-firm commander. It's no wonder these characters exist on

paper and celluloid. They exist in real life, just as the scenes of GIs passing out candy to civilians, sharing their last smoke or holding up a magazine pin-up to troops in a passing convoy.

Clichéd in the context of Bravo 1/5 should be a label of honor, because it mirrors America and is replicated throughout our society and military services. Smith, the commander of Bravo Company, is from Baton Rouge. He fits the image — tall, square-jawed, a good-natured, decent and erudite man who requires things be done correctly. A graduate of Louisiana State University with a B.A. in history, his main goal in Operation Iraqi Freedom — other than accomplishing unit missions — was bringing everyone home. Watching him one night, when troops were out setting an ambush, was like watching a parent of a teenager waiting for his or her child to return home from a New Year's Eve party to which they had driven. The silent pacing was enough to drive one crazy. Any casual mention about how the company had been lucky in the casualty department would result in a quick, sharp look of reproach — don't jinx good fortune by talking about it.

The executive officer is 1st Lt. David Gustafson, a quiet, shy Swede from Maynard, Minn., with a wicked sense of humor. The only graduate of the Naval Academy among the company's officers, his educational background is often a butt of jokes. So too his efforts to conceal the cigarette smoking he'd taken up since crossing into Iraq.

And then there is Gunnery Sgt. Ron "my first name is Gunny" Jenks, the company logistician. Before battle, the Gulf War veteran would sternly but lovingly caution his men on mistakes to avoid and advise on lessons learned the hard way. His "OK, gents, let's get a move on," inevitably followed his barked orders. But for all the sternness, there was the old clichéd heart of gold. Gunny Jenks always had words of encouragement, always knew who was married, who expecting a child and made it a point to inquire about them. He loaded up on cigarettes, parceling them out to his "knuckleheads" when they ran out in the Iraqi desert.

"They're like my own kids," he'd say in quiet moments — not in front of them, of course.

Bravo 1/5 has now left Baghdad. It is heading south toward Kuwait and an eventual return home to California. But there will be no rest for the weary. After an expected parade in Ocean-side and a few weeks of reunion with family, the band of brothers will ship out to Okinawa to complete a previously scheduled deployment. Operation Iraqi Freedom will become just a memory, and another ribbon of honor for men serving their country.

Post script: This reporter took his leave of Bravo 1/5 on April 15. It was one of the hardest farewells I've ever had to make. In the 36 days I spent with them, I had been welcomed and made part of the family. The idea of leaving my band of brothers was wrenching, yet my family at home was also calling. In the end, I left quickly, with few goodbyes. The sight of a blubbering reporter was something best avoided. Speaking with other formerly embedded reporters in Kuwait turned up similar emotional pulls. So how to say thank you? How to say how much I love and respect them? Words can't do it. So, like other reporters, I give them the smartest, snappiest salute I, as a civilian, can muster. Godspeed, Bravo 1/5. Semper Fi (Semper Fidelis, "Always Faithful," the Marine Corps motto).

EPILOGUE

Most wars end with a political honeymoon for the victors. The 21-day victory over Saddam Hussein's regime was an exception. Within days of the fall of Baghdad, the controversy over the looting of Iraq's National Museum, with its treasures of the ancient Babylonian and Sumerian civilizations, cast the first sour note upon the military triumph. In a sense, the victory had been too complete. The Baathist state of Saddam Hussein, along with its policing and food distribution systems and local administration structures, had all collapsed. Water and power supplies were barely functioning. In such circumstances, the difficulty of imposing order on a city of 5 million people with troops still exhausted from their extraordinary efforts became steadily more glaring.

The British and American military authorities, and the civilian teams assembling in Kuwait City under the leadership of former U.S. General Jay Garner, had never expected to inherit quite such a vacuum of power. Even the Iraqi exiles, who had been a prime source of intelligence for conditions on the ground inside Iraq had not reckoned on the almost complete evaporation of Saddam Hussein's administrative regime. And as exhausted military engineers struggled to restore electricity and water treatment plants in Iraq's cities, the military commanders tried to identify local leaders who were not tainted by connections to Saddam. This proved difficult, so complete had been his grip on the country. The traditional tribal leaders, to whom the British instinctively turned in the Basra region, had made their own accommodations with Saddam Hussein. No sooner had the British appointed a leader of the local Beni Hasan tribe to run an interim city council than he was denounced as a tool of the old regime. But it was hard to identify any senior Iraqi engineer or bureaucrat of whom that could not be said. Almost all of the Iraqi professional classes, from doctors and teachers to clerics and factory managers, had either learned to live with and under the regime or had gone into exile.

The Iraqi exiles also struggled to establish their own political credentials in the land that many of them had not seen for years or even decades. Their best-known leader, Ahmed Chalabi of the Iraqi National Council, arrived quickly in a U.S. military transport aircraft. But at his first meetings with prominent locals in Nasiriyah and Baghdad, he found only lukewarm support. In city after city, self-appointed local mayors pronounced themselves in charge, recruited teams of bodyguards, and demanded funds, food and facilities from the U.S. and British troops.

The situation was chaotic. Garner had no authority over the tired and overstretched troops who had won the victory. He could not order the generals to put thousands of troops on the streets to establish order, a task for which the soldiers had not been trained. He had assumed, on the advice of the Iraqi exiles, that with promises of pay and future jobs, the existing Iraqi police force would soon return to work. Uncertain of their own future, and fearing arrest as associates of the Saddam regime, few policemen rallied to the occupying forces. And a handful of assassinations of the police who did return to work, possibly by Baathists still loyal to Saddam Hussein, or possibly by the professional criminals unleashed from prison by Saddam just before war broke out, dissuaded many. In the first three weeks, there were seldom more than 1,800 U.S. troops available for physical security tasks in Baghdad at any given time.

There was one force that seemed ready and able to step into this vacuum of power, despite the predictions of the Iraqi exiles and many regional experts consulted by Garner. This was the Shiite clergy, whose nominal leader was the Najaf-based Ali al-Sistani, who had traditionally refrained from direct political involvement. Those who had played a political role in the Shiite uprising of 1991, immediately after the first Gulf War, had been killed, like Mohammed al-Sadr, or ruthlessly suppressed by Saddam Hussein, or driven into exile, where they began dreaming of a new political role for the Shiites. A striking feature of Iraqi history is that its government has traditionally been dominated by the Sunni minority, rather than by the Shiite majority. Perhaps the most important political consequences of Saddam's overthrow was that the Shiites, and some of their key religious leaders, saw their chance to dominate the new Iraq.

Some of the Shiite mullahs, like Mohammad Bakr al-Hakim, leader of the Supreme Council for the Islamic Revolution in Iraq, had fled into exile in neighboring Iran, where they had come under the influence of the Iranian ayatollahs. Following their example, the exiled Iraqis wanted an Iran-style Islamic state, ruled by the mullahs. These came to be known as the Qom clerics, after the Iranian holy city where they had gathered, and an early rivalry developed with the Najaf clerics, named after Iraq's Shiite shrine, where the mullahs had remained and survived under Saddam Hussein's rule.

SCIRI had some 15,000 trained and armed militia, the Badr brigades, which gave them power on the streets as well as in the mosques. But the Najaf clerics who refused to follow the Qom group quickly found their own leader in Muqtada al-Sadr, the 30-year-old son of the martyred Mohammed al-Sadr. Still a student at Najaf's Kawza seminary, the young al-Sadr used his father's name and the resources of the Sadr Foundation welfare agency to rally support in the main cities of Najaf, Nasiriyah and Karbala. Above all, he established control over Baghdad's vast Shiite slum that used to be known as Saddam city, but has now been renamed Sadr city.

While thanking the British and American forces for toppling Saddam, al-Sadr called for nonviolent resistance to pressure them to leave quickly so that Iraq might become an "Islamic nation." In one dramatic speech in Sadr City, he declared: "Anyone supported by the United States is cursed by us." But rather than opposing all the Qom group, al-Sadr developed close ties to Kadhem al-Husseini al-Haeri, a revered Iraqi-born mullah who has spent the last 30 years in exile in Qom. In a recent fatwa, al-Haeri ordered the Iraqi clergy to "raise people's awareness of Great Satan's plans and of the means to abort them." In Iraq now as in Iran since the fall of the shah in 1979, the Great Satan is the United States.

The British, Americans and exiles had pinned their hopes on a London-based moderate cleric, Majid al-Khoei, who was flown into Najaf even before Baghdad fell and quickly emerged as the main challenger to al-Sadr. On a visit to the shrine of the Imam Ali on April 10, al-Khoei was killed by a mob of al-Sadr supporters, although al-Sadr denied any responsibility for the killing. His death left the moderate and pro-Western clerics, and those who opposed an Iran-style theocracy, with no obvious leader, and left Garner's mission with few points of access to the increasingly important Islamic leadership.

Even while failing to impose security or to reestablish much semblance of normal life, Garner was unable to identify, let alone establish, an interim Iraqi authority that could claim to represent the various Sunni, Shiite, Kurdish and other groups. His team, composed of U.S. officials from different agencies, squabbled among themselves and with the U.S. forces, whom they blamed for the lack of security. Back in Washington, the Bush administration realized that it was in danger of losing the peace and within a month of his arrival in Iraq, Garner was replaced by a former U.S. ambassador, L. Paul "Jerry" Bremer, who was given the authority to deploy troops for security purposes. By the time Bremer arrived, more and fresh troops were available as the 4th Infantry Division and the 1st Armored deployed in Iraq. Bremer decided to concentrate on restoring law and order, the economy, and crucial services like power and water, while putting politics on hold. Instead of trying to invent a national Iraqi council, Bremer focused on the local politics of appointing town councils, but the U.S. and British forces remained firmly in charge. Indeed, the first planned election of a mayor and town council, scheduled for the holy city of Najaf in June, was postponed when the SCIRI-backed candidate looked likely to win.

The one part of Iraq that had showed itself capable of representative self-government, the Kurdish regions of the north, were facing their own difficulties through the slowness of the various bureaucracies to adapt to the end of the U.N.'s oil-for-food program. The United States had scored an important diplomatic success at the United Nations on May 22, when the Security Council agreed to lift the long-running sanctions against Iraq and phase out the oil-for-food program, with the funds going to a new Iraqi Development Fund. But the Kurds were still waiting for the $3.7 billion allocated to them, but not yet paid, from their share of the U.N. program. The end of sanctions, which also ended the Kurds' formerly profitable smuggling trade, disrupted the once thriving economy of the Kurds. And while the end of sanctions allowed the sale of the 10 million barrels of Iraqi oil stored in Turkey, their sale earned just $300 million — a fraction of the estimated costs of $3 billion to repair the country's oil infrastructure alone.

In sum, everything that could go wrong was going wrong, even before the first signs came in May that an organized military resistance was developing to the U.S. occupation. By mid-June, ambushes, sniping and grenade attacks were starting to take an almost daily toll of American lives. In the six weeks after May 1, when President Bush declared "an end to major military operations," 48 U.S. troops lost their lives. By mid-June, the U.S. forces were conducting major raids with armor and helicopters against resistance centers, mostly run by former Republican Guards and other Saddam loyalists. They were well funded. U.S. troops found $8.5 million in cash, jewels valued at over $1 million and other currencies at a resistance center outside Tikrit, where 50 former Republican Guard members were arrested.

These difficulties with the occupation had political consequences. Concern first for the looted museums and archaeological sites, then for the crime wave in Iraq's cities, and then for the failure to locate Saddam Hussein's weapons of mass destruction gave the critics of the war, both at home in Britain and the United States and abroad, new ammunition to condemn Bush and British Prime Minister Tony Blair. The failure to find either the body or the living person of Saddam Hussein, or his two sons Qusay and Uday, was a further embarrassment. Of these, the most serious was the failure to find the weapons of mass destruction that had been cited so often from the White House and from Downing Street — and at the United Nations — as the main justification for the war. Legally, this was not so. There was ample reason for military action in Saddam's failure to fulfill the original terms of the 1991 cease-fire and other U.N. resolutions that

required him to account for the people and loot missing from Kuwait.

Still, the greatest emphasis had been placed on Saddam's nuclear research efforts, his stocks of chemical weapons and his bio-warfare program by the British and American governments, most publicly in Secretary of State Colin Powell's address to the United Nations in January. The British government issued one intelligence report that claimed Saddam Hussein's forces could start using chemical weapons at 45 minutes notice. Bush and Vice President Dick Cheney each claimed before the war that the Iraqi nuclear program still was being pursued. All this became increasingly embarrassing as the weeks after the war failed to find any stocks of significance, beyond two special trucks that seemed to have been designed for chemical warfare. In Britain, the Blair government was forced by pressure in Parliament to open formal inquiries into the allegation that the intelligence assessments of Iraq's weapons of mass destruction had been deliberately inflated. In the United States, one of the leading Democratic candidates for the presidency in the 2004 elections, Sen. John Kerry of Massachusetts, accused the Bush administration of "deliberately misleading the American people."

The critical reaction might have been even worse, but for the constant discoveries of mass graves and evidence of torture that left no room for doubt that Saddam had run one of the most evil and vicious regimes on the planet. Even the sternest critics of the British and American governments acknowledged that the Iraqi people had indeed been liberated from an appalling and brutal rule. The question was whether such issues of the human rights of the Iraqi people alone justified the war, or whether Bush and Blair had between them exaggerated the truth of Saddam's dangers to other countries, whether through his terrorist links or his weapons of mass destruction.

There had always been one broader aspect to the Bush administration's decision to go to war: the tantalizing hope that a liberated Iraq could become a model for reform, democracy and modernization in the rest of the Arab world. The main French criticism of the war, voiced by foreign minister Dominique de Villepin, was that a campaign to overthrow an Arab government and occupy an Arab country, no matter how good the intentions, would be perceived throughout the Arab world as the opening shot in a dreaded "clash of civilizations" between the West and the Arab world, between Christendom and Islam. This, argued Villepin, had to be prevented at all costs.

The Bush administration itself never argued in such terms, but some of its supporters among the neoconservatives saw the stakes of the war in similar terms, but from a different perspective. William Kristol, editor of the Weekly Standard, argued that the only way to prevent a clash of civilizations was for the United States to take the lead in the long, arduous process of modernizing the Arab world. Free markets, free institutions, free media and free trade and freedom of religion were the symbols and the realities of modern, prosperous democracies, Kristol suggested. The Arab world, economically backward even with its oil wealth, run by authoritarian and quasi-feudal regimes and increasingly prey to Islamic extremism, should be saved from itself. And only such a modernized, democratic Arab world could ever be expected to forge a lasting peace with Israel — the issue that kept U.S.–Arab relations in such constant tension. The Bush administration might not have spoken publicly in such terms, but it acted as if this neoconservative view was its strategic guide. In May, Bush proposed a broad free trade agreement with the Arab world, and also put the full weight of his prestige behind a new attempt to craft peace in the Middle East. At two summits in the first days of June, at Sharm el-Sheikh with the Arab leaders and then at Aqaba in Jordan with the Israeli and Palestinian prime ministers, Bush became just as committed to the Middle East peace process as his predecessor Bill Clinton had been. But within days, as Israeli settlers resisted eviction and the Hamas and Islamic Jihad leaders refused to support the new Palestinian prime minister, Mahmoud Abbas, and launched new suicide bomber attacks, the prospects for peace looked as elusive as ever.

It is far too soon to assess the results of the stunning military victory of the Iraq war. The early hopes of a representative Iraqi administration moving toward democracy under Anglo–American stewardship were not fulfilled. The best-organized Iraqi political force

seemed to be steered by Shiite clerics intent on establishing an Iran-style Islamic state. There were increasingly ominous signs that a guerilla campaign was organizing against the occupying forces. The Middle East peace process was sputtering, if not stalled. The crisis in the United Nations as an effective body of global governance and opinion was unresolved. The rifts torn in the Atlantic alliance were only partially healed, even as Polish, Danish, Dutch and other troops began to take their place alongside the British and American forces, with the NATO alliance offering logistical and planning support.

It remains to be seen how long the patience of the U.S. Congress and public will accept the drain of casualties from an occupation that looks to be long and difficult and controversial, with the 2004 presidential election campaign already getting under way. There is an obvious danger that having won the war, the U.S. and British governments could lose the peace. But whatever the eventual outcome of the second Gulf War, at least this time the vicious regime of Saddam Hussein was no longer in place to brutalize its own people and threaten to destabilize the region. One of the three regimes cited by Bush in his January 2002 State of the Union address as the "axis of evil" was overthrown. The other two, North Korea and Iran, drew their own lessons from the two Gulf wars, that the only way to guarantee their security against the American superpower was to develop their own nuclear capabilities. The political crises with Iran and North Korea were building ominously, even as the victors of the war struggled to reestablish order in Iraq.

Commentary: Traitor or patriot?

ARNAUD DE BORCHGRAVE

WASHINGTON, June 16 (UPI) — Did the war to change regimes in Iraq jeopardize the war on terror?

Did the war on Iraq detract from Operation Enduring Freedom in Afghanistan?

Did the war on Iraq rob domestic security of manpower, brainpower and funds?

Did the war on Iraq weaken the administration's counterterrorism alliances abroad?

Did the war on Iraq spawn a new generation of al-Qaida recruits?

Did the administration fail to push the Saudis hard enough to address their own terrorism problems?

Did the war detract from America's international prestige and respect?

Did the war jeopardize the ideals America stands for?

The way the three wars — al Qaida, Iraq and Afghanistan — are being reported, without even having to read between the lines, the answer would have to be affirmative to all eight questions. And most foreign editorials, from Buenos Aires to Berlin and Copenhagen to Cape Town, have reached that conclusion. Administration officials are quick to dismiss these foreign fulminations as gratuitous Bush-bashing. The trouble is former administration officials for two presidents, Ronald Reagan and George Bush 41, make the same points and ask the same questions, albeit sub rosa and sotto voce. None — Democrat or Republican — wants motivations and patriotism impugned.

Until this week, that is. Now Randy Beers — the man who succeeded the legendary Richard Clarke as the White House counterterrorist czar and mysteriously quit after eight months on the job — has gone public. Having served in three Republican administrations, including Reagan and Bush 41, Beers scanned from 500 to 1,000 pieces of "threat information" intelligence that crossed his desk daily — and nightly. He joined the John Kerry for president camp and spilled a few beans to the *Washington Post* — sufficient evidence for Bush loyalists that he was a traitor in their midst. Beers is a registered Democrat but, as his colleagues say, totally apolitical when it comes to counterterrorism.

Former ranking Republican officials are also faulting the current administration for failure to anticipate Iraq's postwar problems. "We should have declared a victory," said one ex–White House and Defense official, "and started pulling out right after Baghdad fell. Now we're trying to get other friendly powers to share the policing burden, but Iraq is already a tar baby."

Two months after President George W. Bush declared the war over, the Pentagon budget assumptions expected to have cut back boots on Iraqi soil to 75,000 troops. Instead, some 150,000 are still deployed to police a country where underground, pro-Saddam resistance appears to be growing.

Republican strategists are ruing the day when more soldiers will have been killed in peacetime action than in the three-week war. Rosy forecasts of Iraqi oil fields pumping out almost 3 million barrels a day by the end of 2003 and 5 million by the following summer have snaffled. Some Republicans can see an economy still heading south and a budget deficit soaring to over $400 billion for the year. Again, ranking Republicans can see the need for supplemental appropriations for a funding bill that has not yet been voted. Budget spending realities are now encroaching on creative bookkeeping.

The House of Saud has also taken a heady plunge back to earth. Recent terrorist bombings in Riyadh by Islamist extremists shook the royal family, as Sept. 11, 2001, never did. Some 100 prominent imams who preach jihad, or holy war, against Christian and Jewish heathens have been called on the royal carpet and told to knock it off. Asked why this wasn't done immediately after Sept. 11, Saudi spokesmen deflect the question with "and look at what else we've done."

The Wahhabi school curriculum is also being revised to eliminate all hateful references to Jews and Christians. For the first time in recent memory, Saudis now tell their American friends they feel sufficiently confident to tell the religious police to mind their own business when their wives are scolded for allowing hair to show.

Millions of Saudi-educated youth — as opposed to U.S.-educated elites — and millions of Pakistanis in the Saudi Wahhabi clergy-funded madrassas have been brainwashed to believe that America and Israel are intrinsically evil. This teaching has gone on since 1979, when the House of Saud reached a "concordat" with the fundamentalist Wahhabi clergy whereby the clerics pledged not to criticize the extravagant excesses of the royal family, and in return the religious chiefs were given free rein to spread their gospel throughout the desert kingdom — and in countries far and near.

The Pakistani fundamentalist bandwagon got rolling in 1980, as the Soviets completed their occupation in Afghanistan. The United States, Saudi Arabia and Pakistan (under President Zia ul-Haq) came up with a great idea to defeat the Soviet army of occupation. They agreed to try to undermine the loyalty of Soviet troops — at first, most of the units were drawn from the Soviet Union's Muslim republics adjoining Afghanistan — by flooding them with the Koran and cheap drugs.

After the Soviets conceded defeat and pulled out of Afghanistan in February 1989, the message of hate was turned against the United States — for leaving Afghanistan in the lurch and for punishing Pakistan for its secret nuclear buildup. Clarke understood the global context of al-Qaida. He also knew there was no nexus between the charnel house of Saddam Hussein and the global terrorism of Osama bin Laden. The invasion of Iraq, like Afghanistan a Muslim country, could only spawn more fresh recruits for al-Qaida.

Maybe Beers is on to something.

Iraqi exiles return to Baghdad

PAMELA HESS

WASHINGTON, June 9 (UPI) — Six Iraqi men and one woman sat at a table in an ascetic conference room in the recesses of a featureless office in an anonymous building near the Pentagon. They are the future of Iraq — or so the Bush administration hopes.

They have volunteered to go back to the country they fled in fear and disgust to help the Americans now in charge of the "coalition provisional authority" restore order. They will help to rebuild a once vibrant healthcare system; to set a course for the new government in the world community; to refresh a drained marsh; to reseed barren wheat fields; and to ease the Kurdish people's entry into Iraq proper after

years of torment and now a decade of almost total independence.

On Monday, another 77 set out to join them, the last and largest tranche from the Iraq Reconstruction and Development Council created in February. Around 60 exiled Iraqis are already at work in Baghdad and elsewhere, providing language, cultural understanding and subject-matter expertise to the Americans in charge of some 20 ministries and government offices. They are aware they may be viewed as carpetbaggers by the Iraqis who stayed and endured under Saddam Hussein. Around 4 million Iraqis fled the country.

"We expect to receive that reception," said Adel Rahoumi, 46, now from Princeton, N.J. "Everyone of us has a suffering story to tell. It's not like we left them to rot. Everyone has suffered somehow."

Saddam Hussein's son Uday killed Rahoumi's brother. It is not something he wants to talk about.

"I feel like it is so small, and other people's agonies are so big. That is the tragedy of our people," he said in an interview in May before setting out for Iraq.

Rahoumi is an artist. Born to an Egyptian mother and Iraqi father, he left Iraq for college in 1977 and did not return. He is now working for the municipality of Baghdad. His task will be to "cleanse the country of so-called artistic statues and murals." Most of the public art pieces are representations of Saddam Hussein. Rahoumi hopes to transform the Saddam Art Center — a city gallery — into a museum dedicated to the regime's many victims, like the U.S. Holocaust Memorial Museum. He would keep the name as it is.

Rahoumi contended the outsiders should be welcomed, as they are the ones who have so long been advocating the ouster of Saddam Hussein.

"The people outside Iraq for the past 12 years, they have been the main reason for this liberation to become actual," he said. "They were the lobby for this liberation to come."

Besides, he said, few of the returning exiles intend to remain in Iraq. Most have made just a few months commitment, and they will return to their businesses and families in the United States.

"Many of us will not stay there. We're established," he said.

Indeed, the group includes a doctor, a pharmacist, business owners and two professors.

In addition to their ostensible jobs with the Ministry of Foreign Affairs, health, agriculture and with the cities of Basra and Baghdad, all seven understand one of their critical purposes will be to ferret out the remaining Baath Party members, and to distinguish between those who joined the party simply to get along in a society controlled by the group and those who participated in its less savory activities.

U.S. Defense Secretary Donald Rumsfeld calls it "de-Baathification" and compares the process to that which was conducted in Germany after World War II. Several high-ranking Baath Party members were initially appointed to important posts by the American counselors — at the Health Ministry and at Baghdad University — but they were quickly fired when Iraqis protested.

Yet the future of the Baath Party divides these seven. They all revile the group that came to power in Iraq in 1969 and promptly began persecuting its enemies. The questions they have are whether an Iraqi democracy can co-exist with the vestiges of the Baath party, or if banning the Baathists outright would undermine the principles of democracy.

"The ideology of the Baath Party was copied from Nazi ideology; you have to melt all the non-Arabs in the crucible of the Arabs," said Mowaffaq al-Tikriti, a pharmacist who left Baghdad for the United Arab Emirates when his string of stores began to flourish and attract government notice. He later settled in Canada, where he now has a business. "That ideology of melting others should be nonconstitutional. Any ideology that calls for ethnic cleanings should be banned."

Al-Tikriti will be working at the Ministry of Health with Dr. Mahmud Thamer, 72, originally from Najaf. Thamer left Iraq in 1969, after the Baathists came to power and tortured and interrogated his brother for weeks. When he was freed, Thamer fled and settled in Baltimore.

"As reprehensible as this may be, this is in clear conflict with the whole idea of democracy. You have to differentiate between the right of the people to believe (in the Baath ideology) and the right to have important posi-

tions" in the government, Thamer said. "We have to be careful. We really don't have a good tradition of tolerating dissent. If a democracy is anything, it is tolerating and respecting of the difference of opinions. We have to really work on that."

The exiled Iraqis appear to have more tolerance for the messy business of democracy than the American powers have evinced so far, at least as far as the Baath Party is concerned. The seven acknowledged that many people may still embrace Baathism, and said they must not be persecuted for it.

"If we are going to have a real democracy, we can't prevent the Baathists from rebuilding," said Rahoumi. "Democracy is not a law. It is a practice."

The session quickly turned into a philosophical debate about the nature of democracy and where its fissures might be in a country with as violent a record as Iraq. But for these seven, the debate has enormous practical implications. They will be the eyes and ears of the Americans in Baghdad who are making the calls that shape whatever government comes next.

"I think we need to set rules for the game. That's what we lacked for 34 years. We have enough Iraqi intellectuals (to do it). It begins with institutions, education, people and practices. It starts with small hamlets and towns. They elect a mayor, a police force," said Ghanim al-Shibli.

Al-Shibli, 62, originally from Baghdad, is working with the Ministry of Foreign Affairs. He was with the Iraqi diplomatic corps and was himself a member of the Baath Party — a distinction he shares with some 15 million other Iraqis. He was assigned to the United States in 1986 when he was recalled to Baghdad. He moved his family to North Carolina because he was told his life was in danger.

"We need to come up with a way to make democracy sacred. That it's a big curse to be 'not democratic,'" Thamer said. "Democracy is an upbringing."

Al-Shibli believes the way to do this is to dramatically expand Iraq's exposeure to information and the Internet.

"The freedom of mind. Access to everything in Iraq would be the best blessing we could ever have," he said.

"There is something about this country — we can jump the moment we get exposed to the world after 35 years of isolation. That will have a big impact on Iraq," added al-Tikriti, the pharmacist. Democracy will succeed if the American authorities don't shove it down the Iraqis throats, he said.

They do not think the differences between the minority, but previously powerful, Sunni Muslims and the majority Shiite Muslims will be difficult to overcome. Those differences were created by Saddam Hussein and the Baath Party, they contended, in order to divide and conquer the country.

"We have many features in history and background that make me hopeful in achieving democracy," Thamer said. "There were poets and writers, there were civil rights and protections. We do have these (in our history). Among the Iraqi people, there was a cultural tolerance. The fighting was between governments. The people themselves didn't fight each other. There was lots of intermarriage, there was a culture of tolerance."

The differences are there, argues Ramadan al-Badran, 41, the most recent refugee from Iraq. A former soldier in the Iraqi army, he went "AWOL" during the Persian Gulf war and then took part in the Shiite uprising in Basra in 1991. It was brutally crushed, but al-Badran said he fought until the end and then fled for a refugee camp in Saudi Arabia. He was the last fighter to escape with his life. He is returning to help the city get back on its feet and to restore the drained marshes in the southern part of the country, a project known as Project Eden Again.

"Let's be clear: We are an old-fashioned society with loyalty to our roots," said al-Badran. "Being clear, being honest will have a good control" on the political situation. "Representation is being clear who you are."

With that declaration, the interview spun out of control as the group argued whether there had ever been an important leader in Baghdad from the southern city of Basra. It was finally decided there had been, some 70 years ago. This seemed recent enough to satisfy everyone at the table.

Two at the table were Kurdish: Sardar Comyon, a Ph.D. in agricultural science who proudly declares he is from "Kurdistan," the

wished-for, but so far unrealized, independent ethnic enclave; and Pakeza Alexander, 38, who has a masters of criminal justice and is the mother of three children in Nashville, Tenn. She fled Iraq in 1975 when the Baathists were cracking down on the Kurds.

"It was hard. I was running. I witnessed a lady dropping a baby without even knowing it. I smelled human flesh burning from the mountains. It still feels like it happened yesterday," Alexander said. She was 10 years old. She married in Iran when she was 12 and had her first son a year later. Alexander is going to Baghdad to run the Iraq Reconstruction Council office there. Comyon will work with the agriculture department.

The Kurds have suffered greatly at the hands of the former Iraqi government. Multiple wars and ethnic cleansing campaigns finally culminated in the mustard gassing of the town of Halabja in 1988, killing as many as 8,000.

"All the time I feel I'm in danger — sometimes I never even feel I'm an Iraqi," said Comyon of his status as a Kurd. Based on his experience with other exiles — Sunni, Shiite, Kurd and Christian — in the nondescript office in Arlington, Va., he has decided he will stay in "Kurdistan," Iraq, forever.

"Now I am starting to feel ... because my friends and colleagues talk to each other about how we can rebuild, really, I feel I'm Iraqi," Comyon said. "We are a part of Iraq now."

Analysis: Blair running out of trust

MARTIN WALKER

WASHINGTON, June 5 (UPI) — For three hours on Thursday afternoon, Tony Blair's full Cabinet talked about whether or not the economic conditions were right for them to call a referendum and recommend to the voters that Britain should join the euro. But somewhere in the back of every Cabinet minister's mind was a rather more urgent question — how far the government in general and Tony Blair in particular still carried much credibility with the public. If they called a referendum and advised the public to vote yes, how many of them would trust Blair's judgment?

Blair on Wednesday, facing "Prime Minister's Question Time" in the House of Commons, put forth his usual accomplished performance against charges that the intelligence evidence about Iraq's weapons of mass destruction had been doctored to strengthen his case for the war. Iain Duncan-Smith, the lackluster and thoroughly decent Conservative Leader of the Opposition, delivered his own customary feeble performance.

On the face of it, Blair won. He denied doctoring anything. He played the patriot card, praising the achievements of the British troops. He turned to human rights, telling the British people they should be proud of toppling such a brutal dictator. And he wallowed in his own triumph and sneered at the discomfiture of his critics.

"They said there would be thousands dead. They said it was my Vietnam. They said that the Middle East would be in flames!" Blair mocked the hapless Duncan-Smith. And the massed ranks of Blair's backbenchers shouted down the opposition. So it was a parliamentary triumph. Yet it was hollow, because one phrase from Duncan-Smith seems to be echoing in Britain with far greater reach and resonance than Blair's defense. "The truth is that nobody now believes a word that the prime minister says." This was the truly devastating remark from the Conservative leader, and people seem to be taking it seriously.

One of Blair's former Cabinet colleagues, development minister Clair Short, who resigned claiming that she had been misled over the Iraq war, has reinforced Duncan-Smith's charge.

"The fact that there was deceit on the way to military action is a very grave accusation I am making. If we can be deceived about this then what can we not be deceived about?" Short said.

The British public seems to agree. Last week, the Daily Telegraph published a poll that showed the Conservatives just one percentage point behind Labor. Blair's own ratings were grim. After the 1997 election, Blair had a positive rating of 60 — that is, 60 percent more voters approved of him than disapproved. Just after his successful 2001 reelection, Blair's approval rating was 18. Last week, it was minus 18.

Worst of all were the poll figures asking whether the government had been honest and trustworthy. Only 29 percent, fewer than one in three, said "Yes."

At the time of the last election, 56 percent thought Blair's government was honest. And 62 percent of British voters polled said the British government was trustworthy.

Those are frightening figures for any politician, but desperate for a leader like Blair, who had managed to forge a close personal link with the British electorate, convincing them of his decency and his integrity. The failure to find Saddam Hussein's weapons of mass destruction, nearly two months after the fall of Baghdad, has corroded the level of personal trust that had been Blair's biggest asset.

Blair has yet to face his biggest test in persuading the British public to put their doubts to one side and trust their prime minister. The decision whether to join the euro is just the half of it. (The chances are that the Cabinet will agree to duck the issue of a referendum, which the polls say they would probably lose.) The issue they cannot duck is the European Union's new constitution, whose draft has just been published by the convention chaired by former French President Valery Giscard d'Estang.

The merits of the new constitution are almost beside the point. The Conservatives and the press and most of the public want a referendum in which they can say yes or no to the new constitution. Blair says no — the constitution will be ratified in the usual way by Parliament, not the public. In effect, Blair is telling the voters, "Trust me," when the issue of Trusting Tony is now at the heart of British politics, and less than a third of the electorate thinks he is honest.

"They fear the government is going to sell them out on Europe and thus will try to do it stealthily," says Robert Worcester, chairman of the MORI polling firm.

So Blair's apparent success at Question Time in Parliament may have been one successful skirmish in a much longer and more serious campaign for the trust of the British public that Blair now seems to be losing. And without it, Blair's plans for Europe, the Middle East, Iraq, domestic reform or anything else will bog down. He seems to be running out of time, just three months short of Aug. 2, the date when he can claim to be running the longest-serving Labor government in British history.

Feature: Iraqi records detail atrocities

P. MITCHELL PROTHERO

BAGHDAD, Iraq, April 27 (UPI) — In "Leviathan", philosopher Thomas Hobbes described life for man living outside the protection of society as "nasty, brutish and short." This is also the life that Saddam Hussein's regime offered the people of Iraq.

Not to say that the Baath regime did not deliver some benefits — cheap food, gasoline and energy — that aided daily life for its people, but overall it was a nasty and brutish rule that lasted far too long, and a new group of Iraqis holds the shocking details in millions of manila office folders.

In what was once the home of the former head of Iraqi military intelligence, an impromptu group called Committee of Freed Iraqi Prisoners now studies the theories and practice of the hell by the former government. When looters first arrived at the home shortly after Baghdad fell, they discovered records that detail the crimes and fates of more than 2 million people persecuted, and mostly killed, by Saddam's men. These records only span the period from 1981 to 1991, but even more were killed from 1991 to 2003, committee officials say.

United Press International was granted access to these records on the condition that it not photograph the researchers or use the names of committee officials. It seems that with no confirmation of Saddam's death, these men who were persecuted so brutally were taking no chances on the return of his regime or the revenge of its supporters. They also requested that United Press International not use the names of prisoners from the records because their families continue to search for information on their fates, and it would be cruel, they say, to learn of them in an article written by a foreign stranger.

Family members come by the carload to loiter in the yard of the house, poring over the lists identifying men killed, and when. About six months ago, Saddam emptied his prisons of most of the criminal and some political offenders in preparation for the American invasion. The families knew what it meant when these men never came home, but they have never received confirmation — which might lead to some information on which mass grave the men were dumped in, which might allow them to find the body for proper burial more than 10 years later.

The scene is one that's both touching and sinister. Emotional old Iraqi women scan the walls and sometimes crumple into a moaning heap as they find a name. Men cry and yell at an American visitor for his government's inexcusable betrayal of the Shiite Muslims when they rose against Saddam in 1991 at former President Bush's urging after the Persian Gulf War, only to be slaughtered by the tens of thousands after Bush changed his mind and allowed Saddam to crush the uprising.

Teenagers with AK-47s roam the yard as a form of very dangerous security to ward off Baath threats. At one point, someone throws a brick through a window of the home, sending the gun-toting man-child at the door into a deadly parody of a soldier as he "patrols" the grounds looking for the offender.

Inside the home, committee officials brief their visitors from the foreign media. They detail their own tales of suffering. Each was related to someone that attended too many Shiite religious ceremonies, which drew regime attention, which led to allegations that they were agents of Iran. Once the allegations were made, each male family member was arrested and most were killed.

Each room of the house is strewn with neat records that in some cases are stacked feet high. Each folder has details of the prisoner on the outside; his name, crime, date of arrest, date of conviction and ultimate fate are stamped with bureaucratic dispassion and efficiency. Most accusations are that they are a Dawa Party member or an assassin supported by a foreign regime. The fates don't vary much: Hanged, hanged, hanged, life in prison, hanged.

Inside the folders are reports from the investigating judge. In one case the judge decides on 20 years in prison, but the next page is a typed letter signed by Saddam himself overruling the judge. Hanged.

"My brother went to mosque," said one man who claimed to be 40, but looked a decade older. "That meant he was a member of the (dissident) Dawa Party. I was in prison from 1981 until this year."

He displays the scars of his torture: burns from cigarettes, electrocution and beatings.

"How can Bush and the Americans support this man Saddam?" he asks, referring to the occasional collaboration between the United States and Saddam prior to 1991 and the ensuing betrayal of the Shiites.

"Why did they do this to us? What do they say in their defense about my four brothers? About me?" he asks. "You are American, what will you say about this to (President George W.) Bush, to (Vice President Dick) Cheney, to the world?" The reporter cautiously offers that the Americans who betrayed him and his people will face God one day and have to account for their actions. But this draws a surprising response from a man tortured for his religious convictions.

"I do not care about that, I do not care about God," he replies.

The man has lost more than just 20 years and four members of his family.

The crowd outside is increasing and grows more dangerous. It's time for the reporters to go, and the tone turns nasty. The committee officials are kind men despite their anger and help ward off some of the passionate demands and intense cries for attention as the reporters struggle into their vehicle. At the car, the group has now stopped moving and almost has to fight to get in. But there is no outbreak of violence, and they depart for the safety of their journalist compound and its four tanks, its four Bradley fighting vehicles.

Analysis: Does terror ever end?

NICHOLAS M. HORROCK

WASHINGTON, May 14 (UPI) — For President George W. Bush, Monday's bombing of apartment complexes in Saudi Arabia was an ugly reminder that the war on terror goes on and perhaps evidence that the victories amassed on the battlefield may be very fleeting indeed. The president heard about the attacks in Riyadh as he toured tornado damage in the Midwest. It was not a surprise to him. U.S. intelligence has warned about attacks on U.S. interests in Saudi Arabia for weeks. Bush did not blame it on al-Qaida, though he, like everyone else, assumes from its methodology, the targets and the venue that it was the work of Osama bin Laden's group or its sympathizers.

It harkens to the original mission of al-Qaida as framed by bin Laden in the 1990s. He wanted to get U.S. troops out of Saudi Arabia and end the Western influence he felt was so corrupting to the home of Mecca and Medina, Islam's two most holy cities.

Now he seems to have achieved both. Quietly, when fighting had ended in Iraq, the United States announced last month that after 12 years it would pull the bulk of its armed forces out of the Arab kingdom. Tuesday, after the bombing, the State Department ordered nonessential diplomatic personnel home, and large numbers of the 40,000 Americans there also began making plans to leave.

The Bush administration always has been suspicious that the Saudi government secretly tolerates al-Qaida, but the truth may be that the Saudi royal family is in as much danger as the enclaves of Americans. Under Islamic teachings, non-Arab troops must not settle in Arabia, and Muslim nations who attack other Muslim nations become infidels. The Saudi royal family has allowed both, supporting the war against Iraq and billeting U.S. forces. The Wahhabi school of Islam, which is dominant in Saudi Arabia, is strong on basic Islamic tenets.

The attack in Saudi Arabia alone, though deadly — 34 people died, including eight Americans — would not be so disturbing to the White House were it in isolation. But it is not in isolation:

• More than a month after hostilities ended in Iraq, Baghdad and much of the nation are in turmoil. Food, water, power, medical care and law enforcement, all basics of civilized life, have not been restored, and the government apparatus is only operating at quarter step.

• Bush quietly had to replace virtually the entire team that the Department of Defense had put together to begin reconstruction, placing a trusted American diplomat, L. Paul Bremer, at the helm.

• Wednesday, Bremer immediately ordered that U.S. troops would fire upon looters, a move that to many who entered Baghdad in mid-April seems a month too late.

• Wednesday, he also set about making sure senior members of Saddam Hussein's Baath Party would not get posts in the new government. That will be a more formidable task than many may think. Jobs throughout government from hospitals to the army command generally required two things: membership in the Baath Party and worshipping as a Sunni Muslim.

• Along with the inability of the U.S. team to get reconstruction briskly under way is the failure to find weapons of mass destruction. Bush and others in his administration argue they will be found. Nevertheless, all the prewar rhetoric about the dangers of Saddam's weapons is as yet coming to naught. The United States is reducing its military weapons hunting teams in Iraq and sending in a smaller, more token force to destroy missiles that have been found and to look further. The most glaring hyperbole here was the report shortly before the war that Republican Guard units guarding Baghdad had access to chemical and perhaps biological weapons. None has turned up.

One of President Bush's primary justifications for waging war against Iraq was to end Saddam's alleged direct and indirect support for terrorists. Evidence of these connections has been lean. Abu Abbas, the man who plotted the Achille Lauro ship hijacking, was picked up in Baghdad, but he had been released over a decade ago in a deal with the Italian government. Other possible al-Qaida members are under investigation there.

The end of major hostilities in Iraq, though brought about swiftly and impressively by U.S. forces, left Saddam's whereabouts a mystery and a sort of open-ended sense that Bush faced in Afghanistan. Nearly two years after the Sept. 11, 2001, attacks, and 18 months after the defeat of the organized forces of the Taliban, U.S. military and British forces still hunt the Taliban and the al-Qaida in Afghanistan and still face stubborn guerrilla attacks there. Last Saturday, for instance, a U.S.-led convoy was attacked in eastern Afghanistan by rebels who killed one Afghan soldier and wounded an American. The Americans and British have had to repeatedly mount search missions to locate Taliban members who often flee over the Pakistani border into tribal regions.

The Afghans have complained that the United States turned away from stabilizing their country in order to wage war against Iraq. Deputy Secretary of State Richard Armitage just completed a visit to Kabul trying to reassure the Afghans that Washington has not abandoned them.

Sen. Bob Graham. (D-Fla.), former chairman of the Senate Intelligence Committee and once an announced candidate for the Democratic Party presidential nomination, said Tuesday the war in Iraq distracted the United States from the war on terror at a crucial moment.

"I would say that al-Qaida had substantially weakened and was on the ropes about 12 to 14 months ago," he said. "As I said last fall, I thought the priority for the United States should be to win the war on terror before we took on the other evils in the Middle East and Central Asia."

Graham may feel that is an issue for the campaign, but the White House dismissed his view by noting there is a Democratic primary going on. Karl Rove, Bush's principal political adviser, sees Bush as a war president who will run and win in 2004 on dealing with the war on terror — no matter how long it takes.

Iraqi group formed to resist coalition

BEIRUT, Lebanon, May 29 (UPI) — An Iraqi group that claims to have elected its command committee from most of the country's provinces has been formed to fight and prevent cooperation with U.S.-led coalition forces in Iraq. The group, called the Unification Front for the Liberation of Iraq, announced its existence with a statement published Thursday by the Lebanese newspaper As Safir.

The group said its principal mission was to "liberate the Iraqi territories from foreign occupation," using "all adequate political and military means." It called on all Iraqi national political forces for quick resistance action, preventing cooperation with the occupation and, boycotting its "agents." It blamed the collapsed Baath Party regime of ousted President Saddam Hussein for the presence of the U.S.-led coalition forces. The group charged that the United States planned to attack Syria and "tear apart Egypt and Saudi Arabia."

Feature: Johnny comes marching home

RICHARD TOMKINS

CAMP PENDLETON, Calif., May 25 (UPI) — It started with worried murmurs of anticipation. It ended with tearful murmurs of joy. And in between was the eruption of sustained cheering from hundreds of cold, tired men, women and children who had milled around for hours in the basketball court of 62 Area Barracks to meet loved ones.

Bravo Company, 1st Battalion, 5th Marines, was home from war. Iraq was now a memory and a service ribbon, no longer a reality of danger, tedium and dust.

"All I want to do is see him," said Anita Hedrick, who was meeting her son, Joseph.

"All I want to do is give him a big hug," Pat Ross said of Joshua, a private first class with the company.

Bravo Company was one of the first two American units to punch into southern Iraq at the start of the ground war on March 20. It captured a gas and oil separation plant in the Rumaila oil field, pushed north and captured the vital Saddam Hussein Canal Bridge and fought a pitched battle after entering eastern Baghdad weeks and hundreds of miles later. In between, its 180 men liberated village after village and helped free children from a prison, some of them incarcerated for refusing to join the militia of dictator Saddam Hussein. It fed hungry villagers and helped stop looting at a hospital on the outskirts of the capital.

"It's a great day to be a Marine," one of them had yelled crossing into Iraq from Kuwait at night, as artillery shells screamed overhead and bright orange explosions from dropped bombs lit the distant, inky black horizon.

The company's casualty toll during the war: just four wounded seriously enough to be medevaced from the grounds of the al-Azimiyah Palace in eastern Baghdad in the middle of a firefight. Nearly a dozen others were treated for less serious wounds and rushed back into the fray.

Call it luck or Divine Providence. Either way, it was a miracle. Virtually every armored vehicle in which the Marines entered Baghdad was hit by rocket-propelled grenades. More than 100 RPGs were fired at them as they held the palace against extremist gunmen firing automatic weapons from alleyways and from windows and balconies and buildings nearby.

At the Saddam Hussein Canal, 120mm enemy mortars exploded just yards away from units, yet the men escaped unhurt as they cleared out Iraqi resistance, opening the way from an armored column's push into the Iraqi heartland.

"Welcome Home Troops," a sign outside a motel in Oceanside, near the main gate to Camp Pendleton, said Sunday. "Job Well Done!"

Saturday evening and well into Sunday, similar signs and banners were hanging from the balconies of barracks surrounding the basketball court in 62 Area, in a part of the base known as Camp San Mateo.

"1/5 No Jive. Welcome Home," said one. "Outstanding Y'all," said another.

"Welcome Home, Daddy," said a third. "We are proud of you."

Analysis: Iraq oil recovery risky, hopeful

BRUCE CHALFANT

NEW YORK, July 31 (UPI) — The good news is Iraq has begun exporting its oil again. The bad news is the war-ravaged country has a long way to go, and events are conspiring to delay the influx of much-needed oil revenues.

Current production levels of about 1 million barrels a day are still far below Iraq's pre-war peak of 1.9 million barrels daily, and very far below what the country is capable of producing and exporting.

The situation has to be frustrating to Iraq's newly formed governing council. Increasing the country's oil exports to their full potential would be a relatively easy job if daily sabotage and sniper attacks were not hobbling efforts, industry experts told United Press International.

That is why technicians from Kellogg, Brown & Root — the U.S. defense contractor in Houston responsible for restoring Iraqi oil — must add soldiers to their convoys before they head out to work each day on the looted and damaged fields, which once pumped 3 million barrels daily and are ranked among the world's most prolific.

Technically speaking, restoring and expanding Iraq's oil flow is a straightforward task. Much of the oil is easily accessible — in pools only 10,000 to 15,000 feet below the surface. The country's overall resource is estimated at 112 billion barrels, nearly half the size of Saudi Arabia's.

More pertinent to the world picture, that much oil could change the pecking order, prestige and power among the members of the Organization of Petroleum Exporting Countries, and perhaps reset the economic and political balance in the Middle East.

"It's not like the North Sea or Sable Island or the Gulf Coast, where you're in deep water and the weather plays hell with your platforms and people," said a former senior oil company executive. "You just drive out to the field and get to work … once the shooting stops."

The potential size of Iraq's reserves and the estimates of short development times frustrate virtually everyone involved. Former Iraqi Oil Minister Issam al-Chalabi called Iraq "one of the least explored among the rich oil countries." In a special presentation for clients, Chalabi, now with Cambridge Energy Research Associates, an international consulting firm, calculated there are 526 potential oil-bearing structures in Iraq, of which only 125 — or 20 percent — have been drilled. He estimated some 4.7 million barrels per day could be produced just from the following short- to medium-term actions:

— Eleven new fields in the south could produce about 3 million barrels per day.

— Eleven new fields in the north could produce 500,000 barrels per day.

— Three fields in the central region could yield 300,000 barrels per day.

— Partially developed reservoirs in existing fields could add another 900,000 barrels per day.

Production levels notwithstanding, oil revenue is the key to the country's recovery. U.S.-led coalition leaders in Iraq have said all along Iraqi oil belongs to the Iraqi people and the first payments will be for food and much-needed aid relief.

There are other calls on the money, however. Iraq owes billions on loans unpaid since 1990. In addition, there are millions claimed in lawsuits over the invasion of Kuwait and by displaced ethnic and religious groups. Right now, production efforts are said to be keeping internal Iraqi demand satisfied. Some 9 million barrels in storage in Turkey have been auctioned and are being exported to refiners in Spain, France, Turkey and to the international company Chevron-Texaco.

Russia and China have additional beefs, too. Iraq had contracted for 418 wells to be developed in joint ventures with the Russian and Chinese national companies. Saddam Hussein's regime had hoped to use the joint ventures as a political wedge to lift the sanctions imposed after the Kuwaiti invasion and boasted of being able to export 6 million barrels per day. That level of output is attainable over the next few years but ownership questions could take even longer to resolve.

Yet though it is barely in business, Iraq remains center stage in world oil politics. Its potential oil resource ranks it second only to Saudi Arabia. As oil exports ramp up, Iraq could demand the chair at OPEC meetings, or skip them altogether and decide to become a powerful but independent market force, as did Russia.

If OPEC is nervous about the long-term picture its members are not showing any signs of it.

"If OPEC did not exist, it would have to be created," Abdullah bin Hamad al-Attiyah, OPEC's president, told reporters after a recent cartel ministerial meeting. OPEC's Middle East members are exporting over 21 million barrels daily; Iraq's output through the next few months will not give them much clout in any of the cartel's pricing and production decisions.

As the OPEC brass philosophizes and the lawyers huddle, technicians from KBR and the U.S. Army Corps of Engineers tackle the rebuilding and renovation. Looting and sabotage have left badly needed production equipment in what the Oil and Gas Journal calls "wretched shape."

Analysts who have seen the facilities report ransacked offices and control rooms, with communications, command and control equipment destroyed, pipeline pumps stolen, oil and gas separation facilities missing important parts.

"You should see the place; it's a goddam mess," the senior oil executive said. Not that Iraq's facilities were all that well cared for to begin with.

Saddam built palaces and Baath party headquarters at the expense of the oil industry. He also left to languish the crucial pipelines that exported oil to neighboring nation seaports. A 1.6-million-barrel-per-day line to Saudi Arabia has been closed since 1990. A 700,000 barrel-per-day line into Turkey was barely operable as coalition forces landed.

"The government started taking the oil revenues and we started losing out," said a senior engineer with the government's national oil company who remembers the country before the Saddam regime.

Phillip Carroll, a former oil company executive and now a consultant to the coalition, says there is one primary task: "Increase security," Carroll told reporters at a recent news conference. Carroll said a diversified global communications capability (to monitor and control pipeline slows) is also high on the list.

Iraqi managers talk of the need for buses to reach their jobs and shooting wars are keeping them home. Most of all they are owed back pay.

Most analysts agree 2004 will see Iraqi oil playing a more important role in world markets — if the attacks stop. An Iraqi coalition government should be in place and important long-term decisions will be deliberated and decided: Who will get the oil, for instance.

Thamir Ghadban, the interim minister of oil, said Iraq is "going to open the door for foreign investment but in accordance with a formula that safeguards the interest of the Iraqi people."

Meanwhile, the convoys leave Baghdad every day. As they head out to the fields, refineries and tank farms, the technicians wear baseball caps displaying the letters "RIO" — "Restore Iraqi Oil."

Commentary: Leaving Iraq is not an option

CLAUDE SALHANI

WASHINGTON, Sept. 2 (UPI) — With American casualties in Iraq surpassing the number killed during the actual offensive, a debate is beginning to brew whether there is a need to dispatch more troops to Iraq or not. Some say yes, while others, such as Secretary of Defense Donald Rumsfeld, say no, the current numbers can adequately do the job. The reality, however, lies somewhere in between.

Following the horrific blast at the Najaf Imam Ali mosque on Aug. 29, which killed Ayatollah Syed Mohammed Baqir al-Hakim and some 100 others, the bombing of the U.N. headquarters in Baghdad on Aug. 19 that killed its representative, Sergio Vieira de Mello, and another 20 people, some voices argued for reinforcing "boots on the ground."

The Najaf and U.N. attacks, which came on the heels of a similar attack on the Jordanian embassy and the sabotage of major water and oil conduits, as well as another car bomb outside a Baghdad police station on Sept. 2, reinforce the belief that the current level of troops — reported to be somewhere around 130,000 U.S. plus 20,000 Brits — is not enough for the task at hand.

Others argued for more international troops from Europe, India and other friendly nations that would allow American soldiers to be less visible, thus less prone to attack.

The counter argument opined that more troops would simply offer those targeting coalition troops greater opportunities to kill American (and other allied) soldiers. The attack on the United Nations, after all, was not aimed at American troops. There is, indeed, something to be said for that.

In truth, it's not more American troops that are needed in Iraq, but rather, speeding up of the process required in order to replace coalition troops with autochthonous forces.

In term of simple numbers, Iraq had the largest army in the Middle East before the U.S.-led invasion abolished it last April. According to a 2003 CIA estimate, Iraq had about 3.5 million men fit for military service. Deduct from that number those who were killed and disabled in the war and those who were too closely linked to the old regime in one way or another. Filtered down, you should easily come up with at least 100,000 able men. Why not mobilize them? And if you really want to revolutionize the country, allow Iraqi women into the armed forces, too. That should easily provide an additional 5,000 to 10,000 troops.

By now, almost five months into the occupation of Iraq, coalition commanders — with assistance from their friends in the Iraqi National Council — should have had no trouble identifying a cadre of friendly Iraqi officers able to lead a reformed military to take over control of much of the country's security. At least as far as high-profile assignments go, such as guarding of government buildings, major intersections, bridges and other sensitive installations. Let the Iraqi people feel they have direct involvement in the rebuilding of their nation, instead of appearing as bystanders with little or no say.

The current situation in Iraq leaves little room for doubt; something needs to be done to prevent the country from becoming a refuge for Islamist militants and other groups opposed to democratic reform. And it needs to be done quickly.

Every day that goes by draws more and more anti-American forces to the region. So much has been acknowledged by American intelligence agencies. Note to those who opposed the United States' unilateral policy or who might regard U.S. policy in the Middle East as neo-colonialist imperialism: Before you begin to applaud America's headaches in Iraq, be advised that continued unrest in Iraq will also weaken the rest of the region. An unstable Iraq will only endanger the whole Middle East. The attack on the United Nations has changed the face of this war.

"If the Americans pull out now, it will open the area to the forces of darkness, the nihilists, the (Osama) bin Laden supporters, and others who will regress the area into the dark ages," said a seasoned Middle East observer.

Or, as President Bush pointed out to an American Legion convention in St. Louis on Aug. 26, "Retreat in the face of terror would only invite further and bolder attacks."

What we are seeing in Iraq in many ways is a repeat performance of what happened in Lebanon in 1982-83 when a multinational force was dispatched to restore order to that war-ravaged country. Lebanon, at the time, was torn apart along sectarian lines with Christian militias opposed to a fractured Muslim-Leftist-Palestinian alliance, much as the Shiites, Sunnis, Assyrians, Kurds and Turkmen are in Iraq. The difference in Iraq is that the various factions are not fighting each other at the level the Lebanese were, at least not yet.

Following the bombing of the Marine and French army barracks attacks in Beirut 20 years ago next month, the multinational force decided to cut its losses and leave, abandoning Lebanon to its own predicament. The Bush administration, however, does not have that luxury in Iraq. Abandonment in its current state is not an option. Which is why two things need to happen with haste.

First, more international troops should be brought in, because security is a concern. The attack on the U.N. building demonstrated that this was not simply an assault on U.S. forces, but also on the international community. And second, Iraqis should be given a more direct role in running of their country sooner rather than later.

APPENDIX

TOTAL FORCES ENGAGED

U.S. — Total: 275,000, including U.S. air and naval forces and 4th Infantry Divison.

Total ground troops engaged in Iraq, 125,000. This includes the 3rd Infantry Division, the U.S. Marines Expeditionary Division, the 101st Airborne Division, elements of the 82nd Airborne Division and 136 Airborne Brigade, Special Forces and corps, logistics and support troops.

The U.S. Navy deployed 5 aircraft carrier task forces, a total of 47 surface ships, and 12 submarines.

U.K. — Total: 45,000, including air and naval forces.

Total ground troops engaged in Iraq, 26,000. This includes the 7th Armored Brigade, the 16th Air Assault Brigade, 3 Commando Brigade (Royal Marines), 102 Logistics Brigade, SAS Special Forces and division, and support troops.

The Royal Navy deployed one aircraft carrier task force (HMS Ark Royal), one helicopter carrier task force (HMS Ocean), a squadron of 15 other warships, and a fleet submarine, which fired 30 Tomahawk cruise missiles.

Australia — The Australian armed forces deployed a total of 2,200 military personnel, including 150 SAS Special Forces on the ground, A Commando unit, 3 warships, and a squadron of F-18 ground support fighter-bombers.

Iraqi forces — Regular army, on paper, 420,000 troops; estimated real deployed number, approx 300,000.

Republican Guard: 72,000
Special Republican Guard: 15,000
Special Security Organization: 8,000
Fedayeen Saddam: 21,000

CASUALTIES

On April 24, the U.S. Pentagon and the British Ministry of Defense issued the following casualty figures:

U.S. — 112 killed in combat
495 wounded in combat

U.K. — 8 killed in combat
74 wounded in combat

U.S. — 21 killed, 66 wounded in noncombat conditions (includes accidents and friendly fire)

U.K. — 24 killed in noncombat conditions, (includes accidents and friendly fire)

Australian — no casualties

Iraqis:

Military — 2,320 in Baghdad fighting alone (U.S. estimate). No other estimates available.

Civilian — 1,254 killed, 5,112 wounded, according to Iraqi official figures as of April 3.

The Web site www.iraqbodycount.net, run by academics and peace activists, estimates: Iraqi civilian fatalities to be between 1,930 and 2,377. Their count is based on incidents reported by at least two media sources.

A total of 7,400 Iraqis were taken prisoner.

7 soldiers recovered, 117 total dead

PAMELA HESS

WASHINGTON, April 13 (UPI) — U.S. Central Command Sunday identified seven U.S. service personnel who were found alive in Iraq.

"Army Chief Warrant Officers Ronald Young and David Williams, Apache helicopter pilots, and Sgt. James Riley, Spc. Shoshana Johnson, Pfc. Patrick Miller, Spc. Joseph Hudson, and Spc. Edgar Hernandez, from the 507th Maintenance Company, were recovered Sunday afternoon," Centcom said in a statement. All were previously confirmed prisoners of war.

Members of the 1st Marine Expeditionary Force returned the seven, who were found near the town of Samar and were flown by helicopter to an airfield near An Numaniyah, south of Baghdad. They were then to be transferred by a C-130 aircraft to Kuwait City, where they were expected to undergo medical treatment. U.S. officials said they were notified of the whereabouts of the seven by Iraqis. Also Sunday, the Pentagon identified three service members killed in action and changed the status of three from missing to killed in action.

Gunnery Sgt. Jeffrey E. Bohr, Jr., 39, of Ossian, Iowa, was killed on April 10 in northern Baghdad while engaging opposition forces. He was assigned to the 1st Battalion, 5th Marine Regiment, Camp Pendleton, Calif.

Cpl. Jesus A. Gonzalez, 22, of Indio, Calif., was killed on April 12 while manning a checkpoint in Baghdad. He was assigned to the 1st Tank Battalion, 1st Marine Division, Twentynine Palms, Calif.

Staff Sgt. Riayan A. Tejeda, 26, of New York, N.Y., was killed on April 11 during combat operations against opposition forces in northeast Baghdad. He was assigned to the 3rd Battalion, 5th Marine Regiment, Camp Pendleton, Calif. Three Marines were confirmed killed in action from earlier missing-in-action status: Pfc. Tamario D. Burkett, 21, of Buffalo, N.Y.; Lance Cpl. Donald J. Cline, Jr., 21, of Sparks, Nev.; and Pvt. Nolen R. Hutchings, 19, of Boiling Springs, S.C. The three were assigned to 1st Battalion, 2nd Marine Regiment, 2nd Marine Expeditionary Brigade, based in Camp Lejeune, N.C. They were engaged in operations on the outskirts of Nasiriyah on March 23.

The Pentagon said Sunday that 117 American service members have died in the war, 12 of which were nonhostile deaths. Not all of the families of the dead have been notified, so some names have yet to be released. Five service members remain missing; there are no prisoners of war.

Previously announced deaths:

Navy Lt. Thomas Mullen Adams, 27, of La Mesa, Calif., was killed when two Royal Navy Sea King helicopters collided over international waters on March 22.

Capt. James F. Adamouski, 29, of Springfield, Va., was killed when his UH-60 Black Hawk helicopter crashed in central Iraq on April 2. He was a member of the 2nd Battalion, 3rd Aviation Regiment, Hunter Army Airfield, Ga.

Spc. Jamaal R. Addison, 22, of Roswell, Ga. He was killed in an ambush of the 507th Maintenance Company on March 23.

Capt. Tristan N. Aitken, 31, of State College, Pa., was killed in action on April 4 in Iraq. Aitken was assigned to the 1st Battalion, 41st Field Artillery, 3rd Infantry Division, Fort Stewart, Ga.

Lance Cpl. Brian E. Anderson, 26, of Durham, N.C., was killed on April 2 in a nonhostile accident west of Nasiriyah, Iraq. Anderson was manning a .50-caliber rifle on top of a seven-ton truck when the vehicle passed under and apparently snagged low-hanging power lines.

Maj. Jay Thomas Aubin, 36, of Waterville, Maine. Aubin was assigned to the Marine Aviation Weapons and Tactics Squadron 1, 3rd Marine Aircraft Wing, Marine Corps Air Station, Yuma, Ariz. Aubin died in a CH-46E helicopter crash on March 20 in Kuwait.

Pfc. Chad E. Bales, 20, of Coahoma, Texas, was killed on April 3 in a nonhostile vehicle accident during convoy operations east of Ash Shahin, Iraq. He was assigned to 1st Transportation Support Battalion, 1st Force Service Support Group, Camp Pendleton, Calif.

Capt. Ryan Anthony Beaupre, 30, of Bloomington, Ill., who was assigned to the Marine Medium Helicopter Squadron 268, 3rd Marine Aircraft Wing, Marine Corps Air Station, Camp Pendleton, Calif. Beaupre died in a CH-46E helicopter crash on March 20 in Kuwait.

Pfc. Wilfred D. Bellard, 20, of Lake Charles, La., died when his vehicle fell into a ravine on April 4. He was a member of the 41st Artillery Regiment, Fort Stewart, Ga.

Sgt. Michael E. Bitz, 31, Ventura, Calif. He was assigned to the 2nd Assault Amphibious Battalion, 2nd Marine Division, Camp Lejeune, N.C. He was killed in action on March 23 near Nasiriyah, Iraq.

Lance Cpl. Thomas A. Blair, 24, of Wagoner, Okla. He was assigned to the 2nd Low Altitude Air Defense Battalion, Marine Air Control Group 28, 2nd Marine Aircraft Wing, Cherry Point, N.C. His unit was engaged in operations on March 24 on the outskirts of Nasiriyah in Iraq. His remains were recovered on March 28.

Spc. Mathew G. Boule, 22, of Dracut, Mass., was killed when his UH-60 Black Hawk helicopter crashed in central Iraq on April 2. He was a member of the 2nd Battalion, 3rd Aviation Regiment, Hunter Army Airfield, Ga.

Cpl. Henry L. Brown, 22, of Natchez, Miss., died April 8. He was assigned to Headquarters Company, 1st Battalion, 64th Field Artillery Regiment, Fort Stewart, Ga. Brown died of wounds received in an opposition rocket attack south of Baghdad on April 7.

Spc. Larry K. Brown, 22, of Jackson, Miss., was killed in action on April 5 in Iraq. Brown was assigned to C Company, 1st Battalion, 41st Infantry Regiment, Fort Riley, Kan.

Lance Cpl. Brian Rory Buesing, 20, Cedar Key, Fla. He was assigned to the 1st Battalion, 2nd Marine Regiment, 2nd Marine Expeditionary Brigade, Camp Lejeune, N.C.

Sgt. George E. Buggs, 31, of Barnwell, S.C., was killed on or about March 23 when the convoy he was traveling in was ambushed in southern Iraq. Buggs was with the 3rd Division Support Battalion, Fort Stewart, Ga., the 507th Maintenance Company, Fort Bliss, Texas.

Sgt. Jacob L. Butler, 24, of Wellsville, Kan., was killed in action on April 1, in Samawa, Iraq, when a rocket-propelled grenade hit his vehicle. Butler was assigned to Headquarters Company, 1st Battalion, 41st Infantry Regiment, Fort Riley, Kan.

Staff Sgt. James W. Cawley, 41, of Roy, Utah, was killed on March 29 during a firefight with opposition forces. He was hit by a U.S. Humvee. He was assigned to F Company, 2nd Battalion, 23rd Marine Regiment, 4th Marine Division, Salt Lake City, Utah.

2nd Lt. Therrel S. Childers, 30, Harrison County, Miss., was killed in action on March 21 in a firefight in the Rumaila oil field in southern Iraq. Childers was assigned to the 1st Battalion, 5th Marine Regiment, 1st Marine Division, Camp Pendleton, Calif.

Capt. Aaron J. Contreras, 31, of Sherwood, Ore., was killed on March 30 in a UH-1N Huey helicopter crash in southern Iraq. He was assigned to Marine Light Attack Helicopter Squadron 169, Marine Aircraft Group 39, Marine Corps Air Station, Camp Pendleton, Calif.

Spc. Daniel Francis J. Cunningham, 33, Lewiston, Maine, died when his vehicle fell into a ravine April 4. He was a member of the 41st Artillery Regiment, Fort Stewart, Ga.

Spc. Michael Edward Curtin, 23, of South Plains, N.J. He was assigned to the 2-7th Infantry, 3rd Infantry Division, Fort Stewart, Ga. Curtin was killed at a checkpoint by a car bomb on March 29.

Staff Sgt Wilbert Davis, 40, of Alaska, died April 3 when his vehicle ran off the road into a canal in Iraq. Davis was assigned to the 3rd Battalion, 69th Armor, 3rd Infantry Division, Fort Stewart, Ga.

Lance Cpl. Jesus A. Suarez Del Solar, 20, of Escondido, Calif. He was assigned to the 1st Light Armored Reconnaissance Battalion, 1st Marine Division, Camp Pendleton, Calif. He was killed when a car bomb exploded at a checkpoint near Najaf on March 29.

Master Sgt. Robert J. Dowdy, 38, of Cleveland, Ohio. Dowdy was killed on or about March 23 when the convoy he was traveling in was ambushed in southern Iraq. He was with the 507th Maintenance Company, Fort Bliss, Texas.

Pvt. Ruben Estrella-Soto, 18, of El Paso, Texas. Estrella-Soto was killed on or about March 23 when the convoy he was traveling in was ambushed in southern Iraq. He was with the 507th Maintenance Company, Fort Bliss, Texas.

Cpl. Mark A. Evnin, 21, Burlington, Vt., was killed in action on April 3 during a firefight in central Iraq. He was assigned to the 3rd Battalion, 4th Marine Regiment, 1st Marine Division, Twenty-nine Palms, Calif.

Master Sgt. George A. Fernandez, 36, El Paso, Texas, was killed in action April 2. He was assigned to headquarters, U.S. Army Special Operations Command, Fort Bragg, N.C.

Lance Cpl. David K. Fribley, 26, Lee, Fla. He was one of nine Marines killed when a group of Iraqis pretended to surrender but then opened fire on Marines near Nasiriyah. He was assigned to the 1st Battalion, 2nd Marine Regiment, 2nd Marine Expeditionary Brigade, Camp Lejeune, N.C.

Cpl. Jose A. Garibay, 21, Orange, Calif. He was assigned to the 1st Battalion, 2nd Marine Regiment, 2nd Marine Expeditionary Brigade, Camp Lejeune, N.C. He was killed on March 23 in a firefight in Nasiriyah.

Pfc. Juan Guadalupe Garza Jr., 20, of Temperance, Mich., was killed in action on April 8 in central Iraq. He was assigned to the 1st Battalion,

4th Marine Regiment, 1st Marine Division, Camp Pendleton, Calif.

Cpl. Jorge A. Gonzalez, 20, Los Angeles. He was assigned to the 1st Battalion, 2nd Marine Regiment, 2nd Marine Expeditionary Brigade, Camp Lejeune, N.C. He was one of nine Marines killed on March 23 near Nasiriyah when Iraqi troops faked surrender but then opened fire on the Americans.

Cpl. Bernard G. Gooden, 22, of Mt. Vernon, N.Y., was killed April 4 during a firefight in central Iraq. He was assigned to the 2nd Tank Battalion, 2nd Marine Division, based at Camp Lejeune, N.C.

Pfc. Christian D. Gurtner, 19, of Ohio City, Ohio, died April 2 from a noncombat weapons discharge in southern Iraq. He was assigned to the 3rd Light Armored Reconnaissance Battalion, 1st Marine Division, Marine Corps Air–Ground Combat Center, Twenty-nine Palms, Calif.

Lance Cpl. Jose Gutierrez, 22, Los Angeles, killed in action on March 21 in southern Iraq. Gutierrez was assigned to the 2nd Battalion, 1st Marine Regiment, 1st Marine Division, Camp Pendleton, Calif.

Chief Warrant Officer Erik A. Halvorsen, 40, of Bennington, Vt., was killed when his UH-60 Black Hawk helicopter crashed in central Iraq on April 2. He was a member of the 2nd Battalion, 3rd Aviation Regiment, Hunter Army Airfield, Ga.

Staff Sgt. Terry W. Hemingway, 39, of Willingboro, N.J., was killed in action on April 10 in Iraq. Hemingway's Bradley fighting vehicle was traveling down a street when a car exploded next to it. Hemingway was assigned to C Company, 1st Battalion, 15th Infantry Regiment, Fort Benning, Ga.

Sgt. Nicolas M. Hodson, 22, of Smithville, Mo., died in a vehicle accident in Iraq. Hodson was assigned to the 3rd Battalion, 2nd Marine Regiment, 2nd Marine Expeditionary Brigade, Camp Lejeune, N.C.

Chief Warrant Officer Scott Jamar, 32, of Granbury, Texas. He was killed when his UH-60 Black Hawk helicopter crashed in central Iraq on April 2. He was a member of the 2nd Battalion, 3rd Aviation Regiment, Hunter Army Airfield, Ga.

Marine Cpl. Evan T. James, 20, of Hancock, Ill. James had been declared missing in action on March 24, near Saddam Canal; his remains were recovered on March 25.

Army Spc. William A. Jeffries, 39, died in a hospital in Spain on March 26 from a sudden illness that came on when he was in Kuwait. He was assigned to D Company, 1st Battalion, 152nd Infantry Regiment of the Illinois Army National Guard.

Pfc. Howard Johnson II, 21, of Mobile, Ala. He was killed on March 23 when his 507th Maintenance Company was ambushed.

Hospital Corpsman 3rd Class (Fleet Marine Force) Michael Vann Johnson Jr., 25, of Little Rock, Ark. Johnson was killed in action on March 25 in Iraq. He was assigned to the Naval Medical Center San Diego, 3rd Marine Division Detachment, San Diego, Calif.

Pvt. Devon D. Jones, 19, of San Diego, died when his vehicle fell into a ravine on April 4. He was a member of the 41st Artillery Regiment, Fort Stewart, Ga.

Staff Sgt. Phillip A. Jordan, 42, Brazoria, Texas. He was assigned to the 1st Battalion, 2nd Marine Regiment, 2nd Marine Expeditionary Brigade, Camp Lejeune, N.C. He was killed on March 23 near Nasiriyah. He was among the nine Marines killed in Iraq Sunday when opposition troops pretending to surrender opened fire.

2nd Lt. Jeffrey J. Kaylor, 24, of Clifton, Va., was killed in action in Iraq on April 7. Kaylor was assigned to C Battery, 39th Field Artillery Battalion, Fort Stewart, Ga.

Spc. James M. Kiehl, 22, of Comfort, Texas. Kiehl was killed on or about March 23 when the convoy he was traveling in was ambushed in southern Iraq. He was with the 507th Maintenance Company, Fort Bliss, Texas.

Capt. Edward J. Korn, 31, of Savannah, Ga., was killed while he investigated the wreckage of a T-72 tank destroyed by his unit in central Iraq. Korn was assigned to the 64th Armor, 3rd Infantry Division, Fort Stewart, Ga.

Sgt. Brad Korthaus, 28, Davenport, Iowa, drowned in a canal on March 24. He was assigned to Engineering Company C, 6th Engineer Support Battalion, 4th Force Service Support Group, based in Peoria, Ill. His remains were found on March 25.

Cpl. Brian Matthew Kennedy, 25, of Houston, was assigned to the Marine Medium Helicopter Squadron 268, 3rd Marine Aircraft

Wing, Marine Corps Air Station Camp Pendleton, Calif. Kennedy died in a CH-46E helicopter crash on March 20 in Kuwait.

Sgt. Michael V. Lalush, 23, of Troutville, Va., was killed on March 30 in a UH-1N Huey helicopter crash in southern Iraq. He was assigned to Marine Light Attack Helicopter Squadron 169, Marine Air Craft Group 39, Marine Corps Air Station, Camp Pendleton, Calif.

Staff Sgt. Nino D. Livaudais, 23, of Utah, died on April 3 from injuries sustained in combat. He was assigned to 3rd Battalion, 75th Ranger Regiment, Fort Benning, Ga.

Spc. Ryan P. Long, 21, died on April 3 from injuries sustained in combat. He was assigned to A Company, 3rd Battalion, 75th Ranger Regiment, Fort Benning, Ga.

Marine Lance Cpl. Joseph B. Maglione, 22, of Lansdale, Pa., died from a noncombat weapons discharge on April 1 in Kuwait. Maglione was assigned to Bridge Company B, 6th Engineer Support Battalion, 4th Force Service Support Group, based in Folsom, Pa.

Sgt. 1st Class John W. Marshall, 50, of Los Angeles, was killed in action on April 8 in Iraq. Marshall was struck by an opposition rocket-propelled grenade during an Iraqi ambush in Baghdad. Marshall was assigned to 3rd Battalion, 15th Infantry Regiment, 3rd Infantry Division, Fort Stewart, Ga.

Chief Warrant Officer Johnny Villareal Mata, 35, of Amarillo, Texas. Villareal Mata was killed on or about March 23 when the convoy he was traveling in was ambushed in southern Iraq. He was with the 507th Maintenance Company, Fort Bliss, Texas.

Staff Sgt. Donald C. May, Jr., 31, of Richmond, Va., of the 1st Tank Battalion, 1st Marine Division, Marine Corps Air-Ground Combat Center, Twenty-nine Palms, Calif.

Pfc. Francisco A. Martinez-Flores, 21, of Los Angeles. Martinez-Florez was assigned to the 1st Tank Battalion, 1st Marine Division, Marine Corps Air-Ground Combat Center, Twenty-nine Palms, Calif.

Marine Sgt. Brian D. McGinnis, 23, of St. George, Del., died on March 30 in a UH-1N Huey helicopter crash in southern Iraq. He was assigned to Marine Light Attack Helicopter Squadron 169, Marine Air Craft Group 39, Marine Corps Air Station, Camp Pendleton, Calif.

1st Lt. Brian M. McPhillips, 25, of Pembroke, Mass., was killed on April 4 during a firefight in central Iraq. He was assigned to the 2nd Tank Battalion, 2nd Marine Division, based at Camp Lejeune, N.C.

Gunnery Sgt. Joseph Menusa, 33, of San Jose, Calif. He was assigned to the 1st Combat Engineer Battalion, 1st Marine Division, Camp Pendleton, Calif.

Pfc. Jason M. Meyer, 23, of Swartz Creek, Mich., was killed in action on April 8 in Iraq. Meyer was assigned to B Company, 11th Engineer Battalion, Fort Stewart, Ga. The circumstances surrounding his death are under investigation.

Pfc. Anthony S. Miller, 19, of San Antonio, Texas, was killed on April 7 by opposition indirect fire in Iraq. Miller was assigned to headquarters and Headquarters Company, 3rd Infantry Division, 2nd Brigade, Fort Stewart, Ga.

Spc. George A. Mitchell, 35, of Rawlings, Md., was assigned to Headquarters Company, 3rd Infantry Division, 2nd Brigade Combat Team, Fort Stewart, Ga. Mitchell died of wounds received in an opposition rocket attack south of Baghdad on April 7.

Marine Lance Cpl. Patrick R. Nixon, 21, of Nashville, has been reclassified as killed in action from missing. Nixon was assigned to the 1st Battalion, 2nd Marine Regiment, 2nd Marine Expeditionary Brigade, Camp Lejeune, N.C. His unit was engaged in operations on March 23 on the outskirts of Nasiriyah in Iraq. His remains were recovered on March 30.

Spc. Donald S. Oaks Jr., 20, of Erie, Pa., was killed in action in Iraq on April 3. He was assigned to C Battery, 3rd Battalion, 13th Field Artillery Regiment (Multiple-Launch Rocket System), Fort Sill, Okla.

Lance Cpl. Patrick T. O'Day, 20, of Sonoma, Calif., of the 1st Tank Battalion, 1st Marine Division, Marine Corps Air-Ground Combat Center, Twenty-nine Palms, Calif.

Lance Cpl. Eric J. Orlowski, 26, of Buffalo, N.Y., was killed by an accidental discharge of a .50-caliber machine gun in Iraq. He was assigned to the 2nd Tank Battalion, 2nd Marine Division, Camp Lejeune, N.C.

Sgt. Fernando Padilla-Ramirez, 26, of San Luis, Ariz., of the Marine Wing Support Squadron 371, Marine Support Group 37, Marine Corps Air Station, Yuma, Ariz. He was last seen conducting convoy operations in the vicinity of Nasiriyah on March 28. His remains were identified on April 10.

Sgt. Michael F. Pedersen, 26, of Flint, Mich. He was killed when his UH-60 Black Hawk helicopter crashed in central Iraq on April 2. He was a member of the 2nd Battalion, 3rd Aviation Regiment, Hunter Army Airfield, Ga.

Pfc. Lori Ann Piestewa, 23, Tuba City, Ariz. Piestewa was killed on or about March 23 when the convoy she was traveling in was ambushed in southern Iraq. She was with the 507th Maintenance Company, Fort Bliss, Texas.

2nd Lt. Frederick E. Pokorney Jr., 31, Nye, Nev. He was assigned to the Headquarters Battery, 1st Battalion, 10th Marine Regiment, 2nd Marine Expeditionary Brigade, Camp Lejeune, N.C.

Pvt. Kelley S. Prewitt, 24, of Alabama, was killed in action by opposition fire on April 6. Prewitt was assigned to Headquarters Company, 2nd Battalion, 69th Armor Regiment, Fort Benning, Ga.

Sgt. 1st Class Randall S. Rehn, 36, Longmont, Colo., was killed in action on April 3. He was assigned to C Battery, 3rd Battalion, 13th Field Artillery Regiment (Multiple-Launch Rocket System), Fort Sill, Okla.

Sgt. Brendon C. Reiss, 23, of Casper, Wyo. He was assigned to 1st Battalion, 2nd Marine Regiment, 2nd Marine Expeditionary Brigade, based in Camp Lejeune, N.C. Reiss, last seen when his unit was engaged in combat operations on March 23 in the vicinity of Nasiriyah, Iraq, had been listed as missing in action. His remains were found on April 11.

Pfc. Diego Fernando Rincon, 19, of Conyers, Ga. He was assigned to the 2-7th Infantry, 3rd Infantry Division, Fort Stewart, Ga. Rincon was killed at a checkpoint by a car bomb on March 29.

Sgt. Duane R. Rios, 25, of Hammond, Ind., was killed on April 4 during a firefight in central Iraq. He was assigned to the 1st Combat Engineer Battalion, 1st Marine Division, based at Camp Pendleton, Calif.

Capt. Russell B. Rippetoe, 27, died on April 3 from injuries sustained in combat. He was assigned to A Company, 3rd Battalion, 75th Ranger Regiment, Fort Benning, Ga. He was from Colorado.

Sgt. Todd J. Robbins, 33, Pentwater, Mich., was killed in action on April 3. He was assigned to C Battery, 3rd Battalion, 13th Field Artillery Regiment (Multiple-Launch Rocket System), Fort Sill, Okla.

Marine Cpl. Robert M. Rodriguez, 21, of Queens, N.Y., was killed in action on March 27 when the tank he was riding in fell into the Euphrates River during combat operations northwest of Nasiriyah. His remains were recovered on March 30. He was assigned to the 1st Tank Battalion, 1st Marine Division, Marine Corps Air-Ground Combat Center, Twenty-nine Palms, Calif.

Cpl. Randal Kent Rosacker, 21, San Diego. He was assigned to the 1st Battalion, 2nd Marine Regiment, 2nd Marine Expeditionary Brigade, Camp Lejeune, N.C. He was killed on March 23 near Nasiriyah.

Spc. Brandon J. Rowe, 20, of Roscoe, Ill., was killed in action on March 31 in Ayyub, Iraq, by opposition artillery. He was assigned to the C Company, 1st Battalion, 502nd Infantry Regiment, 101st Airborne Division (Air Assault), Fort Campbell, Ky.

Capt. Benjamin W. Sammis, 29, of Rehobeth, Mass., was killed in action on April 4 when his AH-1W Super Cobra helicopter crashed during combat operations near Ali Aziziyal, Iraq. He was assigned to the Marine Light Attack Helicopter Squadron-267, Marine Aircraft Group 39, 3rd Marine Aircraft Wing, Camp Pendleton, Calif.

Staff Sgt. Robert A Stever, 36, of Pendleton, Ore., was killed in action by opposition fire on April 8. He was assigned the Headquarters Company, 3rd Battalion, 15th Infantry Regiment, 3rd Infantry Division, Fort Stewart, Ga.

Army Spc. Gregory P. Sanders, 19, of Indiana. He was assigned to the 3rd Battalion, 69th Armored, Fort Stewart, Ga. He died on March 24.

Army Capt. Christopher Scott Seifert, 27, was killed by a grenade when he was sleeping in a tent at Camp Pennsylvania, Kuwait, on March 22. Seifert was assigned to the 101st Airborne Division, Fort Campbell, Ky.

Cpl. Erik H. Silva, 22, of Chula Vista, Calif., was killed in action in Iraq on April 3. Silva was assigned to the 3rd Battalion, 5th Marines, 1st Marine Division, based at Camp Pendleton, Calif.

Pvt. Brandon U. Sloan, 19, of Cleveland, Ohio. Sloan was killed on or about March 23 when the convoy he was traveling in was ambushed in southern Iraq. He was with the 507th Maintenance Company, Fort Bliss, Texas.

Lance Cpl. Thomas J. Slocum, age unknown, Adams, Colo. Slocum was assigned to the 1st Battalion, 2nd Marine Regiment, 2nd Marine Expeditionary Brigade, Camp Lejeune, N.C. He was killed near Nasiriyah.

Chief Warrant Officer Eric A. Smith, 41, of Calif. He was killed when his UH-60 Black Hawk helicopter crashed in central Iraq on April 2. He was a member of the 2nd Battalion, 3rd Aviation Regiment, Hunter Army Airfield, Ga.

Sgt. 1st Class Paul R. Smith, 33, of Tampa, Fla., was killed in action on April 4. Smith was assigned to the 11th Engineer Battalion, Fort Stewart, Ga.

Sgt. Roderic A. Solomon, 32, from Fayetteville, N.C., died on March 28 when his Bradley fighting vehicle rolled off a cliff in a nonhostile accident in Iraq. Solomon was assigned to the 2-7th Infantry, 3rd Infantry Division, out of Fort Stewart, Ga.

Air National Guard Maj. Gregory Stone, 40, of Boise, Idaho, died March 25, from wounds sustained when an American soldier allegedly threw a hand grenade into his tent. Stone was assigned to the 124th Air Support Operations Squadron.

Army Reserve Spc. Brandon S. Tobler, 19. His hometown was not available. Tobler died in a vehicle accident on March 22 in Iraq. Tobler was assigned to the 671st Engineer Brigade, Portland, Ore.

Sgt. Donald R. Walters, 33, of Kansas City, Mo. Walters was killed on or about March 23 when the convoy he was traveling in was ambushed in southern Iraq. He was with the 507th Maintenance Company, Fort Bliss, Texas.

Staff Sgt. Kendall Damon Watersbey, 29, of Baltimore, was assigned to the Marine Medium Helicopter Squadron 268, 3rd Marine Aircraft Wing, Marine Corps Air Station Camp Pendleton, Calif. Watersbey died in a CH-46E helicopter crash March 20 in Kuwait.

Pfc. Michael Russell Creighton Weldon, 20, of Conyers, Ga. He was assigned to the 2-7th Infantry, 3rd Infantry Division, Fort Stewart, Ga. Weldon was one of four Americans killed at a checkpoint near Najaf by a car bomb on March 29.

Lt. Nathan D. White, 30, of Mesa, Ariz., was killed in action April 2 in Iraq. White was assigned to Strike Fighter Squadron One Nine Five, based in Atsugi, Japan, and currently deployed with Carrier Air Wing Five aboard USS Kitty Hawk. White was the pilot of an F/A-18C Hornet lost over Iraq on April 2. The incident remains under investigation.

Sgt. Eugene Williams, 24, of Highland, N.Y. He was assigned to the 2-7th Infantry, 3rd Infantry Division, Fort Stewart, Ga. Williams was killed at a checkpoint by a car bomb on March 29.

Lance Cpl. Michael J. Williams, 31, of Yuma, Ariz. He was assigned to the 1st Battalion, 2nd Marine Regiment, 2nd Marine Expeditionary Brigade, Camp Lejeune, N.C. His unit was engaged in operations March 23 on the outskirts of Nasiriyah in Iraq. His remains were recovered March 28.

As of Aug. 22, the Department of Defense said there were no confirmed prisoners of war or missing personnel.

Combat deaths reported from April 17 to May 1, the date major combat operations were declared over:

Army Spc. Edward J. Anguiano, 24, Brownsville, Texas (previously reported as missing following 3/23 ambush while traveling on Highway 7). He was with the 3rd Combat Support Battalion, Ft. Stewart, Ga.

Marine CWO Andrew Todd Arnold, 30, Spring, Texas. Killed when enemy rocket he was inspecting exploded. He was with the 1st Battalion, 10th Marine Regiment, 2nd Marine Expeditionary Battalion, Camp Lejeune, N.C.

Army Spc. Roy Russell Buckley, 24. Portage, In. Found dead by roadside after exiting truck and entering trailer while traveling in convoy. The incident is under investigation. He was with the 685th Transportation Company, Hobart, Ind.

Marine Cpl. Kemaphoom A. Chanawongse, 22, Waterford, Conn. Killed in action near Nasiriyah on March 23. Previously listed as missing in action. He was assigned to the 2nd Amphibious Battalion, 2nd Marine Regiment, 2nd Marine Expeditionary Brigade, Camp Lejeune, N.C.

Marine CWO Robert William Channell Jr., 36, Tuscaloosa, Ala. Killed near Al Kut April 22 when an enemy rocket he and others were firing for familiarization malfunctioned. He was with the 1st Battalion, 10th Marine Regiment, 2nd Marine Expeditionary Battalion, Camp Lejeune, N.C.

Air Force Capt. Eric B. Das, 30, Amarillo, Texas. Killed in action April 7 when the F15E he was piloting crashed during combat operations. Das was assigned to the 333rd Fighter Squadron, Seymour Johnson Air Force Base, N.C.

Army 1st Sgt. Joe J. Garza, 43, Robstown, Texas. Died in Baghdad April 28 after falling out of vehicle that swerved to avoid civilian vehicle. Garza was assigned to 1st Battalion, 30th Infantry Regiment, Fort Benning, Ga. Marine Pvt. Jonathan Gifford, Macon, Ill. Killed in action near Nasiriyah on March 23. Previously listed as missing. He was with the 1st Battalion, 2nd Marine Regiment, 2nd Marine Expeditionary Brigade, Camp Lejeune, N.C.

Army Pfc Jesse A. Givens, 34, Springfield, Mo. Killed on May 1 in Al Habbaniyah when tank in which he was riding fell into river. He was with 2nd Squadron, 3rd Armored Cavalry Regiment, Fort Carson, Colo.

Army Sgt. Troy David Jenkins, 25, Ridgecrest, Calif. Died April 24 at a hospital in Germany from schrapnel wounds received in Iraq while on patrol April 19. He was assigned to B Company, 3rd Battalion, 187th Infantry Regiment, Fort Campbell, Ky.

Marine Lance Cpl. Alan Dinh Lam, 19, Snow Camp, N.C. Killed when enemy rocket he was inspecting exploded. He was assigned to the 8th Communications Battalion, 2nd Marine Expeditionary Battalion, Camp Lejeune, N.C.

Marine Cpl. Jason David Mileo, 20 Centreville, Md. Shot and killed April 14 when mistaken as an enemy soldier. Incident is under investigation. He was with the 3rd Battalion, 4th Marine Regiment, 1st Marine Division, Twenty-nine Palms, Calif.

Army 1st Lt. Osbaldo Orozco, 26, Delano, Calif. Killed April 25 when vehicle rolled over in rough terrain in Iraq. He was with C Company, 1st Battalion, 22nd Infantry Regiment, Fort Hood, Texas.

Army Cpl. John T. Rivero, 23, Tampa, Fla. Killed in Kuwait April 17 when his vehicle overturned. Rivero was assigned to C Company, 2nd Battalion, 124th Infantry Division, Eustis, Fla.

Army Spc. Narson B. Sullivan, 21, North Brunswick, N.J. Killed by noncombat weapon discharge April 25. Incident is under investigation. He was with the 411th Military Police Company, Fort Hood, Texas.

Air Force Maj. William R. Watkins III, 37, Danville, Va. Killed in action April 7 when the F15E in which he was flying as a weapons officer went down during a combat mission in Iraq. He was assigned to the 333rd Fighter Squadron, Seymour Johnson Air Force Base, N.C.

(Source: U.S. Department of Defense.)

Analysis: Strategic bombing in Iraq war

THOMAS HOULAHAN

WASHINGTON, April 23 (UPI) — Operation Iraqi Freedom provided good news and bad news for advocates of strategic bombing. The good news is that our bombing was more accurate than it has ever been. The bad news is that, dramatically increased bombing accuracy notwithstanding, strategic bombing once again failed to bring Saddam Hussein's regime to its knees. As was the case 12 years ago, victory required significant fighting on the ground.

As with many other systems, in the immediate aftermath of the first Gulf War, the performance of cruise missiles like the Tomahawk was overrated. At the time, the U.S. military reported that of the 288 Tomahawks launched at the Iraqis, eight malfunctioned after launch, 45 missed their targets, two were shot down and 233 scored hits. However, in the years that followed, serious studies found that the Tomahawk's success rate had been significantly overstated. It is now widely believed that Tomahawks destroyed their targets less than 40 percent of the time.

The Defense Intelligence Agency conducted a bomb damage assessment on 357 strategic targets for which sufficient data was available. Some of these targets were engaged by Tomahawks. Of the 34 Tomahawks launched against these targets, 18 destroyed their targets and 16 failed to do so, about a 53 percent success rate. Of the 16 that failed to destroy their targets, the largest portion (the exact numerical breakdown remains classified) experienced guidance failures on the way to the target. The Tomahawks, also known as TLAMs — which stands for tactical land attack missiles — were guided to their targets in 1991 by topographic maps stored in their electronic brains. The missile scanned the terrain in front of it and compared what it saw against digitally coded topographic information preloaded by the Defense Mapping Agency.

The terrain some Tomahawks had to fly over was so flat and featureless that the missiles were unable to properly guide to their targets. It was later disclosed that in some attacks Central Command solved this problem by flying missiles over the rockier terrain of Iran without the Iranian government's permission. For obvious reasons, this was a tactic that had to be used sparingly. Therefore, many missiles had to fly over less than ideal terrain and were lost on the way to their targets.

In the years before Operation Iraqi Freedom, the guidance problem was largely solved. Tomahawks are now guided by global positioning system satellite signals, not terrain features. Though a few Tomahawks did malfunction, landing in Saudi Arabia or Turkey, it appears that the overwhelming majority hit their targets.

Not only were cruise missile strikes more accurate, they were more common. A total of 333 cruise missiles were launched during Operation Desert Storm (There were 45 air-launched cruise missiles, very similar to the Tomahawk, dropped from B-52s). About 800 cruise missiles were launched 12 years later during Operation Iraqi Freedom. The strategic bombing campaign did not suffer from a lack of resources.

Guided bombs also were more common. In Desert Storm, some 9,500 guided bombs were dropped. In the recent war, around 23,000 were dropped. As with cruise missiles, guided bombs were more accurate in the second Gulf War than in the first. Many of the bombs dropped in

Iraqi Freedom were satellite-guided. This cut down on some of the problems encountered in the first Gulf War by airmen trying to guide their bombs optically or by laser under combat conditions. Obviously, it is difficult to guide a bomb when you are dodging antiaircraft missiles.

Of course, combat conditions for allied air crews were much less intense than they were during Desert Storm. At the beginning of the first Gulf War, Baghdad had the second densest concentration of antiaircraft weapons in the world, behind Moscow. However, Iraq's antiaircraft defenses were nearly destroyed during the first Gulf war. They had continued to waste away over the next 12 years as antiaircraft missile sites were destroyed after trying to engage American aircraft patrolling the no-fly zone. The lack of strong air defenses made it possible for pilots to fly at lower altitudes and made delivering non-satellite-guided bombs much easier.

As a result of improvements in guidance and in bombing conditions, it appears that during Operation Iraqi Freedom, guided bombs hit the buildings they were aimed at nearly 100 percent of the time. It should be pointed out that, claims by bombing enthusiasts to the contrary, one cannot sail a bomb through the window of his choice. Guided bombs are not that accurate. However, they will hit within a few meters of their aim point, and that is usually accurate enough to destroy a selected structure.

Figuring out which targets to strike and how to destroy them were the world's top experts on strategic bombing. The U.S. armed forces have strategic bombing down to a science. Based on information collected from a wide variety of intelligence sources, targeteers select which structures to strike. Once targets are selected, weaponeers determine what type of, and how many, bombs or missiles would be necessary to produce the damage they want on a selected structure.

Coalition targeteers had a much better idea of which buildings to strike than they did in 1991. American and British intelligence agencies had been gathering information about potential targets for 12 years. Satellite coverage over Iraq was far more extensive than it was during the first Gulf War. There had also been tremendous advances in the coalition's ability to gather Iraqi signals intelligence. Centcom targeteers knew which buildings were being used for what purpose.

Centcom weaponeers had voluminous information on many targeted structures, to include blueprints showing how the structures were built, with what materials, and what areas were vulnerable. The strategic bombing campaign did not suffer from a lack of information.

In Operation Iraqi Freedom, the tools required for successful strategic bombing were closer to perfect than they have ever been. Conditions for strategic bombing could hardly have been better. The coalition had the world's top bombing experts. These planners had more information about their targets than any planners have ever had before. Yet, with all these advantages, strategic bombing failed to produce the paralysis it was designed to produce. As in 1991, the Iraqi command and control system was disrupted, but not paralyzed.

Strategic bombing enthusiasts have claimed that in the future, wars could be won by bombing alone. This war provided further proof that reports of the death of ground fighting have been greatly exaggerated.

(Thomas Houlahan is the director of the Military Assessment Program of the William R. Nelson Institute at James Madison University. A veteran of the Army's 82nd Airborne Division and the XVIII Airborne Corps staff, he is the author of "Gulf War: The Complete History," Schrenker Military Publishing, New London, N.H., 1999.)

INDEX

ABOUT THE EDITOR

Martin Walker is an author, syndicated columnist and chief international commentator for United Press International, and co-author of "Europe in the New Century: Emerging Superpower," written while he was a public policy fellow at the Woodrow Wilson Center for International Scholars in Washington, D.C. He is also a senior fellow at the World Policy Institute at New York's New School University, a contributing editor of "Europe" magazine, a member of the editorial boards of the "Wilson Quarterly" and of the "World Policy Journal." He is a regular book reviewer for the "Washington Post" and Britain's "Times Literary Supplement" and also contributes to both the French and English services of the Canadian Broadcasting Corporation and to the Voice of America French service.

In 25 years as a journalist with Britain's "Guardian" newspaper, he served as bureau chief in Moscow and the U.S., as European editor and assistant editor. He was awarded Britain's Reporter of the Year prize in 1987. A regular broadcaster on the BBC, Fox News, National Public Radio's "Diane Rehm Show" and "On the Media" and CNN, and panelist on "Inside Washington" and "Capital Gang Sunday", he also scripted and narrated the BBC series "Martin Walker's Russia," and the BBC Analysis special Clintonomics."

He has written for the "New York Times," the "Washington Post," "Foreign Policy," the "New Yorker," the "New Republic," "Die Zeit" of Germany, "El Mundo" of Spain, the "Moscow Times" and "Moskovskii Novosti." He is also a contributing editor of "Demokratisatsiya," the journal of post-Soviet reform, Europe editor of intellectualcapital.com, and contributes columns to theglobalist.com.

Martin Walker has served as vice chairman of the Advisory Board of the European Institute of Washington, D.C. He is also a member of the review board of "International Affairs," the journal "Chatham House," and the Royal Institute of International Affairs, in London. A guest lecturer at the universities of Moscow, Columbia, UCLA, Toronto, New York, and Pittsburgh, he is also a faculty member of A. T. Kearney's Global Business Policy Council.

He also serves on the RAND Corporation's task force on U.S.-European relations and is a member of former Czech President Vaclav Havel's Forum 2000 group, an annual international seminar on global affairs. He also served on the task force for the study of coalition-building run by Georgetown University's Institute for the Study of Diplomacy, and on the U.S. Department of State's Roundtable on the New Europe.

Martin Walker was educated at Balliol College, Oxford, where he was Brackenbury Scholar, and at Harvard, where he was a Harkness Fellow and Resident Tutor at Kirkland House. His book "The Cold War: A History" was short-listed for the Book of the Year prize in Britain in 1993, for the Governor-General's Prize in Canada, and was a "New York Times" Notable Book of the year.

He is married to the novelist Julia Watson, and they have two teenage daughters and a basset hound. They live in Washington, D.C.

LIST OF CONTRIBUTORS

This book is a collective product from the staff of United Press International, one of the world's best known news agencies since its founding in 1907. The headquarters staff and news desk in Washington, the London-based staff of UPI's Arab News Service and UPI U.K., all contributed to the coverage, and without their support the war could hardly have been reported.

Special thanks for their written contributions here are due to:

John O'Sullivan, editor in chief, Washington
Arnaud de Borchgrave, editor at large, in Washington and Jordan
Roland Flamini, international editor, Washington
Elizabeth Manning, deputy international editor, Washington
Pamela Hess, Pentagon correspondent, Washington
Martin Sieff, senior news analyst, Washington
Louis Marano, writer, Washington
Anwar Iqbal, diplomatic correspondent, Washington
Eli Lake, State Department correspondent, Washington
Thomas Houlahan, military analyst, Washington
Krishnadev Calamur, news desk chief editor, Washington
Dan Whipple, science correspondent
Bruce Chalfant, science correspondent
Gareth Harding, chief European correspondent
Anthony Louis, Moscow correspondent
Lisa Bryant, Paris correspondent
Peter Almond, London correspondent
William Reilly, U.N. correspondent
Martin Hutchinson, business editor
Sam Vaknin, business correspondent

The main reporting team in the field included:

Nicholas M. Horrock, chief White House reporter: Turkey, Jordan, Iraq
Richard Tomkins, embedded with the 5th Marines
Jim Bartlett, with the 101st Airborne
P. Mitchell Prothero, Qatar and Iraq
Claude Salhani, features editor, London, Damascus and Beirut
Ghassan al-Khadi, Baghdad correspondent
Joshua Brilliant, Tel Aviv correspondent
Dalal Saoud, Beirut correspondent
Modher Amin, Tehran correspondent
Seva Ulman and Kemal Biritan, Turkey correspondents
Chris Corder, news photographer, Kuwait, Iraq
John Gillis, news photographer, embedded with the U.S. Navy on the aircraft carrier
    Harry S. Truman and the destroyer Anzio

The qualities in this book are all theirs. The errors are all mine.

Martin Walker
Kuwait, Iraq, Washington

THE IRAQ WAR

IRAQ, April 8 (UPI) — A-10 maintenance members from the 392 Air Expeditionary Wing inspect their aircraft for any additional damage after it was hit by an Iraqi missile in the right engine on April 8, 2003, at a forward deployed location in southern Iraq during Operation Iraqi Freedom. The A-10 made it back to the base safely. (U.S. Air Force/Shane A. Cuomo, UPI)

AFGHANISTAN, March 24 (UPI) — As a new war got under way in Iraq, American dead are flown home to Dover Air Force base in Delaware in a grim reminder of the human costs from another war zone where the casualties continued. Army Chaplain (Col.) Richard Rogers performs the last rites for six U.S. airmen killed when their HH-60G Pave Hawk helicopter crashed near Ghazni in Afghanistan, as they flew to pick up two Afghan children for medical treatment at a U.S. field hospital at Bagram Air Base. (U.S. Army/Terri Rorke, UPI)

BASRA, Iraq, April 5 (UPI) — A donkey pulls a wagon of Iraqis just outside of the city of Basra on April 5, 2003, past a checkpoint of British troops. Units of the 7th Armored Brigade moved just outside the city of Basra and had been conducting raids on resistance groups in Iraq's second largest city. (Chris Corder, UPI)

BASRA, Iraq, April 6 (UPI) — A member of the Irish Guard looks on as a Warrior armored personnel carrier from the Royal Scots Dragoon, 7th Armored Brigade, aka Desert Rats, leave a former technical school and Baath Party headquarters they had taken control of only days previous, enroute.

ABOARD THE USS HARRY S. TRUMAN, Eastern Mediterranean, March 21 (UPI) — Ordnance handlers load a F-14 Tomcat with GBU-31 1000 pound bombs on the flight deck of the aircraft carrier USS Harry S. Truman on Friday, March 21, 2003, in the eastern Mediterranean Sea. (John Gillis, UPI)

USS HARRY S. TRUMAN, Eastern Mediterranean, March 31 (UPI) — A pilot of a F-18 Hornet waits his turn to launch from the aircraft carrier USS Harry S. Truman for a strike into Iraq on the early morning of March 31, 2003, in the eastern Mediterranean. (John Gillis, UPI)

ABOARD THE USS HARRY S. TRUMAN, Eastern Mediterranean, March 31 (UPI) — A hook runner gives the all-clear for a F-18 Hornet to move off the flight deck of the aircraft carrier USS Harry S. Truman after it released the arresting cable from its tail hook after returning from a mission over Iraq on March 31, 2003, in the eastern Mediterranean. (John Gillis, UPI)

SOLAYMANYIAH, Iraq, March 23 (UPI) — Kurdish Iraqi refugees from Solaymaniyah, Iraq, camp near Parviz Khan–Qasr-e-shirin, near Iran on March 23, 2003. Approximately 200 families are camping out, hoping to avoid the war and get on with life. (Ali Khaligh, UPI)

PARVIZ KHAN-QASR, Iraqi Ksurdistan, March 23 (UPI) — Close to the Iranian border, 200 families of Kurdish refugees flee the potential war zone near their home in Solaymanyiah for home-made tents in makeshift campgrounds.

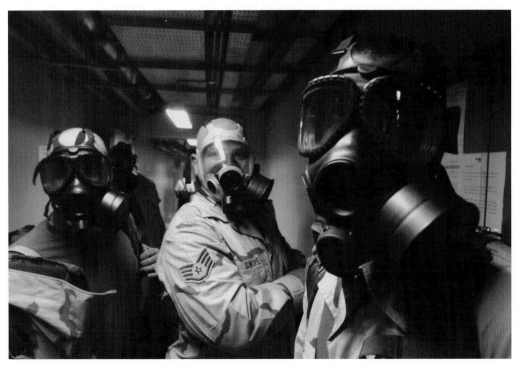

KUWAIT CITY, Kuwait, March 20 (UPI) — Members of the U.S. Army wait out a possible chemical threat in the basement shelter of the Hilton Hotel just outside Kuwait City on March 20, 2003. At least three air raid sirens have filled the airwaves after Iraqis fired missiles in Kuwait's direction. At least one missile was shot down by a Patriot missile, with others landing harmlessly in the desert. (Chris Corder, UPI)

RUMAILA OIL FIELDS, Iraq, April 2 (UPI) — A soldier from the Army helps guard the Rumaila oil field in southern Iraq as firefighters prepare massive water lagoons in the desert to extinguish the last two fires at oil wells sabotaged by the fleeing Iraqi army on April 2, 2003. Teams from Boots & Coots International Well Control and the Kuwait Oil Co. failed to put out the blazes earlier this week, using water from smaller storage tanks. (Chris Corder, UPI)

HILLTOP CHECKPOINT, Kuwait, March 21 (UPI) — Army military M.P.s guard Hilltop Checkpoint north of Kuwait City on March 21, 2003. (Chris Corder, UPI)

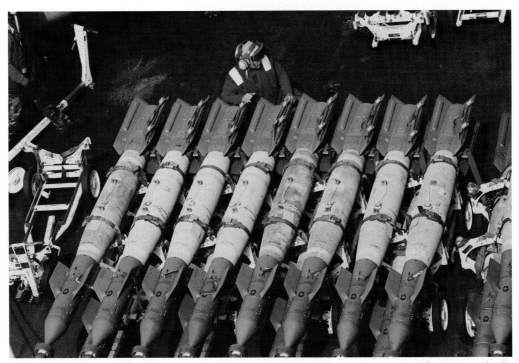

USS ABRAHAM LINCOLN, the Arabian Gulf, March 24 (UPI) — An aviation ordnanceman checks over racks of precision-guided ordnance before moving them to the "bomb farm," on the flight deck of the USS Abraham Lincoln on March 24, 2003. Lincoln and Carrier Air Wing Fourteen are conducting combat operations in support of Operation Iraqi Freedom. Operation Iraqi Freedom is the multinational coalition effort to liberate the Iraqi people, eliminate Iraq's weapons of mass destruction and end the regime of Saddam Hussein. (U.S. Navy photo/Michael S. Kelly, UPI)

USS CONSTELLATION, March 23 (UPI) — A Tomahawk land attack missile is launched from the guided missile destroyer USS Winston S. Churchill on March 23, 2003. (U.S. Navy/UPI)

USS KITTY HAWK, The Arabian Gulf, March 18 (UPI) — An F/A-18C Hornet makes an arrested landing on the flight deck aboard the USS Kitty Hawk on March 18, 2003. Kitty Hawk and her embarked Carrier Air Wing Five are conducting combat missions in support of Operations Southern Watch and Enduring Freedom. Kitty Hawk is the Navy's only permanently forward-deployed aircraft carrier and operates out of Yokosuka, Japan. (Todd Frantom, U.S. Navy/UPI)

NAJAF, Iraq, April 8 (UPI) — U.S. Army military police provide crowd control while Iraqi citizens line up for food and water being distributed to citizens in need near, Najaf, Iraq, on April 8, 2003. The U.S military is working with international relief organizations to help provide food and medicine for the Iraqi people in support of Operation Iraqi Freedom. Operation Iraqi Freedom is the multinational coalition effort to liberate the Iraqi people, eliminate Iraq's weapons of mass destruction and end the regime of Saddam Hussein. (U.S. Navy photo by Photographer's Mate 1st Class Arlo K. Abrahamson)

USS HARRY S. TRUMAN, Mediterranean Sea, April 11 (UPI) — Two F/A-18 Hornets assigned to the "Gunslingers" of Strike Fighter Squadron One Zero Five fly close air support missions for coalition special operations forces on April 11, 2003. (U.S. Navy/Tom Lalor, UPI)

Iraq, March 28 (UPI) — Air Force members from the 621st Air Mobility Group Tanker Airlift Control Element pose in front of a makeshift sign at a forward deployed location in southern Iraq on March 28, 2003. (Shane A. Cuomo/REX FEATURES, UPI)

HARIR AIRFIELD, Iraq, March 30 (UPI) — Paratroopers of the U.S. Army 173rd Airborne Brigade stationed near the Harir Airfield, 45 miles northeast of Irbil in Kurdish-controlled northern Iraq, continue to reinforce their positions on March 27, 2003. An estimated 1,000 paratroopers landed last Thursday and seized the airfield as a possible staging ground for a second front against Saddam Hussein. (Ali Khaligh, UPI)

KHAZER, Iraq, April 4 (UPI) — American troops hold a position near the northern Iraqi town of Khazer, about 20 miles from Mosul, on April 4, 2003. Skirmishes continue as the U.S. military consolidates its position. (Ali Khaligh, UPI)

CENTRAL COMMAND AREA OF RESPONSIBILITY, April 9 (UPI) — U.S. Navy doctor Lt. Cmdr. Bryan Schumacher (*right*) and Senior Chief Hospital Corpsman Zachary Rowe (*left*), assigned to Regimental Aid Station, 1st Marine Division, 5th Marines, renders medical aid to a wounded Iraqi civilian in a northern suburb of Baghdad in support of Operation Iraqi Freedom. (U.S. Marine Corps/Brian Winnett, UPI)

BASRA, Iraq, April (UPI) — A Challenger-2 tank from the Queen's Royal Lancers holds a position as a local biker rides by in Basra, Iraq, in April, 2003. (Rex Features, UPI)

Iraq, April 8 (UPI) — Cpl. Hughes 3 Para making friends with local children on April 8, 2003. (Rex Features, UPI)

UMM QASR, Iraq, March 25 (UPI) — K Dog, a bottle-nosed dolphin from Commander Task Unit, leaps out of the water in front of Sgt. Andrew Garrett during training near the USS Gunston Hall, operating in the Arabian Gulf. (U.S. Navy, Rex Features, UPI)

BASRA, Iraq (UPI) — Soldiers of 3 Platoon, Number 1 Company 1st Battalion, the Irish Guards, escort a group of Iraqi men leaving the city of Basra to check their IDs, and to ensure they are not fleeing Iraqi soldiers or guerrilla fighters. The men were subsequently released. (Rex Features, UPI)

BASRA, Iraq, March 28 (UPI) — A group of Iraqi males are detained at the gateway to the city of Basra by soldiers serving with 3 Platoon, Number 1 Company, 1st Battalion, the Irish Guards. The soldiers manning the checkpoint on the bridge into and out of Basra are there to show a presence and to prevent Iraqi soldiers and militia leaving the city to possibly fight coalition forces. These men were suspected of being soldiers attempting to gain entry into the city. They were released, as no proof could be found. (Rex Features, UPI)

HMS Ark Royal, March 28 (UPI) — Following the tragic deaths of seven aircrew officers of 849 Squadron A Flight early in the morning of March 22, a repatriation ceremony for three of the seven was held onboard HMS Ark Royal on March 28, 2003. Leading the ceremony was the Rev Tudor Bottwood, RN, the members of A Flight acting as pall bearers alongside officers of the ship's company. (Rex Features, UPI)

IRAQ, April 2003 (UPI) — A dead Iraqi soldier lies on the side of a road as members of Naval Mobile Construction Battalion 74 pass by in Iraq on April 3, 2003. (Rex Features, UPI)

BASRA, Iraq (UPI) — A family of Iraqi civilians seek the help of a soldier serving with Number 2 Company, 1st Battalion, the Irish Guards, to locate their other child, caught up in the panic caused by incoming small-arms fire from Iraqi positions in Basra. The family were part of a column of people fleeing the city of Basra when it and the soldiers manning the checkpoint came under small-arms fire from two Iraqi positions several hundred meters away. The Irish Guards were trying to give protection to the local civilians as well as ensure that no Iraqi military or militia slipped through the checkpoint disguised as ordinary civilians. After returning small-arms fire and bringing in artillery fire on the two positions, the soldiers were able to allow free access across the checkpoint. (Rex Features, UPI)

UMM QASR, Iraq, April (UPI) — Damaged and defaced by unknown residents, this billboard stands as a testimony to the deep-seated distaste for the Saddam Hussein regime in Umm Qasr, Iraq, in April 2003. (Matthew Jones/Rex Features UPI)

CAMP PENNSYLVANIA, Kuwait (UPI) — Soldiers of the 1st Brigade, 101st Airborne Division (Air Assault), mourning the loss of Capt. Christopher Seifert at a memorial ceremony at Camp Pennsylvania. Seifert was killed when a grenade was thrown into a sleep tent. The attack left 15 other soldiers wounded. (Rex Features, UPI)